Citizenship and Immigration in Post-war B

Citizenship and Immigration in Post-war Britain

The Institutional Origins of a Multicultural Nation

RANDALL HANSEN

OXFORD
UNIVERSITY PRESS

*This book has been printed digitally and produced in a standard specification
in order to ensure its continuing availability*

OXFORD
UNIVERSITY PRESS

Great Clarendon Street, Oxford OX2 6DP

Oxford University Press is a department of the University of Oxford.
It furthers the University's objective of excellence in research, scholarship,
and education by publishing worldwide in

Oxford New York

Auckland Bangkok Buenos Aires Cape Town Chennai
Dar es Salaam Delhi Hong Kong Istanbul Karachi Kolkata
Kuala Lumpur Madrid Melbourne Mexico City Mumbai Nairobi
São Paulo Shanghai Taipei Tokyo Toronto

Oxford is a registered trade mark of Oxford University Press
in the UK and in certain other countries

Published in the United States
by Oxford University Press Inc., New York

© Randell Hansen 2000

The moral rights of the author have been asserted

Database right Oxford University Press (maker)

Reprinted 2004

ISBN 0-19-924054-X

Preface

THIS book is a study of formal citizenship and immigration in the United Kingdom. It aims to account for the transformation, since 1945, of the UK from a homogeneous into a multicultural society. It focuses on three features of British nationality and immigration policy since 1945: (i) its exceptional liberality and expansiveness between 1948 and 1962 (when some 800,000,000 individuals enjoyed the right to enter the UK); (ii) its rapid reversal after 1962, resulting in one of the most restrictive immigration regimes in the Western world; and (iii) a series of interrelated and unexplained outcomes: the decision to create an imperial citizenship scheme for 800,000,000 British subjects in 1948; the deferral of a distinctive British citizenship until 1981; the reviled and misunderstood concept of 'patriality' and a series of domestic political crises engendered by the expulsions of Asians from East Africa.

The book is intended for three audiences: scholars of Commonwealth migration, comparativists interested in migration, and students of contemporary British history. For those working on Commonwealth immigration, its most noteworthy feature will probably be the explicit challenge to what has become the dominant interpretation of policy-makers' response to non-white Commonwealth migration. According to it, British politicians and civil servants, unanimous in their hostility to black immigration, undertook the task of reconstructing conceptions of British nationality and belonging on racist lines, and then used this 'racialized' conception of Britishness as the pretence for unnecessary immigration controls that they sought from the start.

The argument was developed theoretically in the late 1980s, as the archives concerning Commonwealth migration in the 1950s were opened. The thesis is now common currency among students of migration, and the mantra about official racism and state-led racialization is tirelessly repeated. It is, this book aims to establish, a sloppy and inadequate account. I articulate this claim in the introduction; it is the backdrop to the empirical chapters and I consider its implications in the conclusion.

The argument presented may be misunderstood, and it is worth emphasizing what is not being claimed. I am categorically not arguing that racism was irrelevant to post-war migration controls; these controls were in large measure a response to public opposition to migration, and this opposition was constituted in some measure by racism. Equally, I am not arguing that there were no racists within the major political parties or the civil service. Archival evidence establishes that racism and racists existed. Finally, I am not arguing

that there were not instances in which policy involved the sacrifice of principle to populist hysteria: the Commonwealth Immigrants Act, 1968, a black
spot on the British migration and nationality policy canvas, stands out. What
I am arguing, however, is that such racists as there were did not drive policy
towards Commonwealth migrants; that there were moments when politicians
and civil servants took a principled stand against racism and won the argument; that throughout the post-war period British policy-makers were, taken
as a whole, more liberal than the public to which they owed their office; and
that, as a result, the 'racialization' thesis is too sweeping and exaggerated to
be anything but an impoverished account of the British state's varied
responses to post-war migration.

The focus of the book is on the policy-making apparatus of the British
state; it is not a social history of Commonwealth migrants and their experi-
ences in British society, though there is a need for such a work. It is also not
a book about the role of race within society, or the content and evolution of
Britons' attitudes on questions of race, although some data on the latter are
included. To the degree that racism is considered, it is racism within the state.
The book is about the enactment of a series of public policies that led to a
multicultural Britain that few would have predicted in 1945 and that, although
social scientists are uncomfortable with this, few would have wanted.

It would have been possible to write a very different book, about the
disappointments of Commonwealth migrants, including veterans, who
expected a welcome in the mother country and received the opposite; or
about discriminatory practices in the 1950s, when 'no coloured' signs were
common in London; or about the harassment and intimidation of ethnic
minorities in the 1960s, at the hysterical height of anti-migrant sentiment; or
about contemporary racial violence and racism within the police force.
These are all important historical and sociological topics, and this study does
not suggest otherwise. It is rather that these stories have been told many
times, and are reasonably well known to the academic community. Another
story, about policy-makers in the democratic dilemma, trapped, much to
their discomfort, between liberal impulses and an illiberal public, about hesitance over any immigration restrictions and outright opposition to racist
immigration controls, about a nationality policy that is, for all its contradictions, among the most liberal in Europe, has never been told. The book is
thus written in the same spirit as Rogers Smith's magisterial *Civic Ideas:
Conflicting Visions of Citizenship in U.S. History* (New Haven: Yale, 1997),
a challenge to the conventional argument that American citizenship was (and
is) founded on principles of universalism and inclusion. Smith does not
claim, in the book or in person, that a liberal, inclusionary tradition has
played no role in American citizenship. It is rather that this latter tradition

has competed with its ideological opposite, an exclusionary conception of citizenship founded on race, ethnicity, and gender, and that this tradition has been ignored by a largely Americanophile (and American) scholarly community. In the UK, the opposite is true; the exclusivist impulse among state actors has been catalogued at length, while its inclusionary opposite has been ignored, if not explicitly suppressed. Among other things, this book tells the story of the latter.

Although the book is written as a historical narrative, it falls within an established tradition in political science emphasizing the centrality of contingency, institutions, and path dependence.[1] Comparativists and others interested in the application of theory to immigration will find the introductory chapter most relevant. It considers the British case in the context of opposing claims made in the theoretical literature. One school, associated with globalization theorists, holds that economic interdependence, increased immigration, and the transnationalization of human rights discourse have undermined the capacity of the state to control immigration. A second school counters that the state's capacity to manage immigration remains intact and that such limits as exist are self-imposed; they originate not in the international sphere but in domestic institutions (especially the courts) and the domestic political process. I argue that the British case creates severe difficulties for both schools, but is ultimately a validation of the latter. British success in controlling immigration since the 1960s invalidates globalization theory's key thesis; the country has been subject to globalization pressures identical to the rest of Europe and North America and, yet, it has achieved a degree of policy success, in the form of restrictive immigration policies, unknown to these countries. I explain this success with reference of Britain's institutions. All democratic polities face publics that are hostile to immigration, and all governments have, on the face of it, a rational interest in restricting immigration. The UK succeeds where others fail because its self-imposed constraints are weaker: a timid judiciary and an absence of a bill of rights have enabled

[1] On historical institutionalism and path dependence, see P. A. Hall, *Governing the Economy: The Politics of State Intervention in Britain and France* (New York: Oxford University Press, 1986); Peter A. Hall and Rosemary C. R. Taylor, 'Political Science and the Three New Institutionalisms', *Political Studies*, 44 (1996), 936–57; G. John Ikenberry et al. (eds.), *The State and American Foreign Policy* (Ithaca, NY: Cornell University Press, 1988); M. Levi, 'A Model, A Method, and a Map: Rational Choice in Comparative and Historical Analysis', in M. I. Lichbach and A. S. Zuckerman (eds.), *Comparative Politics: Rationality, Culture, and Structure* (Cambridge: Cambridge University Press, 1997); P. Pierson, 'The Path to European Integration: A Historical Institutionalist Analysis', *Comparative Political Studies*, 29, No. 2 (Apr. 1996), 123–63; P. Pierson, *Path Dependence, Increasing Returns, and the Study of Politics* (revised version of paper presented at European University Institute Apr. 1997, 3 Oct. 1997); S. Steinmo et al., *Structuring Politics: Historical Institutionalism in Comparative Analysis* (New York: Cambridge University Press, 1992).

British governments, once they responded to public demands, to restrict immigration quickly and effectively.

Finally, the book is simply a historical study of Commonwealth immigration since the war. Contemporary historians readily admit the importance of immigration[2] but few have devoted any sustained attention to it. The book traces, on the basis of extensive primary sources and elite interviews, the development of Commonwealth immigration and policies towards it over four decades. It discusses the origin of imperial/British nationality in 1948, the arrival of the first few thousand migrants in the early 1950s, and the agonizing decision to introduce, for the first time in English history, control on the entry of British subjects. It considers the ugliest moments in the history of migration—its surfacing in the 1964 campaign, the demonic campaign of Enoch Powell—and the 1964–70 Labour government's success in securing a consensual approach to Commonwealth immigration. It explains the causes of the expulsions of Asians, from Kenya and Uganda, which dominated migration politics in the late 1960s and early 1970s. Finally, it traces the fitful development, completed only in 1981, of British citizenship. The book is very much political history; it tells the story of immigration as it was seen by politicians and bureaucrats who witnessed, with a mixture of bewilderment, hope, and fear, the transformation of their society from a homogeneous nation at the head of a multiracial empire into a multicultural country shorn of empire.

Oxford and Berlin, R.H.
August 1999

---

[2] P. Hennessy, *Never Again, Britain 1945–1951* (London: Vintage, 1992), 440; K. Morgan, *The People's Peace: British History since 1945* (Oxford: Oxford University Press, 1999).

Acknowledgements

In the time it has taken to write this book I have acquired many debts. The first of these is to Desmond King. Professor King followed the project from its uncertain origins, provided inestimable intellectual support and assistance during the research, and oversaw its completion. I am extremely grateful to Dominic Byatt, Senior Editor for Political Science at Oxford University Press, and his assistant Amanda Watkins. Dominic and Amanda have been unwavering in their support for this project, and ensured its efficient production. My thanks also to the book's anonymous reader and editor. Christian Joppke, under the courage of waved anonymity, wrote a razor-sharp report, laced in equal measure with criticism and encouragement. The book has changed greatly as a result, and he has my sincere thanks.

I owe many others a great debt. Ian Cooper and Iain Maclean read the entire draft once, and parts of it several times, and offered many useful suggestions. Gary Freeman, Jim Hollifield, Ira Katznelson, Robert Lieberman, and Shamit Saggar read the theoretical chapter with care and precision, and it evolved greatly in response to their comments. John Salt gave up several hours of his time to discuss the statistical measurement of migration, and he provided many useful documents. At Oxford, I also owe my thanks to David Butler, Richard Coggins, John Darwin, Matthew Gibney, Robert Falker, David Goldey, Brian Harrison, Rachel Holmes, David Howarth, Tim Hames, Andrew Hurrel, Nien-hê Hsieh, Meira Levinson, Peter Pulzer, Marc Stears, Kurt Strovink, and Alan Ware, all of whom took time to discuss the project. At its inception, Vincent Wright took time from his demanding schedule to analyse exhaustively the original hypothesis and suggested a fundamental, and necessary, change of direction. I am only sorry that Vincent, whose life was cut tragically short, will not see the final product.

Many individuals who lived through the events examined in this book took time to discuss them with me; my thanks to Sir Edward Heath, Lord Jenkins, Enoch Powell, Peter Shore, Lord Merlyn Rees, William Whitelaw, and Baronness Williams. I also spoke with many civil servants, who, in the British tradition of silent service, wished to remain unnamed.

For financial support, I am immensely grateful to the Social Sciences and Humanities Research Council of Canada, the Commonwealth Scholarship Fund (UK), Christ Church, Oxford, and the CEPIC, la Sorbonne. To the archivists who have assisted my work and tolerated my excessive demands, I offer thanks: the Brotherton Library, Leeds, Churchill and Trinity Colleges, Cambridge, the Conservative Party Archives, Oxford, the House of Lords Library, London, the Labour Party Archives, Manchester, the Modern Records Centre, University of Warwick, the Public Record Office, Kew, and the Surrey Record Office.

Parts of the book have been presented at various stages of development in Boston, Baltimore, Glasgow, Oxford, Montreal, Paris, Vancouver, Washington, DC, and Berlin; the comments of the many scholars with whom I spoke have aided me greatly: Donald Blake, Alain C. Cairns, Erik Bleich, John Crowley, Laurent Dubois, Adrian Favell, Romain Garbaye, Andrew Geddes, George Hoberg, Simon Green, Jean Laponce, Samuel Laselva, Oliver Mersch, Rainer Münz, Stephen Legomsky, Robert Lieberman, Antonia Maioni, Jeannette Money, George Ross, Martin Schain, Rogers Smith, and Patrick Weil. Though their remarks have helped me to correct many errors, I am responsible for those that remain.

Chapter 2 first appeared as 'The Politics of Citizenship in 1940s Britain: The British Nationality Act', *Twentieth Century British History*, 10, No. 1 (1999), 67–95, while an expanded version of Chapter 7 appears as 'The Kenyan Asians, British Politics and the Commonwealth Immigrants, 1968', *Historical Journal*, 42/3 (1999), 809–34. I am grateful to Oxford University Press and Cambridge University Press, respectively, for permission to reproduce this material. Part of Chapter 9 was first prepared for a report entitled 'Les Citoyens, les Sujets et les Européens: la loi britannique de l'après guerre sur la citoyenneté', prepared for the French Ministry of Social Affairs. For permission to quote from the R. A. Butler papers, I am grateful to the Master and Fellows of Trinity College, Cambridge. For permission to quote from the Conservative Party Archives, my thanks to David Simpson.

Finally, I offer a last and inadequate word of thanks to Katja, who tolerated my obsession and who learned far more about Commonwealth immigration than she ever wanted to. I dedicate this book to her.

Contents

A Note on Citations and Abbreviations

Citations

The study relies heavily on archival sources. The organization of these varies considerably among archival repositories (in some, pages are numbered, in others, they are loose; in some files are numbered, in others they are named, etc.). In all cases, I have provided as much information as possible, so that the task of anyone who wishes to retrace the citations will be eased. This advantage will, I hope, compensate for any minor stylistic inconsistencies that exist.

Abbreviations

BDTC	British Dependent Territories Citizenship
BNA	British Nationality Act, 1948
BNA 1958	British Nationality Act, 1958
BNA 1965	British Nationality Act, 1965
BNA 1981	British Nationality Act, 1981
BNO	British National Overseas
BNP	British National Party
BOC	British Overseas Citizenship
CIA	Commonwealth Immigrants Act, 1962
CIA 1968	Commonwealth Immigrants Act, 1968
CICC	Citizen of an Independent Commonwealth Country
CUKC	Citizen of the United Kingdom and Colonies
ECHR	European Court of Human Rights
ECJ	European Court of Justice
EU	European Union
FN	Front national
IA 1970	Immigration Act, 1971
NCCI	National Committee on Commonwealth Immigrants
TUC	Trades Union Congress

Archival Abbreviations

CPA	Conservative Party Archives, Bodleian Library, Oxford
LPA	Labour Party Archives, National Museum of Labour History, Manchester
PRO	Public Record Office (national archives), Kew, London
TUC	Trades Union Congress Papers, Modern Records Centre, University of Warwick

PART I

Policy before 1962:
The Laissez-Faire Years

1

Migration and Nationality in Post-war Britain

COMMENTING on the prospect of non-white migration in 1954, Winston Churchill told the Jamaican Governor, Sir Hugh Foot, that Britain 'would have a magpie society: that would never do.'[1] When the British Nationality Act of 1981 was passed some twenty-five years after Churchill uttered these words, multiculturalism[2] was indisputably a fact of British political and social life. The United Kingdom began the post-war years with a non-white population of some 30,000 people; it approaches the end of the century with over 3 million, whose origins extend from Africa, the Pacific Rim, the Caribbean, and the Indian Subcontinent. Together with France and Germany, it has among the largest ethnic populations in Europe, and it shares with France the largest ethnic-minority citizenry.[3]

Casting an eye across modern Britain, a wide range of political issues are linked one way or another with the experience of Commonwealth migration: the inquiry into the botched murder investigation of Stephen Lawrence, a black Londoner; the Rushdie affair and ensuing debates about the role of Islam in

---

[1] N. Deakin, 'The Immigration Issue in British Politics (1948–1964)' (unpublished D.Phil. dissertation, University of Sussex, 1972), 13.

[2] Terms such as 'multicultural' and, even more so, 'multiracial' are contentious. Race is a social construct—there is no obvious reason why meaningful differences attach to the colour of an individual's skin rather than to the colour of his or her eyes—and it is arguable that discussions of 'race' perpetuate the belief that 'race' exists as something 'out there'. In the main, I use the alternative 'multicultural' (which is much more common in, for example, Canadian debates) because it captures reasonably well the sociological transformation that occurred in post-war Britain, and because it is the less offensive of the two terms. A definition of 'multicultural', however inadequate, is given below. For a discussion, see J. Rex, *The Concept of a Multi-Cultural Society* (University of Warwick: Centre for Research in Ethnic Relations, Occasional Papers in Ethnic Relations No. 3, 1985). My use of the term 'race' is limited to instances in which there is no alternative. With the exception of this footnote, I have specifically avoided the habit, common among British scholars of Commonwealth migration, of using the term 'race' in quotes without clarifying their reservations or providing an alternative. Finally, the term 'immigration' often has (at least in Europe) negative connotations, and a generally better alternative is 'migration'. I have in fact used both interchangeably, retaining use of 'immigrant' and 'immigration' because these terms are used in the scholarly literature, press, and public discussion.

[3] The United Kingdom differs notably from Germany in that most of its non-white immigrants are citizens, whereas the acquisition of German citizenship by migrants has been the exception rather than the norm. This may change following the 1999 reform of German nationality law.

British politics, and the threat of Islamic fundamentalism; bilingual education, and separate denominational schools; the issue of positive ethnic minority targets in hiring. Parts of London, Liverpool, Birmingham, and other English cities that were once traditional homes to the white working class are now made up largely of ethnic minorities. All political parties have had to acknowledge the needs of ethnic minorities, even if they would prefer to ignore them. Even the dietary habits of the English have changed greatly (one shudders at the thought of eating out in England before migration); a curry is among the most common of English meals. All of this, and much else that escapes attention because it is taken for granted, would not have happened without Commonwealth migration. The extent and rapidity of the UK's transformation from a largely homogeneous society[4] into a multicultural society is remarkable, unprecedented, and complete.

The story of Commonwealth migration is particularly striking given that few people would have predicted or wanted a multicultural Britain. Christian Joppke distinguishes in a recent comparative study between wanted temporary migration, wanted settler migration, and unwanted migration.[5] During the 1950s and 1960s, France, Switzerland, and Germany facilitated, through guestworker programmes, wanted temporary migration. Since the 1970s, when the guests did not go home, all migration—in the form of family reunification and asylum seekers—has been unwanted.[6] Australia, Canada, and the USA are among the few Western countries in which policy continues to encourage wanted settler migration.

In contrast to all these countries, post-war Commonwealth migration to Britain has been almost entirely unwanted. For the first three decades of the post-war period, polling data demonstrate consistent majority public opposition to New Commonwealth migration.[7] The available primary sources from as early as the late 1940s suggest a consistent uneasiness on the part of Whitehall,

---

[4] Before 1945, the United Kingdom was, of course, a mélange of Anglo-Saxon, Jewish, Irish, Welsh, Scottish, and Huguenots and other European refugees. This patchwork was, however, European and, more importantly, perceived, since 1945 (but not before), to be largely undifferentiated in terms of culture. By contrast, non-white immigrants were viewed as qualitatively different, as alien, and the term 'multicultural' is applied to the arrival in the United Kingdom of substantial persons of non-European origin and culture.

[5] C. Joppke, *Immigration and the Nation-State: The United States, Germany and Great Britain* (Oxford: Oxford University Press, 1999), 19–21.

[6] Ibid. 19–20.

[7] Although there has been variation in the intensity of opposition. See *Coloured People in Britain* (London: Gallup, 1982), NOP (quoted in *LPA, Study Group on Immigration* 'Public opinion and immigration, by Dr. Mark Adams', Jan. 1969), *Immigration and Race Relations* (London: NOP, 1968), *Attitudes towards Coloured People in Great Britain, 1958–1982* (London: Gallup, 1982). Also see D. T. Studlar, 'British Public Opinion, Colour Issues, and Enoch Powell: A Longitudinal Analysis', *British Journal of Political Science*, 4, No. 3 (1978), 371–81. My comments on public opinion are limited to the 1960s–80s. More recent polling data suggests that positions have modified. The claim that Britons opposed New Commonwealth

Labour, and Conservative governments about non-white migration.[8] Finally, most scholarly literature on Commonwealth migration emphasizes, almost without exception, the hostility of successive British governments and civil servants towards New Commonwealth migration.[9] Despite this opposition, the United Kingdom enters the millennium as a multicultural society facing integration imperatives—the encouragement or discouragement of cultural diversity, the acceptance or prohibition of non-Christian edicts in public and private life, the reform of educational forms that grew up in an era before non-European migration—identical to those of self-avowed multicultural societies.

This book offers an account of Commonwealth migration and the politics linked with it. It is divided into two parts. The first, examining the period from 1948 to 1962, focuses on why and how the UK developed into a multicultural society. In doing so, it breaks with the dominant approach in migration scholarship. Implicitly or explicitly, the majority of those writing on Commonwealth immigration treat the adoption of migration control as the dependent variable, and cite public opinion, racism, and/or political opportunism as the independent variables.[10] The first half of this study reverses the relationship: the *absence*, until 1962, of migration controls, is the dependent variable. The reversal is intuitively appealing. That a nation of 50,000,000 would indefinitely keep its doors open to 600,000,000 individuals from developing countries was always incredible; it was doubly so in light of the manifest opposition of British public opinion and the 1945–50 Labour government's explicit rejection of Commonwealth migration as a solution to post-war labour shortages.[11] Though it is extraordinary in light of the considerable amount of ink spilled over Commonwealth

migration should not be equated with the claim that they reject a multicultural society. See Yasmin Alibhai-Brown, *True Colours: Attitudes to Multiculturalism and the Role of the Government* (London: Institute for Public Policy Research, 1999). Also see S. Saggar (ed.), *Race and British Electoral Politics* (London: UCL Press, 1998).

[8] This is discussed in the empirical chapters.

[9] There is almost a consensus in the literature on this point. See, most recently, K. Paul, *Whitewashing Britain: Race and Citizenship in the Post-war Era* (Ithaca, NY: Cornell University Press, 1997) and I. R. G. Spencer, *British Immigration Policy since 1939: The Making of Multi-racial Britain* (London: Routledge, 1997), ch. 4.

[10] See P. Foot, *Immigration and Race in British Politics* (Harmondsworth: Penguin, 1965), Z. Layton-Henry, *The Politics of Race in Britain* (London: Allen & Unwin, 1984); C. Holmes, *John Bull's Island: Immigration and British Society 1871–1971* (Houndmills: Macmillan, 1988), 260–3; R. Ramdin, *The Making of the Black Working Class in Britain* (London: Gower, 1987), 226–9; and E. J. B Rose et al., *Colour and Citizenship: A Report on British Race Relations* (London: Oxford University Press, 1969), ch. 16.

[11] Rather, it relied on European migrant workers. See R. Miles and D. Kay, *Refugees or Migrant Workers? European Volunteer Workers in Britain 1946–1951* (London: Routledge, 1992). On the decision, see H. Booth, 'Immigration in Perspective: Population Development in the United Kingdom', in A. Dummett (ed.), *Towards a Just Immigration Policy* (London: Cobden Trust, 1986). No subsequent government revisited the possibility of drawing on Commonwealth labour as an explicit element of macro-economic policy.

migration, no one has bothered to ask why it was that an outcome that few people would have predicted or wanted came to be. Countless studies in the last fifteen years have underlined elite-level hostility to non-white Commonwealth migration, but none of them has seriously asked why it was that putatively racist policy-makers allowed the free entry of these migrants for fourteen years.

The second part of the study explains the sharp policy reversal after 1962—the fast and definitive restriction of Commonwealth migration—and the politics and legal peculiarities of Commonwealth migration in the era of closed borders. It examines the character of post-1962 migration restrictions, the turn towards anti-discrimination legislation as the focal point of liberal policy (and liberal opinion), the immigration crises engendered by African expulsions of (legally British) Asians, and the deferral until 1981 of a British citizenship for the British, long after the previous imperial citizenship had outlived its usefulness.

POLICY UNTIL 1962: PUBLIC OPINION, INTEREST GROUPS, AND POLITICAL ECONOMY

The maintenance of a free entry policy until 1962 is doubly intriguing given that the government would have faced few domestic constraints in ending it. Public opinion was firmly against non-white Commonwealth migration. It acted, from 1958 if not earlier, as an incentive for an early and definitive end to Commonwealth migration. Likewise, interest groups—which figure prominently in pluralist accounts—played only a limited role in shaping 1950s' policy towards Commonwealth migrants.[12] A few pro-migrant and anti-discrimination organizations—the Coloured Peoples' Progressive Association, an Indian Association (1958), the West Indian Workers' Association (1961), the Pakistani Workers' Association (1962), and other loosely knit organizations campaigned against racial discrimination and migration control.[13] All were joined by the British Council of Churches and umbrella organizations (white and ethnic minority), notably the Coordinating Committee against Racial Discrimination (1962)[14] and the Conference of

---

[12] Pluralist accounts, to summarize briefly, hold that public policy results from the accumulated pressure of the most powerful interest group or coalition of groups. On pluralism, see H. Eckstein and D. Apter, *Comparative Politics* (New York: The Free Press, 1963), part VI.

[13] For a spirited discussion of these groups, see A. Sivanandan, 'From Resistance to Rebellion', in Sivanandan, *A Different Hunger: Writings on Black Resistance* (London: Pluto Press, 1982). Also see Rose et al., *Colour and Citizenship*, chs. 21 and 25.

[14] From 1964, the Campaign Against Racial Discrimination (CARD).

Afro-Caribbean organizations.[15] They were, however, weak and provided no significant check on any restrictionist impulse 1950s governments might have had.[16]

The trade unions, often an important element in Labour Party policy, were also of little importance to the evolution of migration policy and nationality law. Their policy position tended to blow with the wind, but was only mildly either restrictionist or anti-restrictionist. The TUC officially welcomed New Commonwealth immigrants in 1955,[17] yet it soon expressed doubts in private. In April 1955, a TUC delegation, including Arthur Deakin and Sir Vincent Tewson, the General Secretary, met with the Minister of Labour, Sir Walter Monckton. They pressed the government to continue its pursuit of full employment and suggested that some form of migration control might be considered part of this strategy.[18] Several years later, the TUC again raised the issue with the Ministry of Labour. It stated that it was satisfied with West Indian workers on the whole, but that control might be worth examining because of Indian and Pakistani workers.[19] Yet, following racially motivated riots in 1958, it supported the Labour Party's decision to oppose all controls on Commonwealth migration in the late 1950s,[20] and both it and the Scottish TUC opposed the first introduction of migration controls in 1962.[21] As in the case of racial discrimination,[22] the local trade unions

[15] Rose et al., *Colour and Citizenship*, ch. 25.

[16] The importance of pressure groups is never mentioned in the discussions surrounding the first introduction of migration controls in 1962. As for CARD, it was only formed in 1964, after the first adoption of immigration control in 1962. Although CARD was formed after anti-discriminatory legislation was on the agenda, its greatest influence was felt in this area. It, largely through liberal lawyers, such as Anthony Lester, was closely involved in the 1965 Race Relations Act's passage through Parliament. E. Bleich, 'Races or Racists: Ideas and Race Policies in Britain and France', Paper presented to the twenty-second meeting of the Social Science History Association (18 Oct. 1997), 7. Rose et al., *Colour and Citizenship*, ch. 25.

[17] Layton-Henry, *Politics of Race in Britain* 49.

[18] *TUC, 805.91(1)I*, Meeting with Ministry of Labour, 10 Apr. 1955.

[19] *TUC, 805.91(1)II*, Letter from the Assistant General Secretary of TUC to Iain Macleod, 30 Apr. 1958.

[20] *LPA, Race Relations and Discrimination*, 'Commonwealth Sub-Committee of the National Executive Committee: Final Draft Statement on Racial Prejudice,' Sept. 1958, *TUC, 805.91(1)I*, 'Trades Union Congress: Commonwealth Economic Development', 4 Jan. 1959. The latter criticizes migration controls as ineffective and damaging to the Commonwealth, and calls for further British support for economic development in the colonies.

[21] *PRO, CO 1032/300*, Letter from G. Middleton, Scottish TUC, to R. A. Butler, 6 June 1962, G. P. Freeman, *Immigrant Labor and Racial Conflict in Industrial Societies* (Princeton: Princeton University Press, 1979), 222.

[22] TUC policy on the treatment of non-white workers was clear: racial discrimination was opposed. A resolution was passed in the 1950s prohibiting discrimination on the grounds of race, and the TUC was consistent in its opposition to discrimination. As a federated body with limited powers of enforcement, this naturally did not prevent local unions from discriminating against non-white workers. For a discussion of discrimination by individual unions, see D.

pursued at times policies at variance with the TUC,[23] but the unions were not a central player in migration policy.[24]

British economic policy did not, as functionalist theory might predict, link open immigration with the labour market. [25] Unlike France, Germany, and Switzerland, the UK simply did not actively encourage large-scale migration, permanent or temporary. Reliance on Commonwealth migration to fill labour vacancies was considered by Attlee's government, but it was rejected and the UK sought instead to attract European guestworkers.[26] The sole government-initiated programme for sponsoring labour migration from the Commonwealth was, ironically, the Ministry of Health's programmes under Enoch Powell, bringing nurses to the UK, ostensibly temporarily, for training and work.[27] Beyond this, the only link established between migration and economic needs was a negative one: the Ministry of Labour feared continued

---

Brookes, *Race and Labour in London Transport* (Oxford: Oxford University Press, 1975), Z. Layton-Henry, *The Politics of Immigration* (Oxford: Blackwell, 1992), ch. 3 and Rose et al., *Colour and Citizenship*, 313.

[23]   The role of the Transport and General Workers' Union (TGWU), traditionally one of the most influential unions in the Labour Party, was ambiguous. In May 1955, it called at its biennial conference for the strictest control over all migration, and in 1957 a motion in favour of strict control on non-white workers was passed (Layton-Henry, *Politics of Race in Britain*, 49–50). Yet, in 1965, when a Labour government White Paper reduced the number of New Commonwealth immigrants allowed to enter the United Kingdom, the TGWU was alone in delivering its votes against the measure at Labour's Annual Conference. It is possible that the unions' own contradictions on the question of migration contributed to their limited influence. For an early official discussion to the TGWU's reaction to New Commonwealth migration, see *PRO, LAB 8/1898*, 'Working Party on Coloured People Seeking Employment in the United Kingdom. The Employment Position of Coloured Workers: Note by the Ministry of Labour and National Service', 28 Sept. 1953.

[24]   This is not to claim that they did not play a role in integration policy; after 1962, the trade unions were active participants in the debate over anti-discrimination legislation. See E. Bleich, 'Problem-Solving Politics, Ideas and Race Policies in Britain and France', Ph.D. dissertation, Harvard University, Apr. 1999.

[25]   For (Marxist) functionalist interpretations of British migration policy, see L. Kushnick, , in 'The Political Economy of White Racism in Britain', in Kushnick, *Race, Class & Struggle: Essays on Racism and Inequality in Britain, the US and Western Europe* (London: Rivers Oram Press, 1998); R. Miles, *Racism and Migrant Labour* (London: Routledge & Kegan Paul, 1982), 162–4; R. Miles, 'Labour Migration, Racism and Capital Accumulation in Western Europe since 1945: An Overview', *Capital and Class*, 28 (1986), 49–86; Sivanandan, *A Different Hunger.*   [26]   See Miles and Kay, *Refugees or Migrant Workers?*

[27]   According to Edward Heath, Enoch Powell told the Macmillan Cabinet that it could face down British nurses in a pay dispute 'because I can bring in all the nurses we need from the West Indies' (E. Heath, *The Course of My Life: My Autobiography* (London: Hodder & Stoughton, 1998), 292). London Transport and the British Hotel and Restaurants' Association operated private schemes. The UK did not rely on large-scale migration in part because, first, British economic performance was lacklustre relative to continental Europe and labour shortages were never so severe and, second, Ireland served as an industrial reserve army within easy reach of the UK.

migration during periods of high unemployment. The one ministry that might have argued on economic grounds for an expansive migration policy was its consistent opponent.[28]

None of this is to deny that, as neo-classical and Marxist economic theory predicts,[29] migration resulted from dualities in the world economy:[30] Commonwealth migrants were attracted to the UK by the country's economic prosperity in the 1950s. During these years, the country enjoyed extremely low levels of unemployment, and several industries faced labour shortages. The appeal of the British economy does not, however, explain why a government that was putatively opposed to New Commonwealth migration allowed it to fill these vacancies. Migrants fulfil an economic

---

[28] I am not the first to reject functionalist approaches to British migration policy. Stephen Castles and Godula Kosack, in their ambitious comparative study of migration across Western Europe, note that the United Kingdom is the only country in which migration policy was not linked to an active labour market policy. See S. Castles and G. Kosack, *Immigrant Workers and Class Structure in Western Europe* (London: Oxford University Press, 1973). Also see Booth, 'Immigration in Perspective', 121. I address the claim because it retains intuitive appeal and because, as the citations above attest, it has been endorsed since the Castles/Kosack study.

[29] J. Simon, *The Economic Consequences of Immigration* (Oxford: Blackwell, 1989); Castles and Kosack, *Immigrant Workers and Class Structure in Western Europe*; M. Piore, *Birds of Passage: Migrant Labor in Industrial Societies* (Cambridge: Cambridge University Press, 1979).

[30] Earlier versions of dualism focused on dualistic tendencies in the domestic economy. Dual labour market theory in economics argues that the labour market is divided between a 'primary sector', in which the employees enjoy good pay, benefits, agreeable working conditions and low turn-over rates, and a 'secondary sector', in which jobs are poorly paid with few benefits and in which employers invest little in the workers and tolerate high turn-over rates (M. Freeman and S. Spencer, 'Immigration Control, Black Workers and the Economy', *British Journal of Law and Society*, 6, No. 1 (1979), 53–81, 58–61). The bifurcated labour market is necessary to the continued functioning of the free market, particularly in difficult economic times. The secondary sector bears the full brunt of exogenous shocks, shedding jobs and/or lowering wages in times of economic crisis. Dual labour market theory holds that black workers are disproportionately found in the secondary sector, and that this division of labour serves capital's interests by allowing white workers to climb from the secondary sector to the primary as their previous jobs are taken by ill-paid immigrant workers. This internal migration encourages the ascendant white working class to identify with the petite bourgeoisie, a development that weakens the ideological cohesion of the working class. Capital's interests are further served by this division in the working class, which channels bitterness associated with unemployment and eroding living standards away from employers and the state into intra-class conflict. (N. Bosanquet and P. B. Doeringer, 'Is There a Dual Labour Market in Great Britain?'*Economic Journal*, 330 (1973), 421–35; A. Sivanandan, 'Race, Class and the State: The Black Experience in Britain,' *Race and Class,* 17 (1976), 347–68). The debate on dual labour market theory has passed, largely because the evidence is inconclusive. Just after the War, non-white workers were predominantly found in low-paid, unrewarding positions, and they were disproportionately affected by the UK's sharply rising unemployment from the late 1970s. Since then, however, there has been a significant element of occupational mobility, defined as the percentage of male employees in the top professional, manager or employer category, particularly among Asians (T. Jones, *Britain's Ethnic Minorities* (London: Policy Studies Institute, 1993), ch. 4, especially 82; V. Robinson, 'Roots to Mobility: The Social Mobility of Britain's Black Population', *Ethnic and Racial Studies*, 13, No. 2 (1990), 274–86).

function, but the decision governing their entry, particularly in island nations enjoying firm control of their borders, is a quintessentially political one.[31]

RECASTING ACCOUNTS OF THE 1950S: THE 'RACIALIZATION' SCHOOL

The study of Commonwealth immigration and UK migration policy has been theory poor; many if not most accounts are descriptive. [32] Since the 1980s, however, a collection of revisionist scholars has focused on the role of central state actors in migration policy. The account enjoys near-hegemony among British scholars as a theoretical account of Commonwealth migration in the 1950s. It is referred to here, for lack of a better term, as the 'racialization' account. Following several influential articles in the 1980s and 1990s,[33] it holds that governments' responses to New Commonwealth migration in the 1950s were part of an effort at 'racialization': governments, independently of public pressure, defined migration as a question of 'colour', and 'colour' as a 'problem' to be addressed through the introduction of migration controls. As migration controls could not be justified, according to the authors, by the state of the economy or social problems such as housing or crime, British governments 'racialized' migration in order to justify controls.

The thesis was originally cast as an attack on the 'myth' that 'in the 1950s the state was either absent or played a minimal role in the emerging discourse

[31] For some of the newest work on population movements, which examines emigration to the settler countries of Canada, the USA, and Australia through formal methods, see A. E. Kessler, 'Immigration, Internationalization and Domestic Response: Toward an Explanation for the Rise of Restriction in the "New World" ', Paper presented at the Center for the Study of Immigration, Integration and Citizenship (CEPIC)'s conference, sponsored by the German Marshall Fund, on Migration Controls in 19th Century Europe and America, La Sorbonne, Paris, 25–6 June 1999.

[32] See, for example, Z. Layton-Henry, 'Immigration', in Layton-Henry (ed.), *Conservative Party Politics* (London: Macmillan, 1980); Layton-Henry, *Politics of Race in Britain*, Layton-Henry, 'Race and the Thatcher Government', in Z. Layton-Henry and P. Rich (eds.), *Race, Government and Politics in Britain* (Houndmills: Macmillan, 1986); Layton-Henry, *The Politics of Immigration*; Layton-Henry, 'Immigration and the Heath Government', in S. Ball and A. Seldon (eds.), *The Heath Government 1970–74: A Reappraisal* (London: Longman, 1996) and D. Mason, *Race & Ethnicity in Modern Britain* (Oxford: Oxford University Press, 1995).

[33] B. Carter, C. Harris, and S. Joshi, 'The 1951–1955 Conservative Government and the Racialization of Black Immigration', *Immigrants and Minorities*, 6, No. 3 (1987), 335–47, B. Carter et. al., 'The 1951–55 Conservative Government and the Racialization of Black Immigration', in W. James and C. Harris, *Inside Babylon: The Carribean Diaspora in Britain* (London: Verso, 1993); B. Carter et al., 'Immigration Policy and the Racialization of Migrant Labour: The Construction of National Identities in the USA and Britain', *Ethnic and Racial Studies*, 19, No. 1 (1996), 135–57.

about "coloured colonial immigration".'[34] According to it, the British state was not merely responding to racists; it played a central, perhaps the central, role in creating racism:

The [British state's] policy involved direct intervention on some issues and an apparent inactivity on others. . . . This went far beyond the prejudiced attitudes of individuals, albeit individuals holding high office. It amounted to the construction of an ideological framework in which Black people were seen to be threatening, alien and unassimilable and to the development of policies to discourage and control Black immigration.[35]

With this framework in hand, the state sought to justify migration control with reference to crime, unemployment, and housing, and found that a clear link between these social ills and migration could not be established. Lacking any other means to build a 'strong case', it 'racialized' migration: '[t]his "strong case" [in favour of migration restrictions] was built around a racialized reconstruction of "Britishness" in which to be white was to belong and to be black was to be excluded. . . . In building its strong case, the state undertook nothing less than a political project in which notions of "belonging" and "community" were reconstructed in terms of "racial" attachments and national identity organised around skin colour.'[36]

The argument is thus not merely that there were racists in the British 'state', or that public opposition to migration control was motivated by racism,[37] or that such racism as existed in British society was the consequence of imperialism. 'Our argument', they claim, 'clearly points to the need to recover the history of the state's central role in the construction of post-war British racism. This racism was not simply the consequence of an Imperial legacy, even less

[34] Carter et al., 'The 1951–1955 Conservative Government and the Racialization of Black Immigration', 345. There is no citation to those who apparently believe this myth. The article places a great deal of emphasis on informal measures enacted in the 1950s to limit the rate of New Commonwealth migration (campaigns advertising unemployment in the UK, efforts to 'slow up' the issue of passports) in their attack on the 'myth'. There is in fact nothing particularly new about their revelation. Although the precise nature of the informal measures could not be determined until the archives were opened, E. J. B. Rose discusses them at length in his report, sponsored by the Institute of Race Relations, on the arrival and integration of New Commonwealth immigrants. See Rose et al., *Colour and Citizenship*, ch. 16. I discuss informal controls in chs. 2 and 4.

[35] Carter et al., 'The 1951–1955 Conservative Government and the Racialization of Black Immigration', 335 and 345; B. Carter, 'Immigration Policy and the Racialization of Migrant Labour: The Construction of National Identities in the USA and Britain', *Ethnic and Racial Studies*, 19, No. 1 (1996), 135–57. For another restatement of the same argument, see Carter *et al.*, 'The 1951–1955 Conservative Government and the Racialization of Black Immigration', in James and Harris, *Inside Babylon*.

[36] Carter et al., 'The 1951–1955 Conservative Government and the Racialization of Black Immigration', 336 and 345. [37] Ibid. 345–6.

the consequence of a popular concern in the 1960s about numbers.'[38] It is rather argued that the 'state' created racism where none (or perhaps less?) would otherwise have existed, placed racism at the core of British national identity and used the racism it had 'constructed' to justify migration controls:

When [non-legislative controls on migration] proved insufficient, legislative control increasingly became a favoured option amongst Ministers and senior civil servants. For public consent to be won for legislation, however, a 'strong case' had to be built. A consequence of this was an extension of the control and surveillance of the Black population in the United Kingdom. Integral to the policy and these measures was the development of a racialized construction of Britishness which excluded and included people on the grounds of 'race' defined by colour.[39]

At first glance, the thesis appears so simply deterministic as not to merit attention; indeed, most political scientists have simply ignored the argument rather than engaging it.[40] Such a response is inadequate for two reasons. First, radical hypotheses—based on primary sources—that attribute such pervasive racism to politicians and civil servants amount to serious charges that deserve to be taken seriously. If policy-making was shot through with racism, then this cannot be a matter of indifference to students of British politics, institutions and political processes. Second, the Carter et al. thesis is only the boldest and most complete version of an argument that commands widespread support in the British literature,[41] and scattered support abroad. Some theses are more sophisticated—attending to relationship between state racism and public opposition, for instance—but all embrace the claim that British governments have been active participants in a process of racialization.[42] In a

[38] As is argued by M. Dummett and A. Dummett, 'The Role of Government in Britain's Racial Crisis', in C. Husband (ed.), *'Race' in Britain: Continuity and Change* (London: Hutchinson, 1982) and I. Katznelson, *Black Men, White Cities: Race, Politics, and Migration in the United States, 1900–30 and Britain, 1948–68* (London: Oxford University Press, 1973).

[39] Carter et al., 'The 1951–1955 Conservative Government,' 344–5.

[40] See, for instance, Joppke, *Immigration and the Nation-State*.

[41] Specifically, in the literature examining the UK alone. The thesis is not endorsed by comparativists examining the UK as one case among several.

[42] Thus, for instance, Robert Miles argues (with a sociologist's characteristic clarity) that the class interests of the state and capital are served by racializing immigrants and assigning them to a particular position within the capitalist economy: 'Migrants came to Britain to sell their labour power. They were met with an increasingly negative political and ideological reaction, particularly in the 1960s and 1970s, which succeeded in applying the label "race" to the migrants. Consequently, they were negatively racialised and thereby assigned a special position in ideological relations . . . and economic and political relations . . . The process of racial categorisation or racialisation is simultaneously the historical consequence and the site of subsequent struggles between classes and of the formation and reproduction of class fractions. The ideology of racism and the practice of racial discrimination are central components of this process of racialisation which has determinate effects on ideological, political and economic relations.' Miles, *Racism and Migrant Labour*, 168 and 184.

1990 study, one scholar concludes that the only task left for students of Commonwealth migration is more analysis of the racialization process.[43] The most recent book on Commonwealth immigration, by Kathleen Paul, arrives at a variant of the same conclusion. Discussing New Commonwealth migration in the 1950s, she argues—adopting language that is strikingly similar to Carter et al.'s—that governments adopted 'a variety of administrative devices to control migration and an educative campaign designed to inculcate among the resident UK public the dangers of uncontrolled inward colonial migration. There were no formal directives or official offerings of hate literature. Rather, the campaign revolved around the reconstruction of British subjects as immigrants, the transformation of immigrants into "coloureds," and the problematization of "coloured immigration".'[44]

Although the original thesis's research was limited to the 1950s, the arguments have broadly coloured academic judgements of migration and nationality policy more generally. Ending her book with an examination of contemporary British citizenship, Paul concludes that, 'despite its territorial appearance, these [provisions of the British Nationality Act, 1981, which governs current nationality policy] in fact placed greater significance on parentage than on geography and so position the 1981 act within the larger postwar discourse of blood, family and kith and kin.'[45]

One of the goals of this study is the debunking of this thesis. The primary research is seriously flawed, supporting an argument about the state's construction of racism with reference solely to unrepresentative quotations by often marginal figures. The thesis ignores contradicting instances in which a principled stand was made against racism, and it ignores a broader complex of factors that influenced government policy. Other accounts of Commonwealth migration—whether theoretically informed or not—have highlighted the role of public hostility, housing shortages and other local pressures, a lingering attachment to empire in the Conservative party, Commonwealth ideals in the Labour Party and Commonwealth states' opposition to migration restrictions.

---

[43] K. Lunn, 'The British State and Migration, 1945–1951: More Light on the Empire Windrush', T. Kushner and K. Lunn (eds.), *The Politics of Marginality: Race, the Radical Right and Minorities in Twentieth Century Britain* (London: Frank Cass, 1990), 172. For restatements of the same basic thesis, see L. Kushnick, 'The Political Economy of White Racism in Great Britain', in Kushnick, *Race, Class & Struggle: Essays on Inequality in Britain, the US and Western Europe* (London: Rivers Oram Press, 1998); R. Miles and A. Phizacklea, *White Man's Country: Racism in British Politics* (London: Pluto Press, 1984); Sivanandan, *A Different Hunger*; J. Solomos, *Race and Racism in Britain* (Houndmills: Macmillan, 1993), 56–61. Also see J. Rath, 'Political Action of Immigrants in the Netherlands: Class or Ethnicity', *European Journal of Political Research*, 16 (1988), 623–44, 628–9; Rath uncritically reproduces the claim that British immigration laws and rules are racist.

[44] Paul, *Whitewashing Britain*, p. xiii.

[45] Ibid. 183. I return to this particular charge in the conclusion.

A further factor one could add is simple uncertainty about what to do.[46] The 'racialization' thesis will have none of it; the whole history of British policy towards Commonwealth migrants can be traced to a desire to keep blacks out, and the construction of racist definition of nationality in order to do so. As the dominant interpretation of the state's response to Commonwealth migration, it has impeded a balanced and comprehensive understanding of British migration and race relations policy, and it has passed on successive governments a judgement that is largely undeserved.[47]

The claim that migration control was unrelated to public opposition is untenable. From Gallup's first measure of public opinion in 1958, polls consistently demonstrated majority support for stricter migration control, and these demands intensified in the run-up to the first introduction of such controls in 1962.[48] The Commonwealth Immigrants Act of 1968, which denied entry to Kenyan Asians holding British passports, enjoyed strong public support.[49] During the same period, Enoch Powell, a vociferous opponent of Commonwealth migration, was much more popular than the Conservative leader (Edward Heath), and his calls for repatriation were backed by a majority of the public.[50] If Britain had adopted a truly democratic migration policy, migration restrictions would have been introduced sooner, not later.

[46] Uncertainty is a variable that is too often ignored by political scientists.

[47] For examples of sophisticated discussions of race, see A. Favell, *Philosophies of Integration* (Houndmills Macmillan, 1998), ch. 6, Favell. 'Multicultural Race Relations in Britain: Problems of Interpretation and Explanation', in C. Joppke (ed.), *Challenge to the Nation-State: Immigration in Western Europe and the United States* (Oxford: Oxford University Press, 1998); A. Messina, *Race and Party Competition in Britain* (Oxford: Clarendon Press, 1989); S. Saggar, *Race and Public Policy: A Study of Local Politics and Government* (Aldershot: Avebury, 1991); S. Saggar, 'Analyzing Race and Elections in British Politics: Some Conceptual and Theoretical Concerns', in S. Saggar (ed.), *Race and British Electoral Politics* (London: UCL Press, 1998); (in the same volume) A. Geddes, 'Inequality, Political Opportunity and Ethnic Minority Parliamentary Candidacy' and A. M. Messina, 'Ethnic Minorities and the British Party System in the 1990s'. Also see W. James, 'The Making of Black Identities', in R. Samuel (ed.), *Patriotism: The Making and Unmaking of British National Identity* (London: Routledge, 1989).

[48] D. Dean, 'The Conservative Government and the 1961 Commonwealth Immigration Act: The Inside Story', *Race and Class*, 35, No. 2 (1993), 57–74. On the importance of public opinion generally, see C. Holmes, *John Bull's Island: Immigration and British Society 1871–1971* (Houndmills: Macmillan, 1988), 260–3; Ramdin, *Making of the Black Working Class in Britain*), 226–9 and Rose et al., *Colour and Citizenship*, ch. 16.

[49] Gallup asked, 'Do you approve or disapprove of the measures the Government are taking in controlling migration from Commonwealth countries?' 72% approved; 21% disapproved; and 7% did not know. *Coloured People in Britain* (London: Gallup, 1982). National Opinion Polls (NOP) asked, 'Do you think the Government was right or wrong to introduce the new migration bill?' 79% thought it was right; 15% thought it was wrong; and 6% did not know. NOP quoted in *LPA, Study Group on Migration* 'Public Opinion and Migration, by Dr. Mark Adams', Jan. 1969.

[50] See *Attitudes towards Coloured People in Britain*, questions 74–80.

The fact of public opposition renders the argument logically incoherent. If there was little societal opposition to migration restrictions, then the construction of a racist national identity would be redundant. Policy-makers, especially those in a Westminster system concentrating extensive power in the executive, could simply have adopted strict migration controls.

Finally, and most importantly, the thesis finds no support in the archival sources. Although they base their argument on primary materials, Carter et al. provide a selective reading of them; they highlight those quotations that suggest hostility to non-white migration and/or racism, while ignoring those that suggest an opposition to racism and/or a support for New Commonwealth migration. While there were instances of what can be characterized as racism (when this is understood as a desire to exclude black immigrants because they are black), there were more in which individuals took a principled stand against racism and in which the right of non-white British subjects to enter the UK under the same terms as white subjects was defended. The Colonial Secretary in the mid-1950s, Alan Lennox-Boyd, threatened to resign over a proposal to apply migration restrictions exclusively to non-white British subjects.[51] A few years later, the opposition of the Ministry of Labour to non-white migration was checked by the Colonial Office; the latter was a strong supporter of West Indian migration.[52]

Nor does the public action of politicians lend much credibility to the argument. In 1964, the racist campaign of the Conservative candidate in Smethwick, who successfully defeated a prominent Labour incumbent, was condemned in exceptionally strong language by the incoming Prime Minister, Harold Wilson.[53] In the late 1960s and 1970s, Enoch Powell's extremist demand for the active repatriation of Commonwealth immigrants was rejected, he was sacked from the Shadow Cabinet, and unconditional entry was offered to some 50,000 Asians expelled from Uganda.[54] Racism, understood as an assumption of ethnic inferiority, has since the War been marginal and politically insignificant among politicians and bureaucrats. Throughout the post-war period, both were significantly more liberal than the public to which politicians owed their office.

Lest this point be misunderstood, it does not mean that racism was irrelevant to the history of migration. There were several instances in which racism played a role—notably in the victory of the 1964 Conservative candidate in Smethwick, whose supporters told voters that 'If you want a nigger neighbour, vote Liberal or Labour.' It is rather that it played its most powerful role at the

---

[51] See Ch. 3.   [52] See Chs. 4 and 5.   [53] See Ch. 6.
[54] See Chs. 7 and 8.

level of society and not the state. As comparativist scholars have recognized for other countries, politicians were liberal, the public illiberal.[55]

INSTITUTIONS, EMPIRE, AND THE OLD COMMONWEALTH: THE ORIGINS OF MULTICULTURAL BRITAIN

In the light of the inadequacy of much existing theoretical literature on Commonwealth migration, there is considerable scope for new interpretations of this large and historically unprecedented movement, and of the politics linked with it. The account offered here is institutional, and it draws on theoretical advances, particularly in the last decade, realized by European and US scholars. Three aspects of immigration politics and policy require explanation:

- *Its early post-war liberality.* From 1948 to 1962, Britain operated one of the most liberal migration regimes in the world, granting citizenship to hundreds of millions of colonial subjects across the globe. The policy lacked public support, and a number of politicians were increasingly uneasy about it from the 1950s. It was none the less retained until 1962. Why?
- *Its post-1960s restrictiveness.* Once the decision to end unfettered Commonwealth immigration was taken, it was rapidly followed by a series of restrictions that ended, by 1971, almost all privileges once enjoyed by Commonwealth citizens. Once a model of liberality, migration policy is now as restrictive as it can possibly be. How can the speed of completeness of this shift be explained?
- *Its legal peculiarities.* British migration policy until 1981 was characterized by a series of unique (and bizarre) features: from 1948 to 1962, colonial subjects and British citizens were legally indistinguishable; from 1962 to 1981, only a portion of the many British citizens worldwide possessed the right to enter Britain; Britain in the 1960s and 1970s was buffeted by a series of migration crises in which the citizenship rights of East African Asians claiming entry was unclear; and from 1971 to 1981, British identity was founded on the manufactured concept of 'patriality'. How can these British 'exceptionalisms' be accounted for?

---

[55] G. P. Freeman, 'Modes of Immigration Politics in Liberal Democracies', *International Migration Review*, 29 (1995), 881–902, 881–2, D. King, *In the Name of Liberalism* (Oxford: Oxford University Press, 1999).

MIGRATION POLICY PRE-1962

The liberality of British policy between 1948 and 1962 resulted from the intersection of a bipartisan ideological commitment, on the one hand, and the distribution of power within the Conservative Party, on the other. The intersection of ideology and partisan power created an effective veto on migration control. In 1948, the UK created, for reasons that had nothing to do with migration, a definition of citizenship including Britons and colonial subjects under the same nationality. They were both Citizens of the United Kingdom and Colonies with full citizenship rights in the UK. The Labour government enacted the legislation in order to maintain a common definition of nationality throughout the British Empire, and it did so before large-scale migration was considered possible.

When migration began in the 1950s, Conservative governments—sensitive to the political risks associated with a lax migration policy—considered restricting it. Migration controls were, however, checked by a temporal intersection of ideology and power: the attachment of the Conservative Party to the Old Commonwealth mapped on to selective Cabinet-level opposition to racist migration control. The result was the veto throughout the 1950s of restrictions on a Commonwealth migration that few, if any, politicians wanted.

IDEOLOGY AND THE OLD COMMONWEALTH

Paradoxically, the (non-European) colonies were only marginally relevant to the decision to maintain an open door to the whole Commonwealth until 1962. Policy was rather conditioned by an ideological commitment, in both parties but especially among Conservatives, to a previous century's colonies: the 'Old Commonwealth' of Canada, New Zealand, and Australia. Although empire is in the public mind associated with the non-European colonies, above all India—an association encouraged by England's ever-flourishing nostalgia industry—it was the Old Commonwealth that stood at the foundation of Britain's overseas network. The Old Dominions were central to the United Kingdom's economic and foreign policy; they contributed to its international prestige and influence; and they ensured the flourishing of the English language and British culture in the international arena.[56] They were

---

[56] On the United Kingdom's relationship with the Old Dominions, see R. F. Holland, *Britain and the Commonwealth Alliance 1918–1939* (London: Macmillan, 1981); F. H.

Britain abroad, what was called—in the jingoistic heyday of imperialism—'greater Britain'.[57] Attachment to the Old Commonwealth would eventually fade, but, in the 1950s it was firmly entrenched in British political life. The 1948 British Nationality Act was motivated by a desire to shore up this relationship.

One of the most tangible expressions of these distant countries' importance to the UK was intra-Commonwealth migration. The UK actively sponsored the migration of Britons to the colonies, and there was from the beginning a numerically smaller, but symbolically important, movement of Old Dominions' citizens to the UK. At no point did British politicians or civil servants consider restricting Old Commonwealth migration. They were fully committed to the right of Old Commonwealth citizens to enter the United Kingdom freely and to enjoy the full rights of citizenship. By contrast, they were only superficially and residually committed to the entry rights of New Commonwealth citizens. Non-white British subjects were tolerated in small numbers, and even appreciated to some extent as a reflection of the tradition of formally welcoming British subjects from the whole of the Empire, but their arrival was in every sense secondary to the movement of Old Dominions citizens between the UK and the Old Commonwealth.

When New Commonwealth migration picked up in the 1950s, politicians could not bring themselves to apply controls to Old Commonwealth citizens. At the same time, there was selective, but uncompromising, resistance to applying racially discriminatory restrictions, i.e. restrictions solely on the New Commonwealth. The decisive moment was 1955. Powerful members of the Cabinet wished to apply controls exclusively to the New Commonwealth, but the Colonial Secretary, Alan Lennox-Boyd, refused to accept racially discriminatory restrictions. Threatening resignation over the issue, he offered the rest of the Cabinet the choice between migration controls on the whole Commonwealth and no controls at all. Boxed in by their ideological commitment to Old Commonwealth citizens' right to come to Britain, Conservatives opted for no controls.

In almost all cases, opposition to restrictions was articulated by the Colonial Secretary, who had the powerful backing of his department in this effort. The Colonial Office was a partisan of New Commonwealth migration, and above all black migration. The Office assigned itself the task of retaining for West Indians, whom it felt possessed the work ethic and cultural baggage requisite to integration in British society, a right to enter in the face of growing Cabinet

Underhill, *The British Commonwealth: An Experiment in Co-operation* (Durham, NC: Duke University Press, 1956) and H. V. Wiseman, *Britain and the Commonwealth* (London: Allen & Unwin, 1965).

[57]   C. W. Dilke, *Greater Britain* (London: Macmillan, 1869).

scepticism. During the late 1950s, Colonial Office officials worked to resist the position of the avowedly restrictionist Ministry of Labour, appealing to imperial ideology and optimistic economic predictions. The Office naturally lost the battle eventually, and its liberalism was not colour-blind: it was as hostile to Indian and Pakistani migration as it was enthusiastic about West Indian. Its actions none the less contributed to the delay in adopting migration controls and, on a different level, challenge simplistic models attributing crude racism to all politicians and civil servants.

A rather complex mélange of factors thus explains 1950s liberality. British policy-makers were, to be sure, not enthusiastic about non-white migration, and many of them—backed by public opinion—wished to see it restricted. Suggestions made by Enoch Powell in the 1960s and 1970s, to the effect that New Commonwealth migration resulted from some sort of Whitehall conspiracy,[58] are palpable nonsense. Yet, domestic policy concerns about Commonwealth migration were in the 1950s secondary to a larger foreign policy aim—maintaining close relations with the Old Commonwealth—and they lay against the background of selective opposition to racist restrictions. In effect, British politicians faced the choice of casting the net of migration control over the whole of the Commonwealth or accepting New Commonwealth migration as the unavoidable corollary of the Old; they chose the latter. Policy-makers accepted the transformation of the United Kingdom into a multicultural society as the price of supporting the ties between Britain and the Old Dominions.

POST-1960S RESTRICTIVENESS: GLOBALIZATION, CLIENT POLITICS, AND PARLIAMENTARY SOVEREIGNTY

Several chapters are devoted to the 1950s because these were the crucial years ensuring that Britain would become a multicultural society. From 1948 to 1962, some 500,000 primary migrants—migrants without families in the UK—entered the country. Rumours of impending control circulated in 1960–1, and this seems to have doubled the migration figures for 1961, but the arrival would have been in the hundreds of thousands in any event. As governments recognized in the 1960s, this migration effectively guaranteed that the number of persons entering Britain, even if all migration ended, would at least double in the next decade. No liberal democracy has ever

---

[58] Ironically, Powell's accusations of Whitehall duplicity and nefariousness are similar to those of Carter et al.

prevented family reunification, and those, such as France and Germany, that have attempted to do so have failed. A commitment to family reunification is a basic liberal democratic value; only Middle Eastern states have successfully prevented it.[59] Although the Conservative government did not recognize it at the time, the foundations of British multiculturalism were firmly laid as it drafted legislation ending Commonwealth migration.[60]

That said, once the door to the Commonwealth was finally closed, the closure was quick and complete. The rapidity alone is remarkable. In 1962, the Conservatives agonized over migration control. Under a barrage of Labour Party criticism, they instituted a liberal migration policy granting some 60,000 Commonwealth migrants (in addition to aliens) the right to enter the UK. Three years later, the Labour Party sharply reduced this figure; a further six years later, the Conservatives ended the privileged migration status for all but a handful of Commonwealth migrants. Today, the UK operates one of the strictest migration policies in the Western world; annual migration flows are roughly half that experienced by France, a country with a similar population and colonial history, and are much smaller than those received by Germany; family reunification policy is strictly enforced with no Briton enjoying a formal right to it; and all parties agree that the strictest control on 'numbers' is a prerequisite to 'good race relations'.

One way of accounting for the change would be to suggest, as many have, that British governments were simply spineless in the face of public anti-immigrant sentiment. To be sure, both Labour and the Conservative parties were sensitive to the position of votes on Commonwealth migration; only a strange democratic political party would not be. All European governments, however, answer to electorates that take a hostile view of immigration—the UK is in no measure exceptional in this respect—and yet they have enjoyed less success than the British in restricting policy and reducing numbers. Something beyond public sentiment must account for why a policy that had been so generous became so miserly.

[59] On this point, see Dominique Schnapper, *L'Europe des immigrés* (Paris: Éditions François Bourin, 1992).

[60] Ian Spencer's argument that the 1962 legislation was the most important moment in the development of multiculturalism, because it discouraged Commonwealth migrants from return-ing and respected family reunification, is untenable. Family reunification, as noted, was inevitable, and it is extremely unlikely that significant numbers of Commonwealth migrants would have returned. As France, Germany, and Switzerland learned, migrants who promised to return to their countries of origin following the termination of their 'temporary' labour permits reneged on these commitments, and the countries could do little about it. In the British case, when free circulation between this country and the colonies existed, the net migration was always substantially positive. There is little reason to believe that the 1960s, in the absence of controls, would have heralded the voluntary return of hundreds of thousands of New Commonwealth migrants.

The answer might lie in theoretical insights offered by US and European comparativists. Both neo-liberal and globalization theorists have offered accounts of migration control. The former is associated above all with James Hollified. In a series of contributions over more than a decade, Hollifield attempts to account for the 'gap' between the post-OPEC goal of ending immigration and the fact of continued large-scale immigration to Europe.[61] Hollifield argues that migration since the war has resulted from the dynamic influence of markets and rights: demand for labour brought unskilled labour to Europe until the 1970s, and continues to bring skilled labour today; the extension of rights to these workers throughout Europe, irrespective of citizenship, ensured their stay. Hollifield points to both international and domestic factors as the source of these rights, but gives emphasis—particularly in his later work—to the latter.[62] Domestic institutions and actors—and above all the courts—have extended to third country nationals (permanently) resident in Europe social and economic entitlements that have allowed them to resist attempts to repatriate them and to limit family unification.[63] In contrast with globalization theory, which downgrades the importance of states and their role in limiting migration, Hollifield's position remains essentially statist. While rights-based legal regimes guarantee access for certain categories of migrants, and while states trade economic sovereignty for economic gain (higher growth through freer trade, exchange rate stability through monetary union), they are unwilling (and increasingly so) to risk migration; their efforts are consequently aimed, not always successfully, at limiting it.[64]

The British case is in important respects a problem case for Hollifield's model. After the 1962 turn to restrictionism, governments restricted migration quickly and successfully. Numbers dropped from their 1961 peak of 136,000 to half that figure, and they have remained constant—with a few exceptions—

[61] The 'gap hypothesis' was first observed by Hollifield in a 1986 article. See J. F. Hollifield, 'Immigration Policy in France and Germany: Outputs vs. Outcomes,' *Annals*, 485 (May 1986), 113–28.

[62] J. F. Hollifield, *Immigrants, Markets, and States: The Political Economy of Postwar Europe* (Cambridge, Mass.: Harvard University Press, 1992), ch. 1, J. F. Hollifield and G. Zuk, 'Immigrants, Markets, and Rights', H. Kurthen et al., *Immigration, Citizenship, and the Welfare State in Germany and the United States: Welfare Polices and Immigrants' Citizenship* (London: JAI Press, 1998); J. F. Hollifield, 'The Politics of International Migration: How Can We 'Bring the State back in'?', in Caroline Brettell and James F. Hollifield (eds.), *Talking across Disciplines: Migration Theory in Social Science and Law* (London: Routledge, forthcoming).

[63] Hollifield, *Immigrants*, 222–3. Also see W. Cornelius, P. L. Martin and J. Hollifield, *Controlling Immigration: A Global Perspective* (Stanford, Calif.: Stanford University Press, 1994).

[64] See J. F. Hollifield, 'Migration, Trade, and the Nation-State: The Myth of Globalization,' *UCLA Journal of International Law and Foreign Affairs*, 3, No. 2 (Fall/Winter 1998–9), 595–636.   [65] See the Appendices.

to this day.[65] It is the case that numbers in, say, the late 1980s were similar to those of the late 1950s.[66] This has often been taken as evidence of the failure of restrictive immigration laws and regulations; it should not be. The stabilization of migration flows is evidence of their policy success: while the rest of Europe and the USA saw sharply rising numbers from the 1970s and (especially) the 1980s, Britain kept these constant.[67] One never hears the claim—made above all in the USA, but also in Germany—that 'this nation has lost control of its borders' for the obvious reason that it has not. It is this success that makes Britain, in Freeman's words, 'a deviant case',[68] and challenges, on the face of it, the neo-liberal thesis.

Hollifield's neo-liberal thesis has been equated with the argument that states cannot control immigration.[69] This is not quite so: it rather holds that the rights extended to certain categories of migrants—refugees and immediate family members—have placed constraints on the degree of which states can limit their entry.[70] Such analytical restraint has not, however, been characteristic of globalization theorists, who offer near-sweeping dismissals of the state and its role in determining and implementing migration policy. Saskia Sassen, who is most closely associated with this approach, argues that the logic of globalization renders migration controls essentially untenable. There are three elements to her argument. First, important elements of immigration policy have been shifted from states to supranational institutions, most import-antly the European Union (EU) but also the European Court of Human Rights and bi- and multilateral arrangements.[71] Second, consistent with the arguments of post-nationalists,[72]

---

[66] This point was also made by G. P. Freeman, 'The Politics of Race and Immigration in Britain,' Paper given to Faculty Seminar in British Studies, University of Texas, Austin, 1994.

[67] I am basing this claim on 'settlement figures'; that is, people who become permanently resident in the country.

[68] G. P. Freeman, 'Britain, the Deviant Case,' in Cornelius,. Martin, and Hollifield, *Controlling Immigration*.

[69] A. M. Messina, 'The Not So Silent Revolution: Postwar Migration to Western Europe', *World Politics*, 49 (1996), 130–54, 140–1.

[70] For an effort to specify these, see J. F. Hollifield, 'Ideas, Institutions, and Civil Society: On the Limits of Immigration Control in Liberal Democracies', *IMIS-Beitraege*, 10 (1999), 57–90.

[71] S. Sassen, 'The *de facto* Transnationalizing of Immigration Policy', in C. Joppke (ed.), *Challenge to the Nation-State* (Oxford: Oxford University Press, 1998).

[72] D. Jacobson, *Rights across Borders: Immigration and the Decline of Citizenship* (Baltimore: Johns Hopkins University Press, 1997); Y. N. Soysal, *Limits of Citizenship: Migrants and Postnational Membership in Europe* (Chicago: University of Chicago Press, 1994). Postnationalism, to summarize briefly, holds, first, that universal personhood has de-coupled rights, on the one hand, and citizenship and identity, on the other (one can enjoy many of the rights of German citizenship without being German) and, second, that this development resulted from the 'internationalization' and 'universalization' of human rights legislation and discourse (R. Hansen, 'Migration, Citizenship and Race in Europe: Between Incorporation and Exclusion', *European Journal of Political Research*, 35, No. 4 (1999), 415–44). For a critique

an emergent international human rights regime—channelled domestically through the judiciary—limits the capacity of nation-states to limit immigration and refugee movements (thus limiting sovereignty).[73] Finally, the contradiction between increasingly free movement of services, capital, and goods, on the one hand, and the maintenance of limits of the movement of persons, on the other, is likely to render immigration controls unsustainable.[74]

The British case frustrates—totally—the expectations of globalization theory. Unless it is dismissed as *sui generis*, the UK makes clear that globalized markets are consistent with closed borders. Strict migration control on the Commonwealth crystallized in the early 1970s, and rules on family reunification were tightened in the 1980s and 1990s. These, of course, are the decades in which globalization accelerated. International norms and instruments have exercised little if any constraining influence on UK migration policy. The European Court of Human Rights and its Commission have decided two high-profile migration cases against the UK; as discussed, the country ignored one and formally respected another through further tightening family reunification rules. At precisely the moment when, according to the globalization thesis, the UK should have found its restrictionist impulses constrained, it was able to give these near-free reign.

The problems with the globalization thesis extend beyond the UK case. These are threefold. First, the opening of Europe's internal borders has been entirely consistent with the closing of its external borders to non-European and third world migrants.[75] It is not that the EU cannot control, for reasons of logical coherence or human rights, immigration from outside its borders; it is rather that it chooses for reasons of national interest to tolerate and encourage migration among select and wealthy European neighbours. Second, the thesis reifies separate immigration streams: asylum seekers cannot be compared to labour migrants, and labour migrants vary greatly in origin, qualifications, and relationship to the destination country. If globalization is undermining any migration controls, these will most likely be controls on skilled migration. The imposition—again in Europe, as the USA is a more complicated case—of tight controls on non-EU migrants has been accompanied by the relative relaxation of

---

of post-nationalism, see Joppke, 'Immigration Challenges the Nation-State', in *Challenge to the Nation-State*. Soysal's study also examines, and offers an institutional account of, migrant incorporation. On this, and migrant political participation, also see P. Ireland, *The Policy Challenge of Ethnic Diversity* (Cambridge, Mass.: Harvard University Press, 1994).

[73] Sassen, 'The *de facto* Transnationalizing of Immigration Policy', 69–71.

[74] S. Sassen, *Losing Control* (New York: Columbia University Press, 1996).

[75] M. Feldblum, 'Reconfiguring Citizenship in Western Europe', in C. Joppke, *Challenge to the Nation-State*.

controls on skilled migration.[76] In this case, however, 'globalization' becomes a code-word for national self-interest: skilled migration is the sort that every nation has a primae-facie interest in attracting. Finally, it ignores implementation; human rights treaties do exist, but some states sign the treaties without incorporating them into domestic legislation; some incorporate them with severely restraining caveats; and some ignore them altogether. The result, as Joppke put it, is that 'the international human rights regime is not so strong as to make states fear and tremble';[77] lacking incorporation guarantees and enforcement mechanisms, they remain non-binding public international law, often little more than a statement of normative intent.

The inadequacies have led other scholars to seek to account for the gap between restrictionist migration policy aims and expansionist migration policy outcomes. In a series of important pieces, Gary P. Freeman argues that the modest expansiveness characteristic of Western immigration policies results not from international institutions, but from the dynamics of the domestic political process.[78] Applying a model of client politics developed some years ago by James Q. Wilson,[79] Freeman argues that the distributional consequences of migration policy—concentrated benefits and diffuse costs—result, in the context of information scarcity and discourse constraints on those opposed to immigration, in an incentive structure favouring a modestly expansive policy towards migrants and legal permanent residents. Public opinion, though often hostile to immigration, is constrained by incomplete information and limits on discourse, namely the risk of charges of racism and an inability to defend ethnically based migration policies. Extreme-right parties are small and weak, and they are up against a tendency among large mainstream parties to seek a consensus taking immigration off the political agenda.[80] Those benefiting from immigration—businesses and families and

[76] This point was made by Aristide Zolberg at the Center for the Study of Immigration, Integration and Citizenship (CEPIC)'s conference, sponsored by the German Marshall Fund, on Migration Controls in 19th Century Europe and America, La Sorbonne, Paris, 25–6 June 1999. On skilled migration, see K. Koser and J. Salt, 'The Geography of Highly Skilled International Migration', *International Journal of Population Geography*, 3 (1997), 285–303. On Australia, Canada, and the USA, see G. P. Freeman, 'The Quest for Skill: A Comparative Analysis', in A. Bernstein and M. Weiner (eds.), *Migration and Refugee Policies: An Overview* (London: Pinter, 1999); J. Salt, *International Movements of the Highly Skilled* (International Migration Unit, Occasional Papers, No. 3) (Paris: OECD, 1997).

[77] C. Joppke, 'Why Liberal States Accept Unwanted Immigration', *World Politics*, 50 (Jan. 1998), 266–93, 269.

[78] Freeman, 'Modes of Immigration Politics in Liberal Democratic States'. G. P. Freeman, 'The Decline of Sovereignty? Politics and Immigration Restriction in Liberal States', in Joppke (ed.), *Challenge to the Nation-State*.

[79] J. Q. Wilson (ed.), *The Politics of Regulation* (New York: Basic Books, 1980).

[80] Messina, *Race and Party Competition in Britain*.

ethnic relations of those in migrant streams—are well organized and influential; politicians, in turn, have a rational interest in satisfying them. Finally, the costs of immigration, in the short run, fall on the least advantaged members of society with few channels for voice, and, in the long run, are diffuse, falling belatedly on the whole society.[81] For Sassen, autonomy is sharply limited by international variables; for Freeman, it is intact and only partially limited by domestic ones.[82]

Freeman's model is elegant and allows us to account, without reference to weak international institutions or the (somewhat cryptic) concept of universal personhood, for the apparent contradiction between a professed commitment (at least in Europe) to tight migration policies and substantial continuing migration. It nonetheless has a number of weaknesses. First, as Freeman himself concedes, the model works best when applied to the USA, particularly on the issue of lobbying and electoral influence. 'Migrant/ethnic lobbies' enjoy greatest influence in systems characterized by multiple access points and (resulting) porousness to interest group pressure. It works less well in the UK, in which the political system offers fewer access points but greater rewards to the limited number of groups that do gain entry to policy networks.[83] A coordinated lobbying campaign targeting Members of Congress will influence voting patterns in a way that it simply will not in the UK, where party discipline and mechanisms enforcing it are strong. Second, as Joppke has argued,[84] Freeman does not identify the legal process as a separate and powerful source of expansiveness towards migrants; judges are shielded from popular pressure and obligated to apply universal principles with objectivity.[85] The opposite is also true: democratic polities with constrained and/or timid judiciaries enjoy greatly increased autonomy in pursing strict migration policies; this fact is of considerable importance in post-1960s' British migration policy.

The political history of Commonwealth migration accords only partially with Freeman's model. Both political parties did seek a consensus on migration in the 1960s, but only after concentrated opposition to Commonwealth

---

[81] Freeman specifies the model on pages 882–5 of 'Modes of Immigration Politics'; I take these arguments directly from them.

[82] For a similar argument, see C. Joppke, 'Why States Accept Unwanted Immigration', and P. Weil, *The Transformation of Immigration Policies: Immigration Control and Nationality Laws in Europe: A Comparative Approach* (Florence: EUI Working Papers, 98/5, 1998).

[83] D. S. King, 'The Establishment of Work-Welfare Programs in the United States and Britain: Politics, Ideas, and Institutions', in S. Steinmo, K. Thelen, and F. Longstreth, *Structuring Politics: Historical Institutionalism in Comparative Analysis* (New York: Cambridge University Press, 1992).

[84] Joppke, *Immigration and the Nation-State*, 18.

[85] On this, see V. Guiraudon, 'Citizenship Rights for Non-Citizens: France, Germany and the Netherlands', in Joppke, *Challenge to the Nation-State*.

migrants made itself loudly heard in a number of constituencies in the 1964 election.[86] The results terrified Labour, and at least partially affected its decision to turn the restrictionist screw in 1965. At the same time, Commonwealth migrants were in the 1960s and 1970s relatively poorly organized; it is difficult to think of any major politician who faced censure for supporting migration restrictions. Finally, discourse constraints existed—the phrase 'Keep Britain White' was marginal and widely viewed by politicians as disreputable—but politicians were able to justify strict migration controls with legitimate discourse. The policy of 'firm but fair' migration policy, which crystallized in the 1960s, justified strict immigration policy with reference to the need to integrate migrants into British society. 'Integration without control is impossible, but control without integration is indefensible,' as Roy Hattersley slickly put it.

The great strength of Freeman's account[87] is that it focuses attention on national institutions and the national political process as the central factors explaining policy expansiveness or its opposite.[88] In the UK, the variable of greatest importance in explaining current, restrictive migration is the inadequacy of institutional constraints on it. From the 1960s, the main pro-migration client within the Cabinet, the Colonial Office, saw its position reduced. The very fact of having taken the historic decision to control British subjects made further controls easier; the psychological barrier had been crossed and the institutional mechanisms were in place. At the same time, the Office was gradually reduced as a major office of State. The winding down of empire throughout the 1960s undermined its *raison d'être*, and it was merged first with the Commonwealth Relations and later the Foreign Office. By the 1970s, the greatest defender of non-white British subjects' right to enter the UK had disappeared as an institution and elite liberalism no longer expressed itself in favour of open borders.

Liberalism rather became invested in race relations policy. From the 1960s, the UK enacted legislation that created some of the most extensive anti-discriminatory legislation in Europe. By the mid-late 1960s, both parties' front benches accepted, or claimed to accept, the endlessly repeated argument that good race relations (i.e. amicable dealings between Europeans and non-Europeans and an absence of threats to public order) depended on strict

---

[86]   British exceptionalism is conceded by Freeman, 'Modes of Immigration Politics', n. 10.

[87]   In addition to being a general account, something still rare among studies of European immigration. On the need for theory in the study of immigration more generally, see A. Portes, 'Immigration Theory for a New Century: Some Problems and Opportunities', *International Migration Review*, 31, No. 4 (1997), 799–825.

[88]   Also see J. Money, *Fences and Neighbours: The Political Geography of Immigration Control* (Ithaca, NY: Cornell University Press, 1999); here the spatial concentration of immigrants is the independent variable.

migration control. A few isolated individuals continued to carry the charge in favour of open borders, and the Labour Party practised its age-old ritual of condemning migration policies that it later extends. Overall, however, liberal politicians who had once been sympathetic to Commonwealth migration, such as Roy Jenkins, expressed their liberalism in favour of race relations legislation.[89]

To some degree, this experience corresponds to that of the rest of Europe and the USA. All North European countries had ended liberal migration policies by the 1970s, and some of them—notably Holland and France—enacted anti-discrimination legislation. Likewise, both Europe and the USA have populations that are hostile to migration, if somewhat less so in the USA. Yet, none of these nations has been able to achieve the degree of restrictiveness, or control on numbers, associated with the UK. The difference is not accounted for by public attitudes (UK public opinion is squarely within the European restrictionist median) or elite hostility (no north European government has wanted migration since the 1970s) but rather by the absence of institutional constraints on restrictionist governments.

The first of these, well known to comparativists and students of British politics, is the absence of an effective legislature checking the UK's strong executive. The simple fact is that, under conditions of majority government, a single party commanding strong party loyalty and possessing mechanisms to enforce it faces little resistance from the Opposition or its own ranks. In 1962, 1968, 1971, and 1988, British governments, in enacting restrictive legislation, ignored scattered public protests and faced little meaningful parliamentary opposition. As Walter Bagehot argued with justified hyperbole in the nineteenth century, 'there is nothing the British Parliament cannot do except transform a man into a woman and a woman into a man.' Whereas the USA in the 1990s attempted to restrict migration modestly and ended up, following the tortuous American legislative process, expanding it, the UK has consistently adopted migration bills and immigration rules that, though sometimes modified in committee, look broadly the same from beginning to end.

The weakness of channels for pro-migrant opinion is compounded by the absence of a strong judiciary and an entrenched bill of rights. Judicial review does not exist in the UK: British courts rule on the construction, the interpretation, and the meaning of an Act of Parliament, but they cannot strike down laws themselves.[90] They may claim that a law is inconsistent with

---

[89] For the most comprehensive recent study of anti-racism legislation in Britain, see E. Bleich, 'Problem-Solving Politics: Ideas and Race Policies in Britain and France' (PhD dissertation, Harvard University, Apr. 1999).

[90] H. J. Abraham, *The Judicial Process* (New York: Oxford University Press, 1993), 239.

other, existing laws, but there is no higher authority than the common law itself to which they can appeal. Although there is no right to enter a sovereign country in international law, the absence of such an authority, in the form of a particular bill of rights, has considerable implications for migration policy. In countries whose constitutions recognize a right to mobility, to a normal family life or even to equality, all of these rights can be the basis of a claim that citizens have a right to bring family members from abroad; in the UK, there is no right to mobility, equality, or a normal family life, and there is no right to family reunification.

As discussed in the last chapter, Britain's membership in the European Union (EU) changes the picture somewhat. Although pundits and politicians pay tireless homage to parliamentary sovereignty, it vanished in 1973, except in the trivial sense that the UK Parliament might be able to leave the EU unilaterally (though even this is doubtful). The constraint, however, remains weak. The European Court of Justice (ECJ) has been restrained in its rulings on nationality and the rights of third country nationals, and only a fraction of the European Court of Human Rights' (ECHR) decisions address migration. The two most famous of these had doubtful consequences: a 1973 European Commission of Human Rights decision against the exclusion of Kenyan Asians from the UK was effectively ignored, and a 1985 family unification decision was respected only by making policy less generous. The UK's current (1999) incorporation of the European Convention on Human Rights into national legislation may make some difference in the future, but it is likely to be on the edges of migration law and policy. As Christian Joppke has argued, Germany's, the USA's, and (one could add) France's relatively liberal family unification regimes resulted from domestic, not international court decisions.[91] Beyond family unification, the ECJ and the ECHR have limited jurisdiction over migration. Until such a day as the UK enacts a bill of rights, judicial restraint on UK migration policy will remain ineffectual.

Returning to the central point of this section—the transition from liberality to restrictiveness—it should be emphasized that Westminster institutions did not determine in isolation the restrictiveness of post-1960s' migration policy. The legislature and the judiciary were as institutions constant across the 1950s and 1960s and thus cannot alone explain variation in migration policy outcomes between the two decades. It is rather that, once a restrictive course had been agreed upon, these institutions facilitated it in a manner that they would not (and did not) in North America or continental Europe. In addition, there was one institutional change that removed the intra-executive constraint on a restrictionist migration policy: the marginalization of the

---

[91]   Joppke, *Immigration and the Nation-State*, 267.

Colonial Office (following the loss of an intra-bureaucratic competition with the restrictionist Ministry of Labour). This minor institutional shift occurred against a broader attenuation of the Cabinet's commitment to the Old Commonwealth, or at least a weakening of its willingness to tolerate non-white migration in its name. The previous bulwark against immigration control—a commitment among policy-makers to the right of free entry for British subjects—was no longer sufficient to resist the logic and force of the restrictionist argument. Bipartisan support for the free entry of British subjects was based on a system in which Old Dominions/UK movement (both temporary and permanent) dominated and in which a colonial/New Commonwealth migration was limited and temporary. When New Commonwealth migration matched, and then surpassed, Old Commonwealth migration, the open-door policy's days were numbered.

THE LEGAL PECULIARITIES OF BRITISH IMMIGRATION AND NATIONALITY

Citizenship and immigration in post-war UK are the result of an interlocking, and poorly understood, relationship between the feudal basis of British nationality, the post-war experience of decolonization, and the policy instruments chosen to restrict immigration. British migration and nationality legislation has depended on a series of measures that appear alternatively bizarre and sinister, and the politics of immigration have been punctuated by an exceptional series of crises, engendered by expulsions in the former colonies, in which there was general confusion over the UK's legal obligations. All of these have been mentioned in the literature, but there has been no attempt to link them with each other or to identify a common cause. The book examines four exceptional features of the UK experience, and relates these to a common institutional root:

1. Between 1948 and 1962, colonial subjects and British citizens were legally indistinguishable; the former not only had the right to enter the UK, but were in law full British citizens.
2. From 1962 to 1981, the right to enter the UK was not based on citizenship; some British citizens were free from immigration control, others were subject to it, and others were unsure.
3. In the late 1960s and early 1970s, the politics of citizenship were dominated by expulsion crises in which Asians driven out of Africa had or claimed a right to enter the UK; incredibly, British governments were unable to answer a question as basic as whether they had a legal and moral right to enter Britain.

4. In 1971, the British government based the right to enter the UK on the reviled concept of 'patriality'. The status confirmed in critics' eyes the essentially racist character of British migration law and further blocked, until 1981, the creation of a British citizenship for Britons.

Understanding these four features, which were fundamental to the experience of post-war migration and nationality, requires attending to the causal influence of a definition of imperial citizenship, adopted in 1948, on the whole post-war history of Commonwealth migration.

The 1948 legislation created an institutional structure that limited subsequent policy options and militated against its own replacement. In doing so, it led governments to adopt alternative, and flawed policy instruments, which themselves led to migration-related crises, in the form of the Asians' expulsions. The history of Commonwealth migration and nationality law since the war thus powerfully exhibits path dependence—policy options made at one point limit subsequent options and as a result encourage policy continuity—and policy feedback—policies adopted at time t create a new constellation of politics at time $t + 1$.

PATH DEPENDENCE AND THE STUDY OF POLITICS

A number of innovative studies have applied path-dependence theory to political problems.[92] When clearly defined, path dependence does not merely mean that decisions and events today are in some general sense the product of earlier decisions and events. A path-dependent effect can only be said to occur when a previous decision reinforces itself, when it determines in part the future development of events. Margaret Levi, who brings a healthy scepticism to path dependency, puts it this way:

Path dependence does not simply mean that 'history matters.' This is both true and trivial. Path dependence has to mean, if it is to mean anything, that once a country or

---

[92] See in particular K. Thelen, 'Historical Institutionalism in Comparative Politics', *Annual Review of Political Science*, 2 (1999), 369–404. P. Pierson, 'The Path to European Integration: A Historical Institutionalist Account', *Comparative Political Studies*, 29, No. 2 (Apr. 1996), 123–63, 131 and R. D. Putnam, *Making Democracy Work: Civic Traditions in Modern Italy* (Princeton: Princeton University Press, 1993). For classic applications in economic history, see B. Arthur, 'Competing Technologies, Increasing Returns, and Lock-in by Historical Events', *Economic Journal*, 99 (Mar. 1989), 116–31; W. Brian Arthur, 'Self-Reinforcing Mechanisms in Economics', in P. W. Anderson et al. (eds.), *The Economy as an Evolving Complex System* (Reading, Mass.: Addison-Wesley, 1988); and P. David, 'Clio and the Economics of QWERTY', *American Economic Review* 75/2 (May 1985), 332–7. For a critique of path dependence (and especially David's work), see S. J. Liebowitz and S. E. Margolis, 'The Fable of the Keys', *Journal of Law of Economics*, 33 (Apr. 1990), 1–25.

region has started down a track, the costs of reversal are very high. There will be other choice points, but the entrenchments of certain institutional arrangements obstruct an easy reversal of the initial choice. Perhaps the better metaphor is a tree, rather than a path. From the same trunk, there are many different branches and smaller branches. Although it is possible to turn around or to clamber from one to the other—and essential if the chosen branch dies—the branch on which a climber begins is the one she tends to follow.[93]

But why does the original entrenchment create this effect? Krasner, who first popularized the logic behind path dependence among political scientists, suggests a useful standard: '[t]he basic characteristic of an institutional argument is that prior institutional choices limit available future options': the range of options available at any point in time is constrained by extant institutional capabilities, and these capabilities are themselves a product of choices made during some earlier period.[94] To put it another way, path dependence occurs when a decision limits the range of available options at subsequent points and, in so doing, encourages continuity in the form of a retention of the original choice. The decision may be truly 'locked-in', in the sense that reversal is impossible, or, as is more likely in politics, reversal may be rendered more difficult by the path-dependent effect.[95]

Political scientists are divided about whether path-dependence theory predicts, identifies causal mechanisms, or, most sceptically, is little more than a rich metaphor for policy continuity.[96] This debate will not be resolved, and is, indeed, hardly addressed, in these pages. Suffice it to say for the moment that there are at least two prerequisites to speaking coherently, as distinct from merely fashionably, about path dependence: the delineation of moments at which a path-dependent effect is exhibited and the specification of the mechanisms channelling it. In the former, this involves proving causal effect

[93] M. Levi, 'A Model, A Method, and a Map: Rational Choice in Comparative and Historical Analysis', in M. I. Lichbach and A. S. Zuckerman (eds.). *Comparative Politics: Rationality, Culture, and Structure* (Cambridge: Cambridge University Press, 1997), 28. I should like to thank Margaret Levi for allowing me to view and cite this essay in advance of publication. [94] Krasner, 'Sovereignty', 71–2.

[95] There is a lively debate among economists about the applicability of path dependence to economic history, and particularly the claim that increasing returns are common enough to be of any economic significance. For the sceptics, see S. J. Liebowitz and S. E. Margolis, 'Path-Dependence, Lock-in, and History', *Journal of Law, Economics, and Organization*, 11, No. 1 (1995), 205–26, 207; S. J. Liebowitz and S. E. Margolis, 'Should Technology Choice be a Concern of Antitrust Policy?' *Harvard Journal of Law & Technology*, 9, No. 2 (1996), 283–318, 289. Paul Pierson has picked up on this debate and offered a robust defence, whatever the verdict of the economists' debate, of path dependency's role in politics, which is more than economics given to increasing returns. See Pierson, *Path Dependence, Increasing Returns, and the Study of Politics*.

[96] For a review, see Thelen, 'Historical Institutionalism in Comparative Politics'. I owe my thanks to Ira Katznelson and Robert Lieberman for this paragraph.

at the choice points; path dependence is only established when it can be shown that policy divergence was considered and rejected for reasons that cannot be explained without reference to the structure of costs and incentives created by the original policy choice. If at least a residue of path dependency—in addition to the more well-known factors of interest group lobbying, public opinion, incrementalism, and so forth, cannot be isolated—then there was no such effect.

In the history of post-war Commonwealth immigration, there were several choice points at which a path-dependent effect militated in favour of policy continuity. The mechanism was self-reinforcing incentive effects, exercised through government elites;[97] they undertook a sort of cost/benefit analysis and decided that the costs of radical policy change carried the argument in favour of retaining the original policy. The enactment of the British Nationality Act, 1948, for reasons external to immigration, led to the institutionalization of a legal structure whose complexity and legal content served as an independent factor militating in favour of its retention. BNA 1948 determined the evolution of migration politics and policy at three points:

- In 1962, Commonwealth migration was restricted for the first time. The Conservative government, in drawing up the Commonwealth Immigrants Act, 1962, needed a mechanism on which to base controls. The obvious, and most logical, solution would have been the replacement of the common imperial citizenship created in 1948 with a citizenship exclusively for Britons; only individuals possessing this citizenship would have the right to enter the UK. As archival documents indicate, policy-makers considered, and rejected, this option. They decided that the complex legal structure created in 1948 would be too difficult to overhaul, and that doing so might further incite anger in the remaining colonies. Consistent with path-dependency theory, BNA, 1948, which Labour adopted for reasons unrelated to New Commonwealth migration, effectively militated against its own replacement. The government opted to retain the same citizenship for Britons and 'colonial' subjects, and to differentiate among them at the immigration ports on the basis of their passports. If their passports were issued under London's authority (as indicated by a stamp in the passport), they were free from control; if issued under a colonial governor's authority, they were subject to control.
- In 1968, the consequence of BNA 1948's 'stickiness' revealed itself again in what has come to be called the Kenyan Asians crisis. Following

---

[97] For a distinction between causal mechanisms in feedback effects, see P. Pierson, 'When Effect Becomes Cause: Policy Feedback and Political Change', *World Politics*, 45, No. 4 (1993), 595–628.

independence in 1962, the bulk of the Asian community in Kenya, numbering some 200,000, did not apply for or was denied Kenyan citizenship. Several years after independence, the government, reflecting widespread public hostility against the economically successful Asians, enacted a series of measures designed to drive them out of the economy and, ultimately, the country. Since the 1962 British legislation was meant to restrict migration from all parts of the Commonwealth, the Asians should have had no right to enter the UK. However, the interaction of the 1948 and 1962 legislation, in effect, 'created' this right. At independence, the colonial government in Kenya closed shop. Under normal conditions, this would have meant nothing. Because of the 1962 Commonwealth Immigrants Act, however, its consequences were staggering. Asian passports that were issued before independence under the colonial governor's authority were issued after independence under London's authority. As a result, the Asians were immediately 'released' from the 1962 controls. On the night of Kenyan independence the conditions for the Kenyan Asians crisis—one of the most contentious aspects of Commonwealth migration to the UK—were set in place. The 1962 legislation, the character of which was largely determined by BNA 1948, led, in conjunction with Kenyan independence in the context of an absence of inclusive citizenship provisions, directly to the Kenyan Asians crisis.

• In 1971, the Conservative government sought to avoid a repeat of the Kenyan Asians episode by placing migration controls on a more rational footing. It found itself unable, however, to escape the dilemma confronted by its 1962 predecessor: replacing BNA 1948 would require a massive overhaul of nationality legislation in both the UK and the remaining colonies, and it would probably provoke the anger of the latter. Like its 1962 predecessor, the government sought in 1971 to find another basis for control. Rather to its pleasure, the government alighted on the concept of 'patriality'; only 'patrials' would have the right to enter the UK. In order to satisfy those Conservatives still attached to the Old Commonwealth, the government defined patrials as anyone with a parent or grandparent born in the UK. To the government's surprise, the concept provoked a fury of criticism; the special provisions for grandparents, combined with the vaguely ethnic overtones of the word 'patrial', confirmed in its critics' minds both the essentially racist core of the legislation and the government's nefarious intentions. The concept, however, was instrumental and its origins contingent: it was only chosen because the tentacular effects of BNA 1948 prevented its own replacement, and, in the absence of citizenship, the UK government needed some mechanism to distinguish those with the right of entry from those without it.

In all three cases, developments in immigration were not merely path dependent upon previous immigration policies; that would border on the true-but-trivial. It was rather that immigration policy and immigration politics were path dependent upon nationality law.

Lest this appear overly deterministic, it should be emphasized that the institutional effect did not act in isolation from other factors. In 1962, the rush to get immigration control drafted made policy-makers less willing to push for a fundamental overhaul of BNA 1948; in 1968, the crisis was triggered by national policy choices, above all Kenya's exclusivist definition of nationality and its Africanization policies. Path-dependency theory does not require that it be the sole independent variable; it rather holds that the dynamic makes one choice more likely, and at times profoundly so, than another. In British migration policy, path dependency was not the only factor at work in these three instances, but it was the most important one. There was, in addition, a final and broader path-dependent consequence of the 1948 legislation: the boxing-out, until 1981, of a legal definition of UK citizenship exclusively for Great Britain and Northern Ireland. In consequence, a nation that prides itself on its ancient institutions has a definition of national citizenship that is less than two decades old.

2

Imperial Subjects, Imperial Citizens: The British Nationality Act, 1948

THE story of post-war migration is the story of citizenship, which was defined in the United Kingdom for the first time in 1948. The British Nationality Act (BNA) of that year was, as Enoch Powell argues,[1] a revolution in the constitutional status of British subjects within the United Kingdom and Empire and in the institutional links between Britain and the member states of the Commonwealth. It was such for two reasons: first, the legislation, in a manner which was not anticipated, created the conditions that facilitated a mass migration of New Commonwealth citizens to the United Kingdom; and second, it bequeathed to subsequent policy-makers a legal framework that shaped, and ultimately limited, their ability to articulate a policy response to this migration.

The chapter has three aims. The first is to offer an account of BNA's creation. As the Act was the legal framework within which multicultural Britain emerged, an understanding of this process presumes an understanding of the legislation that sanctioned it. Against a lingering misperception,[2] I argue that the enactment of BNA was only peripherally related to immigration. The British Nationality Act was never intended to facilitate mass migration, still less to promote the transformation of Britain into a multicultural society. Its aim was constitutional: the retention of a uniform status, and the possession of uniform privileges, for all British subjects. Canadian legislation altered the definition of British subjecthood throughout the Commonwealth; BNA constituted an attempt to reconstitute a pre-war definition of British subjecthood, and a related system of imperial migration that had been threatened by a unilateral action on Canada's part. The act was a fundamentally backward-looking document reaffirming the status quo as it had existed for decades.

---

[1] For Powell's comments on the act, see E. Powell, *Still to Decide* (London: B. T. Batsford, 1972), 190–2 and 'The UK and Immigration', Address to Sydney University, Sept. 1988, *Reflections of a Statesman* (London: Bellew Publishing, 1991), 411–12.

[2] L. Kushnick, 'The Political Economy of White Racism in Britain', in Kushnick, *Race, Class & Struggle* (London: Rivers Oram Press, 1998), 174, Andrew Roberts, *Eminent Churchillians* (London: Weidenfeld & Nicolson, 1994), 215–16.

Second, the chapter discusses the extent to which there existed a belief on the part of influential policy-makers that the United Kingdom possessed a unique obligation, as the centre of the Empire and Commonwealth, to maintain an open door for all British subjects. It has become fashionable to dismiss out of hand this idea and the corresponding suggestion that immigration restrictions were delayed as a result. One author argues that developments under Macmillan's premiership demonstrate that there never was any principled commitment among British policy-makers.[3] The director of the Institute of Race Relations, Sivanandan, ridicules claims of 'mother-country obligation' as 'a load of bull-shit' taken seriously by 'the tear-stained liberals'.[4] Liberals of the sort, one is tempted to continue, who ran the Institute of Race Relations before its lurch to the Marxist periphery, orchestrated by Sivanandan, in the early 1970s. Sivanandan's polemical tirade hardly constitutes an argument that needs to be taken seriously, but it is important to understand the role of ideas and ideology—attachment to Commonwealth, a belief in Britain's unique obligation as head of the largest empire in the world—in Commonwealth immigration and migration policy. The fact that we find—no doubt rightly—such ideas antiquated, condescending, and hypocritical today does not mean that they exercised no influence on men's thinking and actions in the 1940s.

This chapter considers such questions through an analysis of parliamentary and committee debates surrounding BNA. These make two points, which will continue to come up in this study, quite clear. BNA was not designed to facilitate and did not anticipate non-white immigration. At the same time, a substantive commitment to an open door to the Commonwealth *did* exist. It was, however, a commitment to a system of inter-imperial migration in which the dominant movement was between, on the one hand, the United Kingdom and, on the other, the Dominions of Canada, Australia, and New Zealand. Such movement was expressive of the primary link between the UK and these countries, and their citizens were welcomed in the United Kingdom as a manifestation of it. Colonial migration was tolerated, and in small amounts viewed as part of the grand tradition of *Civis Britannicus sum*[5] in which all British subjects could enter the United Kingdom, but it was in every sense secondary to the movement of individuals to and from the Old Commonwealth.

Third, the chapter sets the context for the remainder of the study. BNA marked a turning-point in the constitutional evolution of imperial and

---

[3]   J. Solomos, *Race and Racism in Britain* (Houndmills: Macmillan, 1993), ch. 3.

[4]   A. Sivanandan, 'Race, Class and the State', in Sivanandan, *A Different Hunger: Writings on Black Resistance* (London: Pluto Press, 1982), 106–7.

[5]   'I am a British citizen.'

Commonwealth nationality. Since migration to the UK was sanctioned by convention before 1948,[6] it did not possess statutory protection until then. The granting of such a status had an important consequence: the mechanism created by the 1948 legislation, a single citizenship for Britons and 'colonial' British subjects, proved extremely complicated to reform, and it encouraged the retention of the status past the point at which it failed to serve its original purpose. In this sense, while the British Nationality Act did not create a right where none had existed,[7] it amounted to more then a mere formalization of past practice.[8] Although it was not known at the time, the enactment of the British Nationality Act amounted to the creation of an institutional structure that would for several decades shape the evolution of British immigration policy and nationality law.

THE ORIGINS OF THE BRITISH NATIONALITY ACT

Events in Canada set BNA 1948 into motion. The Canadian Prime Minister, Mackenzie King, announced the Liberal government's plans to introduce, in 1946, a citizenship act that would define Canadian citizens and declare that they possessed British subjecthood in consequence of their status as Canadian citizens. Although such legislation hardly appears as the stuff of constitutional revolution, it marked the end of a centuries-old definition of British

---

[6] In defining convention, I follow Sir Kenneth Wheare's definition: 'By "convention" is meant a binding rule, a rule of behaviour accepted as obligatory by those concerned in the working of the Constitution.' K. Wheare, *Modern Constitutions* (London: Oxford University Press, 1951), 179. The maintenance of an open door for all British subjects was accepted by the United Kingdom as a duty it had to all British subjects. As it was a convention, free entry was not formally guaranteed but it was implied by statute and legal decision. These are discussed below. On the role of conventions in the British constitution and British politics, see G. Marshall, *Constitutional Conventions: The Rules and Forms of Political Accountability* (Oxford: Clarendon Press, 1984).

[7] It is sometimes claimed, by scholars and politicians, that the great post-war migration could not have occurred without the introduction of the British Nationality Act. See E. Powell, *Freedom and Reality* (London: Batsford, 1969), 213 and Roberts, *Eminent Churchillians* 216. This view cannot, as we shall see, be supported. Free movement from all parts of the Empire to Britain had been ensured at least since 1914 and was generally recognized in the nineteenth century. Others have made a similar point. (N. Deakin, 'The British Nationality Act of 1948: A Brief Study in the Political Mythology of Race Relations', *Race*, 11, No. 1 (1969), 77–83, 77; P. Foot, *The Rise of Enoch Powell* (Harmondsworth: Penguin, 1969), 15–18, and Freeman, *Immigrant Labor and Racial Conflict in Industrial Societies*, 37.) The misunderstanding is, however, still perpetuated in contemporary accounts, including a detailed account by Roberts (see above).

[8] As is claimed by Deakin, 'The British', Foot, *Immigration*, and Freeman, *Immigrant Labor*.

subjecthood. In 1608, the English courts heard a case brought on behalf of a Scottish child, Robert Calvin, over the Scottish possession of English lands. Central to the argument was the question of subjecthood: before 1608, Scots were aliens in England, whether they were born before or after King James I (previously King James VI of Scotland) became King James of England in 1603. The courts (apparently under the influence of the Commons, which sought Scottish legal observance and Scottish taxes) ruled that Calvin was not an alien; all Scots born within King James's rule were English subjects, while those born before were not.[9]

Calvin is recognized by constitutional historians to be the origin of allegiance as a cornerstone of English common law.[10] 'Allegiance' implies two conditions: first, that the bond is a direct, unmediated relationship between king and subject and, second, that any privileges attaching to one's status as subject are granted by the sovereign and are exercised at his pleasure; they are not claimed by the subject against his sovereign. These features distinguish a 'subject' from a 'citizen'; the latter enjoys its status through membership in a community enjoying the same status and makes claims against the state based on this membership.

This essentially feudal concept—that which is within the realm of the lord belongs to the lord—remained unaltered as Britain entered the imperial age.[11] All those born within the sovereign's empire were deemed to be British subjects and enjoyed, in theory, all privileges attached to this status.[12] A basic

---

[9] Those born in Scotland while Queen Elizabeth ruled England were not under the obedience of King James and were, therefore, aliens. See A. Dummett and A. Nicol, *Subjects, Citizens, Aliens and Others: Nationality and Immigration Law* (London: Weidenfeld & Nicolson, 1990), 59–63.

[10] See J. Mervyn Jones, *British Nationality Law and Practice* (Oxford: Clarendon Press, 1947), 41 and C. Parry, *Nationality and Citizenship Laws of the Commonwealth and of the Republic of Ireland*, 2 vols. (London: Stevens, 1957)].

[11] This is something of an oversimplification. The question of distinctions among British subjects (in addition to the fundamental distinction between subjects and aliens) continued to be a matter of controversy into the seventeenth and eighteenth centuries (for example, the status of subjects in Ireland and in Hanover), and the principle of *ius soli* operated with *ius sanguinis* (at times British subjects had to be born within the sovereign's kingdom to a British subject, while persons born to a subject, but outside the sovereign's territory, continued to be British subjects). See Parry, *Nationality and Citizenship Laws of the Commonwealth*, 47–65. The important point is that the principle behind *Calvin* justified the grant of British subjecthood to persons in the dependent territories.

[12] The only precedent for such a conception of membership is, to my knowledge, the Roman. As the Empire expanded, Roman citizenship was conferred on peoples in the occupied territories. Roman citizenship, like the British, recognized no borders within the Empire. On this, see W. H. Hadow, *Citizenship* (Oxford: Clarendon Press, 1923), ch. 7 ('Citizenship and Empire'). The comparison was not lost on British statesmen, who often invoked *Civis Britannicus sum* as a sentimental expression and defence of subjecthood's indivisibility. In 1954, Henry Hopkins (Colonial Secretary) told the House of Commons that '[i]n a world in

feature of the doctrine underpinning allegiance is indivisibility; all subjects enjoy precisely the same relationship with the monarch and no distinction can be made among them. One logical corollary of this was that free movement should have been guaranteed throughout the Empire and Commonwealth. Within the Empire, this was relatively unproblematic. The maintenance of free movement did exist, and the chief beneficiaries of this system were, as one would expect, Britons.[13]

The Dominions were less enraptured with the idea of a common identity throughout the Empire and Commonwealth. Their status as Dominions created a tension in nationality law: because their members enjoyed their privileges through a direct 'grant' from the Crown without passing through local citizenship, they lacked a legal basis for distinguishing between their members and other British subjects; yet their status as Dominions, which entailed autonomy in most domestic matters, implied the ability to control the movement of persons through their territories. This tension manifested itself in the nineteenth century, when the Dominions' restrictionist policies obstructed the migration of Indian labour throughout the Empire.[14] At the Imperial Conference of 1911, the British government sought to harmonize imperial naturalization. By establishing identical conditions for naturalization in all parts of the Empire and Commonwealth, the Conference aimed at reconciling Dominion autonomy in matters of population movement with the principle of non-distinction among British subjects. The result was the British Nationality and Status of Aliens Act of 1914, which defined as a British subject anyone who was a person, or a descendent in the male line of a person, 'born within His Majesty's dominions and allegiance'[15] (i.e. within

which restrictions on personal movement and immigration have increased we can still take pride in the fact that a man can say *Civis Britannicus sum* whatever his colour may be, and we take pride in the fact that he wants and can come to the mother country.' *Parliamentary Debates (Commons)* (532), col. 827, 5 Nov. 1954.

[13] Non-European British subjects in the colonies theoretically enjoyed the right of free movement within the Empire, but few had the resources to avail themselves of it. In the nineteenth and twentieth centuries, this right became increasingly restricted as various colonial immigration laws created for the purposes of immigration control distinctions among British subjects. See Dummett and Nicol, *Subjects, Citizens, Aliens and Others*, 123–4.

[14] Deakin, 'The British Nationality Act', 78. Australia and Canada also enacted restrictions on Chinese immigrant labour. At the Conference of Australia Colonies in 1881, the Australian premiers decided to fine shipowners landing in Australia with an immigrant/tonnage ratio higher than 1 : 100 and charged a landing fee for all immigrants. In 1885, Ottawa enacted the Chinese Immigrant Act, which adopted a similar immigrant/tonnage ratio and imposed a 'head-tax' of $50.00 on Chinese immigrants. This was raised to $100.00 in 1900 and a crippling $500.00 in 1903. On this, see Dummett and Nicol, *Subjects, Citizens, Aliens and Others*, 117.

[15] British Nationality and Status of Aliens Act (*The Law Reports*, vol. lii, 1914), Section 1 (1). The act also granted the status to anyone 'born on board a British ship whether in foreign territorial water or not'.

the Old Commonwealth or Empire). Since the doctrine of indivisibility was maintained, the statutory definition of subjecthood should have, in principle, been strengthened. Under pressure from the Dominions, the Act, however, also gave statutory recognition to the practice of distinguishing among British subjects.[16] This provision contradicted the principle underlying subjecthood—that all subjects have identical rights, obligations, and status due to their allegiance to the Crown—and the British government sought to temper it by securing informal agreement among the Dominions to a 'common code'. This amounted to an undertaking by the Dominions to maintain closely similar nationality laws and to respect the convention that substantial amendments to the common code were 'matters for prior consultation and agreement between members of the Commonwealth'.[17]

Like much legislation concerned with the Commonwealth, the 1914 Nationality Act broke no new ground; rather, it attempted to reconcile in statute extant Dominion practices with past imperial doctrine. And, like most imperial legislation, it was soon called into question by new Dominion initiatives. In 1918, the UK further agreed that each Dominion government should have complete control over immigration, subject to the proviso that British subjects, once admitted, would enjoy reciprocal rights in all territories under the Crown.[18] The system of reciprocity, to minimize contradictions between domestic laws, required that the common code be maintained. No Dominion, in principle, should have unilaterally altered the conditions of citizenship.[19] The Imperial Conference of 1921 further affirmed Dominion autonomy in nationality questions by conceding that each Old Commonwealth Country could settle its citizenship, but it expressed the hope that any deviation from the common code would be insignificant and exceptional.[20] Canada passed legislation in 1921 that came close to violating the agreement to prior consultation and South Africa followed suit in 1927.[21] Other Dominions respected the code only by delaying

---

[16]   Ibid. Section 26 (1) stated that 'Nothing in this Act shall take away or abridge any power vested in, or exercised by, the Legislature or Government of any British Possession, or affect the operation of any law at present in force which has been passed in the exercise of such a power, or *prevent any Legislature or Government from treating differently different classes of British subjects*' (emphasis added).

[17]   *PRO, PREM 8/851*, 'Government Statement on the considerations involved in the proposed change in the British Nationality Law: in Joint Memorandum by the Home Secretary and the Secretary of State for Dominion Affairs', 29 July 1946. The Dominions had incorporated the provisions of the 1914 British Nationality and Status of Aliens Act into their statutes. See Parry, *Nationality and Citizenship Laws of the Commonwealth*, 84.

[18]   Deakin, 'The British Nationality Act of 1948', 78.

[19]   Ibid. 78.

[20]   Patrick Gordon Walker, *The Commonwealth* (London: Secker & Warburg, 1962), 166–9.

[21]   Both acts made local nationality a subdivision of British Nationality ('a small circle within a larger') and therefore maintained the primacy of allegiance. *PRO, HO 213/410*, 'British Nationality Bill. Mr. Ede. Clause 1. Supplementary Note', undated.

or abandoning much-needed reform.[22] Ireland took the most assertive action in 1935. The Irish Nationality and Citizenship Act of that year defined Irish citizens and classified all others, including British subjects, as aliens.[23] This initiative could none the less be dismissed as the impetuosity of a reluctant and disloyal member of the Commonwealth, while all previous decisions could be said to fit, however uncomfortably, within the broad framework of British subjecthood. All subjects possessed their privileges through a direct grant from the Crown, and these privileges, although not equal throughout the Empire and Commonwealth, were (Ireland excepted) at least uniformly unequal. This balance could no longer be supported after Canada's introduction of its own citizenship.

The 1946 Act defined Canadian citizens, declared that 'a Canadian citizen is a British subject'[24] and recognized as a British subject under Canadian law any person who had that status under the laws of any country within the Commonwealth.[25] Canadian citizens would, from 1946, be British subjects in consequence of being Canadian citizens.

The Canadian initiative was regarded by British policy-makers as the first fundamental breach of the doctrine of the indivisibility of subjecthood throughout the Empire and Commonwealth.[26] It could not be argued that the change was an exceptional one affecting only Canadians and that the common code could be maintained among all the nations except Canada, which would have a unique relationship with the Crown whereby allegiance derived from local citizenship. In theory, this was impossible because the binding capacity of the common code stemmed from its holism: its application to all members of the Commonwealth. The Canadian Citizenship Act affected 'the whole Commonwealth and thereby destroys the existing bond of union and substitutes a purely statutory connection'.[27] In practice, such a violation had already occurred as a result of Ireland's Nationality Act. The Irish decision could, however, be dismissed as an exception on the margins of the Commonwealth. Canada was, by contrast, a country at its centre, one 'whose devotion to the Crown [was] above question'.[28] It was 'a revolutionary departure for a country fully in the Commonwealth to define its own citizens in terms that differentiated them from all British subjects'.[29]

---

[22] *PRO, PREM 8/851*, 'Statement on the considerations involved in the proposed change in the British Nationality Law', Appendix to a Joint Memorandum by the Home Secretary and Secretary of State for Dominion Affairs, 29 July 1946.

[23] Ireland left the Commonwealth altogether in 1949.

[24] Canadian Citizenship Act (Statutes of Canada, 1946), Section 26.

[25] *Ibid.*, Section 28.   [26] Walker, *Commonwealth*, 167.

[27] *The Private Papers of Lord Simon*, the Bodleian Library, Oxford, MS Simon 97, 'British Nationality Bill 1948', undated.   [28] Ibid.

[29] Walker, *Commonwealth*, 167. Canada repealed its statute corresponding to the British Nationality and Status of Aliens Act, 1914, on which the common code rested.

For British policy-makers, the consequences were substantial. By defining citizenship without reference to the common code, the act created the possibility of divergent definitions of subject status among Commonwealth nations. People could be British subjects in Canada without being so in other parts of the Commonwealth, and vice versa.[30] In those instances when Canada's citizenship laws denied British subject status to a particular class of persons, but it continued to enjoy that status under the direct-grant system, Britain would be maintaining its status against the wishes of the Canadian Parliament. Labour believed this would be 'tantamount to saying that [Britain] knew better than the other countries concerned what persons belonging to those countries ought to be British subjects and would go perilously near to a claim by this Parliament to legislate on a matter affecting another self-governing country of the Commonwealth, irrespective of the wishes of its government'.[31] In making subjecthood derivative of citizenship, and by failing to link citizenship to the common code, Canada opened a Pandora's box of legal inconsistency.

The act also broke the centuries-old bond between subject status and the Crown. This link had been the essence of subjecthood, the mechanism that theoretically sustained a common identity throughout the Commonwealth and Empire and bound British subjects to the Crown. By making subject status derivative of citizenship, it became possible for Canada, and any Dominion which followed its lead, to grant citizenship (and therefore British subject status) to its citizens while repudiating the attachment of those same citizens to the British Crown.[32] These individuals would enjoy full rights within the United Kingdom without recognizing the legitimacy or authority of the British Crown. Although Britain would soon reconcile itself to the constitutional oddity of an Indian Republic within the Empire, such a notion was viewed with dismay, not to say horror, in 1945.

These constitutional issues were taken extremely seriously within the Cabinet and Whitehall. There was, in addition, a broader political concern voiced in London: Labour detected in the Canadian decision the rumblings of Dominion nationalism. These were not without precedent. Since the end of the First World War, Canada, Australia, and South Africa had asserted their independence and autonomy in foreign affairs. They took a series of initiatives, such as negotiating independent treaties with the United States and appointing legations to non-Commonwealth countries without the consent of

---

[30]   *PRO, PREM 8/851*, 'Memorandum by the Home Secretary', 16 Nov. 1945.

[31]   *PRO, HO 213/410*, untitled memorandum, undated. Such a claim would be offensive to the Dominions, and it would have violated the 1931 Statute of Westminster.

[32]   *The Private Papers of Lord Simon*, 'British Nationality Bill 1948', Lord John Simon, MS Simon 97, 161–5. Note by the Conservative Parliamentary Secretariat.

the Foreign Office, which highlighted the fact that the Dominions were emerging as nations with interests separate from those of Britain.[33] When the Canadian government informed Britain of its intention to create a citizenship bill, Labour believed that Canada's decision reflected a broader dissatisfaction in the Dominions stemming from the slight to their sovereignty implied in the old system.[34] The Dominions' impatience was highlighted by Canada's failure to consult the United Kingdom before unilaterally undermining the common code, an action that caused concern within the Labour government.[35] Labour believed that, were the common status not reconstituted on a new basis, there existed 'a danger that one or more of the Dominions may in the future be disposed to drop [it] altogether and give way to demands from within for completely separate nationhood'.[36] Australia indicated shortly after the Canadian initiative that similar legislation would be introduced,[37] and the Labour government thought that South Africa would follow the same course.[38]

Canada's action, then, marked a further step toward constitutional disengagement from the United Kingdom, and it served as a warning to the British government of things to come. In the light of what we know about the expansion and fragmentation of the Commonwealth in the 1950s and 1960s, any effort to retain Dominion loyalty through a system of subjecthood appears misplaced. In 1945, however, the Old Dominions, and particularly Canada, were central to British foreign and economic policy, and they were viewed

[33] In 1928, South Africa negotiated a convention with Mozambique without consulting the Foreign Office, and the Dominion made a South African/German trade treaty which threatened to undermine the principle of Imperial Preference. Canada, against British protests, appointed a minister to Japan, and in 1930 unsuccessfully attempted to respond to a Chinese request for a Canadian legation. These developments, and the Dominions' opposition to any system of imperial preferences which threatened their economic interest or autonomy, demonstrated a growing Dominion resolve to assert their status as autonomous nations. See R. F. Holland, *Britain and the Commonwealth Alliance 1918–1939* (London: Macmillan, 1981).

[34] *PRO, PREM 8/851*, 'Nationality Law: In Joint Memorandum by the Home Secretary and the Secretary of State for Dominion Affairs', 29 July 1946.

[35] *PRO, PREM 8/851*, 'Canadian Citizenship Bill: C.P. (45) 287'. A Dominion Office paper stated that '[t]he fact that the Canadian Government failed to take the prior step of consultation and agreement before introducing a bill involving such fundamental changes in the common code is itself of some significance as an indication of a breakdown in the working of the principles underlying the present system.' *PRO, DO 35/1384*, 'Statement of the considerations involved in the Proposed Changes in British Nationality Law', Annex to 'Changes in British Nationality Law: Memorandum by the Home Secretary and the Secretary of State for Dominion Affairs', undated.

[36] *PRO, PREM 8/851*, 'British Nationality Law: Memorandum by the Secretary of State for the Home Department', 30 Aug. 1946.

[37] *PRO, PREM 8/851*, 'Cabinet. Changes in British Nationality Law. Joint Memorandum by the Home Secretary and the Secretary of State for Dominion Affairs', 29 July 1946.

[38] *PRO, DO 35/1384*, 'Statement of the considerations involved in the Proposed Changes in British Nationality Law', undated.

with great affection by the British political elite. The imperial nostalgia that exists today recalls the exoticism and romanticism of the Empire, especially its Indian Jewel. For policy-makers in the 1940s, however, the Old Dominions—Canada, New Zealand, Australia, and (though to a lesser degree) South Africa—were the four pillars of Britain's overseas network.[39] It was this relationship, given institutional expression in the doctrine of subjecthood, which was to be preserved in the face of Canadian unilateralism and Dominion nationalism. The Canadian initiative's potential for encouraging such aspirations made it of 'paramount importance' that a common status be created for all British subjects.[40]

On 16 November 1945, Attlee's government considered a proposal for a meeting of experts from Commonwealth countries to consider its implications.[41] The Cabinet approved the proposal on 22 November 1945, and between this date and July 1946 the Dominion governments agreed to reform British nationality law. The British government convened a conference of Commonwealth experts in London during February 1947.[42] They were instructed to create a United Kingdom and colonies' citizenship that would confer British subject status through legislation at Westminster.[43] In defining the principles, the Cabinet followed the Canadian lead: a reconstructed common status would be based on a citizenship system in which a 'citizenship of the United Kingdom and Colonies' would be the 'gateway' through which subject status would be attained in Britain and the Empire.[44] The direct

[39] I owe this point to a conversation with John Darwin.

[40] *PRO, DO 35/1384*, 'Statement of the considerations involved in the Proposed Changes in British Nationality Law', undated.

[41] *PRO, PREM 8/851*, 'Cabinet. Changes in the British Nationality Law. Joint Memorandum by the Home Secretary and the Secretary of State for Dominion Affairs', 29 July 1946.

[42] *PRO, PREM 8/851*, C.M. (46) 80th Conclusions, 9 Sept. 1946.

[43] Ibid. and *PRO, DO 35/1383*, 'Meeting of Prime Minister's Committee of Officials on Nationality Questions'. Old Dominions' representatives and British civil servants participated in the deliberations.

[44] The Cabinet's other principles were the following: (i) that representatives from India, Burma, and Newfoundland (the last of which joined Canada in 1949) be included, and that countries be treated as nations with the right to enact citizenship legislation, (ii) that provisions be created to ensure the preservation of the status of British subjects in Ireland should Eire leave the Commonwealth, and (iii) that all Irish citizens, on the condition of reciprocity, should enjoy all the rights of United Kingdom and colonies' citizens when in the UK. On the question of citizenship, there was in 1945 pressure from India to find a legislative alternative to the term 'British subject', which it viewed as anachronistic and reminiscent of previous patterns of domination. Ceylon supported this change, Southern Rhodesia strongly opposed it, and the Old Dominions were of mixed (and less strident) opinions. See *PRO, PREM, 8/851*, 'Commonwealth Citizen', Memorandum prepared for the Prime Minister, Home Secretary, Chancellor of the Exchequer and Lord Chancellor, 1 May 1948. The legislation ultimately declared that the terms 'British subject' and 'Commonwealth citizen' could be used interchangeably. Thus, while the status of 'Commonwealth citizen' was technically created by the

bond between sovereign and subject was abandoned, to quote a phrase that fell into some disfavour in the 1970s, 'at a stroke'.

THE BRITISH NATIONALITY ACT OF 1948

The Conference's recommendations were presented to the Cabinet in 1947, and published as a White Paper in early 1948. The White Paper formed the basis of the British Nationality Bill, which was introduced into Parliament on 17 February 1948. The Bill was based on six categories of citizenship. These were:

(*a*) Citizenship of the United Kingdom and Colonies (CUKC);

(*b*) Citizens of Independent Commonwealth Countries;

(*c*) Irish British subjects: Although Eire chose not to participate in the 1948 scheme on the same terms as the independent Commonwealth countries (category *b*), citizens of Eire would not become aliens following the passage of BNA if they had previously been British subjects. The Irish could retain their status as British subjects by making a written request to the Secretary of State;

(*d*) British subjects without citizenship;

(*e*) British Protected Persons: BPPs were treated as aliens by the legislation; they were not British subjects.

(*f*) Aliens: all those not coming under categories *a–e*.

The scheme's foundation was the distinction between *Citizens of the United Kingdom and Colonies (*CUKCs*)* and *Citizens of the Independent Commonwealth Countries (*CICCs*)*; the vast majority of British subjects were to fit into either of these categories. Citizens of the United Kingdom and British subjects within the dependent colonies were defined, in a rather unwieldy manner, as CUKCs. Their pre-1949 status as British subjects was subsumed under this designation.

The category of Citizens of the Independent Commonwealth countries included all British subjects who were citizens of independent members of the Commonwealth. When the bill was drafted, this referred only to Canada,

1948 legislation, it was nothing more than another term for British subject and did not grant any additional rights itself, as claimed by Andrew Roberts (*Eminent Churchillians*, 216). It is equally incorrect to claim, as John Solomos has done, that there was a distinction between CUKCs and Commonwealth citizens. CUKCs, like CICCs, were British subjects and thus were Commonwealth citizens (J. Solomos, *Black Youth, Racism and the State: The Politics of Ideology and Policy* (Cambridge: Cambridge University Press, 1988), 31). A careful reading of the act itself would have prevented these errors.

but it was intended to apply eventually to New Zealand, the Union of South Africa, Newfoundland, India, Pakistan, Southern Rhodesia, and Ceylon.[45] Anyone who became a citizen of any of these countries would have the status of British subject bestowed on them as 'Citizens of an Independent Commonwealth Country'. This status was attained through citizenship of an independent Commonwealth country, and the conditions of this citizenship were defined exclusively by the country's domestic legislature. Until this occurred, the British Nationality Act granted them the status of *potential* citizens of the independent Commonwealth countries. This ensured that the members of these countries would continue to enjoy the status of British subject until such laws were passed.[46]

Individuals falling into the bill's two main categories enjoyed broadly identical rights. Their status as British subjects allowed them to enter freely the United Kingdom, to secure employment immediately and, in the case of the Old Dominions, to register as British citizens after a years' residence. British subjects were entitled to stand for Parliament,[47] to vote in election, and to work for the British government.[48]

The Irish category was designed to allow Irish citizens to retain British subject status if Ireland became a republic. As the Irish issue greatly complicated the drafting of the legislation, and as it was material to nationality and immigration policy more generally, it is worth devoting a few words to it. From a scholarly point of view, there are two aspects to the 'Irish question' in 1948. First, the legislation had to grapple with the nationality status of Irish (Republic) citizens, British subjects in Northern Ireland and British subjects born in Ireland before 1922 (when it was part of the UK). Second, the 1948 legislation formed part of a broader policy that gave Irish citizens a place of privilege in the administration of immigration and nationality legislation.

---

[45]   Ceylon, India, and Pakistan were colonies at the time of the British Nationality Act's passing, but their independence was planned.

[46]   L. Fransman, *Fransman's British Nationality Law* (London: Fourmat, 1989), 60. Citizenship laws were passed by Australia and New Zealand in 1948, by South Africa and India in 1949, by Ceylon in 1950, and by Pakistan in 1951.

[47]   One of the quirks of British nationality policy today is that Commonwealth citizens retain this right, even though they lack the right to remain in the UK. Thus, in principle, a Commonwealth citizen without the right of abode could be elected to Parliament then be subject to deportation proceedings for overstaying.

[48]   The difference among the three main classes of subjects—within the UK, the Old Dominions (Canada, Australia), and the colonies (West Indies, Kenya)—was marginal. Indeed, to the extent that differentiation crept in, it was between CUKCs and the Old Commonwealth and to the advantage of the former. CUKCs were de facto naturalized before they landed in Britain, for CUKCs were indistinguishable from people born in the UK. Citizens of the Old Dominions, by contrast, had to wait twelve months or obtain permission from the Secretary of State. This distinction was none the less a nominal one, and all British subjects enjoyed a broad range of privileges within the United Kingdom.

Although the latter has occasioned greater controversy, the first aspect was more important to the drafting and implementation of the legislation. Greater attention is consequently accorded to it.

To the drafters of the legislation, the Irish element presented a multifaceted policy problem. As Ireland had been a constituent part of the UK before 1922, the task of separating British subjects from non-subjects in 1948 was particularly complicated. It was further complicated by the status of Northern Ireland. Both Britain and Eire laid claim to it, and both used nationality law as a mechanism for legitimating that claim. The general result was that, although Irish citizenship did not automatically confer British subjecthood, many Irish citizens were also subjects.

The simplest cases concerned Irish citizens born in the UK or born in Eire of a father born in the UK; in both instances, they would be unambiguously CUKCs.[49] The complex case concerned Northern Ireland. Both Irish legislation and British legislation granted citizenship only to individuals born within (or born of a father born within) the country's respective borders. These borders had been settled as a matter of law (if not as a matter of intention) by the Northern Irish referendum in favour of remaining part of the UK. For Irish nationality purposes, however, 'Eire' was defined to include the twenty-six countries of the Republic *plus* Northern Ireland.[50] Article 3 of the 1922 Irish constitution states that:

Every person, without distinction of sex, domiciled in the area of the jurisdiction of the Irish Free State at the time of the coming into operation of this Constitution, who was born in Ireland or who has been ordinarily resident in the area of the jurisdiction of the Irish Free State for not less than seven years is a citizen of the Irish Free State . . .

Adopting an eccentric reading of Articles 11 and 12 of the treaty establishing the Free State, an Irish Court and the Irish government held that 'the jurisdiction of the Irish Free State' applied to Ireland as it existed between 6 December 1922 (when the Irish Free State constitution came into effect) and 7 December 1922 (when the Northern Irish Parliament declared that it remained part of the UK).[51] In other words, they were Irish citizens.

If this interpretation had gone unchallenged by the British government, it would have technically meant that some British subjects in Northern Ireland would lose that status; the challenge to British sovereignty thrown up by the

---

[49] According to *BNA* (1948), Part II, Sections 4–6.

[50] The Ireland Act, 1949, adopted by the British government following Ireland's departure from the Commonwealth, specifically defines Eire to the exclusion of Northern Ireland.

[51] J. Megaw, 'British Subjects and Eire Citizens', *Northern Ireland Legal Quarterly*, 3/8 (1949), 129–39, 134–5.

Irish interpretation would have succeeded. BNA 1948 holds those who were British subjects before the act took effect, and who did not become CUKCs when it took effect, would be considered such *unless* they were citizens of Eire.[52] If the Irish interpretation had been respected, then considerable numbers of British subjects in Northern Ireland would have lost that status through becoming Irish citizens. This situation led the British government to insert clause 5 in the 1949 Ireland Act, which effectively defined 'Eire' as the twenty-six counties only.[53]

The 1948 Act also includes a further section granting individuals who had been British subjects before 1948, but who lost it as a result of the legislation, the opportunity to reclaim the status by writing to the Home Secretary.[54] Although such individuals had to fulfil one of several criteria (Crown service, associations of descent, holder of a British passport), these were not verified. It is doubtful that the British Nationality Act stripped anyone in Ireland of British subject status.[55] The British government's willingness, even enthusiasm, for granting privileges to the Irish regardless of their repudiation of the Crown is a common feature of the post-war experience, one that created serious difficulties for Macmillan in 1961.

'British subjects without citizenship' was a catch-all category designed to ensure that those who were without citizenship retained British subject status. Although the archival evidence provides no justification for the catch-all clause, it was probably designed to ensure that British settlers who found themselves without either United Kingdom or independent Commonwealth citizenship (because, for example, of the actions of a hostile African nation) would retain British subject status and the right to return to the United Kingdom.

Andrew Roberts has criticized the 1948 Act as a 'cumbersome' piece of legislation riddled with 'loopholes' that allowed hundreds of thousands of British subjects to claim without justification a right to enter the United Kingdom.[56] This view cannot be supported. Given its formidable task— ensuring that millions of subjects across the globe enjoyed the same status and rights in the UK regardless of citizenship—the act has an elegant simplicity. The five categories covered all British subjects in 1948, and their fluidity ensured that any change in nationality or citizenship, including their loss altogether, would leave British subjecthood unaffected. Nor can any element of the bill be described as a 'loophole'. It was of paramount importance to the legislators that no British subject should lose his or her status because of the evolution from the 'direct-grant' to the 'gateway' system.

[52]   Section 12 (4) (c).   [53]   Megaw, 'British Subjects', 136.
[54]   Section 2.
[55]   Parry, *Nationality and Citizenship Laws of the Commonwealth*, 225.
[56]   Roberts, *Eminent Churchillians*, 211–16.

A more probing question is why policy-makers sought with such diligence to ensure the widest application of subject status. The answer relates to the historical conditions under which BNA was formulated and implemented. BNA was enacted during a time of cross-party consensus on the importance of the privileges that had traditionally accrued to British subjects and on the necessity of a common link among them. The act was reactive, and it was designed to retain as much as was possible of the pre-1949 system of British subjecthood. There was never any suggestion, in either public or private deliberations, that the content of British subjecthood should in any sense be altered. On the contrary, the sole concern of BNA's critics was that the legislation failed to retain the privileges associated with British subject status.

THE BRITISH NATIONALITY ACT IN PARLIAMENT

This concern was reflected in both the parliamentary debates and committee deliberations. The debates were noteworthy in two senses. First, there was near-unanimity around the belief that all British subjects—colonial subjects and Old Commonwealth citizens—should formally enjoy full citizenship rights (though they would not be referred to as such) in the UK. Second, there was not a single reference to the possibility that these rights would be exercised by colonial subjects on a significant scale. On 11 May 1948, the Lord Chancellor (Jowitt) moved the second reading of the British Nationality Bill in the House of Lords. In the main, criticism of the legislation centred on its potential for introducing distinctions among British subjects. Lord Altrincham, for example, detected such a differentiation in the distinction between CUKCs and citizens of independent Commonwealth countries:

[W]e on these Benches would lament any tendency to differentiate between different types of British subjects in the United Kingdom. Hitherto, it has been our proud boast that all British subjects have equal rights in the United Kingdom. Whatever you may say at the outset, if you create a distinctive citizenship it is bound to set up a tendency towards differentiation.[57]

When Altrincham's arguments were repeated by others, the Lord Chancellor tried to reassure Opposition members that:

This Bill does not differentiate between British subjects. It is within the competence of this Parliament and it is within the competence of any self-governing Parliament to differentiate. We can say that people who come from one part of the British Empire

---

[57] *Parliamentary Debates (Lords)* (156), col. 998, 21 June 1948.

shall not be allowed in and people from another part shall be allowed in, but in this great metropolitan centre of the Empire I hope we never shall say such a thing . . . [BNA] does not differentiate between any classes of British subjects.[58]

The bill's critics were unconvinced, and it was opposed by a coalition of people who feared variously differentiation among subjects, those who felt that citizenship was alien to the British tradition, and a number who feared the bill's effects on the Old Commonwealth.[59] When the House moved into committee on 21 June, an amendment, put forth by Lord Altrincham and carried by seventy-five votes to twenty-one, substituted the word 'subject' for 'citizen'. Whereas Section 1 (1) of the government's draft read, 'Every person who under this Act is a citizen of the United Kingdom and Colonies', the House of Lords inserted, 'Every person who under this Act is a British subject of the United Kingdom and Colonies.'[60] This undermined the whole purpose of the bill. The government was then defeated a second time and, at the Marquess of Salisbury's suggestion, a subsection was added providing that '[n]othing in this Act shall affect the status by British law of a citizen of Eire in respect of his right to be regarded as a British subject'.[61]

The bill was then introduced into the House of Commons by the Home Secretary, James Chuter Ede. Following the Lord Chancellor, he set the bill in the language of imperial grandeur: 'The maintenance of the British Commonwealth of Nations . . . is one of the duties that this generation owes to the world and to the generations to come.'[62] During the course of the debate, two related sets of criticisms were levelled. The first mirrored those made in the House of Lords, centring on CUKC as a possible source of distinctions among Commonwealth members. Sir David Maxwell Fyfe, later Home Secretary under Churchill, opposed the bill because 'we deprecate any tendency to differentiate between different types of British subjects in the United Kingdom. . . . If we create a distinctive citizenship for Britain and the Colonies, inevitably such differentiation will creep in. We must maintain our great metropolitan tradition of hospitality to everyone from every part of our Empire.'[63]

The second argument focused on the implications of citizenship for the traditional principle of allegiance. By making subject status dependent on

---

[58]   *Parliamentary Debates (Lords)* (156), cols. 1006–7, 21 June 1948.

[59]   Lord Simon in particular objected to the fact that citizens of independent Commonwealth Countries would have to live in the United Kingdom for twelve months before becoming CUKCs, whereas those born in the colonies enjoyed that status at birth. See *Parliamentary Debates (Lords)* (155), col. 766, 11 May 1948. For a summary of the arguments, see *The Times*, 'Citizenship in the Empire: New Proposals Rejected', 22 June 1948, 2d.

[60]   *Parliamentary Debates (Lords)* (156), cols. 992–3, 21 June 1948.

[61]   Ibid., col. 1033, 21 June 1948.

[62]   *Parliamentary Debates (Commons)* (453), col. 397, 7 July 1948.

[63]   Ibid., col. 411, 7 July 1948.

local citizenship laws, allegiance was only preserved through its devaluation. If citizenship were to tie the peoples of the Commonwealth together, then allegiance could not but lose significance. Variants of this argument were presented by Viscount Hinchingbrooke (Conservative), Kenneth Pickthorn and John Foster (Conservatives), all of whom opposed BNA because, they argued, it weakened the principle of allegiance to the Crown.[64]

The British Nationality Act passed from the Commons to a committee which addressed the amendments carried in both Houses. There, outside the public's gaze, the expansive language of imperialism was affirmed. The Committee stated that the fundamental goal of the bill was to maintain the 'vital link', 'the common status possessed by all those who owe allegiance to the King, no matter to what country within the Commonwealth they belong, hitherto known by the term "British subject" '.[65] The Committee took most seriously the objections raised against the substitution of citizenship for British subject status. Foster focused on the provisions for citizenship by descent, which he referred to as the 'catch-all category'. He argued that this provision, when applicable to colonial peoples, was only meaningful at the price of placing colonials in an advantageous position vis-à-vis Old Dominion citizens and forcing CUKC status on people all over the world against their wishes.[66] The only alternative to this would be to claim that no meaning attached to the status of citizenship, that, in effect, it is wholly superfluous, a 'distinction without a difference'.[67] To avoid this confusion, '[t]he sensible thing to do . . . is for the United Kingdom to regard all British subjects, that is, all citizens of other parts of the Dominions, as British subjects, enjoying the fullest rights in this country.'[68]

The Committee defended the citizenship clause as necessary to ensure a broad inclusion of colonial peoples and their descendants as British subjects. For although the British government could legislate for its own citizens abroad, it could not, in the absence of these provisions, legislate for their children.[69] Without the 'catch-all' clause criticized by Foster all existing British subjects who did not become citizens of some part of the Commonwealth

---

[64] See ibid., cols. 418–19 (Hinchingbrooke), cols. 459–63 (Pickthorn) and cols. 466–77 (Foster), 7 July 1948.

[65] *PRO, HO 213/410*, untitled memorandum, undated.

[66] *Parliamentary Debates (Commons)*, (453), col. 466–7, 7 July 1948.

[67] Ibid., col. 467, 7 July 1948.   [68] Ibid.

[69] *PRO, HO 213/410*, 'Notes on arguments used by Mr. Foster' and 'British Nationality. Mr. Ede. Clause 1. Supplementary Note.' A similar process occurred with respect to Sir David Maxwell Fyfe, who suggested deleting the transitional provisions. The Committee argued for the necessity of these provisions because '[u]ntil the other parts of the Commonwealth enact citizenship laws, [they] would not be British subjects under our law.' *PRO, HO 213/410*, 'Notes'.

would lose their ability to transmit British nationality to their descendants born abroad.[70]

The Committee recommended the restoration of 'citizenship'. The status of British subject would after 1 January 1949 be secured through local citizenship laws. The House of Lords accepted the restoration of the bill on 22 July, and the British Nationality Act was given royal assent on 31 July 1948.

While the defeats in the Lords received some attention,[71] the basic structure of British subjecthood was altered in 1948 with little comment, scholarly or journalistic.[72] The Press noted with approval the act's removal of a long-standing injustice against British women. Under an 1870 statute, any British woman who married an alien would lose her British subject status, while men who married aliens retained this status and extended it to their wives. The statute was patently discriminatory, and the wartime coalition government had been under pressure to amend it.[73] Under Section 16 of BNA, individuals who would have been CUKCs or British subjects without citizenship *but* for previous legislation could acquire the appropriate status by declaring 'an intention to resume British Nationality'.[74] The reform was considered long overdue and was welcomed.[75]

THE SILENCES OF 1948

The lack of debate occasioned by the enactment of BNA can be explained by a consensus on both the meaning and purpose of the act. The act was meant

---

[70]   Quoting the Committee: 'In Clause 4 [which grants CUKC status], Parliament can only legislate for the descendants of <u>our</u> citizens. It would not be proper for it to legislate for the descendants of Canadians. It follows that unless a British subject is made our citizen, his children born abroad will not benefit from Clause 4.' *PRO, HO 213/410*, 'Notes'.

[71]   See the editorial in *The Times*, 'Nationality and Citizenship', 22 June 1948.

[72]   Kenneth O. Morgan's *Labour in Power, 1945–1951* (Oxford: Clarendon Press, 1984) does not mention the act, while Peter Hennessy's *Never Again, Britain 1945–1951* (London: Vintage, 1992) accords it passing mention in a brief discussion of post-war immigration. The act is only considered at length in legal texts (see Fransman, *British Nationality Law* and V. Bevan, *The Development of British Nationality Law* (London: Croom Helm, 1986)), which explore the provisions without examining the origins, and in contemporary studies, which mention it as a precursor to current policy.

[73]   See *PRO, DO 35/1385, DO 35/1386,* and *DO 35/1387.*

[74]   Others who had lost their subject status because of pre-1948 legislation could also reclaim it. Section 16 provided that a person who would be British subjects *but* for the operation of Section 12 (1) of the 1914 British Nationality and Status of Aliens Act could also claim this status by declaring 'an intention to resume British Nationality'. See Fransman, *British Nationality Law,* 62–3.

[75]   *The Times,* 'British Nationality', 19 Feb. 1948. The Old Dominions appear to have been dissatisfied with the provisions for women. See *DO 35/1385,* Letter from W. E. Beckett to Markbreiter, 9 Oct. 1945.

to maintain the substance of the pre-1946 arrangement, including the right of all British subjects to enter the United Kingdom. A few welcomed the perceived potential for discrimination in favour of Britain and the Old Dominions, but the majority, including party leaders, rejected it. When it was suggested that Britain's unique position did not imply freedom of entry, members from all parts of both Houses defended this traditional right.[76] The second consensus was implicit in what was not said. The British Nationality Act was never intended to sanction a mass migration of New Commonwealth citizens to the United Kingdom. Nowhere in parliamentary debate, the Press, or private papers was the possibility discussed that substantial numbers could exercise their right to reside permanently in the UK. In defending CUKC as necessary to maintain a common status among British subjects, the Lord Chancellor argued that its importance was not material but symbolic or, in Jowitt's word, 'mystical'.[77] There was no mention of the material advantages that might be achieved through mass migration from the colonies to the United Kingdom; no one imagined such a movement possible.

While this belief appears curious in retrospect, it conforms to a reasonable, historically based, late 1940s understanding of the intra-imperial migratory system. The UK had in 1948 no experience of substantial colonial immigration; the right to enter Britain—a logical corollary of the status of British subject—had previously been exercised by no more than a handful. There had, of course, been colonial immigrants in Britain for centuries. In the late 1940s, these were estimated at 20,000 to 30,000, of which the majority lived in Liverpool, Cardiff, Manchester and in the East End of London.[78] The vast majority of immigrants before the Second World War were, none the less, European.[79] The reversal of migratory patterns, to Britain rather than from,

[76] Deakin, 'British Nationality Act of 1948', 79.

[77] Quoting the Lord Chancellor: 'The conception of an all-pervading common status or nationality is not primarily, not mainly, important because of its material advantages. It is, if you like, rather mystical. But none of us, I suggest, is any the worse for a little mysticism in our life. It is the mark which differentiates the family from mere friends.' *Parliamentary Debates (Lords)*, vol. 155, col. 762, 11 May 1948. For the Press reaction to this statement, see *The Times*, 'British Nationality Bill: Commonwealth Citizenship', 12 May 1948, 2a. To be sure, the Lord Chancellor also mentioned the advantages which could, formally, be achieved through British subject status (free entry to Britain, voting in elections, becoming an MP, etc.). Since these privileges had never been exercised by 'colonials' on a grand scale, however, their application to the whole of the Empire was thought to be of primarily symbolic significance.

[78] *PRO, CAB 129/40*, CP (50) 113, 'Coloured people from the British Colonial Territories', 18 May 1950. This document is part of a Committee of Ministers' report on colonial immigration considered later in the ch.

[79] A surge of East European, particularly Jewish, immigration in the late nineteenth and early twentieth century led to the first introduction of controls on alien immigration in 1905. See B. Gainer, *The Alien Invasion: The Origins of the Aliens Act of 1905* (London: Heinemann, 1972) and J. A. Garrard, *The English and Immigration 1880–1910* (London, 1971).

was made possible by changes in post-war economic conditions, chiefly the achievement of full employment in the UK and the availability of cheap transportation. These were simply not predicted in 1948.

As inter-imperial migration in the 1920s and 1930s had been of a limited scope, one composed almost entirely of Old Dominions citizens, the commitment expressed by parliamentarians to the right to enter Britain must be interpreted in this context. Parliamentarians, *pace* Sivanandan, were committed to an open-door policy, but one that facilitated two specific movements: the permanent movement of Old Dominions' citizens and the temporary, and limited, movement of colonial subjects. Free movement between the Old Dominions and Britain constituted an important manifestation of the affinity felt for these countries by politicians, especially Conservatives,[80] and it was with these individuals in mind that most parliamentarians spoke eloquently of Britain's open borders. This is not to say that colonial British subjects were entirely unwelcome; their movement into the UK was to a degree valued, but it was viewed qualitatively differently from that between Britain and the Old Commonwealth. Whereas the movement of what can be called, for lack of a better term, ethnic Britons between the UK and Old Dominions was valued as both a temporary movement and as a permanent transfer of population, the migration of colonials was intended to be limited and temporary. In defending the right of British subjects to free entry, the precedent considered by politicians was students from the colonies, particularly the West Indies.[81] Their presence in Britain was considered of value, to Britain and to the Commonwealth, and they were for the most part accepted by Britons. With regard to both these movements, and to the constitutional structure which sustained them, policy-makers in 1948 believed that the enactment of the British Nationality Act amounted only to a continuation of the status quo as it had been over the previous two decades.

Several points follow from this discussion of the British Nationality Act. First, we have a more refined understanding of imperial obligation and imperial commitment. To claim that British policy-makers were meaningfully committed to British subject status, and to the rights (including free entry) attached to it, is not to say that they were unanimously and unconditionally committed to the right of every British subject, from every corner of the Empire, to come at any moment to Britain. This is the straw man erected by those who wish to reject both the notion that British policy-makers accepted

---

[80] D. W. Dean, 'Conservative Governments and the Restriction of Commonwealth Immigration in the 1950s: The Problems of Constraint', *Historical Journal*, 35, No. 1 (1993), 171–94, 174.

[81] Before 1954, most New Commonwealth immigrants were students. A. Horne, *Macmillan* (London: Macmillan, 1989), 422.

any obligation to British subjects and the related suggestion that Britain's record in immigration is anything but wholly objectionable; unsurprisingly, on this basis they have found it easy to do so. When British politicians and bureaucrats spoke of the United Kingdom's 'special status' as the centre of the Empire and of Britain's great tradition of freely allowing all British subjects to enter the UK, this was neither vacuous cynicism appealing only to tear-stained liberals nor a purely selfless assumption of a sort of imperial *noblesse oblige*. It was rather a differentiated and conditional, but none the less genuine, attachment to a system of subjecthood from which Britain, as well as the Dominions, derived benefits. The Old Dominions were at the centre of this system, and their members' right to enter the UK as British 'kith and kin' was viewed by major politicians in all parties as unconditional and innately valuable. The right of colonial subjects to entry, by contrast, was passively accepted as a logical consequence and symbolic expression of subjecthood's indivisibility, but it commanded far less enthusiasm and was believed to be rightly limited and temporary. When we speak of special status and obligation, then, we must recognize that these commitments differentiated among British subjects and that those who held them assumed that colonial migration would not be permanent.

Second, there is a point to be made about the importance of political perspective. In framing BNA, policy-makers approached the complex matter of subjecthood from the viewpoint of past migratory experience. The metaphors used to understand, and the words employed in explaining, the legislation were based in their entirety on the system as it had operated before 1948. Policy-makers were unable to consider BNA in any other terms, and it is unreasonable (and profoundly ahistorical) to expect them to have done so. The issues involved in every previous discussion of nationality and intra-imperial migration were primarily constitutional—maintaining the formal indivisibility of British subjecthood—and implicated migration only as a limited and largely Old Dominion/UK phenomenon. To have defined the central issue in 1948 as migration would have been to predict the unforeseeable: the achievement of unprecedented prosperity and full employment in the post-war years and the development of relatively inexpensive, rapid transportation between the UK and the colonies. Failure to recognize these developments—and the migration they encouraged—did not reflect a lack of political prescience; it reflected a reasonable definition and understanding of the issues at stake in the drafting of the British Nationality Act. To put this another way, the act was viewed by the men who drafted it as we would probbly have viewed it were we in their position.

Considering the British Nationality Act as it was considered by its creators suggests that the legislation cannot be understood simply as 'misguided idealism',[82] legal expediency,[83] an attempt to restrain colonial nationalist aspirations,[84] nor as the excessive generosity of a naïve Labour government.[85] Given the perspective from which it was viewed—an expectation of little migration—and the aim it sought to realize (the restitution of a common status for British subjects following Canada's wrecking initiative) the act was neither misguided nor naive, and it was in no sense riddled with loopholes. Its achievement was its aim: the inclusion of all British subjects in a system of common status that resembled as much as was possible the system as it stood before the Canadian Citizenship Act.

In summary, the British Nationality Act was enacted in response to Canada's alteration of imperial nationality's traditional basis, and it was designed to retain the privileges that had accrued to British subjecthood and to ensure that they were enjoyed by all those with a legitimate claim (past or present) to this status. Two implicit processes were under way as the British Nationality Bill became law: first, British politicians assumed that past migratory patterns, dominated by the Old Commonwealth, would continue; and, second, they affirmed a very particular commitment to a laissez-faire policy for the Commonwealth. This implicit commitment was made explicit two years after BNA's passage, when New Commonwealth migration began.

THE FIRST EXAMINATION OF CONTROL

The first post-war New Commonwealth immigrants arrived in London on 22 June 1948. Their arrival was unexpected. The *Empire Windrush* had sailed to

---

[82] Bevan, *Development of British Nationality Law*, 113.

[83] P. Hennessy, *Never Again*, 440.

[84] H. Goulberne, *Ethnicity and Nationalism in Post-Imperial Britain* (Cambridge: Cambridge University Press, 1991), 97. As I have argued, to the extent that it sought to preserve the character of relations within the Empire and Commonwealth, its concern was with the strength of the bond between the UK and the Old Dominions, not the UK and the colonies.

[85] Freeman, *Immigrant Labor and Racial Conflict in Industrial Societies*, 38. Equally unsupportable is the view that 'in sharp contrast to the alien immigration of the earlier part of this century, New Commonwealth immigration arose as a direct result of active encouragement on the part of ... [the] British Government.' (S. Juss, *Immigration, Nationality and Citizenship* (London: Mansell, 1994).) British governments' attitude to New Commonwealth immigration ranged from benign indifference to suspicion. Cabinets recognized at times the value of New Commonwealth immigrants in alleviating Britain's labour shortage, but almost no effort was made to recruit them. To the extent that the British government sought foreign labour at all, they looked to the Continent under the European Volunteer Workers Scheme. Under its conditions, workers were required to obtain a labour permit, to work in specific industries (coal, steel, construction, nursing, and transport) and could only move between jobs with government permission. On the European Volunteer Workers Scheme, see R. Miles and D. Kay, *Refugees or Migrant Workers? European Volunteer Workers in Britain 1946—1951* (London: Routledge, 1992). A similar point has been made by Holmes. See C. Holmes, *A Tolerant Country? Immigrants, Refugees and Minorities in Britain* (London: Faber & Faber, 1991), 53–4.

Jamaica to drop off Jamaican soldiers, and some 500 immigrants boarded for the return trip to England. The Labour government had not expected the migrants, and it was less than pleased. The Minister of Labour, Sir George Isaacs, told Parliament that he hoped 'no encouragement will be given to others to follow their example',[86] but their arrival could not be obstructed.[87] In a Cabinet memorandum circulated on 18 June, Creech Jones, the Colonial Secretary, flatly stated that '[i]t will be appreciated that the men concerned are all British subjects. The Government of Jamaica has no legal power to prevent their departure from Jamaica and the Government of the United Kingdom has no legal power to prevent their landing.'[88] The memorandum also, however, emphasized that the government was opposed to permanent New Commonwealth immigration: '[the movement] was certainly not organised or encouraged by the Colonial Office or the Jamaican Government. On the contrary, every possible step has been taken by the Colonial Office and by the Jamaican Government to discourage these influxes.'[89]

Although statistics on New Commonwealth immigration were inadequately kept until the late 1950s, it is thought that approximately 5,000 New Commonwealth immigrants had arrived by 1950–1.[90] The Labour government viewed this movement with some concern, and on 27 July 1949 the Cabinet discussed for the first time the possibility of limiting the 'time-honoured principle' that all British subjects have the right to enter and remain in the United Kingdom. The impetus for the discussion was partly the growing West Indian presence in the UK, but the immediate consideration was

---

[86]   *Parliamentary Debates* (*Commons*) (451), col. 1851, 5 June 1948.

[87]   Arthur Creech Jones, the Colonial Secretary, is reported to have said, 'These people have British passports and must be allowed to land. [However] there's nothing to worry about because they won't last one winter in England.' The only source for this, however, is anecdotal. It is quoted in Hennessy, *Never Again*, 440, but attributed to Sam King, who is quoted in *Forty Years on: Memories of Britain's Post-War Caribbean Immigrants* (London: South London Press, 1988), 4.

[88]   *PRO, CAB 129/28*, CP (48) 154, 'Arrival in the United Kingdom by Jamaican unemployed: Memorandum by the Secretary of State for the Colonies', 18 June 1948.

[89]   Ibid. In a statement which highlights the importance of British policy-makers' bounded perspective, Creech Jones stated that 'I do not think that a similar mass movement will take place again because the transport is unlikely to be available, though we shall be faced with a steady trickle, which, however, can be dealt with without undue difficulty.' For a (not particularly conclusive) study of the significance of the *Empire Windrush* landing for post-war politics, see K. Lunn, 'The British State and Immigration, 1945–1951: New Light on the Empire Windrush', in T. Kushner and K. Lunn (eds.), *The Politics of Marginality: Race, the Radical Right and Minorities in Twentieth Century Britain* (London: Frank Cass, 1990). The use of the word 'influx' is revealing, because 500 is a rather small 'influx'. This language highlights the extent to which the free entry policy was primarily maintained with an eye to the Old Dominions.

[90]   Hennessy, *Never Again*, 442. The distribution was as follows: 1,200 in 1948, 1,000 in 1949, 1,400 in 1950, and 2,200 in 1951.

Canadian communist seamen who had 'inflicted serious economic loss' by instigating dock strikes in London.[91] It was feared that the communists were taking advantage of the fact that they could not be deported. The issue came before the Cabinet periodically between 1949 and 1950. On 20 March 1950 James Griffiths, Creech Jones's successor as Colonial Secretary, was invited to submit for Cabinet consideration a memorandum on the problems arising from the immigration of 'coloured people', other than students, from the West Indies and other territories.[92]

Griffiths reported on 18 May 1950, and the Cabinet decided on the basis of his report to set up a Committee of Ministers, chaired by the Home Secretary, James Chuter Ede, to explore the means that might be adopted to check 'coloured immigration' into the country.[93] The Griffiths memorandum and the Committee's report warrant consideration because, first, they reveal an approach and attitude among Labour politicians which was remarkably similar to those of subsequent Conservative governments and, second, they underline the differentiated nature of British policy-makers' commitment to the free entry of British subjects.

Griffiths began by noting that the number of colonial subjects living in Britain in 1950 was between 20,000 and 30,000. The community was composed mostly of three groups: colonial subjects who had served in the First World War and settled in the UK afterwards, subjects who had followed the same pattern in the Second World War, and those who had arrived in the UK from 1945 onwards. The integration of those who had arrived since the Second World War had been relatively successful, but three problems had occurred: the concentration of migrants in inadequate inner-city housing, employer prejudice against black workers, and the occurrence of sporadic instances of civil unrest.[94] While these developments were viewed with limited concern in 1948, they were the origins of difficulties that would resurface in the immigration debate over the next two decades.

[91] PRO, CAB 128/16, CM 49 (49) 5, Conclusions of a Meeting of the Cabinet, 27 July 1949. For a discussion of the strikes, and a critique of the government's claim that they were led by communists, see J. Phillips, The Great Alliance: Economic Recovery and the Problems of Power 1945–1951 (London: Pluto, 1996), chs. 3 and 4.

[92] PRO, CAB 128/17, CM (50) 7 13th Conclusions, 'Coloured people from the British colonial territories', 20 Mar. 1950.

[93] PRO, CAB 129/40, CP (5) 113, 'Coloured people from British colonial territories', 18 May 1950. The Committee comprised the Home Secretary (Ede), the Minister for Labour (Isaacs), the Minister for Health (Bevan), the Secretary of State for the Colonies (Griffiths), the Secretary of State for Scotland (Johnston), the Secretary of State for Commonwealth Relations (Gordon Walker), and the Attorney General (Shawcross).

[94] Disturbances broke out in Liverpool between 31 July and 2 Aug. 1948, in Deptford on 18 July 1949, and in a Birmingham hostel on 8–9 Aug. 1949. These generally involved fights between black and white men.

The response of the Colonial Office was to instruct Colonial governments to use informal methods to discourage immigration. This involved warning prospective immigrants of difficulties they would face finding accommodation and employment in the UK and withholding passports from those who lacked the funds for the passage or were deemed unsuitable for regular employment.[95] Those writing about post-war immigration policy have concentrated attention, and based considerable criticism, on Conservative governments' use of informal controls in the 1950s. These are taken as evidence of the Conservatives' indifference to the Commonwealth ideals and their hostility to black immigrants.[96] These measures were, in fact, an extension of initiatives that originated with Labour. A powerful suspicion of black immigration was to be found in both parties, and Labour, despite its professed commitment to multiracialism abroad, was no less apprehensive than the Conservatives about the prospect of large-scale colonial immigration to the UK.[97]

The Committee of Ministers, whose work was initiated after the Griffiths memorandum, reported on 12 January 1951.[98] Despite the Cabinet's belief that an increase in colonial immigration would create serious domestic problems, the Committee recommended against control. The reasons for its decision are revealing. Chief among these was the fact that '[t]he United Kingdom has a special status as the mother country, and freedom to enter and remain in the United Kingdom at will is one of the main practical benefits enjoyed by British subjects, as such.'[99] Although the Cabinet was inclined to limit colonial immigration, this inclination was checked by a belief that it fell to the United Kingdom to preserve the content of British subject status. It is impossible to determine from the archival evidence how widely this belief was held, but the Committee considered it of sufficient importance to list it as the central issue at stake in controlling immigration.

[95] In addition, from 19 Sept. 1949, the Home Office issued instructions to immigration offers that persons without evidence of British subject or British Protected Person status should be refused permission to land. For a full text of the Griffiths report, see *PRO, CAB 129/40*, CP (5) 113, 'Coloured people from British colonial territories', 18 May 1950.

[96] See D. Dean, 'The Conservative Government and the 1961 Commonwealth Immigration Act: The Inside Story', *Race and Class*, 35, No. 2: 57–74 and Carter et al., 'The 1951–1955 Conservative Government and the Racialization of Black Immigration'.

[97] Several documents can be cited to substantiate this point. See for example *PRO, CAB 128/17*, CM 37 (50), 19 June 1950: 'The Cabinet's discussions turned mainly on the means of preventing any further increase in the coloured population of this country. Ministers were apprehensive lest the higher standards of social service in this country should attract here an undue proportion of the surplus population of the West Indies and other Colonial territories. . . . Should not consideration also be given to the wider question whether the time had come to restrict the existing right of any British subject to enter the United Kingdom?'

[98] *PRO, CAB 129/44*, CP (51) 51, 'Immigration of British Subjects into the United Kingdom: Note by the Home Secretary'. 12 Feb. 1951.   [99] Ibid.

This commitment was differentiated. In careful language, the Committee noted that 'it would be difficult to justify restrictions on persons who are citizens of the United Kingdom and Colonies, if no comparable restrictions were imposed on persons who are citizens of other Commonwealth countries.'[100] Controls would be designed to limit the entry of colonial and New Commonwealth immigrants; any control on Old Dominions' citizens was viewed as intrinsically 'undesirable'.[101] As a distinction between the two would not be politically acceptable, colonial and New Commonwealth immigration would be tolerated in the name of the Old Dominions.[102] The evidence from these deliberations confirms that the attachment of British politicians was fundamentally to the Old Commonwealth;[103] New Commonwealth immigrants were accepted, but only in so far as they contributed to a broader structure of subjecthood in which Dominions citizens were the key actors. It also suggests a riposte to those who dismiss the language of imperial commitment as vacuous nonsense.[104] The ultimate failure of politicians' attachment to a common status to prevent the adoption of restrictive immigration measures tells us nothing about the sincerity of this sentiment, for they were only ever partially and contingently committed to its exercise by non-white immigrants.

Although the British Nationality Act's origins were almost entirely unrelated to immigration, its consequences undoubtedly were so related. The decision to enact BNA was an institutional choice taken in response to conditions—migratory patterns dominated by the Old Commonwealth—which turned out to be ephemeral. Once full employment in the UK had been achieved, and cheap transport between the UK and colonies was available, that is, once there existed a powerful inducement to immigrate to the United Kingdom, the implications of the British Nationality Act shifted from institutional relationships and symbolic expression ('none of us is any worse for a little mysticism in our life') to substantial migration. The act was also an institutional choice that limited the scope within which all future govern-

---

[100]   *PRO, CAB 129/44*, CP (51) 51.

[101]   Ibid. The Committee also noted the political controversy that would surround a statutory 'colour bar': 'Any solution depending on an apparent or concealed colour test would be so invidious as to make it impossible of adoption. Nevertheless, the use of any powers taken to restrict the free entry of British subjects to this country would, as a general rule, be more or less confined to coloured persons.'

[102]   The Committee's entire proceedings, including Cabinet discussions and reports submitted to the Committee, are kept in the Public Record Office, *GEN 325*. As the reader will note in the next chapter, there was a considerable degree of continuity in the approach of Labour and Conservative governments to immigration.

[103]   This preference for the Old Commonwealth conforms to what one would expect given the linguistic, institutional, and ethnic ties between Great Britain and the Old Dominions.

[104]   Sivanandan, 'Race, Class and the State'; Solomos, *Race and Racism*.

ments were able to adopt policy responses to this migration. At the very least, policy-makers were bound to work within, even if they would have preferred to reject, this complex structure. By entrenching British subjecthood in statute, and by tying subjecthood to citizenship, the Labour government bequeathed a complex institutional inheritance to successive governments, one which informed and constrained their policy responses to post-war immigration.

3

Immigration in the Indian Summer:
Churchill and Eden

THE age of affluence[1] was a defining period in the history of Commonwealth migration. Commonwealth migration occurred, broadly speaking, in two periods: a 1948–61 wave of primary immigration and a 1962–74 wave of secondary immigration (the spouses and dependants of immigrants already settled in Britain). As family reunification was unavoidable, the second wave of migration was largely the inevitable consequence of the first. The decisive period in the transformation of the United Kingdom into a multicultural nation was the fourteen years during which an open door for all British subjects was maintained.

In keeping with the period's importance, the standard 'racialization' account of British governments' responses to Commonwealth migration is based on primary documents from it. It was during these years that the 'racial-iziation' process is said to have occurred. Requiring (or wanting?) a 'strong case' for its desire to restrict migration, '[t]his "strong case" was built around a racist reconstruction of "Britishness" in which to be white was to belong and to be black was to be excluded. . . . In building its strong case, the state undertook nothing less than a political project in which notions of "belong-ing" and "community" were reconstructed in terms of "racial" attachments and national identity organised around skin colour.'[2] As noted in the intro-duction, the piece has been widely cited as an accurate account of the Conservatives' approach to migration in the 1950s.[3]

---

[1] V. Bogdanor and R. Skidelsky (eds.), *The Age of Affluence: 1951–1964* (London: Macmillan, 1970).

[2] See B. Carter et al., 'The 1951–1955 Conservative Government and the Racialization of Black Immigration', *Immigrants and Minorities*, 6, No. 3 (1987), 335–47, 336 and 345; B. Carter et al., 'Immigration Policy and the Racialization of Migrant Labour: The Construction of National Identities in the USA and Britain', *Ethnic and Racial Studies*, 19, No. 1 (1996), 135–57.

[3] See S. Brooke, 'The Conservative Party, Immigration and National Identity, 1948–1968', in M. Francis and I. Zweiniger-Bargielowska (eds.), *The Conservatives and British Society, 1880–1900* (Cardiff: University of Wales Press, 1996); K. Lunn, 'The British State and Immigration, 1945–1951: New Light on the Empire Windrush', in T. Kushner and K. Lunn

Although less influential, a later study reached diametrically opposed conclusions. Andrew Roberts's explanation of Britain's transformation into a multicultural society is the antithesis of the 'racialization' school. Motivated by a mixture of high-minded patrician liberalism and political expediency, Home Office officials and Cabinet ministers avoided taking the controversial but necessary decision in favour of restricting migration. With the exception of Salisbury, the Commonwealth Relations Secretary, the Oxbridge/public school contingent that monopolized the Home Office and the Conservative Party sacrificed prescience 'to short-term expediency and craving for consensus'. [4] They were able to do so because they represented rural constituencies unaffected by Commonwealth migration.

Although both studies are based on archival documents, neither can be defended with reference to them. There was, to be sure, a deep unease among senior bureaucrats and Cabinet ministers about non-white migration, and few people were enthusiastic about it. Yet, there was an equal amount of confusion among state actors, and a genuine, though not universal, desire to avoid racially discriminatory migration restrictions. There can be little doubt that, behind these deliberations, there rested contradictory preferences and confused thinking. There was something hypocritical in the argument that migration controls were necessary for the New Commonwealth, but that these should be operated in a non-racially discriminatory manner. A truly 'colour blind' policy-maker would have viewed non-white migration with perfect indifference, and it would be naive to claim that policy-makers in the 1950s were unaffected by imperialist assumptions of European superiority. The importance of these attitudes, however, should not be exaggerated. Whatever the ambiguity in policy-makers' positions, archival documentation establishes that non-white British subjects—above all, West Indians—had some defenders in Whitehall and the Cabinet, and that at least one Cabinet member was prepared to resign over the racist application of migration controls. The claim that the 1950s were characterized by an intra-state effort to refound British identity on racist lines is palpable nonsense.

On the other ideological extreme, whatever minor role liberal ideals might have played, they were not behind the decision in late 1954 to abandon the project of restricting migration. It rather reflected a powerful ideological commitment, almost forgotten today, to the Old Dominions. Canada, Australia, and New Zealand are today of small relevance to British policy,

(eds.), *The Politics of Marginality: Race, the Radical Right and Minorities in Twentieth Century Britain* (London: Frank Cass, 1990); K. Paul, *Whitewashing Britain* (Ithaca, NY: Cornell University Press, 1997); and J. Solomos, *Race and Racism in Contemporary Britain* (Houndmills: Macmillan, 1993), ch. 3.

[4] A. Roberts, *Eminent Churchillians* (London: Weidenfeld & Nicolson, 1994), ch. 3.

foreign or domestic. As a result, it is easy to forget that in the 1950s, when the United Kingdom rejected European integration in the name of the Commonwealth,[5] the link between the UK and the Dominions was of central importance to British policy-makers, and the citizens of these countries were viewed with great affection by Conservative politicians. In this environment, the institution of migration controls on Canadians, Australians, and New Zealanders was viewed as anathema by some, and undesirable by all, members of the Conservative government.[6] The story of New Commonwealth/colonial migration in the 1950s is the story of the Old Commonwealth's place in British politics.

This attachment to the Old Commonwealth coexisted with a hesitance on the part of certain Cabinet members to enact racially discriminatory migration controls, and with the steadfast refusal of Lennox-Boyd to countenance them. Had the distribution of preferences been different—had Cabinet members been willing to apply restrictions to the Old Commonwealth or had they been agreed on their exclusive application to the New Commonwealth-migration would have been sharply limited in the early 1950s. As it happened, the result of both was a policy deadlock that kept the door open to the New Commonwealth. In the context of selective anti-racism, increasing New Commonwealth or colonial migration was tolerated in the name of the Old Commonwealth.

MIGRATION POLICY UNDER CHURCHILL

Migration was first addressed by the Churchill government in 1952. The American McCarran Walter Act of this year greatly reduced the ability of West Indians to immigrate to the United States—previously the preferred destination—and Commonwealth migration to the United Kingdom began to increase. The issue was raised for the first time when Churchill, on 25 November, asked 'whether the Post Office were employing larger numbers of coloured workers. If so, there was some risk that difficult social problems

---

[5]   On this point, see A. Seldon, 'The Churchill Administration, 1951–1955', in P. Hennessy and A. Seldon (eds.), *Ruling Performance: British Governments from Attlee to Thatcher* (Oxford: Basil Blackwell, 1987), 86–7.

[6]   South Africa is mentioned less often in the archives. It is possible that the growing hostility against apartheid in the rest of the Commonwealth made Conservative politicians less willing to defend their right of entry. It is also possible that the fact that the South African population was predominantly black led politicians to think of the country as part of the New Commonwealth. In any case, the country is rarely mentioned, and the question disappeared when South Africa left the Commonwealth in 1961.

would be created.' The Postmaster General was invited to report on the matter, and he responded on 16 December. He reported that between 500 and 600 were employed without difficulty, and that the Post Office's main unions raised no objections to their employment at basic grades. If there was any hint in favour of discrimination in Churchill's Cabinet musings, the Postmaster-General rejected the suggestion: 'If it is felt that coloured workers should not be allowed to obtain employment in this country, I should have thought that the proper course would be to deny them entry to the country. The Post Office, alone among Government Departments, could not discriminate against coloured British subjects once they are here nor can I feel that the country would benefit in any way by my discharging the 400 or so that are not established.'[7] The question, he concluded, was not one for the Post Office at all; it was rather whether colonial immigrants should continue to be admitted to the United Kingdom.

Since New Commonwealth immigrants entered the United Kingdom as citizens, no effort was made to record their arrival, and any statistics that now exist are not wholly reliable estimates. The Colonial Office believed at the time that there were approximately 40,000–50,000 non-white immigrants permanently resident in the United Kingdom. The bulk of migration since 1945 had been to London and the industrial midlands, and the Ministry of Labour estimated total unemployment among colonial immigrants to be a tolerable 1,500.[8]

The presence of this community provoked sufficient curiosity and concern for the Cabinet to appoint an inquiry, in the form of an interdepartmental working party, into colonial migration and the possibility of control.[9] The report took thirteen months to prepare, a length of time that leads Roberts to conclude that the government hoped to delay taking action.[10] For this claim to be true, the government must have had a clear idea of the necessary action. For Roberts, restrictions on migration were obviously the necessary course. For the Conservatives, the matter was less clear. Neither they nor their Labour predecessors had expected a substantial migration of British subjects from the colonies/New Commonwealth, and they could not claim to be cognizant of the issues raised by its development. The Working Party was as much as anything an attempt to uncover the aspects of the question that required deliberation. In this effort it succeeded, and its conclusions raised issues that were to resurface in official discussions of migration throughout the decade.

---

[7] *PRO, PREM 11/824*, 'Cabinet. Post Office: Employment of Coloured Workers: Memorandum by the Postmaster General', 16 Dec. 1952.

[8] *PRO, CO 1028/23*, Letter from Henry Hopkinson to Brigadier J. O. Smyth, 30 Dec. 1952.

[9] *PRO, DO 35/5216*, Letter to Sedgwick and Costar, 31 Dec. 1952.

[10] Roberts, *Eminent Churchillians*, 220.

The Report concluded that the efforts of the colonies to discourage immigrants who were unlikely to secure employment and to clamp down on stowaways had continued, but they seemed to have had no great success in substantially reducing migration. African colonies hindered the issue of passports and travel documents to those without a good record of employment and financial solvency. These efforts, which were fairly modest, were the origins of a more ambitious effort to contain the level of migration through non-statutory mechanisms in the late 1950s. In the UK, the police were satisfied with the civil conduct of New Commonwealth immigrants, but there was little social interaction between them and the local community, the latter of which treated the immigrants with an uneasy tolerance. Unemployment among immigrants had increased, and in June it was estimated at 3,336, a small number in itself, but one that was as a proportion higher than the national average.[11]

Of greatest interest in the Report is its discussion of the policy issues involved in any restriction. First among these was, as it had been in the 1950 to 1951 deliberations, the United Kingdom's 'special status as the mother country of much of the Commonwealth', in which 'freedom to enter and remain in the United Kingdom at will is one of the benefits enjoyed by British subjects as such'.[12] Although the commitment to this traditional benefit was stated generally, the Committee was especially concerned about its enjoyment by two groups. The first was emigrants from the United Kingdom and their children, the 'kith and kin' whose 'affectionate feelings towards the mother-country . . . are a source of strength which would be weakened by anything in the nature of a restriction'.[13] The second group, as the discussion in the last chapter implied, was the Old Commonwealth. The Committee concluded that '[a]ny legislation which set up barriers to the free entry of British subjects from other parts of the Commonwealth to the United Kingdom would be particularly objectionable to the citizens of the older self-governing countries within the Commonwealth with which the sentimental ties are the strongest.'[14] The commitment expressed by politicians in 1948 to the traditional laissez-faire policy was a commitment to these individuals' right to enter the United Kingdom. It is unremarkable that, as the right of free entry was exercised in ever-larger numbers by non-white immigrants, civil servants expressed less enthusiasm for it:

---

[11] *PRO, CO 1028/22*, 'Working Party on Coloured People Seeking Employment in the United Kingdom: Draft Report', 28 Oct. 1953. The Working Party was composed of representatives from the Home Office, Colonial Office, Commonwealth Relations Office, the Ministry of Labour and National Service, the Scottish Home Department, the Ministry of Transport and Civil Aviation, the National Assistance Board, and it was chaired by W. H. Cornish of the Home Office.   [12] Ibid.   [13] Ibid.   [14] Ibid.

it may be questioned whether the mother country conception is apt to the present day constitutional relations in the Commonwealth. It has no meaning to the vast majority of the citizens of, e.g. India, Pakistan or the West African colonies. Further, it may well be argued that a large coloured community as a noticeable feature of our social life would weaken the sentimental attachment of the older self-governing countries to the United Kingdom. Such a community is certainly no part of the concept of England or Britain to which people of British stock throughout the Commonwealth are attached.[15]

In its essence and practical application, the open door for British subjects was an expression of the primary link between the United Kingdom and the Old Dominions. To claim that the ultimate introduction of controls violated the principle underpinning the free entry policy is to attribute to it an intent and justification that never existed.

A final issue in the Report concerned the mechanism for restricting migration. The attribution of the same legal status to Britons and dependent British subjects made it necessary to base migration controls on some other test than citizenship.[16] The Committee concluded that:

Administratively, this would not be beyond solution, *and would not in fact conflict with the intentions behind the creation of the common citizenship*, which was the inevitable result of the limitations on the sovereignty of the colonies: nevertheless it might well be contended by critics that legislation directed against British subjects from the colonies was a breach of the principles embodied in this comparatively recent legislation.[17] (emphasis added)

The intentions behind the British Nationality Act, 1948 would not be violated, because its aims were constitutional, not migratory, and it was never designed to sanction New Commonwealth migration. Yet in creating the legislation, policy-makers created a focal point for criticism of limits on migration. As suggested in the last chapter, the British Nationality Act was more than a formalization of previous practice: the statutory entrenchment of British subjects' rights created an independent check against their withdrawal.

The final decision was left, as it is in the case of interdepartmental committees, with the Cabinet. The balance of opinion was against substantial legislation. The Home Secretary, Sir David Maxwell Fyfe, argued that the total number of 'coloured people' in the United Kingdom, approximately 40,000, and their low level of unemployment (3,366) did not justify a 'reversal of

---

[15] Ibid.

[16] Unless, of course, the entire citizenship scheme was overhauled. The complications involved with such a scheme were such that the Working Party did not even canvass it as a realistic option.

[17] These quotations are taken from *PRO, CO 1028/22*, 'Working'.

traditional practices' and the possibility of antagonizing liberal opinion.[18] The Commonwealth Secretary, Viscount Swinton, suggested that the assumption of the power to deport British subjects would probably be tolerated by the Commonwealth, and the Colonial Secretary, Oliver Lyttelton, agreed.[19] Churchill, for his part, felt that a large immigrant population might eventually be resented by a large section of the British public, but accepted the argument that the problem had not reached sufficient proportions to justify restrictive measures.[20] The meeting concluded by requesting the Home and Commonwealth Secretaries to prepare a memorandum on the powers of other Commonwealth and Colonial governments to deport British subjects.

The issue did not remain dormant for long. As the numbers began to increase (reaching 11,000 in 1954, up from 2,000 in 1953), a renewed interest in migration control emerged. In March 1954, the Labour MP for Swindon, Thomas Reid, put down a parliamentary question requesting a committee to look into immigration.[21] When the Cabinet considered the question, the Home Secretary saw some advantage in gathering the facts together and considering them in public, but concluded that these did not outweigh the risks associated with such a decision. The situation was not yet 'sufficiently acute' to demand immediate action, and even the announcement of a committee would be viewed in some quarters as evidence of a willingness to restrict immigration and that 'even to contemplate restricting immigration from the Colonies would be a step toward breaking up the Empire, and in other quarters it would be regarded as evidence that the Government are in favour of a colour bar.'[22] To announce a committee in these circumstances would, Fyfe concluded, only add to the government's difficulties.

The Conservative government's dilemma in early 1954 reflected a broader problem for post-war governments. Although Commonwealth migration was not among the great divisive issues of British politics—such as Europe and Ireland—it generated passions and interests that made the task of securing internal party unity difficult. The intra-party division was one between, on the one hand, those MPs who wished to restrict migration in response to scattered constituency pressure (in the early 1950s) and national public opin-

---

[18]   *PRO, PREM 11/824 CC (54)* 7 Conclusions, Minute 4, 3 Feb. 1954. This anti-restrictionist stance seems to have been the view of the Home Office at the time of the Working Party's creation. *PRO, CO 1028/23*, Letter from J. L. Keith to A. R. Thomas, 5 Dec. 1952. Until later in the decade, the Home Office, which had applied a system of controls to aliens since the early 1900s, was not keen to extend restrictions to British subjects.

[19]   *PRO, PREM 11/824 CC (54)* 7 Conclusions, Minute 4, 3 Feb. 1954.

[20]   Ibid.

[21]   *Parliamentary Debates (Commons)* (525), col. 63, 18 Mar. 1954.

[22]   *PRO, PREM 11/824*, 'Cabinet. Immigration of Coloured People: Memorandum by the Secretary of State for the Home Department and Minister for Welsh Affairs', 8 Mar. 1954.

ion (from 1958) and, on the other, those MPs who refused to accept migration control because of non-domestic political considerations—the importance of the Commonwealth and the fragility of negotiations over decolonization—or (less often) liberal principles. The division mapped to some degree onto one between the front and back benches; the former was motivated to a greater extent by Commonwealth ties and liberal ideals, while the latter, as it happened, represented constituencies with a high concentration of immigrants. In response to this fracture, the Cabinet was forced either to articulate strategies which reconciled the seemingly irreconcilable or to accept inaction as a logical consequence of these competing demands. Under Churchill's last government, when restrictionist pressures were still low, it chose inaction.

In response to the Home Secretary, the Cabinet agreed to decline publicly the appointment of a committee. It none the less invited the Home Secretary and the Commonwealth Secretary (Swinton), who were later joined by the Colonial Secretary (Lyttelton), to consider legislation on the deportation of criminally convicted British subjects and on the control of British subjects' entry into the UK.[23]

The Commonwealth and Colonial Secretaries were unique in that, unlike their Cabinet colleagues, they did not represent any particular domestic interest, such as health or education. They were the institutional manifestation of the Commonwealth's and colonies' voice in the Cabinet, and they articulated opposition to restrictions in this role. When the Commonwealth Relations Office learned of the Cabinet's request, its members met to reach a common position and stressed the deleterious effect that restrictions would have on relations with the Old Commonwealth and the embarrassment of any restriction solely on New Commonwealth migration, at a time when the UK was 'preaching and trying to practice the abolition of the colour bar'.[24] The Commonwealth Secretary urged the limitation of controls to the deportation of British subjects convicted of a criminal offence. On 19 March, he wrote a letter to the Colonial Secretary, Lyttelton, in which he stated this position and suggested that they agree with Salisbury to present a recommendation to the Cabinet against migration control.[25]

Salisbury was unwilling to accept this suggestion. In an articulation of the earliest decisive restrictionist position within the Cabinet, Salisbury argued that legislation on deportation:

---

[23] *PRO, PREM 11/824*, CC, 17 Conclusions, 10 Mar. 1954. The Colonial Secretary was informed nine days later. *PRO, DO 35/5216*, Letter from Salisbury to Oliver Lyttelton, 19 Mar. 1964.

[24] *PRO, DO 35/5216*, Letter to Sir P. Liesching from Swinton, 12 Mar. 1954.

[25] *PRO, DO 35/5216*, Letter from Swinton to Lyttelton, 19 Mar. 1954.

would only be tinkering with what is really becoming a fundamental problem for us all, though it is only just beginning to push up its ugly head above the surface of politics. The figures which we have been given make it clear that we are faced with a problem which, though at present it may be only a cloud the size of a man's hand, may easily come to fill the whole political horizon. . . . Indeed, if something is not done to check it now, I should not be at all surprised if the problem became quite unmanageable in 20 or 30 years time. We might be faced with very much the same type of appalling issue that is now causing such great difficulties for the United States . . . It is true that under your proposed Bill we can get rid of the worst characters. But it is for me not merely a question of whether criminal negroes should be allowed in or not; it is a question whether great quantities of negroes, criminal or not, should be allowed to come . . . [W]e should recognise that this coloured problem is potentially of a fundamental nature for the future of our Country.[26]

Andrew Roberts quotes this letter as evidence of Salisbury's foresight and principle, his Burkean concern for generations as yet unborn. 'Here was a shining exception to the rule that the Tory grandees were getting out of touch with the aspirations of ordinary people.'[27]

It is rather tempting to conclude that Salisbury was motivated by simple racism. Beyond a vague reference to the 'appalling' situation in America (it is unclear whether Salisbury found the treatment of blacks in America or their presence there appalling), the argument for their exclusion appear to derive from colour alone.

Such a statement from Salisbury is not surprising. He expressed concern over the racial character of England throughout the 1950s, and one of his contemporaries suggested that his opposition to New Commonwealth migration might have been a second reason for his resignation from Macmillan's Cabinet.[28] Salisbury is among those cited as evidence of the racist motivation of the British state.[29] What they ignore is the fact that this position was a minority one, and was resisted by Swinton as Commonwealth Secretary, who wished to avoid restrictions, and Fyfe as Home Secretary, who felt that the situation was not of sufficient importance to justify legislation. There existed a plurality of opinion on migration within the Conservative Party, and within it there was until the last few months of Churchill's premiership a majority opposed to restricting Commonwealth migration.

Salisbury met with Lyttelton, Swinton, and Fyfe on 12 April 1954. Salisbury, probably in conjunction with Lyttelton, who shared his restrictionist sympathies, appears to have carried the argument. In keeping with the

---

[26] *PRO, DO 35/5216*, Letter from Salisbury to Lyttelton, 19 Mar. 1954.

[27] Roberts, *Eminent Churchillians*, 225.

[28] Interview with Enoch Powell, Aug. 1995.

[29] Carter et al., 'The 1951–1955 Conservative Government and the Racialization of Black Immigration', 338 (footnote 14).

unanimous view, '[i]t was agreed that there ought to be a power to deport convicted criminals or other undesirable persons or persons becoming a charge,' but they also agreed—against the wishes of Swinton—that '[i]t was thought to be desirable also to have powers of restriction on entry.'[30] They suggested that this operate through a scheme whereby those who intended to stay permanently in the country should be required to pay a £25 deposit. The group was willing to apply these restrictions to the whole of the Commonwealth and Empire, but thought 'it would be desirable, if the "colour bar" objection could be overcome, to limit restriction on entry to Citizens of the United Kingdom and Colonies resident outside the United Kingdom.'[31]

The four recommended another working party to discuss their suggestions, and the whole matter was left for the Cabinet. Shortly after the 12 April meeting, Fyfe and Swinton were informed by Bernard Braine, a Conservative MP, that a Commonwealth Affairs Committee had agreed that it would 'not be unreasonable' for the UK to bring its immigration regulations in line with those operated by the Old Commonwealth.[32] Swinton responded with a temporizing reply: the matter was one about which the government had decided to remain silent but into which considerable thought was going.[33] Swinton remained strongly opposed to any restriction on the Old Dominions' right of entry; in a note on restrictions operated in the Commonwealth, he stated that there 'is a continuous stream of persons from the old Dominions to the United Kingdom who come here, with no clear plans, to try their luck; and it would be a great pity to interfere with this freedom of movement. I see great objection to applying restrictions to Commonwealth European citizens, which the Commonwealth countries do not apply to United Kingdom citizens.'[34]

Migration control vetoed

In 1954, a Cabinet shuffle created the distribution of power and preferences that ensured there would be no immigration control. Sir David Maxwell Fyfe was replaced as Home Secretary by Gwilyn Lloyd-George (son of the former Prime Minister), and Oliver Lyttelton was replaced as Colonial Secretary by Alan Lennox-Boyd. Lloyd-George took a position that was more restrictive

---

[30] *PRO, DO 35/5216*, 'Immigration of British Subjects,' 12 Apr. 1954.

[31] Ibid.

[32] *PRO, DO 35/5216*, Letter from Bernard Braine to Sir David Maxwell Fyfe, 20 Apr. 1954. Note the restrained language, which was indicative of pre-1960s debate about immigration.

[33] *PRO, DO 35/5216*, Letter from Swinton to Bernard Braine, 22 Apr. 1954.

[34] *PRO, DO 35/5216*, 'Immigration Restrictions in Commonwealth countries affecting British subjects', undated.

than his predecessor, and he warned the Cabinet in the autumn that the increase in arrivals throughout the year had altered the migration question greatly. He recommended the establishment of an interdepartmental committee with the following terms of reference: 'To consider and report whether any, and if so, what changes in the law relating to the admission to, and stay in the United Kingdom of any class of British subjects are necessary or desirable in the national interest and in the interests of the immigrants themselves.'[35]

Richard Lamb, in his biography of Macmillan based on recently released Public Record Office files, concludes that Lennox-Boyd 'was the rock on which immigration control foundered' in the Churchill and Eden governments.[36] This conclusion is not quite accurate. Lennox-Boyd was willing to accept migration control; indeed, he stated in November that the government would probably find itself obliged to introduce migration restrictions and that 'the sooner action is taken the better.'[37] Lennox-Boyd would not, however, accept migration restrictions applying exclusively to non-white Commonwealth migrants. He opposed the inclusion of the clause 'any class of' before 'British subjects' in the Interdepartmental Committee's terms of reference, as this might appear to the Committee as an invitation to consider discriminatory proposals,[38] and he informed the Home Secretary that he would 'regard any discriminatory legislation as open to the gravest objections.'[39] Migration control foundered, then, not on Lennox-Boyd's unwillingness to countenance migration restrictions but on the refusal of other Cabinet members to accept their application to the Old Commonwealth.

The Cabinet originally agreed to a departmental committee, though not, as Lloyd-George had suggested, to Labour representation or a statement in the Commons,[40] but they reversed this decision on 6 December. Were the Committee to recommend restrictions, the government would in all likelihood still have to take action in disregard of a minority report; were the Committee to recommend against control, the government would be unable to take any action.[41] The Cabinet instead invited the Colonial Secretary and Home

[35] PRO, DO 35/5217, 'Cabinet. Colonial Immigrants: Memorandum by the Secretary of State for the Home Department and Minister for Welsh Affairs', 20 Nov. 1954.
[36] R. Lamb, The Macmillan Years, 1957–1963: The Emerging Truth (London: John Murray, 1995), 412. The same claim is made by J. Barnes, 'From Eden to Macmillan, 1955–1959', P. Hennessy and A. Seldon (eds.), Ruling Performance: British Governments from Attlee to Thatcher (Oxford: Basil Blackwell, 1987), 110–11.
[37] PRO, DO 35/5217, Letter from Lennox-Boyd to Lloyd-George, 26 Nov. 1954.
[38] PRO, CAB 129/72, 'Cabinet. Colonial Immigrants: Memorandum by the Secretary of State for the Colonies', 6 Dec. 1954.
[39] PRO, DO 35/5217, Letter from Lennox-Boyd to Lloyd-George, 26 Nov. 1954.
[40] Lamb, The Macmillan Years, 411.
[41] PRO, CAB 128/27, CC, 54, 6 Dec. 1954.

Secretary to arrange for the preparation of draft legislation restricting the admission of British subjects from overseas.

MIGRATION POLICY UNDER EDEN

In early 1955, the Cabinet again felt itself under pressure on the migration question. The Home Office met with a deputation of Birmingham city officials concerned over the housing problems created by West Indian migration.[42] Commonwealth migrants concentrated in particular neighbourhoods in Britain's larger cities, and their presence exacerbated housing shortages. At the same time, Cyril Osborne, who began a campaign against immigrants in 1952, created difficulties for the front bench. In January, he requested leave to introduce under the ten-minute rule a private member's bill restricting migration. The matter went to a Commonwealth Affairs Committee, and Osborne's request was denied by a large majority. The Committee felt that the discussion would degenerate into a 'colour bar' wrangle in which the government would appear eager to lower the status of British subjects of colour, and the whole affair would lower the United Kingdom's status in the Commonwealth.[43] There was, as well, something intolerable about discriminating against 'loyal and hard-working' Jamaicans when a far greater number of disloyal Southern Irish entered the country freely. Osborne did not take rejection well; losing his composure, he told the Committee that its refusal was a personal attack on him and a slight against his parliamentary competence. The Committee members dispersed with 'grave disquiet' and 'a feeling that, if Osborne persists, he will, because he is so easily baited by the Opposition, put his foot right in it'.[44]

Certain observers of migration policy have concluded that the Conservatives, particularly after Patrick Gordon Walker (Labour) lost his seat to the Conservative Peter Griffiths' racist 1964 campaign, were hostage to the extremism of men like Osborne who whipped up public hostility and pushed frontbench appeasers into accepting migration controls.[45] The archives

---

[42] *PRO, DO 35/5217*, Letter to the Secretary of State, 19 Jan. 1955. The deputation emphasized that the problem was limited to housing—Birmingham employers were satisfied with West Indian immigration and would resent its termination—and admitted that it stemmed from the local community's prejudiced unwillingness to welcome the immigrants fully.

[43] For the minutes of the meeting, see *PRO, PREM 11/824*, 'Commonwealth Affairs Committee,' 27 Jan. 1955. [44] Ibid.

[45] P. Foot, *Immigration and Race in British Politics* (Harmondsworth: Penguin, 1965), especially ch. 8; M. Dummett and A. Dummett, 'The Role of Government in Britain's Racial Crisis', in C. Husband (ed.), *'Race' in Britain: Continuity and Change* (London: Hutchinson, 1982).

provide little support for this interpretation. Osborne and his accomplice Norman Pannell were viewed with disdain in the 1950s by those at the centre of the Conservative Party's policy-making machine. The quotation also substantiates the view that non-white immigrants enjoyed some support within the Conservative Party. It is difficult to determine its extent, and it is doubtful that Jamaicans' right to enter the United Kingdom was embraced without hesitation by a majority of Conservative Party members. But it equally cannot be said that the history of party policy in the 1950s is but an effort to justify black migrants' exclusion from membership in British society.

Migration control was abandoned under Eden's premiership, as it had been under Churchill's, because of the reluctance of the Cabinet to extend migration restrictions to the Old Commonwealth. The Cabinet found itself in a deadlock over this question. As a Commonwealth relations memorandum in April stated, in the context of a divided Conservative Party,

[t]here is no obvious way round the dilemma which lies at the heart of this question, viz. that there must either be more or less open legislative or administrative discrimination as to which people shall be allowed to enter freely, or else the controls will be liable to keep out a great many citizens of other Commonwealth countries whom no-one wishes to keep out.[46]

This dilemma remained unresolved as a draft bill restricting the migration of British subjects was prepared in early 1955.

In June, the draft bill was prepared. On the surface, the bill appears tame. It empowered Her Majesty's government to make by Order-in-Council 'such provision as appears to Her to be expedient in the public interest' (i) for restricting entry to the United Kingdom of British subjects from outside the UK, the Channel Islands or the Isle of Man, (ii) for the imposition of conditions on subjects that do enter the UK, and (iii) for the Secretary of State, in circumstances specified by Order-in-Council, to deport any British subject.[47] The bill applied to both the Old and New Commonwealth, and therefore did not discriminate on the basis of race, and it provided for the flexible determination of limits.

At a deeper level, the discretionary power of the legislation was considerable. Orders-in-Council are orders issued by the Queen in consultation with the Privy Council.[48] As the Queen's prerogative powers are largely symbolic, and the Privy Council merely approves or records decisions taken elsewhere,

[46]   *PRO, DO 35/5217*, 'Control of Entry of British Subjects into the United Kingdom,' 13 Apr. 1955.
[47]   *PRO, PREM 11/824*, 'Confidential. Commonwealth Immigrants'. Draft Bill to restrict entry of certain British subjects, British Protected Persons and citizens of the Irish Republic and for deportation of such subjects and persons, 23 Oct. 1955.
[48]   H. M. Stout, *British Government* (New York: Oxford University Press, 1953), 70.

such orders are in practice the choice of the minister responsible.[49] The draft bill would have granted to the ministers responsible—most likely the Home Secretary in consultation with the Commonwealth and Colonial Secretaries—unrestrained power to limit migration, impose conditions on entry, and deport British subjects resident in Britain. All British subjects would have been stripped of the privileges associated with their status as either CUKCs or CICCs, and would have in practice been in the same legal position, at least so far as migration is concerned, as aliens.

Perhaps partly as a consequence of the bill's sweeping nature, the Cabinet remained divided over the proper course of action. Lloyd-George had argued that the controversy surrounding the bill would be reduced (and, implicitly, his restrictionist argument strengthened) if the legislation were based on the recommendations of an impartial committee.[50] Ignoring the rather obvious fact that a committee designed in advance to ratify extant conclusions is something less than impartial, he recommended an interdepartmental committee of identical composition and similar terms of reference to the one considered and rejected by the Cabinet in December. The Committee was to (a) report on the economic and social problems associated with migration, (b) examine the administrative measures feasible for purposes of migration control and (c) discuss the consequences of such control for the traditional ties between the UK and parts of the Commonwealth. The Commonwealth Secretary endorsed its recommendation, and the Colonial Secretary accepted it, but expressed his reservations about the terms of reference.[51] Although the Cabinet minutes, which are inevitably a scaled-down version of the full story, do not provide the reasons for Lennox-Boyd's hesitation, it is likely he objected—as he had in the past—to the inclusion of 'any class of' British subjects as a possible basis for discrimination. The Colonial Secretary was sending another indication to his Cabinet colleagues that he would find it impossible to accept racially discriminatory migration controls.

---

[49]   H. Morrison, *Government and Parliament: A Survey from the Inside* (London: Oxford University Press, 1959), 81. Orders in Council are issued by the Privy Council, and they may be either judicial (reporting a judgment of the Judicial Committee of the Privy Council) or legislative; the majority are the latter, that is, they are made in pursuance of powers delegated to Her Majesty in Council by statute. They have a status identical to regulations made by ministers under delegated legislative powers, but they enjoy greater prestige as they are formally made by the sovereign. Unless they concern an exceptionally important matter, they are drafted by the legal advisers to the relevant department. Draft Orders are read out by the Lord President, they are approved orally by the Queen, and they are authenticated by the signature of the Clerk of the Council. See S. A. de Smith, H. Street and R. Brazier (eds.), *Constitutional and Administrative Law* (London: Penguin Books, 1985), 165–6.

[50]   *PRO, PREM 11/824*, 'Cabinet. Colonial Immigrants: Memorandum by the Home Department and Minister for Welsh Affairs', 10 June 1955.

[51]   Ibid.

The Committee reported in August 1955, and it offered conclusions that on the whole should have surprised no one. Legislation could be justified, it argued, because the UK's greater prosperity acted as a magnet, and the UK was unique in its lack of control on migration; yet, any control would be criticized as racial discrimination and would be impossible to justify on purely economic grounds (the Committee found no evidence that immigrants were an undue burden on National Assistance). Race relations might also deteriorate were the 'coloured population' to continue its increase, and it seemed unlikely that the rate of arrivals would slow. The Committee concluded with the argument that the Irish, who provided much-needed labour and whose control would be difficult to administer, should be exempted from control.[52]

The Committee had been intended by Lloyd-George to provide a justification for the restrictions he desired, but it only restated arguments which were widely known and sent the whole matter back to the Cabinet. Of those members of the Cabinet responsible for migration, the Commonwealth Secretary was willing to accept restrictions on migration that discriminated against West Indian and African British subjects, but was less sanguine about their application to the Indian subcontinent. 'I', he stated, 'myself would argue that we should not take any action which would give the impression that citizens from India, Pakistan and Ceylon are less favourably treated than citizens from the older Commonwealth countries.'[53] He justified his opposition with reference to Indian willingness to check working-class emigration and the possibility of retaliatory measures against the entry of the British business community.[54]

The Commonwealth Secretary assumed—as many in Cabinet did—that migration restrictions would *not* apply to the Old Commonwealth: '[i]t would probably be quite easy to discriminate in favour of white members of the "old" Commonwealth countries.'[55] The entire Cabinet viewed an Old Commonwealth exemption as desirable, and immigration as a political issue was created by substantial migration from the New Commonwealth. Had post-war migration been solely Old Dominions' citizens, there would have

---

[52] For the full report, see PRO, *CAB 129/77*, 'Cabinet. Colonial Immigrants: Note by the Secretary of State for the Home Department and Minister for Welsh Affairs', 18 Aug. 1955.

[53] *PRO, PREM 11/824*, 'Cabinet. Colonial Immigrants: Memorandum by the Secretary of State for Commonwealth Relations', 2 Sept. 1955.

[54] Ibid. There are several references in the documents to the concerns of the British business community about migration restrictions, and these seem to have been one among several arguments against restricting migration. It is difficult to be certain of the business community's importance, but it probably made some lobbying efforts to persuade the Commonwealth Relations Office of its case. Documents after 1958 make no reference to this matter, so it seems that its importance decreased in the later 1950s, perhaps as UK business interests looked to Europe and the UK government downgraded the importance of settler communities in its overall policy.   [55] Ibid.

been no interest in restricting it. When the draft bill and report of the Interdepartmental Committee were considered by the Cabinet in early November 1955, Alan Lennox-Boyd made it clear that he would find the exclusive application of migration restrictions to colonial immigrants intolerable. Arguing that discriminatory legislation would be 'fiercely resented' in West Indian, African, and Pacific dependencies, he stated that 'I must therefore record that I could not agree to legislation confined to Colonial immigrants.'[56]

Lennox-Boyd's conclusion, in effect, vetoed migration control. The memorandum contained an implicit threat of resignation,[57] and the Cabinet was unwilling to incur the negative consequences of a resignation over the issue (not least because the public was unaware of the deliberations). As Cabinet ministers were not more willing than they previously had been to apply controls to the Old Dominions, the result was a deadlock. Norman Brook advised the Prime Minister to appoint a committee of ministers, chaired by the Lord Chancellor, to analyse the problems associated with legislation. Such a body would clear away technical issues that would have to be dealt with in any case, and it would, more importantly, create a delay during which the case for legislation might become sufficiently strong to break the Cabinet deadlock.[58] It would also, for the moment, bury the issue. Eden agreed; in a note scribbled on Brook's letter of 10 November he stated that '[a commmmittee] is, I think, the best we can do'.[59]

When the Committee reported the following June, it paradoxically provided the sort of intellectual justification that Lloyd-George had hoped to secure through committee deliberations. It concluded that the argument in favour of legislation centred around the fact that the traditional right of free entry had become anachronistic. The principle 'grew up tacitly at a time when the coloured races of the Commonwealth were at a more primitive stage of development than now,' when there was no likelihood of a 'coloured invasion of Britain'.[60] Since then educational opportunities had improved in the New Commonwealth/Colonies, incomes had increased, and transport facilities had improved. As there was an obvious limit to Britain's capacity to absorb the influx there was, the Committee argued, every reason to believe that controls would be inevitable.

---

[56] *PRO, PREM 11/824*, 'Cabinet. Colonial Immigrants: Memorandum by the Secretary of State for the Colonies', 1 Nov. 1955.

[57] Lamb, *The Macmillan Years*, 415.

[58] *PRO, PREM 11/2920*, Letter from Norman Brook to Eden, 10 Nov. 1955.

[59] Ibid.

[60] *PRO, CAB 129/81*, 'Cabinet. Colonial Immigrants: Report of the Committee of Ministers', 22 June 1956.

This amounted to the claim that the right of free entry for Commonwealth citizens of colour was only applicable at a time when they lacked the capacity to exercise it. While it seems curious logic to argue that a right is nullified through its exercise, it is consistent with the character of the dominant commitment to the Commonwealth. The right of entry had been viewed as the institutional expression of the primary relationship between the UK and the Old Dominions, and it was given statutory backing in 1948 because politicians and bureaucrats believed that migration to the UK would be dominated by British subjects from the Dominions. As in 1950, it was the Old Commonwealth that continued in 1956 to work against ending the right of free entry. If restrictions were extended to immigrants from Canada, Australia, or New Zealand, 'the legislation would need very full and careful handling to explain it to public opinion in those countries'.[61]

A lack of clear public support for controls, and opposition among liberal opinion, also militated against the introduction of legislation. With the exception of Salisbury, who called for immediate restrictions, the Committee came out against control.

MIGRATION POLICY UNDER CHURCHILL AND EDEN

It has been argued that migration controls were not enacted because Eden lacked the will, and failed to demonstrate the political leadership, necessary to take the difficult but essential decision in favour of restrictions.[62] It has also been suggested that Eden failed where Churchill might have succeeded, and that his attachment to moderation and the rhetoric of a multiracial Commonwealth undermined his willingness to act.[63] In truth, it is doubtful that Churchill would have enacted legislation had he remained beyond his already extended term in office. Migration control failed not because of political weakness; rather, it failed because of political division. Lennox-Boyd, as Colonial Secretary, would not accept racially discriminatory restrictions, while Lord Home, as Commonwealth Secretary and with the support of the rest of the Cabinet, would not countenance restrictions on the Old Dominions.

Migration controls were thus delayed, and British multiculturalism furthered, by an elite attachment to the Old Commonwealth in the context of

---

[61] *PRO, PREM 11/824.*

[62] See *The Times*, D. Walker, 'Why Wait Thirty Years?', 2 Jan. 1986

[63] Lamb, *The Macmillan Years*, 416. Henry Pelling disputes this view of Churchill. H. Pelling, *Churchill's Peacetime Ministry, 1945–1951* (London: Macmillan, 1997), 183. Like Lamb, however, he views Eden's failure to act as a sign of weakness.

selective, but none the less genuine, opposition to racially discriminatory restrictions. By the early 1960s, it was increasingly clear that the Old Dominions saw their economic and security interests in regional rather than Commonwealth alliances: Canada with the United States, New Zealand and Australia with the United States and the democratic nations of the Pacific Rim. By 1962, Britain was willing to take the step of applying to the European Community, an implicit admission that its future was a European one. But in the mid-1950s, when Whitehall and the Conservative Party were dominated by men who defined their political selves in the Second World War, the Commonwealth—and particularly the Old Commonwealth—was the foundation of Britain's economic and security future. To have enacted migration control in the early 1950s in a manner acceptable to the Colonial Secretary would have been to conclude, or so it was believed, that the association between the United Kingdom and the Old Commonwealth was not worth preserving. Such an admission was for many inconceivable. Robert Skidelsky, in an essay on Britain's relationship with the Continent, concludes that in 1939 'Hitler, in effect, offered England the alternatives of falling back on the undisturbed enjoyment of Empire and embarking on a European War in which defeat was a real possibility: the choice between Commonwealth and Europe. England chose the latter.'[64] In the 1950s, the United Kingdom turned again to its overseas network of Dominions and colonies.[65] Britain faced a choice between the Commonwealth and Europe twice: politically over the European Coal and Steel Community and symbolically over migration control. In the former, Britain had the opportunity to join the process of European institutional and economic integration; in the latter, it had the chance to admit to itself and its former and current dependencies that England's future could only be a regional one. In both cases, Conservative politicians chose the Commonwealth.

[64] R. Skidelsky, 'The Choice for Europe', *Interests and Obsessions: Selected Essays* (London: Macmillan, 1993), 342.

[65] Indeed, it is arguable that the War itself was central to this development. The conflict drew the Empire and—especially—the Dominions into the United Kingdom, and the country's success convinced many of the centrality of the Commonwealth to the UK's future. I owe my thanks to Brian Harrison for suggesting this point.

4

The Decline of an Ideal: The Conservatives and Immigration, 1958–1960

SHORTLY after replacing Anthony Eden as Prime Minister, Harold Macmillan sent a note to Rab Butler stating, 'I have no doubt you will be reporting to the Cabinet . . . about the situation in London and elsewhere in what are called the "race riots". . . . [W]e agreed not long ago to look again at the immigration question in a few months' time. Perhaps we should look at it now.'[1] The migration issue was examined after the riots, and it continued to be until the introduction of restrictive legislation in 1962. This chapter focuses on two eventful years—1958 to 1960—during which a divisive argument within Whitehall and the Cabinet was carried in favour of control. The two years are of considerable scholarly interest, as they produced a rich abundance of documents on Commonwealth immigration. They demonstrate that a lengthy argument was waged between the Colonial Office and the Ministry of Labour over the legitimacy and necessity of migration controls. The right of free entry had its defenders in the British bureaucracy, and the argument in favour of control was won against their objections.

This flurry of argument and activity, which preoccupied certain Cabinet ministers and bureaucrats for the better part of two years, was set in motion by the crack of a Molotov cocktail.

THE NOTTINGHAM AND LONDON RIOTS

In late August 1958, an altercation in a public house ignited tensions that had been growing between the poor indigenous populations of Nottingham and London and the recent West Indian arrivals.[2] The experience of immigrant

---

[1] H. Macmillan, *At the End of the Day, 1961–1963* (London: Macmillan, 1973), 74.

[2] For fuller, and somewhat contradictory, accounts of the riots' origins, see D. Hiro, *Black British White British* (London: Grafton, 1991), 39; E. Pilkington, *Beyond the Mother Country: West Indians and the Notting Hill White Riots* (London: I.B. Tauris, 1988), 106–7; and R. Ramdin, *The Making of the Black Working Class in Britain* (London: Gower, 1987), 204–14.

communities in Notting Hill was typical of post-war British cities. After the War, immigrants and a dwindling proportion of working-class Britons lived in squalid conditions. Grand old Victorian houses were rented to Commonwealth migrants who found themselves crowded into them; at the same time, generally rising standards of living allowed more white families to leave the area. Those that remained associated its continued decay with the West Indians, while the conditions in which the latter were forced to live (most houses had a single lavatory and bathroom) intensified racist assumptions about hygiene and living habits.

It was against this background that the events of late August and early September 1958 took place. Following a fight outside a bar, the white youths went on self-described 'nigger-hunts', beating West Indians in the streets and attacking frightened individuals who had locked themselves in their homes. Crowds of some 1,500 to 4,000 were believed to have participated in the Nottingham disturbances,[3] which occurred on the weekend of 23 August. On Monday, 1 September, Notting Hill—then largely a West Indian neighbourhood—experienced the worst civil unrest in the 1950s. Gangs moved through the area, more West Indians were attacked, and various neo-fascist groups, including Mosley's Union movement, are reported to have distributed inflammatory anti-West Indian propaganda.[4] The police attempted to maintain order and protect the West Indians, but the lines between aggressor and victim blurred as West Indians began defending themselves.

On 2 September, an uneasy calm returned. Although relations within both communities remained tense, there were no further incidences on a comparable scale. The experience was, nonetheless, a tremendous shock to the British public and all political parties. In retrospect, this reaction seems exaggerated. Although a number of thuggish incidents occurred, and racist attitudes were openly demonstrated, the 'race riots' were, comparatively speaking, not especially riotous. There were no fatalities, and the overall level of damage pales in comparison with the American Watts riots in the late 1960s or the 1981 Brixton riots. But they occurred after a lengthy period of peaceful prosperity and shattered the Edwardianesque calm, personified in Macmillan, of 1950s Britain.[5] They also forced British elites to question assumptions about oft-invoked (but rarely substantiated) English tolerance. The process was made more painful by the smugness of South Africa and other racist settler regimes,

---

[3] On the Nottingham incident, see *The Times*, ' "irresponsible actions" at Nottingham' (27 Aug. 1958), 'Renewed calls for changes in immigration law' (28 Aug.), 'Race riots in Nottingham' (30 Aug.) and 'Clashes in the streets' (5 Sept.).

[4] Pilkington, *Beyond the Mother Country*, 117–18.

[5] For an analysis of Macmillan's aesthetic, see the chapter by L. Siedentop in V. Bogdanor and R. Skidelsky (eds.) *The Age of Affluence, 1951–1964* (London: Macmillan, 1970).

which found it difficult to contain their glee at what they took to be further proof of the instability inherent to multiracial societies.[6]

An immediate consequence of the riots was the transformation of migration from a regional into a national issue. The riots' extensive coverage in the Press ensured that all citizens of the United Kingdom were well aware of them. Certain commentators concluded, rather perversely, that because the victims were on the whole West Indians, the time had come to reconsider the tenability of Britain's open borders. The fact that the attacks were executed largely by white men (and a few women) against blacks led commentators to suggest that a threshold of tolerance had been reached and that the British public would not accept a larger immigrant presence.[7]

Backbenchers from both parties echoed these arguments. The riots allowed Pannell and Osborne to claim that their warnings had been justified, and they were assisted by a few Labour MPs. James Harrison (Labour, Nottingham North) called the open-door policy anachronistic and impractical.[8] He was joined by George Rogers (Labour, Notting Hill), who described the riots as the work not of 'Teddy-Boy' hooligans, but of a community legitimately hostile to undesirable sections of the black population.[9] He called for legislation providing mechanisms for deporting immigrants convicted of crime and limiting the right of entry to those with accommodation.[10] Osborne naturally revelled in this unexpected boost. After the first disturbance, he stated publicly that '[w]e are sowing the seeds of another Little Rock and it is tragic. To bring the problem into this country with our eyes open is doing the gravest disservice to our grandchildren, who will curse us for our lack of courage. I regard the Nottingham incident as a red light to us all.'[11]

It has been claimed that the riots gave the restrictionist campaigners within the party a great boost.[12] The immediate result was in fact the opposite: the riots served as a constraint on restrictionist legislation.[13] The Conservatives had been concerned over Notting Hill since early 1958; on 20 January, a deputation of individuals from local and central government, including the Labour MP George Rogers, spoke with David Renton about the tensions in the area.[14] The cause of greatest concern was housing, and particularly the

---

[6] See The Times, ' "The biter bit" in racial clashes: S. African comment on Nottingham', 28 Aug. 1958, and 'Racial lesson for Britain: reactions to clash at Nottingham', 30 Aug. 1958.

[7] Layton-Henry, Politics of Immigration, 38–9. See for example 'Why Racial Clash Occurred', The Times, 27 Aug. 1958.

[8] 'Nottingham M.P.s urge curb on entry of immigrants', The Times, 27 Aug. 1958.

[9] Pilkington, Beyond the Mother Country, 133.   [10] Ibid. 134.

[11] 'Renewed call for changes in immigration law', The Times, 28 Aug. 1958.

[12] Layton-Henry, Politics of Immigration, 39–41.

[13] PRO, CO 1032/196, Letter for Sir John Macpherson's signature, undated.

[14] PRO, CO 1032/3931, 'Note of a Meeting', undated.

unscrupulous actions of Paul Rachman. Rachman was one of the few land-lords who freely rented rooms to West Indians, but he charged them exorbitant prices for squalid accommodation. The housing conditions faced by West Indians intensified prejudices among the indigenous population, including those who had denied them accommodation.[15] Following a familiar pattern, Renton expressed concern and sympathy, but he told the deputation that the government saw no justification in departing from its traditional policy towards British subjects.

Those who wished to use Notting Hill as a platform for restrictionism did not get far. Post-war settlement patterns meant that immigrants congregated for the most part in the constituencies of backbench MPs with little access to the instruments of government and party policy. In addition to their obvious exclusion from the Cabinet, they did not serve on the various committees that examined the migration question; indeed, they were often ignorant of their existence. These individuals' extremism ensured that they would not be embraced as part of the Conservative mainstream. This was because these individuals were tainted with racism,[16] and frontbench ministers of a party espousing a commitment to the Commonwealth and engaged in delicate negotiations over decolonization could not, whatever their personal prejudices, associate themselves with the Osborne/Pannell position. They found no more sympathy among bureaucrats; in Whitehall correspondence, Osborne and the others were referred to dismissively as the 'lunatic fringe'.[17] With the exception of Salisbury, they received no support among the aristocratic members in Parliament. They viewed the rantings of Osborne and Pannell with a patrician distaste, and they felt little pressure from their constituents on the question of migration. 'The knights of the shires', Enoch Powell commented later, 'were little affected.'[18]

[15] The mechanisms for checking these abuses were weak, and the local authorities were reluctant to invoke them. Under 1946 legislation, the local authorities had powers to initiate proceedings on their own initiative before a rent tribunal in instances of suspected abuse. The Borough Council had, however, decided that to do so would infringe the tenants' freedom of contract, and it had limited its efforts to a warning letter. Certain living conditions were a breach of the Public Health Acts, but there were insufficient local authorities to enforce these. See *PRO, CO 1031/3931*, 'Note of a Meeting', undated.

[16] Discussing the immigration of Irish and Jews, Pannell argued that their success in integrating into British society provided no positive lesson. For '[w]hatever their peculiarities, habits or customs when they first arrive, they have been able to adapt themselves to the British social pattern and have gained full acceptance in the community because, to put it baldly, their skins are white' (N. Pannell and F. Brockway, *Immigration: What is the Answer?* (London: Routledge & Kegan Paul, 1965), 40). Osborne, in an interview with the *Daily Mail*, flatly stated that Britain 'is a white man's country, and I want it to remain so'. See 7 Feb. 1961.

[17] See *PRO, 1032/196*, Letter for Sir John Macpherson's signature, undated, and *PRO, CO 1032/196*, Letter for Mr Roger's signature to Governors of the West Indies, British Guiana and British Honduras, undated.

[18] Interview with Enoch Powell, Aug. 1995.

The shift in frontbench Conservative attitude was not associated with the lobbying efforts of these politically impotent individuals. It rather began with a fracturing of the anti-restrictionist consensus within the Cabinet and Whitehall. The first element in this was a hardening of the Ministry of Labour against unrestricted migration. Although the Labour Ministry recognized at times the usefulness of colonial and New Commonwealth migration in relieving unemployment, it was to a far greater extent preoccupied with the possibility of a migration-driven surge in unemployment during periods of recession. In August 1958, the ministry reported that employment prospects for immigrant workers were deteriorating rapidly. It put pressure on the Colonial Office, which had the greatest responsibility for the West Indians and the greatest interest in avoiding migration control.[19] At an interdepartmental meeting, the Labour Ministry proposed that the West Indian governments be persuaded to withhold, for a fixed period, all passports from those intending to travel to the UK in search of employment.[20]

As passports had been withheld from Indians and Pakistanis since 1955, it was difficult for the Colonial Office to resist this suggestion.[21] Yet resist it they wished to do. To the dismay of the Colonial Office, migration from the Indian subcontinent had begun to increase in 1958 and a fear emerged, one which was later realized, that the UK would be forced to accommodate a second, substantial influx of New Commonwealth migration. The Colonial Office was especially anxious to prevent such a development, because it would give credence to a nascent restrictionist position within the Cabinet,[22]

[19]   This position was consistent with that of the TUC, which considered pressing for immigration control in the mid-1950s (though it reversed its position after the riots). See *TUC, 805.91(1)I,* Meeting with Ministry of Labour, 10 Apr. 1955, *TUC, 805.91(1)II,* Letter from Assistant General Secretary of TUC to Iain Macleod, 30 Apr. 1958.

[20]   *PRO, CO 1032/196,* 'Colonial Immigrants: Brief for the Secretary of State for Cabinet', 8 Sept. 1958.

[21]   *PRO, CO 1032/196,* 'Colonial' and *PRO, CO 1032/196,* Letter for Mr Roger's signature to Governors of the West Indies, British Guiana and British Honduras, undated. Quoting the letter: 'Our feeling is that the administrative measures as such, i.e. the tightening up of passport controls, can only have a marginal effect and that much more effective results may be expected from deliberate publicity. ... Nevertheless we cannot, frankly, get away with this argument here under present circumstances. The Commonwealth Secretary has already made public reference to the steps taken by the Governments of India and Pakistan to restrict emigration, and the Secretary of State [for the Colonies] may well be pressed fairly soon to say what positive steps are taken by the Governments of the West Indies.' This document appears to have been drafted before the riots, an event which undermined much of the case in favour of passport restrictions on West Indians.

[22]   Quoting *PRO, CO 1032/195,* Letter from Ian Watt to Marnum, 1 May 1958: '[w]hat has, I think, made Ministers take a sharper look at the problem has been the great increase in arrivals from India and Pakistan, nearly all of them feckless individuals who have neither the "British" backgrounds of the West Indians, nor their abilities, nor their intention to come here and do a hard job of work and be paid for it.' Also see *PRO, 1032/196,* Letter to Sir Kenneth Blackburne, 29 Aug. 1958.

and because the department was less than enthusiastic about Indian and Pakistani migration. To a striking degree, the Colonial Office defined itself as a partisan of the West Indians and their right to enter the United Kingdom. To be sure, part of this reflected the obvious fact that the West Indies remained colonies, while India and Pakistan were independent Commonwealth countries and, as such, were represented by the Commonwealth Relations Office. But there was more to it than this. For the Colonial Office, a distinction between the two types of migration was necessary because of the character of the immigrants themselves. Immigrants from the Indian subcontinent were 'hardly fit to compare with the West Indians either socially or as industrial workers', and they were, 'most embarrassing to us in the Colonial Office'.[23] Whereas West Indians were viewed as industrious, reliable, and talented, Indians and Pakistanis were seen to be lazy, feckless, and difficult to place in employment.[24] Should migration control have been applied in 1958, certain members of the Colonial Office wished to contrast 'the skilled character and proved industry of the West Indians with the unskilled and largely lazy Asians' in order to secure an exemption for immigrants from the West Indies.[25]

Although the above comments on Asians possess all the nuance of barroom prejudices, they demonstrate that black immigration, far from inciting fear and loathing across parties and the bureaucracy, had strong support within at least one major office of state. One Home Office official has even suggested that, had Commonwealth migration remained purely West Indian, there would have been no end to free entry.[26] The West Indians spoke English, many had had a British education in the West Indies, and they were viewed by at least some British bureaucrats as part of the British family.

The Colonial Office's response to these pre-riot developments was to communicate with the West Indian governors in order to secure agreement on

---

[23] *PRO, CO 1032/196*, Letter for Mr Roger's signature to Governors of the West Indies, British Guiana and British Honduras, undated.

[24] See *PRO, CO 1032/195*, Letter from Ian Watt, 3 Mar. 1958 and *PRO, CO 1032/196*, Letter from Ian Watt to Marnum, 1 May 1958. Most of these negative letters were written by Watt, but he appears to be an important figure at the Colonial Office level (given his consistent presence in correspondence) and these letters are marked up by other officials expressing agreement.

[25] *PRO, CO 1032/195*, Letter from Ian Watt, 21 Feb. 1958. The contrast in Colonial Office attitudes is interesting, because it highlights, if more evidence were needed, the extent to which racial assumptions are socially constructed. The experience allowed them to escape, at least to some extent, the racist assumptions and treatment endured by, for example, African Americans. If the tabloid press is to be taken as an indicator of the public mood, public prejudices have reversed in favour of immigrants (and children of immigrants) from the Indian subcontinent and to the detriment of those from the West Indies.   [26] Confidential interview.

the use of non-statutory methods for discouraging emigration to the UK.[27] This raised the possibility of restricting migration along the lines followed by India and Pakistan. The Colonial Office was suspicious of such a policy, which enjoyed some support in the Cabinet,[28] but it accepted the need for some form of informal means of tempering the rate of emigration. A Colonial Office letter was sent on the eve of the riots, an experience that, as we have seen, altered greatly the place of the migration issue in British politics.

Thus, two restrictionist streams emerged on the eve of the riots: a politically impotent backbench and an influential frontbench restrictionism. The effect of the riots was paradoxical; while increasing public pressure against migration, they decreased the government's ability to respond to either this pressure or the Ministry of Labour's arguments within the Cabinet. The liberal wing would not accept a panicked response to the riots (and its underlying racist sentiment),[29] and the Colonial Secretary, Lennox-Boyd, remained strongly opposed to restrictions.[30] His position was reinforced by anti-restrictionism within the colonies. Although substantial informal controls might have been acceptable before the riots, the events ensured that any substantial informal controls would meet extensive local opposition.[31] In particular, any restrictions on passports would be viewed, falsely but widely, as a direct response to the riots, and it would inflame already emotional public opinion in the West Indies.[32] West Indian opposition was emphasized when Prime Minister Manley of Jamaica arrived in London shortly after the riots.[33] His ostensible purpose was to reassure the West Indian community and to

---

[27]   *PRO, CO 1032/196*, 'Brief for the Secretary of State for Cabinet', 8 Sept. 1958.

[28]   *PRO, CO 1032/196*, Letter for Sir John Macpherson's signature, undated.

[29]   *CPA, CRD/2/44/20*, 'A Bow Group Memorandum on Coloured People in Britain', Oct. 1958.

[30]   The Prime Minister's position is unclear. His memoirs suggest that he might have been sympathetic to controls (Macmillan, *At the End of the Day*, 74–5. Nigel Fisher, however, argues that Macmillan was reluctant to impose them throughout the period (N. Fisher, *Harold Macmillan* (London: Weidenfeld & Nicolson, 1982), 285.). Whatever Macmillan's attitude, it is not easily determined.

[31]   *PRO, CO 1032/196*, Letter for Sir John Macpherson's signature, undated. Quoting the document: 'We did in our discussions cast a general fly over the West Indies Ministers, to see whether or not the proposals in the draft savingram enclosed with my letter would be acceptable, but we soon realised that to ask them to turn off the passport tap completely, as a positive and explicit measure of policy, would no longer [i.e. after the riots] be acceptable.'

[32]   *PRO, CO 1032/196*, Letter from Ian Watt to Sir J. Macpherson, 8 Sept. 1958 and *PRO, CO 1032/196*, Letter to Mr Rogers, 15 Sept. 1958. The Governors of Barbados (Sir R. Arundell), Jamaica (K. Blackburne), Windward Is. (Sir C. Deverell), British Guiana (Sir P. Renison), Leeward Is. (Sir A. Williams), the West Indies (Lord Hailes), and the Acting Governor of Trinidad all agreed that the riots made passport controls politically impossible.

[33]   A few days earlier, the Home Secretary, R. A. Butler, produced at Macmillan's request a statement timidly affirming government opposition to immigration control. *PRO, CO 1032/196*, 'Racial Disturbances. Note of a Meeting held in the Home Secretary's Room'. 8 Sept. 1958.

promote interracial harmony, but he and other West Indians leaders also met with the Conservative government.[34] Part of Manley's purpose in visiting London was to ensure that the riots would not occasion an end to Jamaicans' ability to enter the United Kingdom, a policy of which they were the chief West Indian beneficiary. The Home Secretary assured the West Indian ministers that the UK would not alter its traditional policy, but stressed the need for discouraging migration 'in substantial numbers' during a period of rising unemployment. The West Indian ministers agreed to two measures: (i) the West Indians would emphasize to all those applying for passports the desirability of securing a job in advance and to regulate the pace of passports granted; and (ii) extant efforts to ensure that no one with a serious criminal record was granted a passport to come to the UK would be increased.[35] These efforts had little long-term effect on pressure to emigrate.

LABOUR AND THE 1958 RIOTS

In the late 1950s, any restriction on Commonwealth migration would have been strongly opposed by Labour. The party had responded to the riots with a decisive stand against migration control and racial discrimination, one that was to be at the foundation of party policy through to the 1962 Commonwealth Immigrants Act. While Labour seems to have devoted comparatively little attention to race relations and migration before 1958, a Working Party on Racial Discrimination had existed since at least 1957,[36] and it had undertaken studies of race relations in Birmingham.[37] This body served as an institutional forum for responding to the riots and for providing the evidence on which the National Executive Committee (NEC), the party's key policy-making body, made its decision. The NEC met in September, received

---

[34] Ibid.

[35] Two positive measures were also agreed to: (i) the British Caribbean Welfare Service, an agency designed to address the needs of West Indians at the community level in the UK, would be expanded; and (ii) the local authorities should take more active steps to foster 'inter-racial community development'. For a full summary of the meeting and its conclusions, see *PRO, CO 1032/196*, 'From the Secretary of State for the Colonies. To the Governor-General, THE WEST INDIES', undated.

[36] *Labour Party Archives (LPA)*, National Museum of Labour History, Manchester, *Race Relations and Discrimination* (file), Letter from John Hatch to Members of the Working Party on Racial Discrimination, 23 Jan. 1958.

[37] See *LPA, Race Relations and Discrimination*, 'Working Party on Racial Discrimination. The Coloured People of Birmingham: A Public Opinion Poll', undated and 'Working Party on Racial Discrimination: Information from the Report of an Enquiry Undertaken by the Race Relations Group of Fircroft College, Birmingham.'

reports from local districts, and produced a statement that guided party policy until 1962. It condemned the Notting Hill disturbances and opposed any restrictions on Commonwealth migration:

We are firmly convinced that any form of British legislation limiting Commonwealth immigrants to this country would be disastrous to our status in the Commonwealth and to the confidence of the Commonwealth peoples.[38]

There was, as one would expect, opposition within the party to such an unequivocal line. A small group of MPs—John Hynd, Harry Hynd, George Rogers, Albert Evans, and James Harrison—demanded an end to free entry, and they were supported by certain local London districts.[39] Unlike the Conservative Party, however, in which backbench hostility resonated to some degree with the Minister of Labour (and, later, the Home Office), opinion within Labour was divided between a front bench which was wholly committed to an open-door policy and a marginalized contingent on the back benches. The very fact that an obvious link was seen to exist between racial discrimination and migration control is a reflection of the strength of this position within the Labour Party. It was not until 1963 that a tenable restrictionist position emerged from Labour's front bench.

While the Conservatives, in theory, could have used Labour's opposition as a chance to place migration at the centre of an adversarial contest, few Tories were interested in doing so. The majority of Conservative politicians viewed exploitation of the immigration issue as divisive and morally objectionable. Macmillan preferred to secure bipartisan support for legislation,[40] and the government attempted to adopt a compromise position. By reducing migration through informal controls in the colonies, the government could satisfy public opinion and the Ministry of Labour; by eschewing statutory mechanisms for controlling migration, it would formally retain its commitment to a right of free entry for all Commonwealth citizens[41] and avoid the impression of caving in to the rioters and backbench restrictionists. The front bench closed ranks around this stance, and in early January the Home Office

---

[38] *LPA, Race Relations and Discrimination*, 'Commonwealth Sub-Committee of the National Executive Committee: Final Draft Statement on Racial Prejudice', Sept. 1958. The Committee, however, accepted the government's efforts to warn colonial British subjects of the unemployment and housing difficulties in the UK.

[39] See for example *LPA, Race Relations and Discrimination*, 'Racial Disturbances in London,' Report by London District Organizer of the Labour Party, 11 Sept. 1958.

[40] *PRO, PREM 11/824*, 'West Indian Immigration', 14 Jan. 1955.

[41] The Bow Group's policy summary suggested acceptance of this sort of approach: 'No restriction should be placed by the British Government on Commonwealth immigration into this country. But Commonwealth governments may find it in their interests to regulate the flow of immigrants to the U.K.' *CPA, CRD 2/44/20*, 'A Bow Group Memorandum on Coloured Peoples in Britain', Oct. 1958.

told George Rogers that the government saw no justification in departing from its traditional position as the open metropolitan centre of the Empire.[42]

MIGRATION POLICY AFTER THE RIOTS

In the months following the events of late summer 1958, the migration issue receded from the public's attention.[43] In private, however, the issue was given sustained consideration. The intra-bureaucratic consensus in favour of an open-door policy, which had come under strain over the summer of 1958, continued to fracture. Shortly after the riots, on 8 September 1958, the Home Secretary, under Cabinet pressure, instructed the Committee on colonial immigrants (chaired by the Lord Chancellor) to consider the desirability of assuming statutory powers to deport 'undesirable' Commonwealth immigrants. The Committee reported on 20 January 1959. It considered the arguments in favour and against such a measure and concluded that the ultimate decision on its importance rested with the Cabinet. Two of the arguments against legislation, interestingly, were the need for a 'comprehensive Immigration Bill' which would be delayed by a separate bill for deporting colonial immigrants and the fact that such a measure might be criticized for 'failing to deal with the real problem—that of limiting the number of immigrants'.[44] The government chose not to legislate along the lines suggested by the Committee primarily because public concern had decreased with the

[42] *PRO, CO 1031/3931*, 'Note of Meeting', 20 Jan. 1959.

[43] The issue was of little importance in the general election. See D. E. Butler and R. Rose, *The British General Election of 1959* (London: Frank Cass, 1970).

[44] *PRO, CAB 129/96*, 'Cabinet. Commonwealth Immigrants: Memorandum by the Lord Chancellor', 20 Jan. 1959. The other arguments against were: (i) it would differentiate among British subjects and would thus be 'a major departure from principle' and (ii) the race riots have died down and there is no great public demand for legislation. The arguments in favour were: (i) such a bill would alleviate public anxiety about crime, (ii) it would improve race relations by removing those few who sully the immigrant community's name, (iii) failure to do so could encourage extremist action in the UK and would decrease the colonies' incentive to reduce emigration, (iv) it would be better for the government to enact the legislation itself rather than being forced to do so by further riots, and (v) limited legislation would likely receive little parliamentary opposition. In a pattern typical for the time, the back bench appears to have known nothing of these deliberations. When Cyril Osborne asked the Home Secretary on 11 June if he would report on his negotiations with the Commonwealth governments on the repatriation of known criminals, Butler coldly responded that he had nothing to add to a 26 February reply. When Osborne pushed him further, Butler stated that there would be a 'considerable value' to having such a power, if it applied to the whole Commonwealth, but stated that he did not accept 'that there is universal support for this. As it would be a major change in our national policy, I should expect to get general support before I proceeded further with it.' See *Parliamentary Debate (Commons)* (606), cols. 1168–69, 11 June 1959.

passage of time, as had the number of New Commonwealth immigrants, particularly from the West Indies.[45] It is difficult to know how significant this report was; such committees are formed frequently, sometimes with the aim of burying an issue, and no legislation was placed before Parliament until 1962, when a comprehensive migration bill was introduced. When the Committee reported for the last time three months later, its conclusions on the question of control were typically inconclusive. The apparent success of informal controls and the reduction in racial tensions had satisfied the Committee that the immediate need for legislation had passed, but it remained concerned about future dangers of continued immigration.[46] This consideration was, however, checked by the view that the introduction of control 'would have important implications for Colonial and Commonwealth Policy' and that 'there were strong arguments against modifying in any way the traditional right of British subjects to enter and settle in the United Kingdom without restrictions.'[47] The conflicting imperatives associated with the migration question militated against any clear action, and the government took refuge in indecision.

The Committee considered a final issue in passing. It mentioned the possibility, which had some support among liberal opinion in Britain, of using public funds to improve the conditions (particularly housing) of immigrants already resident in Britain. It was rejected, however, because it was felt that it would create a magnet effect and would undermine the colonies' efforts to reduce to rate of emigration. It was doubtful, the Committee concluded, that 'without such control [of migration], it would be possible to tackle effectively the problem of improving the conditions under which coloured immigrants lived here and of integrating them fully into the community'.[48] The argument, made constantly in the 1960s, 1970s, and 1980s, that good race relations depended on tight controls on migration was beginning to take shape.

This attention to the government's examination of migration should not

---

[45]   During the last four months of 1958, the net arrival (i.e. total arrivals minus departures) from the West Indies was 1,373 (vs. 7,074 in the same period for 1957 and 3,222 in 1956), while the net arrival from India was 940 in the four months (vs. 1,508 the previous year). The net balance of Pakistanis was negative; 174 left the UK. *PRO, CAB 129/96*, 'Cabinet'. Note that immigration in this period was still a largely West Indian phenomenon.

[46]   Ibid. Committee on Colonial Immigrations, 22 July 1959.

[47]   Ibid. This anti-restrictionist conclusion was in line with liberal, not to say general, public opinion. *The Times*, which knew of the Committee's existence, stated in June that '[m]ost controversial is the question of legislation. It would be unthinkable to introduce discriminatory immigration laws against Commonwealth citizens.' *Times*, 'Awakened to danger', 5 June. Norman Pannell duly responded, in a letter to the Editor five days later, that what was needed was discriminatory legislation (i.e. restrictions on immigration) that applied in a non-discriminatory way (i.e. to the whole of the Commonwealth and colonies). See *The Times*, 10 June 1959.

[48]   *PRO, CAB 134/1467*, 'Cabinet'.

obscure the fact that its main preoccupation for 1959 was securing a third parliamentary majority. Under Macmillan's skilful leadership (1959 was the zenith of the 'Super-Mac' phenomenon), the Conservatives achieved a feat that appeared impossible in the divisive and acrimonious post-Suez atmosphere two years earlier: the Conservatives returned to power with an increased parliamentary majority. With a little help from the Chancellor of the Exchequer, economic growth increased in 1959, and the Conservatives successfully presented themselves as the party that had engineered affluence. To Labour's further detriment, it was considered unpatriotic to mention the Suez crisis.[49] The stick with which the party hoped to beat the Conservatives had been taken from it,[50] and the Conservatives easily returned to power with a majority of almost 100 seats.

Following the election,[51] restrictionist pressure within the Cabinet increased. In December, the Ministry of Labour reapplied pressure to the Colonial Office. After reaching a low point of 9,656 in August 1959, unemployment among immigrants of colour had risen to 10,156.[52] This increase, and alleged future trends, led the Labour Ministry to conclude that the British economy could no longer absorb large-scale migration.

It should be emphasized that this pressure was independent of backbench restrictionism. As the Conservative front bench equivocated on the appropriate response to migration, and as the Colonial Secretary and Minister of Labour carried on a sort of intra-Cabinet argument, the back benches were not

---

[49] A. Sked and C. Cook, *Post-War Britain: A Political History* (London: Penguin, 1993), 157.

[50] Not for the last time, Labour found itself in trouble over the tax issue. Gaitskell promised that he would increase social spending without raising income tax rates. The Conservatives seized on and successfully exploited this ill-considered commitment. See P. M. Williams, *Hugh Gaitskell: A Political Biography* (London: Jonathan Cape, 1979), ch. 20.

[51] Immigration was not an issue during the campaign (Butler and Rose, *The British General Election of 1959*). Central Office instructed candidates to provide two standard, slightly evasive, answers to questions on immigration. To the question, 'Would you restrict the entry of coloured immigrants into the United Kingdom?', the suggested answer was 'It is not possible under the law as it stands to prevent British subjects from entering this country. Any legislation that sought to alter that position would be both complex and controversial. Moreover, we have always prided ourselves on the fact that a British subject, wherever he lives, is free to come to the Mother Country if he wishes to do so. The Government has had useful and helpful discussions with the Colonial and Commonwealth Governments principally concerned and many difficulties have been overcome.' To the question, 'Are you in favour of the deportation of Commonwealth citizens convicted of certain criminal offences?', the suggested answer was 'At present there is no power to deport Commonwealth citizens convicted of certain criminal offences. The Conservative Government has recently been in consultation on the matter with Governments in the Commonwealth and Colonies.' See *Conservative Party Archives (CPA)*, CCO4/8/138, Bodleian Library, Oxford, 'General Election 1959. Questions of Policy: Coloured Immigrants', 19 Sept. 1959.

[52] *PRO, CO 1031/2546*, Letter from E. J. Toogood to M. Z. Terry. 14 Dec. 1959.

kept abreast of developments. An exchange between James Watt, MP for Manchester, and Butler, the Home Secretary, is typical of attitudes at the Cabinet level. In response to a standard letter from Butler in which he provided the usual tepid response emphasizing the complexity of the situation and the importance of maintaining the traditional policy towards British subjects, Watts responded testily that '[it] completely disregards the grave disquiet felt, as the Report from the Special Committee set up by the Home Office admits, in all industrial cities about the great increase in crimes of violence.'[53] The tone of the letter was aggressive; playing on the fact that Butler was both Chairman of the Party and Home Secretary (a division of responsibility about which he complained in another letter of the same day), Watt addressed 'My dear Chairman of the Party' and began by saying that he had received an unsatisfactory letter from the Home Secretary (i.e. Butler himself) and requested that the Chairman of the Party raise the matter with the Home Secretary. Butler responded with a cold letter assuring Watts that he was able to fulfil both functions.[54] When Watts requested a meeting to discuss corporal punishment and immigration, Butler had his private secretary inform Watts on 20 December that the Home Secretary could not see him soon, but might be able to arrange a meeting in January.[55] Watts responded three days later that he was 'naturally at call' as far as an interview with the Home Secretary was concerned. Butler, apparently conceding that Watts would not go away, scribbled on the latter's missive a note to his private secretary instructing him that he would agree to a casual talk with Watts but only if he was clear that this was not a formal interview.[56] Although this exchange was of course an isolated one, it was indicative of the response of Cabinet Members to backbench concerns on migration. Such concerns were not taken seriously; those complaining were not informed of the front bench's own examination of the issue; and they were not welcomed into the policy-making apparatus. There is no evidence to suggest that the front bench was pushed into controls by the tenacity of back bench restrictionism.

The turn to migration occurred instead at the Cabinet and departmental level. The central actor in late 1959 was again the Ministry of Labour. Its doubts were triggered by an increase in arrivals. Informal controls appeared to be doing their job in 1959, and the intensity of concern over migration

---

[53] For these exchanges, see the *Private Papers of Lord Butler*, Trinity College, Cambridge, *RAB E 15/42*[10(2)], Letter from James Watts to Butler, 12 Dec. 1960. For the accompanying letter, see *RAB E 15/42* [10(1)]

[54] *Private Papers of Lord Butler, RAB E/42/15*[11] Letter from Butler to James Watts, 14 Dec. 1960.

[55] *Private Papers of Lord Butler, RAB E/15/42*, Letter from Watts to Butler, 20 Dec. 1960.

[56] *The Private Papers of Lord Butler, E15/42*[14], Letter from Watts to Butler, 23 Dec. 1960.

decreased,[57] although it did not disappear. This respite was short-lived. In late 1959, the number of immigrants began to increase.[58] In early December, a meeting of an interdepartmental committee on West Indian immigrants agreed that the Ministry of Labour should produce a statement on projected employment prospects for West Indians and that these findings should serve as the basis for a dispatch to West Indian governments.[59]

Although the unemployment and economic growth figures were positive in late 1959, the Ministry of Labour spoke mostly of negative future trends. Four developments were believed to bode poorly for the future prospects of immigrant workers: (1) the process of automation, which would reduce the need for unskilled labour, (2) an unprecedented number of school-leavers, which was to reach a peak between 1961 and 1963, (3) the end of National Service, which would lead to an additional 200,000 young men ready for employment, and (4) the continued arrival of workers from the Irish Republic, estim-ated at 60,000 per year. These trends led the Ministry of Labour to conclude that 'there must be a limit to the extent to which the economy can go on absorb-ing unskilled labour' and that there should be no relaxation in administrative checks on Indian, Pakistani, and West Indian migration.[60]

The Ministry of Labour's position in the migration debate is curious. From the earliest recorded mention of Labour Ministry positions, the department was sceptical about Commonwealth migration. Its conclusions were based either on current employment statistics or their projected future deterioration. What the Ministry of Labour does not ever appear to have done is defend an open migration policy as necessary in a time of cyclical labour shortages.

[57] While West Indian immigration decreased from 23,000 in 1957 to 15,000 in 1958, the number of arrivals increased to 16,400 in 1959 and 49,650 in 1960. See House of Commons, *Commonwealth Immigration to the United Kingdom from the 1950s to 1975: A Survey of Statistical Sources,* Library Research Paper, No. 56, HMSO, 1976.

[58] In the case of immigration from the Indian subcontinent, a part of the movement was illegal. A growing traffic in forged passports, at times sold to Indians and Pakistanis at the then-astronomical sum of over £200, allowed some to evade the passport restrictions in place in India and Pakistan. For many others, usually the poorest illiterates, the result was tragic. Their forged documents were recognized, either in India (most of the traffic was conducted in Dehli and Bombay) or Britain, and the individuals were sent back to their villages destitute. See *The Times*, 'Doubt about Passports of Indians Held in Ship', 2 Nov. 1959, and 'Traffic in Misery', 4 Nov. 1959. The Indian government was embarrassed by revelations about this practice. Nehru admitted on 26 November that his government had been 'caught napping' over the issue. See *The Times*, 'India "Caught Napping" over Passports', 27 Nov. 1959.

[59] *PRO, CO 1031/3932*, Letter from M. Z. Terry to Mackintosh, 5 Dec. 1960. For the statement, see *PRO, CO 1031/3932*, 'Employment Prospects in the United Kingdom for West Indian Immigrants', 1 Jan. 1960. The dispatch was sent on 14 Mar. 1960.

[60] *PRO, CO 1031/2456*, Letter from E. J. Toogood (Ministry of Labour) to M. Z. Terry (Colonial Office), 14 Dec. 1959. Also see *PRO, CO 1031/2456*, Extract of (interdepartmental) Meeting held in the Colonial Office, 11 Dec. 1959.

Although it might be tempting to attribute the ministry's behaviour to a given minister, the evolution of Iain Macleod's position suggests otherwise. Although Macleod would later defend the open-door policy from the perspective of the Colonial Office (1959–61), as Labour Minister (1957–9) he claimed to see a limit to the UK's ability to absorb migration and supported the maintenance of administrative checks on emigration.[61] This change suggests that there was an important place for institutional position in forming preferences on the migration question. The Colonial and Commonwealth Secretaries were the voice of the Empire and Commonwealth within the Cabinet, and they articulated a defence of free entry in this role. Likewise, the Ministry of Labour, for reasons that are less clear, defined itself as the watchdog against unemployment and did so irrespective of who held the position. It is possible that the ghosts of the 1930s haunted civil servants; full employment had only existed since the late 1940s—approximately ten years—and confidence in its maintenance was not yet general. Whatever the reasons, the Ministry of Labour emerged sometime in 1958 as the clearest exponent of a restrictionist case within the Cabinet.

The Colonial Office had placed confidence in informal controls as a mechanism capable of reducing the rate of arrival to a point at which the Ministry of Labour's case would be undermined. The increase in migration, despite the existence of disincentives to migrate, placed the Colonial Office in a difficult position. Lacking any other means to reduce migration, and believing that inaction would be tantamount to conceding the restrictionist case, they agreed to a second set of dispatches.[62] These were sent out between March and May 1960. They emphasized the concern about long-term trends and, as most of the increase could be attributed to Jamaica, emphasized the need for special attention in this area. In early June the Colonial Secretary met with the Jamaican Cabinet to discuss additional

[61]   *PRO, CO 1031/3932*, Letter from Iain Macleod to R. A. Butler, 13 July 1960. Macleod appeared reluctantly willing to accept controls at this point: 'You [Butler] said in your letter that the alternative course [to further administrative checks] was the introduction of United Kingdom legislation to control the numbers of immigrants from the Commonwealth. I think we must recognise that nothing short of such legislation is likely to achieve a substantial or rapid reduction in the present flow, and that in its absence we must be prepared to expect that immigration from the West Indies is likely to continue on something like the present scale for some time to come.' Macleod stated, however, that he was 'reluctant' to end the traditional policy.

[62]   This was likely to be a difficult decision, because even informal restrictions were a matter of some controversy in the West Indies. 'The matter is one of the greatest political delicacy in the West Indies, as well as being a very touchy one in the U.K.' *PRO, CO 1031/3932*, Letter from Roger to Sir H. Poynton, 12 Feb. 1960. On the whole, the West Indies seems to have cooperated with the British government. The exception to this was British Guiana, which refused the second dispatch. It may even, the Colonial Office suspected, have encouraged immigration to alleviate its unemployment problem. *PRO, CO 1031/3932*, Letter from M. Z. Terry to Dawson, Hammer and Mackintosh, 20 June 1960.

measures for limiting migration without recourse to UK legislation.[63] These initiatives were the last, ultimately unsuccessful, attempts by the Colonial Office to reduce migration without recourse to legislation.

INFORMAL RESTRICTIONS AND THE COMMONWEALTH IDEAL

In the late 1980s, the Public Record Office released the files concerning the Conservative government's contemplation of migration control in the mid-1950s and the government's reaction to the riots. These files were unknown to the public, and their release occasioned considerable surprise. Scholars who have written on this period since the mid-1980s have consistently concluded that the files demonstrate that there was little if any principled commitment on the part of policy-makers to the right of British subjects to enter the United Kingdom. The debate in the 1950s, writes Solomos, 'was never about principle. Labour and Conservative Governments had by 1952 instituted a number of covert, and sometimes illegal, administrative measures to discourage black migration.'[64] This conclusion, which is based on a selective reading of the archival materials, overlooks the documented motivation, at least among Colonial Office officials, for informal controls. Informal controls were not an abandonment of an elite commitment to the free entry policy; rather, they were an effort to preserve free entry by undermining the restrictionist case against it. Only if the number of entrants were perceived to be related to the UK's capacity to absorb immigrants, on economic and social (especially housing) grounds, could the Labour Ministry, backbench, and public case against formally unfettered migration be deflected. By conceding ground on the practice of migration (the rate at which West Indians entered the UK), the Colonial Office and other anti-restrictionists hoped to gain on the fundamental issue of *principle*: the statutory right of all British subjects to enter and remain in the United Kingdom.

[63] *PRO, CO 1031/3932*, 'Extract from the record of a Cabinet Meeting held in Jamaica', 6 June 1960. The Jamaican Minister of Labour suggested asking the United States to allow Jamaicans to use the unused portion of Britain's quota. The Prime Minister appealed to President Kennedy and the Canadian government without success.

[64] J. Solomos, *Race and Racism in Britain* (Houndmills: Macmillan, 1993), 57. K. Paul, *Whitewashing Britain: Race and Citizenship in the Postwar Era* (Ithaca, NY: Cornell University Press, 1997), chs. 5 and 6. Solomos cites as evidence for this claim B. Carter et al., 'The 1951–1955 Conservative Government and the Racialization of Black Immigration', *Immigrants and Minorities*, 6, No. 3 (1987), 335–47. I have critically examined this article in the previous chapter. Also see (although the case is put in more considered language) D. Dean, 'The Conservative Government and the 1961 Commonwealth Immigration Act: The Inside Story', *Race and Class*, 35, No. 2 (1993), 58–74.

The numbers increased nonetheless, reaching a record of 5,000 West Indians in May.[65] It was becoming clear that West Indian governments could do no more to reduce emigration. The British economy's demand for labour created a migratory incentive too great to be checked through informal means. This conclusion was even accepted by the Colonial Office officials, some of whom saw the choice as one between the acceptance of a large immigrant presence in the UK or legislation against it.[66] At the same time, the Home Office, which had traditionally been more agnostic on the question of control than either the Colonial Office or the Ministry of Labour, was becoming 'increasingly disturbed' about the number of West Indians coming to the United Kingdom.[67]

As the Conservative government began to lose confidence in informal controls, the intra-bureaucratic and intra-party case for control was joined by an organized extra-parliamentary campaign. In October 1960, the Birmingham Immigration Control Association (BICA) was founded. BICA brought into a mass organization a number of local figures who had lobbied for migration control.[68] Its first demand was a cessation of migration for five years. The less influential Vigilant Immigration Control Association and British Immigration Control Association joined BICA, and the three organized a protest campaign of meetings, postcards, and mass petitions directed against the Conservative Party and local Conservative MPs.[69] Although the groups acted as a further indicator of public hostility to continued migration,[70] they were too weakened by internal disputes to have any significant impact.[71]

By the autumn of 1960, the Conservative government remained divided and indecisive. The Colonial Secretary came under pressure from the West Indians, whom he assured in October that he would never accept restrictive legislation.[72] The Colonial Office continued to resist legislation, but admitted

[65] *PRO, CO 1031/3932*, 'Immigration from the West Indies', 8 July 1960.

[66] See *PRO, CO 1031/3932*, Letter from M. Z. Terry to Dawson, Hammer, and Mackintosh, 20 June 1960. The only option short of statutory restrictions was passport control by the colonies; West Indian governments refused to do this. *PRO, CO 1032/302*, 'Cabinet. Coloured Immigration from the Commonwealth: Brief for the Secretary of State', Oct. 1960.

[67] *PRO, CO 1031/3932*, Letter from M. Z. Terry to Pettit, 30 June 1960.

[68] Rose, *Colour and Citizenship*, 217.

[69] S. Patterson, *Immigration and Race Relations in Britain 1960–1967* (London: Oxford University Press, 1969), 380. For a fuller description of these organizations, see Foot, *Immigration and Race in British Politics*, ch. 9.

[70] Rose, *Colour and Citizenship*, 217.

[71] Patterson, *Immigration and Race Relations in Britain*, 379. The influence of these groups is mentioned nowhere in the archives.

[72] *PRO, CO 1031/3932*, Letter from M. Z. Terry, 7 Oct. 1960.

again that the choice was between legislating and tolerating the inflow.[73] Butler was under considerable pressure from both the pro- and anti-restrictionist camps in the party, but appeared for the moment to adhere to the open-door principle.[74] When Osborne put forth a motion recommending the control of Commonwealth migration, the government did not know how to respond, and there was considerable relief in the Colonial Office when it was withdrawn.[75]

The following month a new set of figures were released, and these confirmed the Colonial Office's reluctant conclusion of the previous June. Migration for the first nine months of 1960 was estimated at 38,100, and the West Indian portion alone was expected to reach 50,000 by the end of 1960.[76] The West Indians continued to refuse passport controls,[77] and the Indian and Pakistani governments had been under powerful domestic pressure to relax theirs.[78] This pressure culminated in an Indian Supreme Court decision which declared it illegal to withhold passports from Indian citizens.[79] The massive population of India appeared ready to travel to Britain's shores.

BUREAUCRATS AND BRITISH SUBJECTS IN THE LATE 1950S

The terms of political debate in the 1950s were of a world we have lost. Today, the need for some form of migration control is almost a truism. Critics dispute the degree of control required, the mechanisms for appeal, the racial or class biases of a particular arrangement for control. Yet, with the exception of marginal proponents of open borders, few seriously object to some form of control; most members of the public and even of informed opinion would express surprise at the fact that Britain's doors were once entirely open to some 800 million British subjects. Even those most vociferous in their attacks

[73] *PRO, CO 1031/3938,* Letter from M. Z. Terry, 28 Nov. 1960.

[74] Ibid.

[75] *PRO, CO 1031/3931,* 'General Review of the position in areas where there are large concentrations of West Indians', 22 Nov. 1960.

[76] *PRO, CO 1032/302,* 'Cabinet. Coloured Immigration from the Commonwealth. Memorandum by the Home Secretary,' undated.

[77] *PRO, CO 1031/3938,* Letter from M. Z. Terry, 28 Nov. 1960. As migration from the West Indies to Britain was viewed as an essential safety valve in combating unemployment, restricting passports was highly sensitive politically. *PRO, CO 1031/3925,* Letter from Hugh Fraser to Charles Grey, MP, 26 Feb. 1962.

[78] *PRO, CO 1032/302,* 'Cabinet. Coloured Immigration from the Commonwealth: Memorandum by the Home Secretary', undated.

[79] Layton-Henry, *Politics of Immigration,* 75.

on immigration control remain evasive on the question of whether they seriously expected open borders to the Commonwealth, in the context of inexpensive transportation and massive wealth disparities, to continue indefinitely. In late 1950s, however, the decision was extremely controversial. Ministers were loath to admit what seems perfectly obvious today: that affluent nations require some formal check if economic migration is to remain within manageable limits. They did so partly because they hoped that informal control would allow them to avoid such a decisive step altogether, but also because they feared its consequences. In politics, as in life, the fear of decisions that we cannot avoid can paralyse. In late 1960, most believed that legislation would be necessary, and most feared that it would irreversibly alter Britain's relationship with its former possessions. For many in the Conservative government, the introduction of migration control was the end of the Commonwealth.[80] At the same time, members of the Cabinet, as well as the bureaucracy, recognized that the only choices were inaction in the face of large (and increasing) numbers of arrivals or statutory restrictions.[81]

Scholars of migration have largely forgotten the role of the Colonial Office in articulating a policy towards Commonwealth migrants, and they have consequently exaggerated the degree of agreement over migration within Whitehall and the Cabinet.[82] The Colonial Office was a vocal and consistent defender of West Indian migrants' right to enter the UK free of formal controls. Its firm opposition, moreover, lay against a broader reluctance—motivated by liberal, patrician, and imperial sentiment—to end the traditional free entry policy. Even the Minister of Labour, the closest thing to an uncompromising restrictionist following Salisbury's departure, based his opposition on a technocratic view of the matter.

The competition between the Colonial Office and the Ministry of Labour casts light on both the history of Commonwealth migration and the nature of liberal democratic politics. The Colonial Office was the focal point of intra-Cabinet opposition to migration, and its decline in subsequent years removed one of the important institutional constraints on a restrictive migration policy. Its contest with the Ministry of Labour also highlights the extent to which—

---

[80]   Confidential interviews. The Home Secretary told the Cabinet in November that legislation, in addition to being a matter of great political controversy, risked destroying the bonds that united the Commonwealth. *PRO, CO 1032/302*, 'Cabinet. Coloured Immigration from the Commonwealth: Memorandum by the Home Secretary', undated.

[81]   *PRO, CO 1031/3932*, West Indian Immigration, Dec. 1960. On 7 Oct. Butler had decided to bring the issue from the Committee to the Cabinet level; from this point until the decision to restrict, the question of control was at the centre of domestic British politics. *PRO, CO 1031/3938*, Letter from M. Z. Terry, 28 Nov. 1960.

[82]   To my knowledge, there is no historical scholarship which gives attention to the contest between the Colonial Office and Ministry of Labour from the mid-1950s to 1962.

even in a polity taken to be the model of bureaucratic neutrality—the prefer-ences of the state cannot be reified and cannot be reduced to those of the ministers of the day.

The short period between 1958 and 1960 constitutes an interlude between the first half of the decade, during which *Civis Britannicus sum* continued to move men and women to defend the traditional rights of British subjects, and the early 1960s, when the pressure for control had become irresistible. It was in a period in which the commitment to laissez-faire weakened—the expres-sions of attachment to the Old Commonwealth which dominated earlier discussions are markedly less frequent—but in which the Colonial Office articulated a final objection in an argument that was clearly no longer going its way. Never again would the argument be made with comparable convic-tion by those in power; never again would it be taken seriously.

5

Same Citizenship, Contrasting Rights:
The 1962 Commonwealth Immigrants Act

BY January 1961, it was clear that the free entry policy's days were numbered. Efforts to regulate the rate of migration through informal measures appeared to have broken down, the Ministry of Labour continued to press the restrictionist case, and public opposition was growing. The ultimate introduction of controls took over a year, finally being enacted in April 1962. This chapter examines this period, and offers an explanation of both the delay itself and the institutional character of the controls ultimately adopted. The former highlights, for the final time, the importance of Colonial Office opposition to restrictions in facilitating further New Commonwealth migration, while the latter—a point that will be developed at length—was the direct result of the causal influence exercised by BNA 1948.

The delay resulted in part from continued Conservative Party hesitance, but also from the last-ditch efforts of the Colonial Office to delay restrictions on migration. Iain Macleod was one of the main post-war advocates of rapid decolonization (a position that earned him the undying hatred of some sections of the Tory right), and he and Macmillan wished to secure West Indian independence in the context of a multinational federation. This transcendent foreign policy objective allowed Macleod to argue that migration controls in advance of the federation would lead to a West Indian, specifically Jamaican, rejection of it. Migration controls were thus postponed. This postponement in turn encouraged further migration: rumours of impending restrictions circulated throughout the Commonwealth, and a 'beat the ban' rush sharply increased migration figures in 1961.

Of equally important long-term significance was the character of the controls adopted. However odd it may appear from today's perspective, BNA 1948 rested on a logic common to European and North American nationality law: it was founded on the distinction between citizens and aliens.[1] Citizens

---

[1] As always, the exception to this was the Irish, who were formally mostly aliens (i.e. non-British subjects) but in practice treated like citizens (right to vote, work, etc.). In addition, those Irish citizens who opted to retain British subjecthood under the British Nationality Act, 1948 were also British subjects.

possessed full rights in the UK; aliens possessed discretionary and alienable privileges; and all individuals fell into either category according to British nationality law. The Commonwealth Immigrants Act, 1962 transformed this arrangement. It retained the status of 'Citizens of the United Kingdom and Colonies' and distinguished between British subjects' rights to enter the United Kingdom according to the manner in which their passports were issued. Britons and colonial British subjects continued to hold identical citizenship, but only citizens with British-issued passports enjoyed the full rights of citizenship. In the history of British nationality law, the introduction of immigration control without the reform of citizenship was a revolutionary moment.

This defining act, which determined in part immigration policy and nationality law until 1981, was the result of the continuing influence of the citizenship scheme introduced in 1948. The British Nationality Act of 1948 viewed citizenship as instrumental: the concept was introduced into British law in order to retain a uniform content and application of British subject status. Yet once entrenched in law, the concept could only be altered through a costly and complex process: the United Kingdom would face the immensely complicated task of devising (yet another) provisional status for colonial British subjects, and it would have to enter lengthy negotiations with the remaining colonies, which would have objected strenuously to any attempt to alter unilaterally their members' status. The institutional structure of 1948 set in place an incentive structure which encouraged the maintenance of the 1948 scheme after the point at which its *raison d'être*, the maintenance of formal equal privileges for all British subjects, had passed. As we will see in subsequent chapters, the 1962 decision itself exercised a powerful influence on subsequent migration politics and policy.

THE CONSERVATIVE PARTY IN THE PRELUDE TO THE COMMONWEALTH IMMIGRANTS ACT

The first immigration debate of 1961 occurred in February, when Osborne requested leave to introduce another bill restricting immigration. David Renton, responding for the government, repeated the (now rather unconvincing) argument about the importance of the UK's traditional policy towards British subjects and stated that the government would not introduce controls on Commonwealth immigration. Macleod also stated in public that 'the Government . . . have at present no plans to introduce legislation bringing immigration from any Commonwealth country to a halt'. These statements became the government's referents throughout the year, both in its answers to backbenchers in Parliament and in its communications with the colonies. When Manley suggested in April that immigration controls, and perhaps even repatriation measures, were likely if the West Indies did not substantially reduce immigration, the government said in response that it had no intention of introducing restrictions.[2] At the June Commonwealth Prime Minister's Conference, the government decided in advance to state in response to all questions on immigration that its view was as it had been expressed in the 17 February parliamentary debate.[3] This was despite the fact that the government almost surely knew that legislation would be introduced in the next session of Parliament. This secrecy, not to say duplicity, explains in part the bitterness of Jamaica's reaction to the announcement in November of immigration controls.

The Mechanism of Control

The need for control had been accepted by the Home Office in February 1961;[4] the argument that remained concerned its timing and form, and the question was debated in working parties and committees. In March, a working party on the socio-economic consequences of immigration requested a series of ministerial reports on the various forms of potential control.[5] It considered a labour voucher scheme, a health check, and restrictions based on housing certificates.[6] In the end, the working party recommended a labour voucher scheme whereby immigrants would be allowed into the country according to their level of skill and the state of the British economy. A health check was rejected because it would involve considerable delay and would not reduce sufficiently the number of arrivals, while a housing certificate scheme was considered unworkable in practice. The working party argued that employment control would provide the government 'a flexible instrument

---

[2] *PRO, CO 1031/1924*, 'West Indian Emigration to the UK', 21 Apr. 1961. The West Indies privately lobbied the government for a retention of the open-door policy throughout the year. See for example *CO 1031/3924*, 'Extract of note of meeting between Mr. Macmillan and the West Indies Federal Cabinet', 25 Mar. 1961.

[3] *PRO, CO 1032/303*, 'Meeting of the Commonwealth Prime Ministers, 1961... Note for the Secretary of State', 13 Mar. 1961.

[4] *PRO, CAB 134/1469*, 'Memorandum by the Secretary of State for the Home Department', 8 Feb. 1961. The paper, signed by Butler, also accepts as inevitable the exclusion of the Irish from any immigration controls.

[5] *PRO, CO 1032*, 'Meeting of Commonwealth Prime Ministers, 1961... Note for the Secretary of State', 13 Mar. 1961.

[6] *PRO, CO 1032/303*, 'Working Party to report on the social and economic problems arising from the growing influx into the United Kingdom of coloured workers from other Commonwealth Countries: Note by Secretary', 1 Mar. 1961.

which would enable them to limit the flow of immigration severely as soon as economic conditions began to deteriorate'.[7]

On 16 February 1961, at a meeting of the Commonwealth Migrants Committee, a fateful decision was made. The Committee was to choose the mechanism on which controls would rest; individuals with work permits would have a privileged entry. But how would immigration officers otherwise differentiate between different CUKCs? It discussed the possibility of adopting the most logical control mechanism—a British citizenship for Britons and to the exclusion of the colonies. The vexing problem was what to do with the colonies. The Committee considered two options: a collective citizenship for the whole of the colonies plus British citizenship, or British citizenship plus local citizenship in each of the remaining colonies (Kenyan citizenship, Ugandan citizenship, etc.). It rejected both options because of the complications associated with acting on them. The colonies themselves would resent a collective colonial citizenship as an inferior alternative to CUKC.[8] The creation of local citizenship for each colony would lead to constitutional difficulties in colonies such as Gambia, which contained both colonies and protectorates, and might encourage separatist movements.[9] In addition, some members of the Committee also believed that, since CUKC had supplanted British subjecthood as the constitutional tie binding the Commonwealth, its replacement would remove the Commonwealth's last tenuous binding mechanism at a time when the cohesion of the organization was threatened by immigration control itself.[10] Finally, some argued that the gains from this

---

[7] *PRO, CO 1032/304*, 'Working Party to report on the social and economic problems arising from the growing influx into the United Kingdom of coloured workers from other Commonwealth Countries: Draft Report to the Ministerial Committee', undated. The working party considered and rejected a scheme in which employers would apply for the permits. They believed that few employers would bother to apply, and the result would be a too drastic limitation on immigration.

[8] In addition, the colonies without the UK would be 'a too artificial grouping' to be subsumed under a single citizenship *PRO, CO 1032/303*, 'Working Party to report on the social and economic problems arising from the growing influx into the United Kingdom of coloured workers from other Commonwealth Countries: Citizenship in Relation to the Commonwealth Immigrants Bill', Appendix to Draft Report to Ministerial Committee, undated. For a discussion of a citizenship-based scheme's effect on subsequent generations born abroad, see *PRO, CO 1031/3924*, 'Further notes on the possibility of creating a "citizenship of the United Kingdom" as a criterion for exemption', undated.

[9] *PRO, CO 1032/303*, 'Working Party to report on the social and economic problems arising from the growing influx into the United Kingdom of coloured workers from other Commonwealth Countries: Memorandum by the Home Office', 24 Mar. 1961.

[10] *PRO, CO 1032/303*, 'Working Party to report on the social and economic problems arising from the growing influx into the United Kingdom of coloured workers from other Commonwealth Countries: Citizenship in Relation to the Commonwealth Immigrants Bill', Appendix to Draft Report to Ministerial Committee, undated. A technical problem is also mentioned: as British passports had been granted without distinction to colonial subjects and

exercise would be limited, as the colonies would introduce local citizenship at independence.[11] The number of Citizens of the United Kingdom and Colonies subject to immigration control would continually fall, and UK citizenship would emerge.

In addition to the constitutional and practical complexities associated with reforming citizenship, the Irish question further discouraged the creation of a distinctive UK citizenship. As the Working Party had recommended against the application of restrictions to the Irish,[12] the new citizenship would have to include the United Kingdom and Ireland. The inclusion of Ireland would 'blur the concept of citizenship',[13] and it would be anathema to the Irish government. Ireland had refused to participate in the 1948 scheme as an independent Commonwealth country, as this would have implied a degree of allegiance to the Crown; a common citizenship could only intensify this concern, and it would be bitterly rejected by the Republic.[14]

It is debatable whether or not these objections were insurmountable. To some degree, British policy-makers were in 1962 still uncomfortable with the concept of citizenship, viewing British subjecthood as their still-primary legal status. As a result, the oddity of the same citizenship with different rights raised fewer objections than it would have in Germany, France, or the United States. But there was nonetheless sufficient support for a distinctive British citizenship for it to be actively considered in committee. It would have succeeded were it not that the 1948 citizenship scheme militated against its own replacement. BNA 1948 generated support for its retention in the colonies and could only be replaced through a complicated process that risked political instability within the dependent territories. These disincentives led the government to conclude that it had no option but to retain the same status—CUKC—for all members of the United Kingdom and the remaining colonies and yet to differentiate among these citizens for the purposes of immigration. The institutional structure created in 1948 created a tendency in 1962 towards policy continuity.

Britons, it would take as long as five years, the period during which a passport is valid, for the UK to ensure that all those holding British passports were members of the British isles. Immigration control would, therefore, be evaded in large numbers, and the immigration officers could not be expected to hold an inquiry into the nationality of each UK passport holder.

[11] *PRO, CO 1032/303*, Letter from Ian Watt to J. M. Ross, undated.

[12] *PRO, CO 1032/303*, 'Working Party to report on the social and economic problems arising from the growing influx into the United Kingdom of coloured workers from other Commonwealth Countries', undated.

[13] *PRO, CO 1032/303*, 'Working Party to report on the social and economic problems arising from the growing influx into the United Kingdom of coloured workers from other Commonwealth Countries: Memorandum by the Home Office', 24 Mar. 1961.

[14] *PRO, CO 1032/303*, 'Working Party to report on the social and economic problems arising from the growing influx into the United Kingdom of coloured workers from other Commonwealth Countries', Minutes of a meeting held at the Home Office, 29 Mar. 1961.

The employment control scheme did not go unchallenged; the Colonial Office firmly resisted it. The Office opposed both the discretion of the Ministry of Labour, in issuing labour vouchers,[15] and the discretion of immigration officials at the ports, in deciding on the admission of immigrants who arrive without entry certificates.[16] As is often the case, a department that had lost on the question of principle attempted to fight it out on the details. However, the Office's influence in Cabinet had been reduced,[17] because of the loss of Macleod and broad Cabinet disillusionment with immigration and failed promises on informal control, and its protests on the basic choice were ignored. Once the issue of control had been decided, policy leadership shifted from the Colonial Office to the Home Office and, to a lesser extent, the Ministry of Labour. The Colonial Office, none the less, was able to exercise some influence. It insisted that the legislation place British subjects, as much as was possible, in an advantageous position vis-à-vis aliens.[18]

On 26 May, the Lord Chancellor's Committee came out in favour of control via a labour voucher scheme.[19] The Committee, however, recommended delay in the light of a London conference on the West Indies Federation[20] and the importance of securing a positive result in the Jamaican referendum on joining a West Indies Federation.[21] A month later, the Home Secretary attended a joint Home Office Affairs/Commonwealth party Committee meeting and found the traditional restrictionists, John Hall and Norman Pannell, leading a decisive majority in favour of immediate restrictions.[22] Butler, the Home Secretary, was most likely the Chair of the powerful Home Affairs Committee, and its opinion

---

[15] *PRO, CO 1032/306*, Letter to the Colonial Secretary, 4 Oct. 1961. Quoting the document: 'the method of control proposed puts enormous powers of administrative discrimination into the hands of officials of the Ministry of Labour in the issue of permits for jobs and I fear that we shall never escape criticism that a piece of legislation ostensibly non-discriminatory is being operated in a discriminatory manner.'

[16] *PRO, CO 1032/306*, Letter from M. Z. Terry to Thomas, 22 Sept. 1961.

[17] Interview with a Home Office official.

[18] Interview with a Home Office official.

[19] *PRO, CAB 129/105*, 'Cabinet. Commonwealth Immigrants: Memorandum by the Lord Chancellor', 26 May 1961.

[20] At the Conference, Macleod did in fact hint at the imminence of control. He told the West Indies ministers that the British government had made no decision but that the great increase in numbers could not be ignored. See *PRO, CO 1032/308*, 'Consultations with Colonial Governments about Proposed Commonwealth Immigrants Bill', 16 Nov. 1961.

[21] *PRO, CAB 129/105*, 'Cabinet'.

[22] *PRO, CO 1032/304*, 'Minutes of the Joint Meeting of the Home Office Affairs and the Commonwealth Committees', 6 July 1961. Nigel Fisher, who was consistently among the most liberal voices in the Conservative Party, and Christopher Chataway opposed controls because of reactions in the Commonwealth, especially the West Indies. Should any legislation be introduced, they continued, it should be accompanied by legislation against racial discrimination in the UK. This link between restrictive controls and positive measures did not have sufficient appeal among Conservatives. Only Wilson's Labour government realized the social (and political) benefits of it.

would have been extremely influential.[23] Its conclusions reinforced those of a Home Affairs Committee meeting earlier in the year, in which a well-attended meeting expressed a majority opinion in favour of some form of restrictive legislation.[24] This represented a reversal of the majority decision of two years previous, a change which was largely occasioned by the sharp increase in arrivals as informal controls broke down. By the summer of 1961, the Conservative Party had more or less accepted that for which it had little enthusiasm: some measure of immigration control.[25]

Immigration and the Politics of Decolonization

In 1961, the most credible opposition to immigration control came from Iain Macleod, who replaced Lennox-Boyd as Colonial Secretary.[26] Macleod's opposition to controls was motivated by developments in the colonies. West Indian independence was scheduled for 1962, and Macleod and Macmillan sought to achieve this within a framework uniting the various nations of the West Indies in a loose federal structure.[27] The establishment of the West

[23]   Confidential interview.

[24]   *PRO, CO 1032/298*, Letter from Nigel Fisher to Iain Macleod, 6 Feb. 1961. Fisher expressed his reluctance to accept this position: 'I quite understand this point of view [concern over immigration] but I confess that it seems to me inconsistent for us as a nation to preach multi-racialism in the Commonwealth if we do not practice it in the United Kingdom.' This tension between Conservative governments' commitment to multiracialism abroad and their trepidation over the same policy at home has been commented on by S. Brooke, 'The Conservative Party, Immigration and National Identity, 1948-1968', in M. Francis and I. Zweiniger-Bargielowska (eds.), *The Conservatives and British Society, 1880-1900* (Cardiff: University of Wales Press, 1996).

[25]   For Butler's contribution to the discussions leading up to the act, see *CPA, CRD 2/44/1*, Minutes of the Home Office Affairs Committee Meeting, 2 Feb. 1961.

[26]   One MP referred to a division in the parliamentary party between 'restrictionists' (who accepted the need for controls in practice), 'last ditchers' (who opposed any control of Commonwealth immigration), and 'hedgers' (who agreed with the last ditchers in principle, but were swayed to the restrictionist cause because of numbers). (*PRO, CO 1032/304*, 'Report to Home Secretary and Colonial Secretary on meeting at the House of Commons, June 8th, 1961, between Parliamentary Members of the British Caribbean Association and West Indian Ministers'). He does not, however, state their number or position, so it is impossible to determine their influence. Macleod's was the most credible simply because he was the only clear frontbench anti-restrictionist.

[27]   British interest in a West Indies Federation dates to the inter-war period. It was believed in the UK that the poverty-stricken West Indies could only be economically viable, and thus politically viable, within a larger economic structure providing the requisite basis for economic development. Certain West Indian leaders shared this view, believing that only a federation capable of marshalling the resources of the whole of the British Caribbean could execute economic planning and development, while others saw a common West Indian nationality and a federation as the only means to wresting independence from the reluctant British. See J. Darwin, *Britain and Decolonisation: The Retreat from Empire in the Post-War World* (London: Macmillan, 1988), 217-21. Also see J. Mordecai, *The West Indies: The Federal Negotiations* (London: George Allen & Unwin, 1968).

Indies Federation depended on a referendum in Jamaica, and it was widely believed that a restriction on West Indian migration to the United Kingdom would lead to a Jamaican reaction against the Federation.[28] For this reason, Macleod and the Colonial Office continued to resist restrictions on immigration,[29] and the Cabinet agreed that restrictions should be delayed until at least the establishment of the Federation.[30]

For a period of several months, migration controls, which had the full support of the public and the back benches, as well as the reluctant assent of the Cabinet, were frozen by the need to respect developments in the colonies. Cabinet ministers and their departments had consented to this delay, and in order to achieve this agreement the Colonial Office had dropped its suggestion that the legislation only apply to the independent Commonwealth countries.[31] The Colonial Secretary was unlikely to retract this demand, despite the government's fears of a backbench-led revolt at the Annual Conference. He had agreed to control reluctantly, and securing a West Indies Federation was viewed by him and the Office as a necessary achievement.

An element of contingency broke the deadlock. In a 21 September referendum, the Jamaican electorate voted against joining the West Indies Federation. This removed the foundation of the remaining anti-restrictionist position within the Cabinet and undermined Macleod's position as Colonial Secretary.[32] Macleod agreed to legislation, and he was later moved by Macmillan to the leadership of the House of Commons. This failure of the Federation removed the final impediment to the adoption of immigration control.[33] The plans which had been circulating in committee since the

[28] See *PRO, CO 1032/304*, 'Political Repercussions in West Indies', undated, 'Working Party to report on the social and economic problems arising from the growing influx into the United Kingdom of coloured workers from other Commonwealth Countries', Minutes of a Meeting held at the Home Office, 10 May 1961, 'C.C.M. (16) 8. Commonwealth Migrants Committee: Further Report by the Inter-Departmental Working Party' (Brief for the Secretary of State), 16 May 1961.

[29] According to his biographer, Macleod was the last to be convinced of the need for legislation. R. Shepherd, *Iain Macleod: A Biography* (London: Pimlico, 1995), 267.

[30] *PRO, CO 1032/305*, Letter from Ian Watt to Vile, 3 Aug. 1961.

[31] Ibid.

[32] E. J. B. Rose et al., *Colour and Citizenship: A Report on British Race Relations* (London: Oxford University Press, 1969), 219.

[33] Certain members of the Colonial Office attempted to continue resisting on the question of timing, but this threat was no longer taken seriously. *PRO, CO 1031/3946*, Letter from M. Z. Terry to Thomas and Hammer, 21 Sept. 1961 and Letter from E. R. Hammer, 22 Sept. 1961. In particular, the Colonial Office wished to defer until they secured the agreement of Dr Eric Williams (Trinidad) to an Eastern Caribbean Federation. The Colonial Office felt these negotiations depended on Trinidad's willingness to make concessions on freedom of movement, and that this willingness would be threatened by immigration restrictions. The argument, however, was beginning to wear thin and domestic considerations triumphed, as they often do, over foreign.

summer were organized for presentation, and on 19 September a Legislation Committee agreed that legislation on the basis of employment control was necessary.[34]

The 1961 Annual Conference

When the delegates arrived in Brighton, it was widely believed that Commonwealth migration would be debated. Cyril Osborne was in fine form, and on the morning of the immigration debate he handed each delegate a copy of his letter to the *Daily Telegraph* entitled 'Immigration Lunacy: Even Nearer an Afro-Asian Britain', which contained the usual arguments about housing and colour. He would later claim that the eloquence and persuasiveness of this piece tipped the balance in favour of control,[35] but this is baseless. The party leadership's only reaction to Osborne in 1961 was fervently (but vainly) to wish, as it had wished throughout the 1950s, that he would go away.

Forty resolutions on immigration had been submitted to the Conference, and all but one demanded stricter control. The Conference carried by a large majority a resolution stating '[t]hat this Conference expresses its concern at the very serious problems being created by the uncontrolled number of immigrants flowing into the United Kingdom. It asks Her Majesty's Government to take action quickly on this matter.'

With two exceptions, one in which a Manchester MP referred to immigrant children as 'six delightful piccaninnies round [the immigrant father's] knees' and one in which Pannell suggested that immigrants were 'not necessarily inferior to us', the speeches and the resolution itself were moderate. Tribute was paid, however hollowly, to the Commonwealth and the role of immigrants in the British economy, and one speaker defended the open-door and condemned Pannell's and Osborne's 'carefully fostered campaign'. The liberal Tory, Nigel Fisher, sensing that his battle against restrictions was lost, pleaded for controls which did not discriminate between the Old and New Commonwealth. When Butler spoke before the final vote, he offered a cryptic speech which, on the whole, suggested the government's willingness to restrict immigration. Promising the 'fullest consultations' with the Commonwealth and overseas governments, he concluded that 'it may be that we can work out a system which is humane, unprejudiced and sensible and which meets some of the undoubted rising social and economic problems which otherwise may become too much for certain parts of our country'.[36]

---

[34] *PRO, CO 1032/306*, 'Legislation Committee: Commonwealth Immigrants Bill (L.C.(61)64),' 19 Sept. 1961.

[35] Rose et al., *Colour and Citizenship*, 219.

[36] For the full text of the immigration debate, see *National Union of Conservative and*

Butler's speech negotiated a path between capitulation and defiance. By emphasizing the seriousness of the issues at stake, the importance of immigrants to the British economy, and the value of the Commonwealth, he offered a sop to liberal opinion. Yet he also made clear to the Conference, and the country, that the Conservative government was prepared to see an end to its traditional free entry policy.[37]

THE COMMONWEALTH IMMIGRANTS ACT

The legislation, which was to be temporary, had two main sections.

Part I: Control of Immigration

The first part of the act specifies which Commonwealth citizens were subject to control. Out of a complex process of specifying by default, restrictions were applied to any Commonwealth citizen who (*a*) had not been born in the UK, (*b*) does not hold a United Kingdom passport as a citizen of the United Kingdom and Colonies or a Republic of Ireland passport, and (*c*) is not included in the passport of (*a*) or (*b*).[38]

The second requirement was linked with the question of a passport's 'issuing authority'. As CUKC had not been replaced, there was no such thing as a British passport. Rather, there were CUKC passports held by Britons. To 'exempt' such individuals from restrictions, 'passport' was defined in Section 1 (3) as a passport issued by the United Kingdom government. This in itself did not go far enough. It would have restricted citizens of independent Commonwealth countries (Australians, Indians, Canadians, and so forth), but it would not have excluded colonial citizens. It was here that the question of 'issuing authority' came into play. If CUKCs received passports under the authority of colonial governments, they were subject to control; if CUKCs received them under the authority of London (all CUKCs—British-born or not), then they were not.[39] This bizarre mechanism, a triumph of British prag-

Unionist Associations, 80th Annual Conference, 11–14 Oct. 1961, 26–33. The convention that governments could not reveal the contents of the Queen's Speech in advance of its delivery was stronger in 1961 than today, and the substance of Butler's speech reflected an effort to respect this constraint. Interview with a Home Office official.

[37] For a less favourable reading of Butler's speech, see B. Levin, 'The Image and the Search', *Spectator* (20 Oct. 1961), 529–31.

[38] Such as dependants, for example.

[39] In practice, this meant that Britons and others excluded from controls would have a stamp in their CUKC passport to the effect of 'issued under the authority of Her Majesty's

matism over Cartesian logic, opened another Pandora's box of future policy problems. Most importantly, though it was poorly understood at the time and continues to be, it was at the heart of the Kenyan Asians crisis of 1968.

All of this was a rather tortured way of saying that Britons, including those born in the country and those who had migrated before 1962, were free from migration controls. The act then went on, in Section 1 (2), to include the employment voucher scheme. Individuals who had successfully applied for one of three categories were free to enter the UK:

- Category A for people promised a specific job by a specific employer;
- Category B for individuals with training, skill, or educational attainments deemed useful to Britain; and
- Category C for all unskilled workers without a job in the United Kingdom.[40] This last provision was subject to a variable limit, defined according to the employment situation in the UK,[41] and it was to be operated on a 'first-come, first served' basis, with no preference for any part of the Commonwealth. The first quota for category C was set at 10,000 vouchers per year, while the quota for A and B together was 20,800.

Other privileged individuals, both Commonwealth citizens and aliens, included students attending full-time courses or substantial part time courses, the independently wealthy and members of the armed forces.

Finally, there was a halfway house of individuals who, in some cases even if they held a labour voucher, could be refused admission:

- those individuals who, in the judgement of a medical inspector, are suffering from a mental disorder or are otherwise undesirable for medical reasons.
- those believed to have been convicted of any crime which is subject to extradition.
- individuals whose admission would, in the view of the Secretary of State, be contrary to national security.

Government in the UK' or 'issued under the authority of the British High Commission in [for example] Ottawa'. Passports subject to control would have a stamp to the effect of 'issued under the authority of the Colonial Government in [for example] Kenya'. The latter stamp could be issued either in the colony concerned, or in London; it was the authority that was central, not the specific location. None the less, certain CUKCs attempted to evade controls through securing the former stamp. Thus, a Hong Kong student in the United Kingdom might renew his or her passport in London in the hope that a negligent official would stamp the passport incorrectly. If this occurred, as the Home Office believes it did in a few instances, the student could escape immigration restrictions. Interview with a Home Office official.

[40] CIA, Section 3(*a*).
[41] *CPA, CRD/2/44/20*, 'The Commonwealth Immigrants Bill', HAC (61) 3, 2 Nov. 1961.

These measures drew on aliens' law, which had, after the First World War, granted the Home Secretary substantial discretion in excluding individuals on security grounds. They were the starting point in a process, culminating in 1971, that would extend provisions of aliens' legislation to Commonwealth citizens.

Part II: Deportation

The second part of the Act provides provisions for deportation; these had not existed, although they had been considered, before the 1962 Act. All those subject to control could be deported if they were over 17 years old and were convicted of an offence punishable with imprisonment. Any court could recommend the offender's deportation. Only those Commonwealth citizens who had been normally resident in the UK for more than five years, could not be deported. As CUKCs entered with a British passport, this meant that colonial citizens were effectively, and automatically, naturalized as full British citizens after five years' residence.

THE COMMONWEALTH IMMIGRANTS ACT IN PARLIAMENT

The decision to restrict was announced in the Queen's Speech on 31 October, and Butler moved the Second Reading of the Commonwealth Immigrants Bill on 16 November. The justification for the bill, he told the House

> is that a sizeable part of the entire population of the earth is at present legally entitled to come and stay in this already densely populated country. It amounts altogether to one-quarter of the population of the globe and at present there are no factors visible which might lead us to expect a reversal or even a modification of the [current] immig-ration trend.[42]

Whatever credit the Conservatives may have taken for the act later in the decade, the legislation was viewed as a distasteful necessity of which they were not proud. Butler had no enthusiasm for control,[43] and many in the party shared Macleod's view that it was a detestable bill.[44] This attitude of

---

[42] *Parliamentary Debates (Commons)* (649), col. 687, 16 Nov. 1961.

[43] Interviews with Home Office officials; confidential interview.

[44] *PRO, CO 1032/306*, Letter from Iain Macleod, 4 Oct. 1961. The bill was publicly opposed by Nigel Fisher, and Reginald Maudling, who succeeded Macleod as Colonial Secretary, later revealed that his attachment to the idea of free entry made him extremely reluctant to support the bill. R. Maudling, *Memoirs* (London: Sidgwick & Jackson, 1978), 157–8.

unenthusiastic and reluctant agreement left the Conservatives ill-prepared for Labour's attack.[45]

The Labour Party had three objections to the bill: (i) it harmed relations between Britain and the New Commonwealth, (ii) it was prejudicial to good race relations throughout the world, and (iii) it damaged economic prospects in the West Indies.

The bill's damage to the New Commonwealth was said to result from the fact of control itself, and it was believed by Labour to be exacerbated by the failure to ensure proper Commonwealth consultation. This point was raised several times in the debates,[46] and Gaitskell, the Labour leader, spoke with Sir Grantley Adams of Jamaica after the Second Reading. He received a telegram from Adams stating that 'I categorically deny that West Indies Government was ever consulted in any way whatever about form or detailed provisions of Bill [sic].' Gaitskell informed Macmillan of his intention to publish the letter and requested a statement in the House.[47] Macmillan responded with an icy letter claiming that telegrams exchanged between the UK and the West Indies, some of which Adams showed to Gaitskell, 'provided information of Her Majesty's Government's intentions, invited comments and sought the co-operation of Colonial Governments in implementing the scheme outlined in them. This is what I understand to be consultation.'[48] The charge unsettled the government; Macleod noted with annoyance Gaitskell's efforts to 'make a great fuss about Commonwealth consultation',[49] and somewhat defensive letters circulated between ministers in an effort to rebut the charge.[50] Labour's criticism was in fact a legitimate one; the colonies were not informed until early October, a few weeks before the bill was announced in

---

[45]   The Home Secretary had consulted the Opposition in October and concluded that 'some sections' would find the bill less objectionable if it were subject to annual renewal. Butler thought this was impossible (though annual renewal ultimately was incorporated during the bill's passage through Parliament), but he agreed to a five-year renewal by Order-in-Council. *PRO, CO 1032/307*, 'Commonwealth Immigrants Bill', Admiralty House meeting, 19 Oct. 1961. It is possible that this concession encouraged the government to believe that the bill's passage would be a less difficult one.

[46]   See, for example, *Parliamentary Debates (Commons)* (649), cols. 692–4 and 716, 16 Nov. 1961. In the latter, Gordon Walker stated that '[w]e bitterly oppose the Bill and will resist it. It has been rushed. There has been no inquiry, no consultation with the Commonwealth. It is widely and rightly regarded as introducing a colour bar into our legislation. It will do great harm to the Commonwealth. It is so ill-conceived that it will not achieve even its own mis-begotten purposes.'

[47]   *PRO, CO 1032/323*, Letter from Gaitskell to Macmillan, 22 Nov. 1961.

[48]   *PRO, CO 1032/323*, Letter from Macmillan to Gaitskell, 22 Nov. 1961.

[49]   *PRO, CO 1032/308*, Letter from Macleod to Butler, 15 Nov. 1961.

[50]   See for example, *PRO, CO 1032/308*, 'Consultations with Colonial Governments about Proposed Commonwealth Immigrants Bill', 16 Nov. 1961.

the Queen's Speech, and the government was not prepared to countenance changes.[51]

The Opposition argued that the bill harmed race relations because it was racially discriminatory. Its application, which favoured (skilled) Old Commonwealth immigrants, was itself discriminatory, and the bill's racist intent was confirmed by the exclusion of immigrants from the Irish Republic.

Control on immigration between the Irish Republic and Great Britain (I use this term deliberately) had existed only once: during the Second World War. By 1960, following the dismantling of wartime controls, Ireland and Britain formed a 'common travel area' in which people could travel freely without identity documents. There were two options for controlling the movement of persons between Ireland and the United Kingdom. The first was to patrol the border between the Republic and Northern Ireland. This had never occurred; the government felt that the extensive number of crossings would make border controls expensive and cumbersome, while the thousands of people who crossed every day would be forced to carry identity papers. Such papers were considered both cumbersome and continental; it is not clear which was the greater offence. The second option, which was implemented during the Second World War, was to allow free movement between the two Irelands but to patrol the border between Great Britain and Northern Ireland (as well, of course, as the border between Great Britain and the Irish Republic). The government argued that this was highly undesirable because it would offend the patriotic sentiments of the Northern Irish and would create the anomaly of border controls within a democratic polity.[52]

The government, which had never intended to apply controls to the Irish Republic, anticipated strong opposition to its exclusion. Its extremely weak strategy was to introduce controls on Ireland in the original bill but to make clear in Parliament that, in practice, controlling Irish immigration was impractical and thus would not occur.[53] This attempt convinced no one. After

[51] *PRO, CO 1031/3946*, Letter from Colonial Secretary to all Governors and Administrators, the West Indies, 13 Oct. 1995. The telegram also stated that the government hoped that the 'telegram under reference will not be interpreted as inviting Colonial Governments to propose to the British Government any policy changes'. It is rather 'intended to give your Government the opportunity to raise questions about the implementation of the measures proposed'. Consultation appears rather like directive.

[52] The difficulties associated with controlling Irish migration come up frequently in official discussions. See, for instance, *PRO, PREM 13/2157*, Letter from Harold Wilson to the Archbishop of Canterbury, 18 Jan. 1967, concerning the Archbishop's complaints about the absence of migration restrictions on Ireland.

[53] *Parliamentary Debates (Commons)* (649), cols. 700–1, 16 Nov. 1961. This strategy followed the recommendation of the working party. *PRO, CO 1032/303*, 'Working Party to report on the social and economic problems arising from the growing influx into the United Kingdom of coloured workers from other Commonwealth Countries', undated.

Butler explained this position, Patrick Gordon Walker, who would later regret his stridency, came out swinging:

Why did the right hon. Gentlemen put this in the Bill in the first place[?] . . . I think I know. He put it in as a sort of fig leaf to preserve his reputation for liberalism. Now he stands revealed before us in his nakedness. He is an advocate now of a Bill which contains bare-faced, open race discrimination. He advocates a Bill into which race discrimination is now written—not only into its spirit and its practice, but into its very letter.[54]

Gordon Walker ended his speech with a tirade against a bill that he claimed could only be described as a 'ramshackle monstrosity'.[55]

The Irish question was an extremely sensitive one for the government. Relations between Dublin and London were poor in the 1950s,[56] and many Conservatives resented the privileges enjoyed by the Irish. Ireland had remained neutral during the Second World War and, shortly thereafter, had repudiated allegiance to the Crown and declared itself a republic. These acts of disloyalty angered individuals on both government benches, and their feelings were exacerbated by the Conservative Party's own doubts about the effect of the bill on the Commonwealth, of which it remained fond, and its suspicions of Macmillan's turn to Europe. It was especially difficult to accept the exclusion of the Irish from restrictions in the context of their application to the Old Dominions. This anger was exploited by John Biggs Davidson, who organized Conservative opposition against the Irish exemption. There was a very real danger that Conservatives would vote against the bill if it maintained the Irish exemption unaltered.[57]

In concluding the Opposition's case, Gaitskell drew on the full power of his oratorical skill in a stinging rebuke of government policy:

Do the Government deal with [integration difficulties] by seeking to combat social evils, by building more houses and enforcing laws against overcrowding, by using every educational means at their disposal to create tolerance and mutual understanding, and by emphasising to our own people the value of these immigrants and setting their face firmly against all forms of racial intolerance and discrimination[?] . . .

---

[54] *Parliamentary Debates (Commons)* (649), col. 706, 16 Nov. 1961.

[55] *(Commons)* (649), col. 716.

[56] There existed the possibility that immigration controls would have been undermined by the provisions for the Irish. Since there were no controls between Ireland and Great Britain, it might have been possible for Commonwealth citizens to travel to Ireland and then to the UK. The Home Office pressed their counterparts in Ireland to enact legislation requiring their port officials to control Commonwealth immigration bound for the UK. This agreement was, in the last weeks, finally secured. The fact that the Commonwealth Immigrants Bill provided the formal means to control Irish immigration might have served as a useful prod with which to encourage the Irish government. Interview with a Home Office official.

[57] Interview with a Home Office official.

[T]here is no shred of evidence that the Government have even seriously tried to go along this course and make a proper inquiry into the nature of this problem. They have yielded to the crudest clamour, 'Keep them out.'[58]

The Labour back benches were euphoric, an (already guilt-ridden) government was on the defensive, and Butler doubted that he would be able to get the bill through Parliament.[59] For Gaitskell's enthusiasts, it was the party leader at his best, and subsequent critics of Labour immigration policy have pointed to the speech as the party's finest hour, a golden age followed only by compromise and appeasement.[60] The fact that Gaitskell died without ever having to demonstrate the courage of his convictions, and that he was succeeded by the unreconstructed pragmatist, Harold Wilson, has served to reinforce the mythology surrounding the speech and cement Gaitskell's reputation as an unyielding man of principle.

In truth, Gaitskell was given to taking extreme and politically unwise decisions which even his admirers found difficult to comprehend. Gordon Walker, who was among Gaitskell's closest allies, recorded in his diary that 'I began to fear that Gaitskell has the seeds of self-destruction in him. . . . He is becoming distrustful and angry with his best friends and wants to take up absolute and categorical positions that will alienate all but a handful.'[61] There was something of the impulsive in Gaitskell's speech, and something of the hypocrite. Gaitskell was Chancellor the Exchequer during Labour's 1950–1 Cabinet discussions over immigration, and he was in all likelihood party to their conclusion that a substantial increase in immigration would be cause for legislation. Gaitskell was only able to make this case convincingly because Labour's early post-war doubts and deliberations were unknown; they were not (as they would almost certainly be today) leaked, and the prohibition on one government examining the files of another prevented the Conservatives from knowing of their existence.[62] For Gaitskell to treat the notion that social problems might require limits on immigration with such high-minded derision was, at the very least, revisionist.

But, of course, none of this was known, and the government was shaken. Its latent divisions had been successfully exploited by Labour, and the Irish question threatened to wreck the bill. Butler, moreover, made life worse for himself by his ignorance of the figures for arrivals; he was unable to tell Parliament whether they represented gross or net immigration, and his ignorance made

[58] *Parliamentary Debates (Commons)* (649), col. 801, 16 Nov. 1961.

[59] R. A. Butler, *The Art of the Possible: The Memoirs of Lord Butler* (London: Hamish Hamilton, 1971), 206–7.

[60] See P. Foot, *Immigration and Race in British Politics* (Harmondsworth: Penguin, 1965).

[61] *Private Papers of Patrick Gordon Walker*, Churchill College, Cambridge, *GNWR 1/14*, 12 May 1960.   [62] Interview with a Home Office official.

him appear extremely foolish.[63] When the issue was put to a vote, the 'Ayes' carried by a substantial majority—283 to 200—but only because the front bench manœuvred skilfully in the last hours of the debate. A 1922 Committee meeting was arranged so that the issue could be discussed there, the Whips worked strenuously, and the front bench inserted, at the last moment, two paragraphs into John Hare's closing speech promising that the government would try to find a practical way to deal with the Irish problem.[64] Without these efforts, Macleod predicted, the majority would have been less than half that attained.[65] At the close of the second reading, Home Office officials felt they might not sustain majority support for the measure.[66]

After the disastrous debate, the government organized a hasty ministerial meeting.[67] The ministers agreed to, first, commission a survey of the extent of Irish immigration to the UK,[68] and, second, highlight the fact that Irish citizens arriving from somewhere other than Ireland *would* be subject to control.[69] The Irish, along with aliens and British subjects not resident in the UK, would pass through immigration control when they arrived in the United Kingdom from anywhere but Ireland; they would pass through no border controls, for none existed, when travelling from Ireland. Thus, Irish citizens travelling into the United Kingdom from Ireland, whether via Holyhead or Heathrow, would enter freely; Irish citizens travelling, for instance, from Paris to Dover could theoretically be refused admission.[70] In practice, however, most would be 'cleared' by an immigration officer as residents returning to Britain after a holiday abroad, or as individuals in transit to the Irish Republic.[71] This did not impede either their mobility once in the UK or

---

[63] *Parliamentary Debates (Commons)* (649), cols. 687–92. The figures were net (immigration minus emigration), and the Home Office had assumed that Butler knew this.

[64] *PRO, PREM 11/3238,* Letter from Macleod to Macmillan, 17 Nov. 1961. For the inserted text, see *Parliamentary Debates (Commons)* (649), col. 809.

[65] *PRO, PREM 11/3238,* Letter from Macleod to Macmillan, 17 Nov. 1961.

[66] Confidential interview.

[67] Confidential interview.

[68] The survey was done by Thomas of the Central Office of Information; he would have liked to publish it, but public demand was gone and the government had no desire to rekindle the issue. The government eventually discharged its obligation by publishing the statistics in the back of Hansard in response to a parliamentary question. Interview with a Home Office official.

[69] During closing speech in the Second Reading, John Hare went so far as to suggest that, were the practical difficulties involved in administering controls at the ports overcome, some additional measures might be introduced. See *Parliamentary Debates (Commons)* (649), col. 809, 16 Nov. 1961.

[70] Were the government to have operated border controls between Northern Ireland and the UK, it would have been necessary to amend the 1920 Aliens Order, which created powers to control the entry of aliens 'landing' in the UK. Crossing the border between the Republic and Northern Ireland is not 'landing'.

[71] Interview with a Home Office official.

their right to work,[72] as the United Kingdom and Ireland remained a common travel area, and the right of Irish citizens to work in the UK had not been rescinded. None the less, the strategy mollified enough Conservative MPs to secure strong support for the bill. Had it not been for this compromise, the government almost certainly would have been defeated.

The exclusion of Irish citizens from control was the most controversial aspect of the 1962 legislation. For many, it confirmed their belief that it was a racist act designed to exclude immigrants of colour.[73] The matter was in fact more complicated than this. There is no doubt that the act was designed to reduce New Commonwealth immigration, because this movement was associated with social problems in the inner cities and was the target of public hostility. In restricting third world and colonial migration, Britain did in 1962 what every other European and even North American nation has done since. The Irish exclusion had powerful political and economic considerations in its favour, chief of which was potential opposition from the Northern Irish government and among Ulster Unionists. The only reliable means of controlling Irish immigration would have been to treat the Republic and Northern Ireland as one for immigration purposes and to control movement from the island to Great Britain. British citizens resident in Northern Ireland would have to pass through immigration control to travel to Great Britain. Border controls within the United Kingdom would have been bitterly opposed by Ulster Unionists, and it would have been unthinkable for the Conservative and Unionist Party to impose such restrictions.[74]

A secondary consideration was economic. Irish citizens were well represented in British industry and services, of which construction is an obvious example, and the government feared that control would impede this movement and exacerbate labour shortages.[75] Irish immigration was, moreover, qualitatively different from New Commonwealth immigration in this respect. Whereas the latter was largely a permanent movement of citizens to the United Kingdom, Irish labour was mobile and responsive to the level of demand in the British economy. In recessionary periods, Irish labour could be

---

[72] The Irish also remained subject to the deportation provisions. In the absence of border controls, however, such provisions were ineffective. Deported Irish citizens only had to catch a train to Dublin and return to the UK from there. None the less, to do so would be an offence, and the offenders could be arrested if found by the police.

[73] K. Paul, *Whitewashing Britain* (Ithaca, NY: Cornell University Press, 1997), 109.

[74] *PRO, CO 1032/308*, 'Commonwealth Immigrants Bill: The Irish Problem', undated.

[75] *PRO, CAB 134/1469*, 'Application of Commonwealth Immigrants Bill to the Irish Republic', 8 Nov. 1961; *PRO, CO 1032/303*, 'Working Party to report on the social and economic problems arising from the growing influx into the United Kingdom of coloured workers from other Commonwealth Countries. Application of Commonwealth Immigrants Bill to the Irish Republic: Memorandum by the Home Office', undated.

expected, to an extent far greater than that from the New Commonwealth, to return to the Republic until conditions improved.[76]

Finally, it must be recalled that many politicians and bureaucrats were extremely unhappy about the Irish exemption. The Colonial Office consistently opposed this decision,[77] and the government very nearly faced a back bench revolt over it. To the extent that the Conservatives longed for a racist exclusion, it was Canadians, Australians, and New Zealanders whom they wished to see exempted. The Old Dominions were viewed with much greater affection in 1962 than the disloyal Irish.

The Commonwealth Immigrants Bill passed through Parliament slowly, and as it did the number of arrivals increased. The 'beat-the-ban' rush, which began early in 1961 as rumours of control circulated throughout the Commonwealth, reached its climax. By the end of 1961 a record 136,000 New Commonwealth immigrants (net) had arrived in the United Kingdom, and the bill was still being debated in Parliament. It was finally guillotined in a Committee of the whole House (it was debated there because Labour insisted that the bill was constitutional) in February. The Commonwealth Immigrants Act received Royal Assent on 18 April 1962 and became law on 1 July.

Butler views a softening in Labour's tone as important to the Conservatives' ultimate success.[78] By the final debate, the party concentrated on technical questions and remained ambivalent on the question of whether Labour would repeal the act. It claimed credit for five minor amendments: easier entry for residents, the institution of entry certificates, the publication of instructions to immigration officers, and the exemption of wives and children from controls. Denis Healey gave a final, tepid, speech for Labour, in which he offered only stifled opposition to the act.[79]

The reasons for the change in Labour's stance are unclear. It is possible that the party had only intended on the second reading to create an opportunity for amendments and was satisfied with the changes in the Irish provisions. These amendments were, however, a response to Conservative divisions rather than Labour pressure, and the latter probably recognized this.[80] Another possibility, suggested by those who witnessed the act's

[76]   This point should not be exaggerated. There were and are large numbers of Irish citizens permanently resident in the UK. The proximity of Ireland, however, allows for a level of circulation that never existed between the UK and colonies.

[77]   See *PRO, CO 1032/307*, 'Cabinet. Commonwealth Immigrants Bill: Application to the Irish Republic (C (61)180): Brief for the Secretary of State', 8 Nov. 1961, Letters to Thomas and Bourdillon 8 Nov. 1961 and 27 Oct. 1961.

[78]   Butler, *The Art of the Possible*, 206.

[79]   *Parliamentary Debates (Commons)* (654), cols. 1264–71, 27 Feb. 1962.

[80]   Had the Conservative Party been united, there would have been no need for the amendments, the primary purpose of which was to mollify John Biggs Davidson and his supporters. Interview with a Home Office official.

passage, is that Labour belatedly recognized the extent of public hostility to immigration control.[81] In late August, Gordon Walker was subjected to considerable hostility on a programme entitled 'Listeners Answer Back'. He found himself continually heckled; the words 'nigger', 'blackies', and the phrase 'Keep Britain White' were used; and he admitted the case for restricting immigration control when the numbers are too large.[82] During the passage of the immigration bill, Gallup's second poll on attitudes to immigration estimated its approval at between 62 and 67 per cent.[83] These indicators of the public mood may have convinced certain Labour members that little could be gained through its original categorical opposition. Whatever the reason, the Conservatives found their job significantly easier after the Second Reading.

THE COMMONWEALTH IMMIGRANTS ACT: CONSIDERATIONS AND CONSEQUENCES

To the extent that the timing and form of immigration restrictions are remarkable at all, they are so for the degree to which politicians and bureaucrats passively accepted the transformation of Britain into a multicultural society. Immigration was restricted a full four years after all measures of the public mood indicated clear hostility to a black presence in Britain, and even then it was only done with hesitation. The legislation, moreover, was liberal: the limits under the three categories were generous (allowing somewhere between 30,000 and 40,000 immigrants to enter each year), and dependants, including grandparents, enjoyed the unconditional right of entry.

The politicians who were consistently hostile to black immigration were a handful, numbering less than ten, of backbenchers. The fact that Osborne demanded immigration control in 1952 (and beyond) and immigration control was enacted in 1962 has led scholars to conclude that their persistence won the Conservative Party over; they were the proverbial drip that wears away the hardest stone.[84] These individuals' importance was in fact minimal. They were relevant to migration policy only insofar as they served as one among a host of indicators that alerted the government to the public mood. They were

---

[81] Interview with a Home Office official; interview with Peter Shore.

[82] *CPA, CRD 2/44/20*, Listeners Answer Back, 'Mr. Gordon Walker on Immigration', 31 Aug. 1961.

[83] *Attitudes towards Coloured People in Great Britain*, question 35. The percentage of those disapproving ranged between 12% and 21%.

[84] Foot, *Immigration and Race in British Politics*, and Freeman, *Immigrant Labor and Racial Conflict in Industrial Societies*, 49–52.

not consulted by ministers in the decision to restrict legislation, their input on its form and timing was not solicited, and they were not represented on the policy-making organs of the party and government. Macmillan's snub of Osborne in 1957 is indicative of the frontbench attitude to the Osborne/Pannell faction,[85] and it can be said with confidence that had Commonwealth migration (and its attendant social problems) remained at its early 1950s level, the Commonwealth Immigrants Act would not have been enacted.

When the decision was ultimately taken, it reflected in part the pressure of numbers, in part the usual pluralist pressures.[86] The government faced a hostile public,[87] a housing shortage,[88] and a tremendous surge in arrivals, particularly from India and Pakistan,[89] which had doubled in both years since 1959.[90] This increase exacerbated the housing crisis in Britain's cities and amounted to a figure in excess of what the United Kingdom was thought able to absorb.[91] The party- and bureaucracy-wide admission in mid- to late-1960 that informal controls would not keep immigration within what were regarded as manageable limits marked the end of Britain's open door for all British subjects.

The previous bulwark against immigration control—a commitment among policy-makers to the right of free entry for British subjects—was no longer sufficient to resist the logic and force of the restrictionist argument. Among the factors contributing to this change was the fact that the migratory patterns on

[85] See *Parliamentary Debates (Commons)* (563), col. 392, 24 Jan. 1957. Quoting the Prime Minister: 'It would not be right for the Government to impose any restriction on emigration which has contributed so much to the development of the Commonwealth. . . . I would deprecate any reflection that may be cast on the standards of health and conduct of these immigrants.'

[86] For a discussion of the latter, see J. Money, *Fences and Neighbours: The Political Geography of Immigration Control* (Ithaca, NY: Cornell University Press, 1999), ch. 4.

[87] *PRO, CAB 134/1469*, 'Cabinet. Commonwealth Migrants Committee. Coloured Immigration: Memorandum by the Secretary of State for the Home Department', 8 Feb. 1961.

[88] *PRO, PREM 11/3238*, Letter from Norman Brook to Macmillan, 24 Nov. 1960.

[89] The large increase in Indian and Pakistani immigration was central to the decision to introduce immigration controls. *PRO, CAB 134/1508*, 'Cabinet. Commonwealth Immigration Committee: Review of First Year of the Control', 3 July 1963. One Home Office official subsequently speculated that had New Commonwealth immigration remained largely West Indian, no immigration controls would have been introduced in 1962. Interview with a Home Office official.

[90] *PRO, PREM 11/3238*, Letter from Norman Brook to Macmillan, 9 Oct. 1961.

[91] *CPA, CRD/2/44/20*, 'Commonwealth Immigrants Bill,' HAC (61) 4, 13 Nov. 1961. A less significant factor, but one that was mentioned, was the failure of economic development in the colonies and New Commonwealth in reducing the motivation to emigrate. *CPA, CRD 2/44/20*, 'The Commonwealth Immigrants Bill,' HAC (61) 3, 2 Nov. 1961. There had at one time been faith among Conservatives in economic development as a means to reducing emigration pressures, but a lack of demonstrable success in the short-term disillusioned them. See *CPA, CC04 6/151*, 'The West Indian Immigrant' and *CRD 2/44/20*, 'West-Indian, Asian & Southern-Irish Immigrants', undated.

which this commitment was premissed had altered. Bipartisan support for the free entry of British subjects was based on a system in which Old Dominions/UK movement (both temporary and permanent) dominated and in which colonial/New Commonwealth migration was limited and temporary,[92] and the overall migratory framework was seen to be expressive of this primary UK-Old Dominions attachment.[93] When New Commonwealth/ Colonial immigration matched and then surpassed that from the Old Dominions, the British Nationality Act of 1948 was legitimizing an unintended and unwanted mass migration. The free entry principle originated during a period in which colonial and New Commonwealth British subjects were unable to migrate to the United Kingdom on a large scale,[94] and the 1948 entrenchment of the right of free entry for all British subjects was never intended to facilitate the transformation of Britain into a multicultural society. It should be no surprise that, when this occurred, support for the policy fatally weakened. The only surprise is that controls were introduced relatively liberally, and so late.

THE COMMONWEALTH AND THE EUROPEAN ECONOMIC COMMUNITY

The importance of the Commonwealth and the European Economic Community (EEC) for the decision to introduce immigration controls is often raised in the scholarly literature. The EEC is frequently mentioned, but an argument about its importance has never been convincingly developed.[95] Two possibilities present themselves. The first is the argument that a weakening attachment to the Commonwealth, as a basis of British pride, power, and prestige, and an increased interest in Europe as the arena in which a previous world power could exercise influence in the manner to which it had become accustomed, rendered policy-makers more predisposed towards immigration control.[96] This argument is certainly plausible. Many of those who criticized the Commonwealth Immigrants Act did so in the name of the Commonwealth, and Gaitskell's bitter (if fleeting) opposition is thought to have been founded

[92]   CPA, CRD 2/44/20, 'The Commonwealth Immigrants Bill', HAC (61) 4, 13 Nov. 1961.
[93]   See ch. 2.
[94]   PRO, CAB 129/81, CP (56) 145 'Colonial Immigrants: Report of the Committee of Ministers', 22 June 1956.
[95]   D. Dean, 'The Conservative Government and the 1961 Commonwealth Immigration Act: The Inside Story', Race and Class, 35, No. 2 (1993), 57–74, 73.
[96]   D. W. Dean, 'Conservative Governments and the Restriction of Commonwealth Immigration in the 1950s: The Problems of Constraint', Historical Journal, 35, No. 1 (1993), 171–94, 193.

on his attachment to the Commonwealth.[97] It is conceivable that those who supported immigration restrictions did so in part because they were disillusioned with the Commonwealth as heir of Empire. Unfortunately, in the absence of clear evidence,[98] this takes one into the fuzzy realm of personal psychology and makes it extremely difficult to draw any firm conclusions.

A second possibility is that the restriction was enacted with an eye to the European negotiations; the decision was designed to send a signal to Bonn and Paris that Britain was prepared to accept the consequences of its European future (a claim De Gaulle consistently denied) and that the Continent would not be affected by the migratory relics of its imperial past.[99] This is an interesting idea, but there is unfortunately no evidence to support it.[100] Commonwealth immigration was simply not terribly relevant to the European question. Of far greater consequence was sterling and imperial preference. Had the UK wished to create a symbol of its freedom from the constraints of Empire, it should have devalued sterling and abandoned all preferences for the Commonwealth and colonies.[101] In the end, the Conservatives did neither, and any sop on immigration would have been of very little symbolic or political value.[102]

[97]   Interview with Peter Shore.

[98]   The only ones, to my knowledge, who made this link explicit were Pannell and Osborne. In the February 1961 debate, the latter argued that '[t]he greatest argument that will be used against me from both sides of the House will be the mother country tradition. It will be said that people have been allowed to come back to their mother country and that they must always be allowed to do so. That argument is completely and utterly out of date. The mother country argument arose from the Kipling ideal, the imperialist ideal, which is now utterly rejected by hon. Members opposite and by the countries from which the immigrants come. We no longer talk of "Empire" now. We no longer dare use the term "Empire" and "Imperialistic ideals." It is now "Commonwealth". We talk about these countries being sister States. Therefore, the "obligation of the mother" has gone . . . Either we go back to the Kipling concept of the mother country, with all that that involved, or we accept the restrictions inherent in the idea of sister States'. *Parliamentary Debates (Commons)* (634), col. 1940, 17 Feb. 1961.

[99]   Dean, 'The Conservative Government and the 1961 Commonwealth Immigration Act: The Inside Story', 57–74, 71.

[100]   The fact that Macmillan does not mention any connection in his memoirs is not a decisive strike against the suggestion, for he might—even more than ten years on—have wished to avoid the political controversy that such an admission might have engendered. More damning, however, is the absence of any Cabinet, departmental, or party papers.

[101]   On the question of preferences, see C. Johnson, 'The Common Market: Way in for Britain?' *Crossbow*, 14, No. 1 (1961), 29–32.

[102]   Regarding a 'Commonwealth effect', the Commonwealth had a small but measurable influence on migration restrictions' timing. The establishment of a West Indies Federation was considered to be of sufficient importance to prevent the announcement of immigration restrictions until its foundation, despite the fact that the arrivals had reached record numbers and pressure for immigration restrictions was at its most intense. *CPA, CRD 2/44/1*, 'Minutes of the Joint meeting of the Home Office Affairs and the Commonwealth Committees', 9 July 1961, *PRO, CO 1032/302*, Letter from G. P. Lloyd to MacKintosh, 15 Feb. 1961, *PRO, CO 1032/304*, 'Political Repercussions in the West Indies', undated.

The Commonwealth Immigrants Act was a turning-point. It ended permanently the privileges which Commonwealth citizens and colonials had enjoyed for centuries, and it gave institutional expression to that which the British Nationality Act had sought so strenuously to avoid: the division of subjecthood. There was for the first time a formal difference between subjects born in, or otherwise belonging to, the United Kingdom and those of the Commonwealth and colonies. While this fact is of considerable historical interest, the mechanism adopted to check their entry was of great practical consequence. Because of the difficulties associated with its reform, the government opted to work within the framework of the 1948 British Nationality Act—to retain CUKC status—rather than to overhaul this system radically in favour of a distinctive United Kingdom Citizenship. Britons and colonial subjects continue to possess the identical citizenship, but the latter enjoyed fewer privileges in the United Kingdom. In other words, from 1962 there was a large category of second-class United Kingdom and colonies' citizens scattered around the globe. Although the very notion of second-class citizenship is normatively indefensible, it remained politically tolerable so long as all British subjects in the colonies exercised in practice the rights associated with citizenship—employment, education, etc.—in the various dependent nations of the Commonwealth, and so long as the transfer to independence involved the assumption by *all* colonial CUKCs of local citizenship.[103] In Africa, such a process failed to occur, and when (predominantly Asian) CUKCs who did not take local citizenship found themselves ousted from the local economy (sometimes gradually, sometimes brutally), they turned naturally and inevitably to the United Kingdom.

There is a second sense in which the act was a turning-point. The argument for control had been won; the question from 1962 onwards was to centre on the appropriate degree of restriction. New Commonwealth immigrants were, however, not only a substantial presence in British society; they were an incentive in favour of its augmentation. The year 1962 marked by and large the end of large-scale primary immigration to the United Kingdom—the immigration of persons with no personal connection to the country. The 1962 Act guaranteed the right of spouses, children, and grandparents over 65 to migrate to the UK, and after 1962 they began to do so in substantial numbers. Wives joined their husbands, husbands joined their wives, children joined their parents, and secondary immigration remained a political issue throughout Labour's two terms in office. In a manner similar to the British Nationality Act, at least superficially so, the Commonwealth Immigrants Act

---

[103] The assumption that this process would occur, it will be recalled, was at the foundation of the 1948 Act.

missed its policy target. In aiming to reduce primary immigration, the act entirely ignored the potential for large-scale secondary immigration. As a result, the relatively generous limits under the labour voucher scheme were filled, and they were supplemented by a substantial movement of spouses and dependants and the number of arrivals remained as high as they were in 1960, a year that was only exceeded by the great 1961 rush. But to tell this story, it is necessary to turn to Harold Wilson's Labour government.

PART II

Policy after 1962:
Effective Restrictionism

6

Labour and Party Competition: The Race Relations Act, 1965

IN the end, the sound and fury of Gaitskell's embittered attack on immigration control signified nothing, and both parties settled into a quiet acceptance of the 1962 system of control. The Colonial Office continued to resist the Ministry of Labour's position—it disagreed with the Ministry of Labour's pessimistic view of the economic situation in early 1962[1] and argued for a generous quota on Category C vouchers[2] (for the unskilled)—but its influence was on the wane. It had decisively lost the argument over control, and the process of decolonization led inevitably to its marginalization within the Cabinet. The winding down of Empire removed the Colonial Office's *raison d'être*; the ministry was merged with the Commonwealth Relations Office (CRO) in 1966, closed in 1967, and the CRO was in turn merged with the Foreign Office in 1968. There was after 1962 no question of rescinding the 1962 Act. The continued pressure of immigration, particularly from India and Pakistan,[3] meant that no one would seriously consider abandoning controls that had been presented as temporary. *Il n'y a rien d'aussi permanent que le provisoire*, as the French say.

The Labour government enacted two measures during its first government: the 1965 White Paper reducing the Commonwealth Immigrants Act's quotas

---

[1] *PRO, CO 1031/3934*, Letter from M. Z. Terry, 7 Mar. 1962. Terry, who consistently defended New Commonwealth and colonial immigration stated that '[t]he Ministry of Labour as usual paint a gloomy picture, and as usual make no effort to compare the unemployment figures with the net immigration figures over the same period' (which were exceptionally high because of the 'beat the ban' rush).

[2] *PRO, CO 1032/341*, Letter from E. R. Hammer to Mr McGee, 24 Apr. 1962 and Letter from A. R. Thomas, 1 May 1962.

[3] *PRO, CAB 134/1508*, 'Cabinet: Commonwealth Immigration Committee. Review of the First Year of Control: Memorandum by the Home Secretary', 3 July 1963. While the Committee expressed satisfaction with the implementation of the act and the overall operation of the categories, there was concern over 'considerable migration from India and Pakistan', countries with an 'inexhaustible immigration potential'. The Home Office estimated net immigration from the whole of the Commonwealth at 30,250; this figure was subsequently revised upwards (see Appendices).

and the 1965 Race Relations Bill.[4] This chapter analyses both these measures in the context of 'bipartisanship' and its role in Labour's overall approach to immigration politics.[5] A scholarly consensus holds that the centrepiece of Labour's two terms in office was bipartisanship, or an effort to keep race out of party politics.[6] There is a good deal of evidence to support this argument, but the term must be used with precision. If 'bipartisan' is intended to refer to some sort of formal agreement, a concordat, between the two main parties, or to a system of routinized and formal meetings, then such a description is inappropriate.[7] It was rather a largely informal process in which both parties saw it in their own interest to keep immigration and race out of party politics. Although it is difficult to date broad attitudinal shifts in party politics precisely, the foundations of the bipartisan consensus were in place by 1966 election. The consensus would suffer a great deal of strain in the coming years: Margaret Thatcher fleetingly attempted to make immigration a political issue after assuming the Conservative leadership, and a number of lesser politicians—notably Norman Tebbit and Kenneth Baker—have sought a few political points through attacks on black and Asian Britons and on Labour's laxity on immigration. Yet, despite these efforts, the bipartisan consensus survived, and in the late 1990s Britain is unique in Europe in that it is a country with no significant far-right party and in which immigration plays no significant role in national elections. Indeed, one of the remarkable aspects of the Thatcher years was that a government that was bent on deriding and sweeping away all vestiges of consensus politics left the bipartisan approach to immigration, race, and multiculturalism largely untouched.[8]

Bipartisanship originated in a deft policy linkage orchestrated by Labour, and above all its maligned Home Secretary Frank Soskice. The goal of the strategy was to make the maintenance and extension of immigration controls

---

[4] It should be noted that the White Paper did *not* introduce new controls; it rather reduced the quotas available under the Commonwealth Immigrants Act. No new legislation was introduced until the Commonwealth Immigrants Act, 1968.

[5] The reader will note that I give a disproportionate amount of attention to the 1965 Race Relations Act, devoting less attention in subsequent chapters to the 1968 and 1976 extensions of it. The reason is simple: the 1965 Act was one pillar of the two-pillar origin of the intellectual and policy linkage of restrictionist and integrationist measures. Confidential interview.

[6] P. Foot, *Immigration and Race in British Politics* (Harmondsworth: Penguin, 1965); I. Katznelson, *Black Men, White Cities: Race, Politics, and Migration in the United States, 1900–30 and Britain, 1948–68* (London: Oxford University Press, 1973); Z. Layton-Henry, *The Politics of Immigration* (Oxford: Blackwell, 1992), ch. 4, *The Politics of Race in Britain* (London: George Allen & Unwin, 1984), ch. 5; A. M. Messina, *Race and Party Competition in Britain* (Oxford: Clarendon, 1989), ch. 2; and J. Solomos, *Race and Racism in Contemporary Britain* (London: Macmillan, 1989), 52–8.

[7] Interviews with Home Office officials.

[8] On this, see A. Favell, *Philosophies of Integration: Immigration and the Idea of Citizenship in France and Britain* (Houndmills: Macmillan, 1998), ch. 4.

more acceptable by linking these with positive measures for integrating migrants. Migration controls were necessary because past migration had locked the UK, by 1964, into substantial future migration: the inevitably of family reunification meant that migration, even if the borders were entirely closed, would continue at around 30,000 per year. Positive measures were necessary because the 1964 campaign had made it abundantly clear that racism existed and threatened to destabilize British politics. Both immigration restrictions and anti-discrimination measures had independent arguments in favour of them. It was Soskice's contribution to link them together in a coherent framework, and to use this as an offer to the Conservatives to take immigration and race out of party politics.

The enactment of anti-discriminatory legislation refracted the liberal thrust of government policy, which had supported open borders before 1962, towards race relations policy. The 1965 Race Relations Act, and related measures announced in a White Paper of that year, provided the institutional basis for official measures against racism and in favour of integration. Liberal activists and sympathetic politicians, who before 1962 would have sought to maintain an open door to the Commonwealth, sought in the 1960s and 1970s to secure the consolidation and extension of this legislative framework.[9] The 1965 Act was followed by substantial extensions in 1968 and 1976; both became part of the bipartisan framework. Although, as evidence of the strange bedfellows encouraged by politics, the far left and the far right continue to attack the laws as ineffective, they enjoy broad support, and even a measure of official pride, in contemporary Britain.

IMMIGRATION POLICY AFTER THE COMMONWEALTH IMMIGRANTS ACT

Hugh Gaitskell's death in January 1963 meant that the new leader, Harold Wilson, faced the decision of whether to oppose the annual renewal of the

---

[9] The only exception is radical Marxists and other marginal partisans of open borders; when the liberal Institute of Race Relations reconciled itself to immigration controls in the late 1960s and concentrated its efforts on aiding the government in developing integration measures, it was part of a broader shift in liberal opinion from open borders to integration. Only the Marxist and radical fringe, which took over the Institute and took it, stripped of resources, out of policy altogether, remained partisans of open borders. On the split, see A. Sivanandan, *Race and Resistance: The IRR story* (London: Race Today Publications, 1974). On the Institute today, see L. Fekete, 'The Surrogate University', in C. Prescod and H. Waters (eds.), *A World to Win: Essays in Honour of A. Sivanandan*, special issue of *Race and Class*, 41, Nos. 1–2 (1999), 123–30.

Commonwealth Immigrants Act (in the Expiring Laws Continuance Bill). The moment contained a certain irony; Labour had demanded annual renewal in its opposition to the act, and the party was now forced to confront its own doubts about immigration in the public eye. Its clever solution was to offer support for renewal, but only if the Conservatives agreed to renegotiate the matter with the Commonwealth. The Conservatives rejected this offer, as Wilson no doubt knew they would, and Labour voted against renewal.[10]

Labour's fickle attitude towards immigration reflected its own contradictions on the matter. The intellectual and anti-colonialist element in the party instilled in Labour a powerful opposition to anything suggesting racial prejudice; immigration control was itself associated, though briefly, with such sentiment. Yet, the trade unionist element in the party harboured suspicions of large-scale immigration and integrative measures to cope with it. The Trades Union Congress (TUC) viewed race relations legislation as an interference in free collective bargaining,[11] and the workers at the grass-roots level instinctively viewed New Commonwealth immigrants, the majority of whom were unskilled, as a threat to their standard of living.[12] The TUC also complained that West Indian workers were reluctant to join unions, although it provided no figures to substantiate this claim.[13]

Despite its opposition to legislation on the matter, the TUC was formally opposed to any racial discrimination. It passed a resolution prohibiting discrimination on the grounds of race, but this prevented neither the practice

---

[10]   T. Benn, *Out of the Wilderness: Diaries 1963–1967* (London: Hutchinson, 1987), 76–7 and *LPA, Study Group on Commonwealth Immigrants: Minutes 10 February–6 June 1964.*

[11]   S. Castles and G. Kosack, *Immigrant Workers and Class Structure in Western Europe* (London: Oxford University Press, 1973), 141–2. Also see the *TUC Papers (TUC), Modern Records Centre, University of Warwick,* 805.91(1)2, 'Trades Union Congress: National Joint Advisory Council to the Minister of Labour', 22 July 1958, 805.9(1), 'Letter from General Secretary, TUC to Mr J. G. Stewart, Ministry of Labour', 28 Mar. 1957, and 805.9(1)VIII 'Trades Union Council: Race Relations Act', 3 July 1969. When race relations acts were passed in the 1960s, however, the Labour front bench persuaded the TUC, which was unenthusiastic, not to oppose the legislation. See E. Bleich, 'Problem-Solving Politics, Ideas and Race Policies in Britain and France' (Ph.D. dissertation, Harvard University, Apr. 1999).

[12]   R. Ramdin, *The Making of the Black Working Class in Britain* (London: Gower, 1987), 200. The first TUC action on immigration appears to have occurred on 1 Apr. 1955, when a deputation visited a minister. On 30 Apr. 1958, George Woodcock, later General Secretary of the TUC, wrote to the government, stating that the TUC membership was worried about the poor health of Indian and Pakistani immigrants and that the organization believed 'that the controls adopted by other Commonwealth countries should be studied and that it would be suitable for us to adopt some measures of control over would-be immigrants for whom no job is waiting or is likely to be available. We also ask you to consider including medical examination within these immigration controls.' *PRO, PREM 11/290*, 'Note on Trades Union Congress Representations about Commonwealth Immigrants', undated.

[13]   *PRO, CO 1031/3942*, Record of a Meeting held at the Colonial Office, 10 Mar. 1961.

of racism of the shop-floor[14] nor its institutionalization in the craft unions.[15] The latter held that anyone who belonged to a union was to serve an approved apprenticeship. 'Approval' was at the discretion of the union, and it allowed the widespread exclusion of New Commonwealth immigrants from the craft unions; two-thirds were estimated to have operated a 'closed shop'.[16]

By the time the Labour Party entered the 1964 election, the party platform stated that controls on the numbers of immigrants were necessary; no mention was made of Commonwealth negotiations.[17] This shift in Labour's policy has been traditionally explained as the consequence of Hugh Gaitskell's sudden death, an event that is believed to have removed the anchor of Labour's anti-restrictionist consensus and facilitated a policy reversal under Wilson.[18] Although it is true that Wilson and an influential circle of individuals—Richard Crossman, Roy Hattersley, and Frank Soskice—accepted entry restrictions as a political necessity,[19] it remains uncertain that Gaitskell would have maintained his uncompromising opposition. Those closest to him believe that the great increase in numbers would have ultimately driven him to accept immigration control.[20] Labour's realist volte-face had, however, not prepared it for the experience of Smethwick.

[14] There were a number of instances of explicit shop-floor racism. Two strikes in the 1950s captured popular attention: in Feb. 1955 workers at the West Bromwich Corporation began a series of token Saturday strikes to protest the employment of an Indian trainee conductor; seven months later, Wolverhampton transport workers banned all overtime to protest the increased use of black workers, and they demanded a 5 per cent 'colour quota' (there were 68 black workers out of a total of 900). In both cases, the Transport and General Workers' Union policy was one of non-discrimination. See Ramdin, *The Making of the Black Working Class in Britain*, 200–1.

[15] *TUC, 805.9(1)*, 'Coloured Workers', 15 Apr. 1955. It is also true, however, that certain local unions passed their own anti-discriminatory resolutions and urged the TUC to take a firm line against racism. See, for example, *805.9(1)*, Letter from Croydon Trades Council to Sir Vincent Tewson, General Secretary of TUC, 27 May 1958.

[16] E. J. B. Rose, et. al., *Colour and Citizenship: A Report on British Race Relations* (London: Oxford University Press, 1969), 313.

[17] See F. W. S. Craig (ed.), *British General Election Manifestos 1959–1987* (Aldershot: Dartmouth, 1990), 56. The party had reached this decision by at least Dec. 1963. The Home Policy Subcommittee, one of the NEC's two main policy-making committees, stated that 'The Labour Party accepts the need for control over the number of Commonwealth immigrants entering this country. The vital question is not control itself but how this control should be operated.' *LPA, NEC Minutes*, 'Home Policy Sub-Committee: The Labour Party and Commonwealth Immigration', Dec. 1963.

[18] N. Deakin, 'The Politics of the Commonwealth Immigrants Bill', *Political Quarterly*, 39 (1968), 25–45, 42. Also see Katznelson, *Black Men, White Cities*, 144.

[19] Messina, *Race and Party Competition in Britain*, 32.

[20] R. Jenkins, *Nine Men of Power* (London: Hamish Hamilton, 1974), 180; P. M. Williams, *Hugh Gaitskell: A Political Biography* (London: Jonathan Cape, 1979), 784; interview with Peter Shore. As I noted in the last chapter, Labour began to move away from its categorical opposition to the bill as it passed through Parliament. Denis Healey's final intervention was a restrained one, and the party refused to promise to repeal the act.

SMETHWICK AND THE POLITICS OF LEARNING

The incumbent in the Midlands constituency of Smethwick was Patrick Gordon Walker, a Labour veteran and Gaitskellite who had been tipped by Wilson to be Foreign Secretary. Although his majority had declined in the last four elections, Gordon Walker was expected to retain his seat in an election that seemed likely to produce a significant swing to Labour. The seat was in fact lost to Peter Griffiths, who placed immigration at the centre of an unashamedly racist campaign. Griffiths spoke of 'voters in their turbans and saris' deciding Smethwick's future, attacked Gordon Walker for his alleged indifference to the impact of immigration on the local economy, and made political capital out of Gordon Walker's opposition to the Commonwealth Immigrants Act.[21] At the campaign's nadir, he refused to disassociate himself from campaign posters that stated: 'If you want a nigger neighbour, vote Liberal or Labour.' The slogan, he told a *Times* correspondent on 8 March 1964, 'is a manifestation of the popular feeling. I would not condemn anyone who said that. I would say that is how people see the situation in Smethwick. I fully understand the feelings of the people who say it. I would say it is exasperation, not fascism.'[22] Gordon Walker was defeated by a 7.2 per cent swing to Griffiths, one which occurred against a national swing of 3.5 per cent to Labour. When Gordon Walker left for his home after conceding defeat, Griffiths' supporters gathered around the defeated Gordon Walker, jeering and chanting: 'Where are your niggers now, Walker?'; 'Take the Niggers away!'; 'Up the Tories!'

It is difficult to exaggerate the shock to Labour. On 11 September 1962, Gordon Walker had spoken to Gaitskell about the danger that Labour might lose Smethwick over the question of 'colour',[23] but no one had expected such a squalid campaign. Race also appeared to play a role, though an ambiguous one, in Southall, Perry Barr, and Eton/Slough; in the last Fenner Brockway, who had sponsored several private member bills against racial discrimination, lost his seat.[24] The reaction partly concerned the electoral consequences of

[21] See Foot, *Immigration and Race in British Politics*, 46, 63–79 and Messina, *Race and Party Competition in Britain*, 34–5.

[22] *The Times*, 'Immigration Main Issue at Election', 9 Mar. 1964.

[23] *The Private Papers of Patrick Gordon Walker*, GNWR 1/14 (Churchill College, Cambridge). Gordon Walker's diary, 1960–1.

[24] F. Brockway, 'Fenner Brockway Writes', *Tribune* (9 Oct. 1964), 9; Layton-Henry, *The Politics of Race in Britain*, 57; A. Nicholas, 'Immigration and the Election', *Tribune* (23 Oct. 1964), 8. The influence of race was not, of course, unmediated. Other factors competed with immigration/race, and two restrictionist Conservative candidates with long records of opposing Commonwealth immigration—Leslie Seymour and Norman Pannell—lost their seats. For an examination of the seats in which immigration and race were of central concern, see N. Deakin (ed.), *Colour and the British Electorate 1964: Six Case Studies* (London: Pall Mall, 1965).

immigration: Richard Crossman recorded in his diary that '[e]ver since the Smethwick election it has been quite clear that immigration can be the great-est potential vote-loser for the Labour party if we are seen to be permitting a flood of immigrants to come in and blight the central areas in all our cities,'[25] and others have concluded that Gordon Walker's defeat was of considerable importance in turning Labour to immigration control.[26] The lesson was about more than electoral considerations; it concerned fear of race as a political issue,[27] the role it could play the political process and the limits of any competition over an issue as emotional, divisive, and potentially ugly as race.[28] The lesson appeared to be confirmed a few months later, when Gordon Walker lost a 21 January by-election in Leyton and had no choice but to resign the Foreign Secretaryship. In retrospect, most agree that the loss of Leyton reflected carpet-bagging—Reginald Sorenson, a popular Labour MP, was given a peerage against his will and the wishes of the constituency—and Gordon Walker's poor campaigning skills.[29] But in January 1965, before the shock from Smethwick had worn off, the result was interpreted as further evidence of race's effect on politics and on the prospects of a party holding power with a tiny majority.

Labour's Response to Smethwick and the Immigration Issue

Wilson's response to Smethwick was decisive. He sent a telegram in the early hours of 16 October 1964 assuring Gordon Walker that he would retain his place at the Foreign Office, and he publicly paid tribute to the hapless man: 'The whole country knows why you lost and all honour to you. All your colleagues look forward to your early return to the House of Commons for neither the House nor the country can afford to be without your services.'[30] In Parliament, Wilson launched a stinging attack on Griffiths. In classic style, Wilson encouraged his opponents to provide the springboard for his assault: in the debate on the Queen's Speech, he noted that '[w]hen foreign Affairs are

---

[25] R. Crossman, *Diaries of a Cabinet Minister*, i: *Minister of Housing 1964–1966* (London: Hamish Hamilton and Jonathan Cape, 1975), 149–50.

[26] Messina, *Race and Party Competition in Britain*, 32.

[27] Confidential interview, interview with Peter Shore.

[28] There is a body of literature that views these fears as constructed; immigration and race were only 'problems' because political elites saw them as problems. For such constructivist approaches, see J. Solomos, 'From Equal Opportunity to Anti-Racism: Racial Inequality and the Limits of Reform', Policy Paper in Ethnic Relations No. 17 (Warwick: Centre for Research in Ethnic Relations, 1989).   [29] Interview with Peter Shore.

[30] *Private Papers of Gordon Walker, GNWR 1/16*, Telegram from Liverpool, 16 Oct. 1964, 2.34 a.m. Wilson is reported to have turned white upon hearing the Smethwick result. R. Pearce (ed.), *Patrick Gordon Walker: Political Diaries, 1932–1971* (London: The Historians' Press, 1991), 41.

debated my right hon. Friend the Foreign Secretary will not, I am sorry to say, be taking part in the debate.' This comment elicited predictable laughter, and the Prime Minister attacked:

I am surprised that hon. Gentlemen opposite should laugh at that, because the reasons why he will not be taking part—making every allowance for the freedom of electors to make their choice and the freedom of political parties to seek to influence that choice—will leave a lasting brand of shame on the Conservative Party. . . . Is [the Conservative Party leader] proud of his hon. Friend the Member for Smethwick? Does he now intend to take him to his bosom? Will the Conservative Whip be extended to him, because if he does accept him as a colleague he will make this clear: he will betray the principles which not only his party but the nation have hitherto had the right to proclaim. And if he does not, if . . . the right hon. Gentlemen [Sir Alec] takes what I am sure the country would regard as the right course, the Smethwick Conservatives can have the satisfaction of having topped the poll, and of having sent here as their Member one who, until a further General Election restores him to oblivion, will serve his term here as a Parliamentary leper.[31]

The attack was founded in Wilson's disgust with a contemptible campaign,[32] but it also reflected considerable generosity towards Patrick Gordon Walker. Gordon Walker was a member of the inner circle of Gaitskellites, and he made no attempt to hide his distaste for Gaitskell's unworthy successor. In his tribute to the fallen leader, he stated that '[n]o-one was a greater realist than Hugh Gaitskell but no-one was less of an opportunist. He fought for his profound beliefs regardless of consequence.'[33] The 'opportunist' line was a clear swipe at Harold Wilson.

Labour continued to keep Griffiths in its sights during the debate over the Expiring Laws Continuance Bill, when Michael Foot and Tom Driberg continued to attack Griffiths,[34] but the Commonwealth Immigrants Act, to no one's surprise, was none the less renewed.

The tone and language of Wilson's 'parliamentary leper' intervention was exceptional, and the anger behind it reflected a general distaste on Wilson's part for racial prejudice,[35] one that was widely held within the party. If Smethwick singled the potential for demagogues to exploit latent (and not so

---

[31] *Parliamentary Debates (Commons)* (701), cols. 70–1, 3 Nov. 1964. In the uproar that followed, Wilson refused to withdraw the statement.

[32] H. Wilson, *The Labour Government 1964–70: A Personal Record* (London: Weidenfeld & Nicolson, 1971), 29, interview with Peter Shore.

[33] *Private Papers of Gordon Walker, GNWR 1/14*, Tribute to Hugh Gaitskell, 19 Jan. 1963.

[34] *Parliamentary Debates (Commons)* (702), cols. 362–73 and 390–3, 17 Nov. 1964.

[35] Interview with Peter Shore; B. Pimlott, *Harold Wilson* (London: HarperCollins, 1992), 367.

latent) public hostility to unfettered immigration, it equally affirmed in Labour minds the necessity of turning attention to the position of New Commonwealth immigrants within the British community. After the election, Wilson assigned Maurice Foley, at the Department of Economic Affairs, the task of coordinating departmental activities relating to the integration of Commonwealth immigrants.[36] The Department of Economic Affairs (DEA) was a creation of Wilson's first government, and it was intended to execute a national plan (planning was, briefly, the rage in Labour circles) for transforming the UK into a 'high-investment, dynamic economy',[37] and to do so free from the interference of a sceptical Whitehall. The department, which was to be responsible directly to the Prime Minister and the Cabinet, proved ineffectual for a number of reasons, including Treasury hostility and a sterling-driven deflation that robbed planning of the necessary resources.[38] The DEA was none the less responsible for Labour's first efforts to tackle the matter of immigration. Foley was a well-liked, union-sponsored MP with political skill but no proficiency in economics.[39] At the same time, the Home Office viewed integration with suspicion (one Home Office official patronizingly advised the Prime Minister to 'gently discourage' Foley from demonstrating too much enthusiasm for the subject,[40] and Wilson was determined to keep the matter out of its hands.[41] It was a fairly limited affair; Foley operated with a tiny staff—Jack Howard Drake and Valarie Nicholls—that attempted to create informal contact and consultation with local government, churches, and prominent members of the immigrant community. But it was the beginning of more substantial efforts and belies the claims of critics that Labour did nothing to prevent deterioration in relations between immigrants and indigenous communities.[42]

---

[36] *PRO, PREM 13/382*, Letter from J. T. A. Howard-Drake to J. Trevelyan, 26 Mar. 1965.

[37] Thomas Balogh, economic adviser to Wilson responsible for creating a department with responsibilities independent of the Treasury, quoted in Pimlott, *Harold Wilson*, 278.

[38] A 1968 Mahood cartoon in *The Times* showed Roy Jenkins, then Chancellor of the Exchequer, as a seeing-eye dog pulling along a blind Harold Wilson clutching a DEA briefcase; the Prime Minister helplessly shouts 'Heel!' *The Times*, 26 Mar. 1968.

[39] He did, however, lobby for a thorough study of the economic advantages and disadvantages of Commonwealth immigration. See *PRO, HO 376/127*, 'Commonwealth Immigration,' C(65)111, 26 July 1965, *HO 376/127*, 'The Economic Implications of Commonwealth Immigration,' undated and *HO 376/127*, 'The Survey of Race Relations conducted under the auspices of the Institute of Race Relations', undated. The last was published as Rose et al., *Colour and Citizenship*.

[40] *PRO, PREM 13/382*, Letter to the Prime Minister, 24 Feb. 1965.

[41] Confidential interview.

[42] See A. Dummett and M. Dummett, 'The Role of Government in Britain's Racial Crisis', in L. Donnelly (ed.), *Justice First* (London: Sheed & Ward, 1969); and Foot, *Immigration and Race in British Politics*, 233–4.

THE ORIGINS OF THE 1965 WHITE PAPER AND THE RACE RELATIONS BILL

The results of the 1964 election provided an argument in favour of immigration restrictions, but of greater significance in the government's mind was the failure of the 1962 controls to reduce substantially the annual arrival of immigrants. Net immigration from the colonies and new Commonwealth in 1960 was approximately 58,000. Leaving aside 1961–2, during which rumours of impending control inflated the number of arrivals to 136,000, the figures for 1963 and 1964 were over 50,000. The numbers, which were believed by the public and many in both parties to be too high, were largely unaffected by the 1962 legislation. The Commonwealth Immigrants Act appeared, from a restrictionist point of view, to be singularly ineffective.

Central to its failure was the distinction between primary and secondary immigration. The 1962 Act allowed 20,500 to be admitted under Categories A and B of the labour voucher scheme (those with a job and those with skills, respectively) and issued Category C vouchers at a discretionary pace. Assuming an issue rate of 200 per week for Category C (a rate that was felt to be unduly restrictive by many at the time), approximately 30,000 'places' were reserved for immigrants with or without any familial connections to the United Kingdom. Yet, the act also guaranteed the entry of spouses, children under 18, and grandparents over 65, and it did so in the context of migratory patterns that had up to 1962 been dominated by the arrival of immigrants without their families.

The potential for continued heavy secondary immigration was grasped early in 1965 by the new Home Secretary, Frank Soskice. In a letter to Wilson on 4 January 1965, he argued that the United Kingdom, unless it withdrew the rights of dependants, was committed to an annual intake of approximately 30,000 dependants for the immediate future.[43] When Soskice presented the matter to the Cabinet later in the month, he raised further concerns about those who evaded the 1962 controls. These were individuals who either misrepresented their case at the ports (for example, claiming falsely to be students or dependants) or were admitted for a temporary period but decided later to remain in the United Kingdom (for example, students who finished their course and sought employment). There were no mechanisms to prevent the latter, and the former, although they could technically be deported by an order of the courts, were rarely discovered. Although immigration officers

---

[43]   *PRO, PREM 13/382*, Letter from Frank Soskice to the Prime Minister, 4 Jan. 1965.

could attach conditions to the entry of students and visitors, the weak enforcement mechanisms (tracking the individual down, securing a deportation order
from the courts), gave officers little incentive to do so. Soskice concluded that
'we shall not be able to deal effectively with the main body of those who
evade the control. . . . I think we should have a wider use of the power to
impose time limits on them, and better means of enforcing the limits imposed.
We need power to require Commonwealth citizens to leave identifying particu-
lars with immigration authorities and to register with the police; and the
Home Secretary should have the power to repatriate, without criminal
proceedings, a Commonwealth citizen who has outstayed the period for
which he has been admitted.'[44] Soskice accepted the Commonwealth
Immigration Committee's recommendation that there should be no further
legislation against immigration.[45]

Frank Soskice was widely regarded by members of the Cabinet and the
Home Office as an extremely incompetent Home Secretary.[46] He brought a
lawyer's pedantry to a job that required flexibility and decisiveness. During
the drafting of the Race Relations Bill, Soskice obsessed over the wording
and ground the work of his department to a halt as he did so.[47] At one departmental meeting, he examined twelve drafts with different wordings. An exas-
perated Attorney General, Elwyn Lloyd, said, with as much patience as he
could muster, 'pick one Frank, just pick one.'[48] Sandwiched between two
successful and respected Home Secretaries who made a mark on policy and
politics, R. A. Butler and Roy Jenkins, Soskice has largely been forgotten.[49]
Even race relations legislation, of which Soskice was the first author, is linked
in the public mind with Jenkins and the liberal hour.

Soskice was nonetheless the first person to make the equation between
tighter controls and positive measures as a means to managing the central
dilemma of any immigration policy: that any restriction was, in its effect, a
racialist (but not necessarily racist) exclusion.[50] In the letter to Wilson cited
earlier, Soskice called for a linking of the two sets of measures, the creation
of a sort of 'package deal': 'I mean the more or less simultaneous announcement by others of my colleagues and myself of a number of measures,
designed not merely to make the control effective, but to integrate the

---

[44] *PRO, CAB 129/120*, 'Cabinet. Commonwealth Immigration: Memorandum by the
Secretary of State for the Home Department', 29 Jan. 1965.

[45] *PRO, PREM 13/382*, Letter from Burke Trend to the Prime Minister, 30 Jan. 1965.

[46] Confidential interviews; Crossman, *Diaries of a Cabinet Minister,* i. 149. Quoting
Crossman: '[Soskice] is a disaster as Home Secretary and he has to deal with the hottest potato
in politics—the problem of immigration.'   [47] Confidential interview.

[48] Confidential interview.

[49] Along with Henry Brooke, Butler's immediate successor, who was also not respected.

[50] I discuss this distinction in the Conclusion.

coloured immigrants in a genuine sense into the community as first and not second class citizens.'[51] Soskice suggested all the components which were to become part of Labour's two-pronged strategy: a race relations bill, financial aid to communities for purposes of integration, amending the 1936 Public Order Act to prohibit racial incitement, the announcement of discussions with the Commonwealth and departmental measures in the fields of health, housing, and education. The Colonial Secretary, Anthony Greenwood, the Commonwealth Relations Secretary Arthur Bottomley, and the Minister for Overseas Development, Barbara Castle, were 'apprehensive' about any extension of control, administrative or statutory, and they insisted on two conditions: they must apply to the Old and New Commonwealth and aliens must not appear to be in a better position than Commonwealth immigrants. There was continuity in the approach of overseas departments to immigration controls under Labour and the previous Conservative government: the Colonial and Commonwealth Relations Offices insisted on precisely these conditions during the drafting of the Commonwealth Immigrants Act.

Labour's acceptance of control and its endorsement of race relations legislation had predated the election, and the election demonstrated the level of latent public hostility in certain sections of the electorate. It was Soskice who linked these three disparate pieces of the immigration puzzle into a single, coherent strategy and policy. Immigration restrictions and integrative measures could be presented as intellectually and politically linked, and both were explicable with reference to public opinion: the extension of control as the acceptance of its ultimate verdict, and the introduction of positive legislation to affect its content and check its most extreme manifestations.

RACE RELATIONS LEGISLATION

Legislation against discrimination on the grounds of race had first been considered by Macmillan's Conservative government. Fenner Brockway's tenacity in sponsoring such Private Members' Bills led the Home Office to give the matter some thought, or at least to adopt a position, and there was a small section in the Conservative Party, led by Nigel Fisher, which was supportive in principle of statutory prohibitions. In early 1960, Fisher suggested an amendment to the Public Order Act of 1936 to prohibit the distribution of racist leaflets. The act prohibited 'in any place or at any public meeting' the use of abusive or insulting behaviour with intent to provoke a

---

[51] *PRO, PREM 13/382*, Letter from Frank Soskice to the Prime Minister, 4 Jan. 1965.

breach of the peace, or whereby a breach of the peace was likely to result. Butler consulted the Home Office, which opposed the legislation because it would either be too limited to be effective or create an unjustifiable limitation on the freedom of contract,[52] and concluded that 'I do not think we should be justified at present in limiting in this way our traditional freedom of expression.'[53]

Labour committed itself to legislation outlawing racial discrimination, on the basis of Fenner Brockway's bill, on 15 February 1964.[54] A committee under the chairmanship of Professor Andrew Martin was then set up by the Society of Labour Lawyers to consider the matter. The Committee drew up a draft bill (which differed from Brockway's in that it left untouched discrimination in the sphere of private housing) that suggested the linking in the same bill of prohibitions on discrimination by public bodies (National Health Service, municipal housing, public transport, schools, and employment exchanges) with a strengthening of the Public Order Act.[55]

When Labour took office in 1964, the Home Office responded to the party's promise on race relations legislation with suspicion and uncertainty. Many within the department viewed the promise as the manifesto baggage of a naive party, and they saw it as their task to inject realism (which amounted to a profound scepticism) into Labour's plans.[56] Others were simply wholly uncertain of how to move forward. Legislation against racial discrimination was viewed as something alien to the English legal tradition, and there appeared to be no adequate British precedent from which guidance could be drawn.[57]

Soskice moved on legislation against racial discrimination early in 1965. After discussions with the Lord Chancellor and Law Officers, he secured the general agreement of the Home Affairs Committee at its 12 February meeting, and went to the Cabinet on 22 February. Soskice's proposals contained two elements: first, a prohibition on racial discrimination if practised in places to which the public have access—hotels, public houses, restaurants,

---

[52] *PRO, CO 1032/349*, 'Colour Discrimination', Interdepartmental Meeting, 28 Jan. 1960 and Letter from J. S. Bennett, 4 Jan. 1961. The Home Office also took the view, which was widely accepted in the 1950s, that legislation against discrimination was inherently ineffective because it could not change attitudes.

[53] *PRO, CO 1032/321*, Letter from R. A. Butler to Nigel Fisher, 27 Jan. 1960.

[54] *LPA, Study Group on Commonwealth Relations* (Minutes 10 Feb.–4 June 1964), 'Home Policy Committee. Race Relations: Interim Report on Bill to Outlaw Racial Discrimination in Public Places and Incitement to Racial Hatred or Contempt'.

[55] Ibid.   [56] Interview with a Home Office official.

[57] New York and Ontario had passed anti-discriminatory legislation, and these measures were examined by the Home Office before the 1965 Race Relations Act was passed.

and places of entertainment or recreation;[58] and, second, an extension of the Public Order Act to prohibit 'the dissemination of written matter which is threatening, abusive or insulting, with intent to provoke a breach of the peace or whereby a breach of the peace may be occasioned'[59] and the definition of it as an offence 'for a person, with intent to stir up hatred against an ethnic or racial group, to disseminate written matter, or in a public place or at a public meeting to use speech, which is threatening, abusive or insulting and likely to stir up hatred against that group on grounds of race or colour'.[60] The Cabinet accepted these principles, and the Race Relations Bill was prepared for presentation to Parliament.[61]

Labour presented its twofold strategy, and attempted to forge bipartisan agreement on it, in several stages. On 4 February 1965, Soskice told the House of Commons that he intended to tighten restrictions on the entry of dependants and that he was seeking powers to deport illegal immigrants, a power that was justified because of widespread evasion.[62] On 9 March, Wilson presented to Parliament the 'package deal' to which the Cabinet had agreed earlier in the year. Four measures were promised: (i) the appointment of Maurice Foley as minister in charge of coordinating action on assimilation and improving community relations; (ii) the introduction of a bill prohibiting racial discrimination and creating penalties for incitement to racial hatred; (iii) an examination of the mechanisms for controlling immigration in light of evidence suggesting a serious problem of evasion; and (iv)

[58] Soskice admitted that such discrimination was a small matter in comparison with the refusal of landlords to rent accommodation to lodgers of colour, but concluded that such discrimination could not be included in the legislation 'without interfering unjustifiably with the rights of the individual'. *CAB, 129/120*, 'Cabinet. Racial Discrimination and Incitement to Racial Hatred: Memorandum by the Secretary of State for the Home Department', 17 Feb. 1965.

[59] This would involve amending Section 5 of the act, which provided that '[a]ny person who in any public place or at any public meeting uses threatening, abusive or insulting words or behaviour with intent to provoke a breach of the peace or whereby a breach of the peace is likely to be occasioned, shall be guilty of an offence.' The penalties, which were increased under the 1963 Public Order Act, were a maximum of three months' imprisonment and/or a £100 fine on a summary conviction and twelve months' imprisonment and/or a £500 fine on conviction and indictment.

[60] *PRO, CAB, 129/120*, 'Cabinet. Racial Discrimination and Incitement to Racial Hatred: Memorandum by the Secretary of State for the Home Department', 17 Feb. 1965.

[61] The Trades Union Congress (TUC) was unhappy with the legislation, viewing it as interference in free collective bargaining. See Castles and Kosack, *Immigrant Workers and Class Structure in Western Europe*, 141–2. Also see the *TUC Papers (TUC), Modern Records Centre, University of Warwick, 805.91(1)2*, 'Trades Union Congress: National Joint Advisory Council to the Minister of Labour', 22 July 1958. It was unable, however, to prevent the Labour government from enacting either the 1965 legislation or its bolder 1968 extension. On this, see E. J. B. Rose et al., *Colour and Citizenship*, 529–31. For the TUC's reaction to the legislation at the time, see TUC, *805.9(1)*, II, III, and VIII.

[62] *Parliamentary Debate (Commons)* (705), cols. 1284–5, 4 Feb. 1965.

a mission to the Commonwealth with the aim of discussing matters of immigration control.[63]

On 23 March, when Thorneycroft initiated a parliamentary debate on immigration, the government struck a conciliatory tone that appeared to be reciprocated by the Opposition. The dual policy of maintaining tight controls while expanding efforts to integrate resident immigrants appealed to members on both sides; Nigel Fisher stated that 'I am myself a believer in a bipartisan approach to the problem. I think that as far as possible it should be taken out of party politics.'[64] Labour agreed, and Soskice concluded with a ringing endorsement of bipartisanship:

[T]here has been disclosed in the course of the debate a very great degree of unanimity on the broad aspects of the problem with which we are faced. . . . [First,] the Government accept that there must be—simply because of the scale of possible immigration—effective control of numbers. . . . [Second,] our aim should be to see that there is only one class of citizen, each with equal rights, each with equal respect, each with equal opportunity and each with an equal career of happiness and fulfillment in his life in the community. We all agree that we should aim [at] that.[65]

THE CONSERVATIVES AND THE AFTERMATH OF SMETHWICK

At first these measures met with limited initial interest in the Conservative Party, and the development of bipartisanship was far from linear. Labour felt the bruise of race at Smethwick, and it was eager to remove the matter from party competition. The Conservatives, by contrast, had no such immediate inclination. It would be incorrect to claim that Conservative Central Office or the party's front bench was pleased with the content of Griffiths's campaign; on the contrary, several Conservative members were as unhappy with their candidate's populist racism as Labour. But the Conservatives did not suffer politically from Smethwick, and they instinctively viewed themselves as the party that would not lose from immigration. The Conservatives had ended the right of all British subjects to enter the UK, and they considered extending the controls before they lost the October election.[66] Their position appeared

---

[63] *Parliamentary Debate (Commons)* (708), cols. 248–9, 9 Mar. 1965.
[64] *Parliamentary Debate (Commons)* (709), col. 385, 23 Mar. 1965.
[65] *Parliamentary Debate (Commons)* (709), cols. 443–4, 23 Mar. 1965.
[66] See deliberations of the Commonwealth Immigration Committee in *PRO, CAB 134/1468.* Henry Brooke, the Home Secretary, urged control for the same reasons that his Labour successor would: an excessive rate of arrival occasioned by a large number of dependants and evasions.

securely close to that of the (restrictive) median voter. The party would, however, soon come to accept Labour's bipartisan gestures.

The Conservative Party's response to Smethwick was ambiguous. Immigration surfaced sporadically during the campaign—the Prime Minister, Sir Alec Douglas-Home, claimed on 6 October that 300,000 immigrants would have entered the United Kingdom were it not for the Commonwealth Immigrants Act[67]—but the issue was not one of great national concern. The questions that dominated the last days of the campaign were prosperity and a strike on London's underground.[68] When Conservative Central Office was questioned over the 'If you want a nigger neighbour, vote Liberal or Labour' slogan, it quoted Douglas-Home's statement that 'I would most certainly deplore any attempt to create or exploit racial tensions for political purposes. . . . I personally deprecate the whole concept of racial discrimination, and I hope the exploitation of racial tension will play no part in the election campaign of any candidate,' but rather feebly added that in 'a great Party such as ours . . . there must be a certain liberty to practice,' and that, moreover, overcrowded housing conditions engender intolerance regardless of race.[69]

Despite the embarrassment of the party's patrician and liberal wings over Griffiths's campaign, the Conservatives saw some advantage in taking political issue with Labour's approach to immigration and race relations. Wilson's 'parliamentary leper speech', possibly unintentionally, had the effect of perpetuating the use of immigration as a chip in a game between the parties, and it encouraged the Conservatives to use the matter to their advantage.[70] In early 1965, Sir Alec Douglas-Home made four restrictionist demands: (1) the repatriation of all illegal immigrants; (2) government funds for those wishing to return; (3) statistics on dependants; and (4) a reduction in the numbers.[71] The call served to nullify any gains that might have accrued to the Labour Home Secretary's announcement that the numbers admitted under Category C (unskilled labour) would be reduced. It cannot be known if Sir Alec was motivated by a desire to create a competition between the two major parties over immigration or by the need to satisfy the demands of restrictionists within the Conservative Party who demanded a hard-line approach to immigration. In

He concluded: 'I do not think that things can be left as they are. The rate of net immigration is too great.' See 'Cabinet. Commonwealth Immigration Committee. Control of Commonwealth Immigration: Memorandum by the Secretary of State for the Home Department', 21 July 1964.

67 *Guardian*, 'Sir Alec ploughs through the din', 7 Oct. 1964.

68 *Guardian*, 'Sir Alec returns to the old themes,' 14 Oct. 1964.

69 'Racial Discrimination' (Conservative Central Office publication), 30 Apr. 1964.

70 *CPA, CRD 3/11/2*, Text of speech by Thorneycroft at Central Council meeting Westminster, 5 Mar. 1965.

71 *CPA, CCO4 9/225*, 'Extract from Speech by Sir Alec Douglas-Home to the Central Council Meeting', 6 Mar. 1965.

either case, the decision lent momentum to the latter. Douglas-Home replaced Edward Boyle, a liberal enthusiast for race relations legislation, as frontbench spokesman on Home Affairs with Peter Thorneycroft, an uncompromising restrictionist. Thorneycroft immediately demanded further legislation to restrict immigration, and he repudiated Labour's bipartisan overtures in March.[72] When Sir Cyril Osborne requested, yet again, leave to introduce a bill restricting all immigration with the exception of those with parents or grandparents born in the United Kingdom until local authorities had dealt with immigration, the front bench did not reject it outright. Instead, it maintained the content of the bill while encouraging Osborne to couch it in delicate wording, and it granted him permission to seek leave to introduce the bill.[73] The measure, however, did not gain the overwhelming support of the Opposition. In the absence of any whip, seven Conservative MPs voted with Labour, and approximately fifty members abstained or absented themselves from the vote.[74] The result was a refusal of leave to introduce by a majority of 261 votes to 162, i.e. ninety-nine votes.[75]

The Conservatives continued for a short while to tinker with the possibility of using immigration in party competition. In drafting the Report, Selwyn Lloyd expressed concern over the possibility of Labour adopting the Conservative's restrictionist stance,[76] and, had the report been enacted, would have retained a policy space between the parties. Although the Report, which Heath viewed as a candidate for inclusion in the next election manifesto,[77] claimed to base itself on a principle that was to inform both parties' policies—linking firm control with positive steps for integration—it was the document's recommendation that 'at least over a period of years the numbers entering do not exceed those returning' which captured attention.[78] The Report offered detailed proposals for integratory measures, including hostels for unmarried immigrants and additional staff for schools and a substantial increase in the grant to the National Committee for Commonwealth Immigrants (a body encouraging the integration of immigrants), but these were on the whole lost in the Press reaction to the 'one in, one out' proposal;[79] the *Guardian* and *Economist* were particularly scathing.[80] Sir Cyril, true to form, called for a

---

[72] S. Patterson, *Immigration and Race Relations in Britain 1960–1967* (London: Oxford University Press, 1969), 38.

[73] On the bill, see *The Economist*, 'The Osborne Affair', 6 Mar. 1965, 979–80.

[74] Ibid.   [75] Patterson, *Immigration and Race Relations in Britain*, 37.

[76] *CPA, CRD 3/11/2*, Letter from Edward Heath to Selwyn Lloyd, 3 June 1965.

[77] Ibid.

[78] *CPA, ACP/65/11*, 'Policy Group on Immigration—Interim Report', 14 July 1965. The Group's minutes and discussion papers are contained in *CPA, CRD 3/11/2*.

[79] Patterson, *Immigration and Race Relations in Britain*, 39.

[80] *The Economist*, 'Incoming Tide', 10 July 1965, 140.

ban on all immigration with the exception of students and professionals whose stay would be temporary. None of this, however, saw the light of day. Selwyn Lloyd's proposal was quietly dropped, and the 1965 Annual Conservative Party Conference was a moderate affair concentrating on the favourable aspects of integration.[81] The Conservatives' moderation was eased by Labour's articulation of its bipartisan offer.

THE RACE RELATIONS ACT

When Frank Soskice published his Race Relations Bill on 7 April 1965, it contained the provisions outlined in his February memorandum to the Cabinet: incitement to racial hatred, including through the use of written material, was to be a crime punishable by a fine of up to £1,000 and/or two years in prison, while discrimination in the provision of public services was to be illegal and punishable by fines up to £100. Prosecution in the latter could only be undertaken with the authority of the Director of Public Prosecutions. In introducing the bill's second reading, he justified it with reference to Labour's dual policy. The government's approach, Soskice argued, has two aspects. One is the exercise of an effective control on the numbers who come to our shores, and measures were announced on 4 February this year to achieve this. . . . The other aspect of our policy is that directed to achieving the task of settling the new arrivals into our community as in every sense first-class citizens. It is to the achievement of this task that the bill is directed.[82]

In addressing the government's bill, the Conservatives were divided between those associated with the Edward Boyle/Nigel Fisher position, which strongly advocated support for the bill, and those on the libertarian or restrictionist right, such as Enoch Powell and Sir Cyril Osborne, who demanded complete opposition to the bill. The Conservative front bench, eager to avoid a split over the issue, secured, through two Home Affairs Committee meetings, agreement to a compromise motion that deplored discrimination on

---

[81] Christopher Brocklebank-Fowler moved '[t]hat this Conference, recognising that firm restrictions on new entrants are now necessary to prevent exacerbation of the overcrowding problem in areas of immigrant concentration, urges that this must be coupled with positive and wide ranging measures for the integration of existing immigrants in the fields of housing, education, employment and the social services, backed up by the generous resources of the central Government.' The motion, which Thorneycroft welcomed, was carried by an overwhelming majority. *National Union of Conservative and Unionist Associations, 83rd Annual Conference*, 78–83.

[82] *Parliamentary Debates (Commons)* (711), cols. 926–7, 3 May 1965.

racial and religious grounds, but which still opposed the Race Relations bill because of its dependence on criminal sanctions.[83] Sanctions became a focal point of Conservative opposition to the bill during its second reading on 3 May 1965.[84]

The Conservatives' compromise position gave Labour, which was still interested in securing cross-party support for its bill, the opportunity to address the Opposition's criticisms while still maintaining the integrity of its anti-discriminatory legislation. While the Second Reading of the Race Relations Bill was carried with the criminal sanctions attached, Soskice struck a conciliatory note at the beginning of his opening speech: '[W]e will listen most closely to the arguments advanced in favour of the introduction of a conciliation process. If we feel that it is practicable and in the public interest, we will, either before or during the Committee stage, amend the Bill to give such effect as we feel able to the general wish of the House.'[85] Soskice had examined the issue of conciliation in advance of the second reading, although he originally conceived of it as a mechanism for addressing discrimination in additional areas, such as employment or housing, which he viewed as 'unsuitable' for treatment by the act's penal clauses.[86] Following the 3 May debate he reconsidered the issue, and agreed that it could replace criminal sanctions as the chief mechanism for combating racial discrimination.[87] The Conservatives' opposition to the penal clauses, as well as the sympathy of many Labour supporters to conciliation procedures as a 'first step' before recourse to the courts, led Soskice to amend the bill.[88]

The matter remained difficult for the Conservative Party. Criminal Sanctions were replaced by conciliation in the form of a Race Relations Board, which worked through local committees that reported to it. This

---

[83] Layton-Henry, *Politics of Immigration*, 126.

[84] *Parliamentary Debates (Commons)* (711), cols. 943–1062, 3 May 1965. Thorneycroft, early in the debate, begged to move that 'this House deplores discrimination whether on racial or religious grounds but declines to give a second reading to a Bill which introduces criminal sanctions into a field more appropriate to conciliation and the encouragement of fair employment practices while also importing a new principle into the law affecting freedom of speech [col. 943].'

[85] *Parliamentary Debates (Commons)* (711), col. 929, 3 May 1965.

[86] *PRO, PREM 13/383*, 'Note by the Secretary of State', Frank Soskice, 26 Apr. 1965.

[87] For an ideational account of the reasons behind this shift, see E. Bleich, 'Problem Solving Politics: Ideas and Race Policies in Britain and France, 1945–1998'. Paper delivered at the 'Politics and Ideas', Panel, 1998 Annual Meeting of the American Political Science Association, Boston, 3–6 Sept. 1998.

[88] *PRO, CAB 129/121*, 'Cabinet. Race Relations Bill—Conciliation Machinery: Memorandum by the Secretary of State for the Home Department', 18 May 1965. Quoting Soskice: 'The [3 May] debate served to confirm the general feeling in favour of conciliation machinery, with a preference that any proceedings that might follow failure of conciliation should be of a civil rather than criminal nature.'

concession to the Opposition made it, paradoxically, difficult for the Conservatives to hold this moderate position. Opposition to criminal sanctions united the Conservatives precisely because it was opposition; now that Labour had removed the policy space between themselves and the Conservative Party, members of the latter wished to press further amendments. The Shadow Cabinet agreed that, as their main objection had been addressed, the proper course would be to abstain from voting on the remaining stages of the bill; however, several Conservatives told the Chief Whip, William Whitelaw, that they intended to vote on precisely that in the Report Stage or the Third Reading. The Shadow Cabinet felt that this would undermine the fragile agreement among Conservative members, and would encourage those supportive of race relations legislation to respond with support for the government. There was a danger of a Conservative split, and the party responded,[89] successfully, by instructing the Whips to discourage all members from voting on the Bill.

THE MOUNTBATTEN REPORT

Early in 1965, after Soskice had presented statistics on secondary immigration, the government turned its attention to reducing the rate of arrival. Since further legislation had been ruled out by the Home Secretary in late January,[90] the government turned to the possibility of administrative restrictions. It was decided to send a mission to Commonwealth governments to determine their attitudes to further control and the possibility of exercising further restrictions by the Commonwealth governments. In implementing its plan, the government had an eye on its broader bipartisan objectives: Wilson suggested R. A. Butler as leader of the mission.[91] The signature of a former Conservative Home Secretary, a respected moderate who had instituted the first controls on Commonwealth immigration, would have lent considerable cross-party appeal to the proposals. In the event, Butler declined the invitation,[92] and

---

[89]   CPA, LCC 65/61, 30 July 1965. Quoting the document: 'Mr Whitelaw explained that several Members said they wanted to vote on some Amendments on the Report Stage, or on the Third Reading, and there was a danger that we would be split or even that there would be some Conservatives in the Government Lobby.' There was a great deal of emotion on both sides of the House, and part of the Whips' success lay in allowing feelings to cool before the Report stage.

[90]   PRO, CAB 129/120, 'Cabinet. Commonwealth Immigration: Memorandum by the Secretary of State for the Home Department', 29 Jan. 1965.

[91]   PREM 13/382, Letter from Derek Mitchell to D. J. Trevelyan, Lord President's Office, 8 Feb. 1965.

[92]   Apparently for health reasons. PRO, PREM 13/382, 'Commonwealth Immigration', 28 Feb. 1965.

Labour placed another figure of exceptional stature, Lord Mountbatten of Burma, in charge of the proceedings.

Mountbatten visited the capitals of Malta, India, Nigeria, Canada, Jamaica, Trinidad, and Cyprus and reported in June 1965. Pakistan refused to greet Mountbatten, and he met no success in encouraging the Commonwealth to limit emigration to the United Kingdom. The Report ignores this failure and offers the following recommendations:

(a) While the Government works to assimilate immigrants into the community, there should be a 'marked restriction' in the number of vouchers, to about 10,000 a year of which 6,000 should be reserved for Category A (those with jobs) and 4,000 for category B (those with skills). Category C (unskilled) should be abolished altogether, though this should not affect seasonal workers.

(b) The concessionary extensions to the statutory right of dependants between 16 and 18 should be withdrawn, but 'rare exceptions' on compassionate grounds should be within the discretion of the Home Secretary.

(c) The Home Secretary should be given power to repatriate Commonwealth citizens without the need for a criminal conviction or court recommendation [which was required under Section 6 (1) of the Commonwealth Immigrants Act, 1962].

(d) All immigrants, their dependants and students should have to pass a health check under the supervision of the British High Commission in their country of origin.

(e) Commonwealth visitors should be allowed in for six months, a length of stay that would give them a clear advantage over aliens, who are restricted to three months, and extensions should be liberally granted.[93]

The Report ended with a warning and, as it happened, a prophecy: 'I believe that these drastic restrictions will be accepted with understanding so long as they only remain in force during the breathing space needed for assimilation. If the full scale of restrictions is continued beyond the time period which Commonwealth countries understand I consider there will be a real risk that this could do lasting damage to Commonwealth relations.'[94] As it turned out, the Mountbatten mission was the last hurrah for the Commonwealth as a substantial influence on domestic British politics.[95] It was never again consulted on immigration control, and tributes to the Commonwealth ideal became less frequent and less convincing.

The influence of Mountbatten on the ultimate decision to restrict was

---

[93] In addition, entry certificates should be encouraged (though not required), High Commissions should be encouraged to vouch for bona fide students, and intending immigrants should be required to satisfy the British High Commission in their country of origin that they possess a level of English satisfactory to assimilate into British society.

[94] *PRO, PREM 13/383*, 'Copy of Minute from Lord Mountbatten of Burma to the Prime Minister', 13 June 1965.

[95] Layton-Henry, *Politics of Immigration*, 64.

minimal; it was taken while he was jetting between capitals. Herbert Bowden's Commonwealth Immigration Committee agreed to a reduction of Labour Ministry vouchers in April,[96] and the UK High Commissioners were told of it while the Mountbatten mission was under way.[97] The government took pains to ensure that this decision was not revealed to the Commonwealth governments, as it would have made a mockery of the notion of consultation underlying the mission.[98] Mountbatten's Report, nonetheless, had implications for the form of the White Paper.

The Commonwealth Immigration Committee examined Mountbatten's recommendations. The Committee was, overall, sympathetic to the Report's conclusions, but it differed on two points: (i) 10,000 vouchers per year was too high, and a more 'realistic' figure would be 7,500;[99] and (ii) although repatriation, following Mountbatten, should be possible without a criminal conviction or recourse to the courts, it should be tied to a right to appeal.[100] Some committee members expressed concern over two other aspects of the Report: (i) the possibility that the skill-based voucher system would 'cream off' Commonwealth citizens who were of value to their countries while placing unskilled aliens (who faced no quota) at an advantage vis-à-vis British subjects; and (ii) the possibility that the rigid nature of the categories and their skill bias would disproportionately harm small territories, the economies of which depended on their ability to send unskilled workers to the UK.[101] These concerns were registered, but they seem to have had little effect on the eventual proposals, a reflection, most likely, of the small number who shared them and the determination of the Home Office (and possibly the Ministry of Labour) to carry the reductions through.

---

[96] *PRO, PREM 13/383*, 'Confidential. Mr. McIndoe. Cabinet Office', 9 Apr. 1965.

[97] *PRO, PREM 13/385*, 'General & Migration', undated.

[98] Herbert Bowden, in typically understated official prose, noted that '[t]he introduction of such a radical change as we contemplate before the Mission had completed its task would cause considerable feeling in capitals the Mission had already visited, on the grounds that the British Government had not bothered to wait to hear the result of the discussions with the Mission before going ahead with a drastic new decision. On the other hand Governments still to be visited might well question the usefulness of the Mission and might even find difficulty in receiving the Mission if there were to be serious public reactions. In both cases the chances of our obtaining the active co-operation of Commonwealth Governments in checking evasion would be seriously affected.' For this reason, he concluded, no change should be introduced until Mountbatten returned. The contents of the Report, however, were irrelevant to the decision: 'This does not of course mean that we should not meanwhile press on with our efforts.' *PRO, PREM 13/382*, Letter from Herbert Bowden, 14 Apr. 1965.

[99] This figure, the Committee argued, should be checked against the arrival of aliens, which amounted to 9,000 in 1964.

[100] *PRO, CAB 129/121*, 'Cabinet. Commonwealth Immigration: Memorandum by the Lord President of the Council', 6 July 1965.

[101] Ibid.

Soskice suggested one more turn of the restrictionist screw. In keeping with his fears about the United Kingdom's commitment to the future immigration of dependants, Soskice argued for a distinction between the dependants of immigrants already in the United Kingdom, who should enjoy an unqualified right to enter the country, and the dependants of future immigrants whose (then) unqualified right to enter should be made conditional upon proof of adequate provision for housing. To restrict the rights of the former would be a 'breach of faith', while to maintain the rights of the latter without regard to the social consequences of their arrival, 'to allow dependants to come to overcrowded conditions in an atmosphere of developing ill will and friction with the indigenous population could I think be described as immoral.'[102] Soskice accepted the recommendation of an appeal machinery, but he felt that it should be limited to that available to aliens: with the exception of matters of security or criminal court recommendations, an immigrant resident in the UK for over two years could make an appeal to the Chief Magistrate. On the question of evasion, one (with numbers) of the two justifications for a reform of the administrative machinery, Soskice made a strong plea for increased powers: to deal with the chief cases of evasion—students and visitors who overstay—immigration officers must be able to limit to length of stay, to require registration with the police, to limit a student's study to a specific course, and so forth.[103]

The Cabinet considered Soskice's memorandum on 8 July. The paper was supported in the Cabinet by Wilson, Crossman, James Callaghan, and George Wigg.[104] Opposition to it came from ministers associated with the Overseas departments: George Brown, Barbara Castle, Tony Greenwood, and Arthur Bottomley; their wishes were overruled, except on the issue of dependants.[105] While the Cabinet accepted Soskice's basic endorsement of the Mountbatten Report, it rejected the central contention of his memorandum: that the social consequences of immigration necessitated a restriction of dependants' rights, current or future, to enter the country. They agreed to remove the discretionary right of those between 16 and 18 to enter the country, but maintained intact the right of spouses and children under 16 to enter the United

---

[102] *PRO, CAB 129/121*, 'Cabinet. Commonwealth Immigration: Memorandum by the Secretary of State for the Home Department', 7 July 1965. The change would have resulted in an equation of the rights of aliens' dependants with those of Commonwealth immigrants.

[103] Ibid.

[104] B. Castle, *The Castle Diaries, 1964–1970* (London: Weidenfeld & Nicolson, 1984), 50.

[105] Ibid., and Crossman, *Diaries of a Cabinet Minister,* i. 270–1. With the exception of Brown and the Lord Chancellor, who also weakly protested, the anti-restrictionists were all responsible for the Commonwealth and colonies.

Kingdom.[106] As a reflection of the side constraints on even British immigration policy, the Cabinet was united in the view that preventing family unification was morally unacceptable.

THE WHITE PAPER

The government's White Paper, 'Immigration from the Commonwealth',[107] was published on 2 August 1965. The paper followed the recommendations of the Mountbatten Report, Committee and Cabinet discussions, and it linked the extension of controls with the introduction of further positive measures. It contained two sets of provisions: on integration and control. The integration measures received little attention, but they included calls for increased use of migrants in the Health Service to address language difficulties, increased funds for hospitals in needy areas, and financial assistance for local authorities in which significant numbers of Commonwealth migrants lived. The paper also created the National Committee for Commonwealth Immigration (NCCI), replacing the Commonwealth Immigrants Advisory Committee set up in 1962. The NCCI was to promote the integration of immigrants through liaisons with existing local communities, the creation of new ones, the organization of conferences and workers in the field, and the examination of particular problems.

The heart of the paper, and the one that received the greatest attention, was control. Four measures were announced: the quota for Categories A and B was reduced to 8,500, including 1,000 that were reserved for Malta. No more than 15 per cent of Category A countries could go to any one country (this reflected the experience of the Commonwealth Immigrants Act; India and Pakistan took a disproportionate share under the 'first-come, first-served' system). Category C (unskilled) vouchers were abolished altogether.[108] The right of dependants under 16 to enter the UK was maintained, but the practice of allowing children between the age of 16 and 18 to join their parents on a discretionary basis was, except in cases of hardship, ended. There could be a health check for any immigrant, both in the country of origin and at the UK port, but entitled dependants could not be refused entry on medical grounds. Immigrants whose residence in Britain was less than five years were subject

---

[106]   *PRO, CAB 129/122*, 'Cabinet. Commonwealth Immigration: Memorandum by the Lord President of the Council', 23 July 1965.

[107]   HMSO, Cmd. 2739, Aug. 1965.

[108]   Because of the volume of applications for Categories A and B, no Category C vouchers had been issued since Sept. 1964.

to deportation at the Home Secretary's discretion if they evaded immigration controls. Immigration officers could require immigrants suspected of evasion to register with the police.[109]

Among Labour's traditional supporters in the Press, the reaction was one of disappointment and hostility. The *New Statesmen* accused the government of entrenching a 'colour bar'[110] and the *Tribune* called the paper 'as white as leprosy'.[111] Three members of the British Overseas Fellowship, which was created by the NEC to assist immigrants and advise the government, resigned in protest.[112] The Labour Member for Wandsworth Central, Dr David Kerr, criticized it in the Commons as a 'grave and bitter disappointment', while Lord Brockway wrote in the *Tribune* (13 August) that he felt ashamed to be a member of the party.[113] Crossman recorded the extent of party anger: 'I can't overstate the shock to the Party. This will confirm the feeling that ours is not a socialist Government, that it is surrendering to pressure, that it is not in control of its own destiny.'[114] The publication of the White Paper was a moment of disillusionment, in some quarters profound, among Labour's supporters in the liberal Press, the immigrant communities and those that worked with them and on the back benches.

By contrast, the paper was a clear success with the voters and the Opposition. The public responded with an overwhelming endorsement: Gallup published a poll that estimated its approval rating at 87 per cent.[115] The paper's aims were threefold: to bring the rate of arrival down to what was believed by Labour (and particularly the Home Office) to be a manageable number, to satisfy public opinion[116] and to contribute to the bipartisan policy developed by Labour since coming to power. Crossman, noted for his frankness, makes this point quite clear: 'Politically, fear of immigration is the most powerful undertow today. . . . *We felt we had to out-trump the Tories by doing what they would have done and so transforming their policy into a bipartisan policy' (emphasis added).*[117]

---

[109]   Instructions to Immigration Officers were issued a year later. See *PRO, CAB 129/126*, 'Cabinet. Revised Instructions to Immigration Officers: Memorandum by the Secretary of State for the Home Department', 12 July 1966.

[110]   M. S. Jones, 'Britain accepts a colour bar,' *New Statesman* (6 Aug. 1965), 175–6.

[111]   6 Aug. 1965. The act was also condemned by the *Spectator*, which derided it as a 'surrender to racial prejudice, vilely dressed up as reasonable' ('Keeping Britain whitish', *Spectator* (6 Aug. 1965), 168).

[112]   *LPA, Race Relations Working Group Minutes and Papers, 6 April–22 June 1967.*

[113]   Patterson, *Immigration and Race Relations in Britain*, 46.

[114]   Crossman, *Diaries of a Cabinet Minister,* i. 299.

[115]   *Attitudes toward Coloured People in Britain* (London: Gallup, 1982), question 50.

[116]   *PRO, CAB 129/121*, 'Cabinet. Commonwealth Immigration: Memorandum by the Secretary of State for the Home Department', 7 July 1965.

[117]   R. Crossman, *Diaries of a Cabinet Minister,* i. 299.

The strategy was a success. The Conservatives welcomed the White Paper in Parliament,[118] and approached the 1966 election with a policy broadly similar to Labour's. The Conservative Policy Group abandoned the 'one-in, one-out' principle and avoided any further mention of restriction on numbers.[119] Edward Heath, the new party leader, made it clear that there would be no repeat of Smethwick in the 1966 election, and when the election manifesto, *Action not Words*, was published it promised a combination of restrictionist and integrationist measures: the strengthening of health checks, the introduction of a probationary period on which an immigrant's stay was conditional, better statistics on entry, the provision of funds for voluntary repatriation, ensuring that all immigrants were treated with respect and without discrimination and the provision of 'special help' for those areas with a high concentration of immigrants. In a policy document that could have been written by either party, the Shadow Cabinet stated that:

[a] society must have new entrants, but entry must be sensibly controlled if the entrants and the country to which they come are to benefit. The Conservative Party stands firm on a two-fold policy for immigrants: (i) positive steps must be taken to fit into our community the immigrants already there; (ii) firm control must be established for the entry of new immigrants, and for the conditions under which they enter.

The passage concluded smugly with a reference to the cross-party agreement that had emerged: '[w]e welcome the Labour Government's belated conversion to this humane and socially responsible point of view.'[120]

---

[118] *Parliamentary Debates (Commons)* (717), col. 1061, 2 Aug. 1965.

[119] *CPA, ACP 3/14*, 'Party Policy on Immigration and Race Relations', undated. (Previously filed as *ACP 67/37*).

[120] *CPA, LCC* 65/42, 'Policy Document: Breakthrough for Britain', 9 Sept. 1965.

7

The Kenyan Asians Crisis of 1968

IN late February 1968, there was a sense of panic among the Asian community in Kenya. The euphemistically termed 'Africanization' policies pursued by the Kenyan government had for several years been designed to drive them out of key positions in the economy. Asians had found that their work permits were no longer renewable; they were restricted to certain sectors of the economy; they were sacked from the civil service. Until 1968, their ultimate security had been guaranteed by their possession of British passports, which gave them unrestricted entry into the United Kingdom. On 22 February, this guarantee collapsed; the Home Secretary, James Callaghan, announced that the British government would no longer respect the Asians' passports. Just over a week later, legislation ending the Asians' unqualified right to enter went into force, and on 1 March the fully booked aeroplanes that had been carrying Asians to the UK for months were turned away. Some 200,00 individuals holding only British citizenship were abandoned, effectively stateless, in Africa or India, and some of these individuals are still waiting to enter the United Kingdom today.[1]

The passage of the Commonwealth Immigrants Bill, 1968 was among the most divisive and controversial decisions taken by any British government. For some, the legislation was the most shameful piece of legislation ever enacted by Parliament, the ultimate appeasement of racist hysteria.[2] For others it was the Labour Party and, particularly, Callaghan at their finest—purposeful and decisive in the face of immense pressure, and at last in touch with the working- and lower middle-class voters to whom the government owed its office.[3]

---

[1] Under 1981 legislation, they and others were given British Overseas Citizenship (BOC); the new status did not affect their right to enter the UK. It is roughly estimated that there are 50,000 BOCs in the world, including Asians and others. Interview with an Immigration and Nationality Directorate official, Home Office, Jan. 1999.

[2] This position was taken by Iain Macleod, Sir Edward Boyle, Nigel Fisher, and Ian Gilmour in the Conservative Party and by Andrew Faulds (a Birmingham MP), Michael Foot, Anthony Lester, and Shirley Williams in the Labour Party. See Kenneth O. Morgan, *Callaghan* (Oxford: Oxford University Press, 1997), 309–10.

[3] Within the Labour Party, the legislation enjoyed majority support among Cabinet ministers (with the exception of those specified in fn. 2) though many of them probably viewed it as a regrettable necessity rather than a cause for joy. The bill had strongest support, again with the

PLEDGES, LOOPHOLES, AND OBLIGATIONS

The Kenyan Asians episode was a political crisis of tremendous significance, politically and intellectually. Politically, it was of immeasurable consequence for the life chances of Asians who were unable to scramble through the closing door; intellectually, it is a sort of prism through which several broader currents of post-war British political history are illuminated.[4] Most importantly, the episode raises the question of the government's obligations to what one Conservative Party researcher later called the 'detritus of Empire':[5] individuals who found themselves without local citizenship following the colonies' independence. At the time, the debate among politicians, intellectuals, activists, and the broader public focused on the existence, content, and status of a 'pledge' allegedly made by the Conservative government in 1963, at Kenyan independence. Those opposed to the 1968 legislation maintained that it violated a commitment made to minority communities in Kenya at the time of its independence, when the Asians were deliberately exempted from immigration controls instituted by 1962 legislation controlling Commonwealth immigration. Those supporting the government retorted that no enforceable pledge had been made (though some non-enforceable assurance may have been foolishly given), and that the Labour government was both entitled and obligated to restrict the flow of Asians entering the UK with British passports. It was entitled because no parliament can bind its successors, and it was obligated because the overwhelming majority of the British public demanded restrictions on Asian entry. The debate about the Labour government's obligations, and the Conservative government's promises, is very much alive today.

The episode also highlights the fact that, from the point of view of British politics, the Commonwealth was by 1968 in its twilight. The party that had a year earlier claimed that the Commonwealth was 'the greatest multi-racial association the world has ever known',[6] was now stripping British subjects possessing only British citizenship of the fundamental right linked with this

exception of Andrew Faulds, among MPs such as Richard Crossman representing constituencies (notably in the Midlands) with a high concentration of Commonwealth migrants. Interview with Peter Shore, Sept. 1995; Richard Crossman, *The Diaries of a Cabinet Minister,* ii: *Lord President of the Council and Leader of the House of Commons 1966–68* (London: Hamish Hamilton and Jonathan Cape, 1976), 679; Morgan, *Callaghan*, 308–9.

   [4] I discuss these at greater length in R. Hansen, 'The Kenyan Asians, British Politics, and the Commonwealth Immigrants Act, 1968', *The Historical Journal*, 43, No. 3 (1999), 809–34.
   [5] *Conservative Party Archives (CPA), Bodleian Library, Oxford, CRD 3/16/4,* 'Memorandum by Patrick Cosgrave for Edward Heath', 19 Mar. 1970.
   [6] *Labour Party Archives (LPA),* National Museum of Labour History, Manchester, *Race Relations* (July 1967).

citizenship, and it was doing so in response to public opposition to the entry into Britain of non-whites. If there was ever a moment confirming that the Commonwealth—the 'great and glorious heir of Empire', as Powell acidly referred to it—was no longer a political entity and ideal for which British politicians were prepared to make domestic sacrifices, it was 1968. The fact that the legislation was passed within a year of Callaghan's devaluation of the pound, which was a great disappointment to those countries in the sterling area,[7] and of the Labour government's unsuccessful application to join the European Economic Community (EEC), confirms the importance of 1968 as a landmark year in the withering of the Commonwealth.

Finally, the crisis casts light on competing strains within the 1960s Labour Party. The success of Roy Jenkins in securing parliamentary approval for progressive legislation on a range of social issues secured him the undying support of liberal intellectuals, journalists, and activists intoxicated by the heady optimism of the 'liberal hour', but it alienated Jenkins and his supporters from working-class and middle-class voters who held conservative views on homosexuality, race relations legislation, and non-white immigration. For Jenkins, the first was a matter almost purely of individual choice, while immig-ration and race were to be managed by an enlightened elite leading and shaping public opinion.[8] By contrast, Callaghan exhibited a profound distaste for what he viewed as the moral permissiveness manifested in premarital sex, gay and lesbian relationships, and the use of soft drugs, and he viewed immigration as, in the words of his biographer, 'an issue to be handled in a way attuned to public opinion, rather than on the basis of abstract liberal political theory'.[9] There is little doubt that public opinion, Labour's traditional supporters and much of middle-class England sided with Callaghan. During the passage of the Commonwealth Immigrants Bill, Gallup and National Opinion Polls (NOP) found support for the bill among 69 per cent of respondents, with greatest support among the aged and working class.[10] The 1968 immigration act was the product of a Home Secretary who, though viewed with intellectual disdain by Jenkins, closely reflected the preferences of this core constituency. After indulging a year of Roy Jenkins's social liberalism, the party had returned to its roots.

This chapter will concentrate on the first of these issues, reconsidering a public debate that took place between Iain Macleod and Duncan Sandys in

[7] S. Strange, *Sterling and British Policy* (London: Oxford University Press, 1971); Morgan, *Callaghan*.

[8] R. Jenkins, *A Life at the Centre* (London: Macmillan, 1991), 188–9.

[9] Morgan, *Callaghan*, 308.

[10] *Coloured People in Britain* (London: Gallup, 1982), question 56; NOP quoted in *LPA, Study Group on Immigration*, 'Public opinion and immigration, by Dr. Mark Adams', Jan. 1969.

1968. In 1968, the sharpest debate about the government's obligations to British Asians in Kenya occurred, oddly, not between representatives of opposing political parties but between two members of the Conservative Shadow Cabinet. Iain Macleod, who accelerated the African decolonization process during his 1959–61 tenure as Colonial Secretary, argued that the Labour government was bound by a solemn pledge made by him and his party; Duncan Sandys (with Enoch Powell's support), Colonial Secretary from 1962 to 1964, argued that James Callaghan and the Labour government were free to satisfy public demands for restrictions. Neither man wavered from his uncompromising position, and both went to the grave claiming that the other was palpably mistaken.

This chapter attempts to resolve the debate between these two individuals and to comment on the broader issues raised by it. There are two questions underlying the Sandys/Macleod argument. First, why was it that the Kenyan Asians were able to enter the United Kingdom in the late 1960s despite the introduction of immigration control on the whole of the Commonwealth in 1962? Was their exemption the result of accident or design? Second, whether or not the Asians were first subject to controls in 1962, did the Conservative government promise them, at independence or perhaps before, that they would be allowed to enter the United Kingdom if the Kenyan government discriminated against its minorities? Answering the first question requires attending to the path-dependent effect of the British Nationality Act, the second to the intentions of British politicians as documented in official sources.

These questions are addressed in three sections. The first section briefly examines the origin of the Asian community in Kenya, considers the Asians' position within Britain's pre- and post-war imperial nationality frameworks, and traces the events leading up to their exclusion from the United Kingdom. The second pays particular attention to the arguments made by Iain Macleod in a public intervention in the midst of the crisis. Macleod argued at the time that the government had foreseen the possibility of a Kenyan Asian migration to the United Kingdom and had specifically exempted them from immigration controls; Sandys entirely denied this claim. The section examines the evidence Macleod cited to support his argument, and it argues that this evidence does not prove that the British government made any pledge to the Asian community in Kenya. The third section argues that Macleod's position is none the less tenable, though not for the reasons he put forward in the 1960s. Contrary to what is widely believed,[11] and what Macleod seemed to

---

[11] It is frequently claimed that the Kenyan Asians' passports were exempted from 1962 immigration controls. See A. Dummett and A. Nicol, *Subjects, Citizens, Aliens and Others* (London: Weidenfeld & Nicolson, 1990), 199; C. Holmes, *John Bull's Island* (Houndmills:

suggest in 1968, Asians in Kenya and other East African nations were placed under immigration restrictions first enacted against Commonwealth immigrants in 1962. Their 'release' from these controls was not, as many have claimed, a matter of design; it was rather the unintended consequence of the mechanism chosen to restrict immigration in 1962. The 1962 decision (determined by the complexity surrounding the replacement of BNA 1948) to base immigration controls not on citizenship, led, in the context of an exlusivist definition of post-independence citizenship in Kenya, directly to the Asians' exemption from the 1962 controls. It was a consequence, however, that was recognized by civil servants at the time of the Commonwealth Immigrants Act, 1962's passage and accepted by key figures in the British Cabinet, including Duncan Sandys himself. The position taken by Sandys and the majority of the Conservative Party in 1968 was, behind the safety of the Official Secrets Act, a betrayal of commitments made and pledges given only a few years earlier.

THE KENYAN ASIANS: THE JEWS OF AFRICA?

Asians had lived in East Africa for centuries before European powers divided the continent amongst themselves, but the majority of the Asian community arrived after the expansion of British hegemony over the area from the mid-nineteenth century.[12] As in the rest of East Africa, they came to Kenya as labourers[13] and traders. After the Second World War, they were to be found in all occupations: in business, in the police force, in the bureaucracy, and the professions, both in Nairobi and the townships.[14] Their commercial skills contributed to the economic development and prosperity of Kenya and the rest of East Africa,[15] and their success bred suspicion and resentment. The

Macmillan, 1988), 265–7; D. Mason, *Race & Ethnicity in Modern Britain* (Oxford: Oxford University Press, 1995), 28; John Solomos, *Race and Racism in Contemporary Britain* (London: Macmillan, 1989), 54. Others note that the Asians were free from immigration control after independence, but they are not clear on whether the Commonwealth Immigrants Act, 1962 applied to them and they often imply that the Asians' exemption was intentional. See D. Hiro, *Black British, White British* (London: Paladin, 1991), 212; K. Paul, *Whitewashing Britain* (Ithaca, NY: Cornell University Press, 1997), 179.

[12] D. A. Seidenberg, *Uhuru and the Kenya Indians* (New Delhi: Vikas Publishing House, 1983), 3–9.

[13] Indian 'coolies' were instrumental to the construction of the Kenyan railway. They were brought to camps along the line, where they lived an isolated existence until the railway was completed. Then, as dictated by their contracts, they returned to India, or they took the option of local discharge from indenture. J. Murray-Brown, *Kenyatta* (London: George Allen & Unwin, 1972), 64.   [14] Ibid. 83.

[15] J. S. Mangat, *A History of the Asians in East Africa* (Oxford: Clarendon Press, 1969), ch. 1.

nineteenth-century British explorer, Sir Richard Burton, echoed widely held
sentiment when he derided Indian merchants as 'local Jews',[16] one sect of
which was 'unscrupulous and one-idea'd in the pursuit of gain', given to
using false weights and measures and receiving stolen goods.[17]

In terms of nationality, Kenyan Asians, along with all other members of the
colonies, were British subjects before the War, citizens of the United
Kingdom and colonies after. Kenya became independent in 1963, and it
altered its nationality law accordingly. Individuals of African descent, and
others whose families had long lived in Kenya, acquired citizenship automatically. All others, including the majority of the Asians, were given two years
to apply for Kenyan citizenship. Dual citizenship was not allowed (CUKC).[18]
The UK put little if any pressure on the Asian and European communities to
apply for local citizenship. Both were slow to do so, and the majority opted
to retain their CUKC status. Out of approximately 185,000 Asians and 42,000
Europeans, fewer than 20,000 had submitted applications by the deadline.[19]
Those who remained in Kenya after December 1965 continued to work, but
their place within post-independence Kenya was precarious, and it was
resented—at times bitterly—by Africans. Large numbers of the African
community believed that Asians had not participated in the struggle for independence,[20] and that they used their economic position to exploit the
Africans.[21] Whichever citizenship the Asians opted for served as a confirma-

---

[16]   The phrase 'Jews of Africa', frequently applied to the Asians, has possessed varied
connotations. It was originally coined by European settlers as a term of disparagement channelling prejudices commonly held about European Jews against the Asians (Seidenberg, *Uhuru
and the Kenyan Asians*, 14). Following the expulsions of Asians from East Africa, the phrase
has been closer to an expression of sympathy, linking the irrational bigotry aimed at a successful European minority (and its ultimate consequence) with that experienced by the East African
Asians.

[17]   Quoted in Mangat, *A History of the Asians in East Africa*, 22.

[18]   Kenyan constitution, Section 2 (5). From 1948 until 1981, British citizenship was
formally entitled 'citizenship of the United Kingdom and colonies'. The nationality status
(though not the same rights after 1962) was shared by Britons and 'colonial' subjects. Also see
CPA, LCC (68) 169, 'Immigration of Asians from Kenya', 9 Feb. 1968. In this text, I use the
terms 'CUKC', British citizenship, and British passport interchangeably.

[19]   Ten thousand of these were in the last month (Donald Rothchild, *Racial Bargaining in
Independent Kenya* (London: Oxford University Press, 1973), 188). Statistics on the Asian presence in Kenya were inadequately kept, so these figures should be viewed as conservative estimates.

[20]   In fact, at least part of the Asian elite in Kenya supported the independence movement.
The African nationalist elite, however, was unwilling to accept Asians as equal partners in the
independence movement. See Mangat, *History*, ch. 6 and, on the Freedom Party, Seidenberg,
Uhuru, ch. 7.

[21]   This suspicion reflected in part the division of labour in Kenya. As the colony developed,
Asians assumed the role of 'middlemen' purchasing African farmers' goods and selling them in
large urban markets. As the African farmers never met the consumers who bought their product,
they easily believed that the Asians were reaping huge profits at their expense. These feelings

tion of these views. Those who failed to apply for citizenship confirmed in African minds Asian disloyalty to the Kenyan *Gemeinschaft*, while those who did apply were believed to have done so for purely strategic reasons.[22] Many of those who applied for citizenship met obstacles and delays,[23] and large numbers of their applications for citizenship were simply never processed. Although the exact reasons for this administrative failure are uncertain, it is almost certain that Kenyan hostility towards Asian naturalization led civil servants to ignore deliberately many Asian applications.

Although Asians with Kenyan citizenship enjoyed some statutory protection (though little social acceptance),[24] those without soon felt the tightening vice. Their work permits were gradually withdrawn, and they found themselves squeezed out of the Kenyan economy. The Kenyan Immigration Act, 1967 required all those without Kenyan citizenship to acquire work permits;[25] a Trade Licensing Act passed in the same year limited the areas of the country in which non-Kenyans could engage in trade; [26] and Asians in the civil service were sacked in favour of Africans.[27] Without a future in Africa, and with no right (or, in many cases, strong inclination) to migrate to India or Pakistan,[28] they began to travel to England. In early 1967, Kenyan Asians were arriving at the rate of approximately 1,000 per month.[29]

seemed to be confirmed by the Europeans' and Asians' economic progress relative to the African farmers, and the last saw the Asians as the cause of their poverty. Seidenberg, *Uhuru*, 12–13. On the role of the British in creating this stratification, see O. Nnoli, *Ethnic Politics in Nigeria* (Enugu, Nigeria: Fourth Dimension, 1978), ch. 1.

[22]   D. Rothchild, 'Citizenship and National Integration: The Non-African Crisis in Kenya', in *Studies in Race and Nations* (Center on International Race Relations, University of Denver working papers), 1/ 3 (1969–70), 1.

[23]   R. G. Gregory, *Quest for Equality: Asian Politics in East Africa, 1900–1967* (Hyderabad: Orient Longman, 1993), 99.

[24]   Under the Kenyan constitution (discussed below), Asians (and all others) born in Kenya to at least one parent born there become automatic Kenyan citizens (Rothchild, *Racial Bargaining*, 40). Citizenship did not provide a full guarantee against discrimination, as many Asians suspected it would not. Non-Africans with citizenship were at times denied permits, and a number of Asians were stripped of their citizenship and deported stateless for having 'shown themselves by act and speech to be disloyal and disaffected towards Kenya [Section 8 (1) (a) of the Kenyan constitution]'. See Rothchild, 'Citizenship', 20.

[25]   Gregory, *Quest*, 99.

[26]   A. Dummett and A. Nicol, *Subjects*, 199. For a discussion of the Asians' ability to carry on in Kenya despite Africanization, see R. L. Tignor, *Capitalism and Nationalism at the End of Empire* (Princeton: Princeton University Press, 1998), chs. 10 and 11.

[27]   D. Himbara, *Kenyan Capitalists, the State, and Development* (Boulder, Colo.: Lynne Rienner, 1994), 116–17.

[28]   India was in fact suspicious of their permanent entry, particularly in large numbers. *PRO, PREM 13/2157*, Notes of meeting between Colonial Office and T. N. Kaul, Indian Foreign Secretary, 20 Feb. 1968.

[29]   Home Office statistics cited in *The Times*, 'Citizens from Kenya', 16 Feb. 1968.

LABOUR AND THE COMMONWEALTH IMMIGRANTS ACT, 1968

The first signs of the Kenyan Asians crisis appeared while Roy Jenkins was still Home Secretary. In 1967, when some 13,600 Asians arrived in Britain,[30] Jenkins, indecisively, brought the issue to an October Home Affairs committee meeting.[31] It decided that the Home Secretary was to 'work out appropriate policies and consider the practicality of legislation'.[32] *Fortuna*, in the form of a 1967 devaluation crisis, spared Jenkins a gruelling decision.[33] In the early hours of 14 November 1967, Wilson, Callaghan, and their advisers agreed to devalue sterling from US$2.80 to $2.40. Callaghan had been the last to accept the argument in favour of devaluation. He had promised on several occasions that sterling's value against the American dollar would be maintained, and the decision was a tremendous personal blow.[34] He insisted on resigning from the Treasury, and Wilson, to avoid a massive Cabinet shuffle (and the promotion of Anthony Crosland, still a serious challenger on the right of the party), gave Callaghan the Home Office and brought Jenkins to the Treasury.[35]

When Callaghan entered the Home Office, he was under intense emotional strain. The devaluation debacle had thrown him into the blackest gloom,[36] and he was determined to avoid a situation in which he would again be a slave to events. It was in this context that the government passed the Commonwealth Immigrants Act.

When Callaghan arrived at the Home Office, officials believed that approximately 2,000 Asians per month were leaving for Britain.[37] Stories of their arrival dominated the news, and the 'flood' that had been predicted in

---

[30] Home Office statistics.

[31] Crossman, *The Diaries of a Cabinet Minister*, ii. 526.

[32] Ibid. At this point, there was at least some opinion within the Home Office in favour of legislation. See *PRO, HO 376/125*, 'Asian Immigration from East Africa', T. Fitzgerald, Sept. 1967 and (more equivocally) 'Application of Immigration Control to Certain Citizens of the United Kingdom and Colonies', Note by the Home Office, undated. In both documents, the major argument in favour of control was that legislation might be needed to prevent a deterioration of race relations; Callaghan later chose this as his chief justification for a restrictive bill.

[33] J. Campbell, *Roy Jenkins* (London: Weidenfeld & Nicolson, 1983), 93. Jenkins had let slip in April 1967 that if 100,000 Asians had tried to enter Britain, he would have had to revise legislation governing their movement. The comment caused further alarm in East Africa. *PRO, HO 376/125*, 'Jenkins warning alarms Asians', 24 Apr. 1967 (cut out of the *Observer*).

[34] J. Callaghan, *Time and Chance* (London: Collins, 1987), 214–25.

[35] Ibid. 222.   [36] Morgan, *Callaghan*, 274.

[37] Callaghan, *Time*, 264.

anti-immigrant propaganda and speeches seemed to manifest itself. British viewers saw nightly pictures of Asians scrambling for tickets in Kenya, forming long queues at airports and pouring off planes in the UK.[38] The public demanded that they be stopped. [39]

Callaghan responded swiftly and rushed a restrictive bill through Parliament. Normally the matter would have gone to a Home Affairs committee, but a special Cabinet committee on immigration was set up, on 13 February, with Callaghan in the chair. He dominated the proceedings and was contemptuous of his critics; according to Crossman, the Home Secretary dismissed anyone opposing him as a 'sentimental jackass'.[40] The committee meeting was an extraordinary moment. The party that had championed the Commonwealth ideal of racial equality and interracial cooperation, the party that had bitterly attacked the Commonwealth Immigrants Act, 1962, and the party that had justified opposition to Rhodesia's Unilateral Declaration of Independence (UDI) on the grounds of opposition to racism was on the verge of passing legislation denying entry to British citizens because of the colour of their skin. As Crossman put it, '[a] few years ago everyone there would have regarded the denial of entry to British nationals with British passports as the most appalling violation of our deepest principles. Now they were quite happily reading aloud their departmental briefs in favour of doing just that.'[41]

In a Cabinet memorandum, Callaghan defended the legislation as necessary because,

Our best hope of developing in these Islands a multi-racial society free of strife lies in striking the right balance between the number of Commonwealth citizens we can allow in and our ability to ensure them, once here, a fair deal not only in tangible matters like jobs, housing and other social services but, more intangibly, against racial prejudice. If we have to restrict immigration now for good reasons, as I think we must, the imminent Race Relations Bill will be a timely factor in helping us to show that we are aiming at a fair balance all round. Conversely, I believe that the reception of the Race Relations Bill will be prejudiced in many

---

[38] Dummett and Nicol, *Subjects*, 200.

[39] See the public opinion poll, *Coloured People in Britain* (London: Gallup, 1982), question 56 and NOP (quoted in *LPA, Study Group on Immigration* 'Public opinion and immigration, by Dr. Mark Adams', Jan. 1969) indicating 72 and 69 per cent support, respectively. Also see Callaghan, *Time*, 267. To be sure, the public is constituted in part by politicians whose privileged position may allow them to shape it. Another politician more beholden to abstract principles might have attempted to move public opinion in the direction of a more migrant-friendly stance. None the less, there can be little doubt that Callaghan's actions enjoyed the support, as measured by public opinion data, of a majority of Britons in the late 1960s.

[40] See Crossman, *Diaries*, ii. 679.   [41] Ibid.

minds, and support for it weakened, if people think that the numbers entering are unlimited or unreasonably high.[42]

In an attached annex, Callaghan made two other arguments in favour of legislation. The first, which testifies Callaghan's indifference over international law and the rights of citizenship, was that the Asians had 'no greater claim on merits' to settle in the United Kingdom than have Commonwealth citizens living in independent Commonwealth countries or CUKCs living in colonies.[43] The second was that, as the Asians contributed to the total number of 'immigrants' arriving each year, they added to strains in the schools, youth employment, and local housing.

At the 15 February Cabinet meeting, uncompromising opposition to Callaghan came from the Commonwealth Secretary, George Thomson, who officially recorded his dissent.[44] Michael Stewart, the Foreign Secretary, argued that a final appeal should be made to Kenyatta, the Kenyan leader. The argument was still overwhelmingly in favour, however, until Jenkins, to the surprise of the other ministers, agreed with Stewart, and argued for delay. The Prime Minister sided with Callaghan,[45] but the Cabinet agreed to send Malcolm Macdonald, the UK's special representative in East Africa (and former colonial governor), to Nairobi with the aim of securing Kenyatta's cooperation in stemming the outflow.[46]

When the Cabinet met again on 22 February, Macdonald reported that Kenyatta had categorically refused to compromise.[47] Callaghan demanded immediate legislation,[48] and his position was resisted only by George Thomson, who argued again against the bill.[49] Jenkins made a final appeal for a yearly figure of 2,000 immigrants (the level before the rush began) but Wilson silenced the debate.[50] The quota would remain at 1,500. Barbara Castle, once a passionate defender of Commonwealth immigration and of the Commonwealth, was absent from the previous meeting and fell asleep at this one.[51] All ministers, whatever their doubts, fell in behind the decision.[52]

---

[42]   *PRO, CAB 129/135*, Home Secretary's memorandum C(68) 34, 12 Feb. 1968. Also see *PRO, HO 376/118*, Letter to Dr David Pitt, drafted for the Home Secretary's signature, undated.

[43]   *PRO, CAB 129/135*, Annex to Callaghan's memorandum, 12 Feb. 1968.

[44]   *PRO, CAB 129/135*, Commonwealth Secretary's memorandum C(68)35, 12 Feb. 1968.

[45]   Crossman, *Diaries*, 685.

[46]   Barbara Castle, *The Castle Diaries, 1964–1970* (London: Weidenfeld & Nicolson, 1984), 377, *The Times*, 'Rapid rise in influx from Africa', 16 Feb. 1968.

[47]   Castle, *Diaries*, 377; *PRO, PREM 13/2157*, Telegram from Macdonald, 19 Feb. 1968.

[48]   *PRO, CAB 129/136*, Home Secretary's Memorandum on East African Asians C(68) 39, 21 Feb. 1968.   [49]   Castle, *Diaries*, 377.   [50]   Ibid. 378.

[51]   Ibid. 377–8.   [52]   Interview with Peter Shore, Sept. 1995.

Kenyan Asians who knew no other citizenship than British would no longer have access to the UK.

From that moment, the pace quickened. The Conservative Shadow Cabinet had agreed on 21 February to support a phased entry of Kenyan immigrants if talks with Kenyatta failed.[53] When Callaghan announced the government's intention to introduce a bill after the 22 February Cabinet meeting, Quintin Hogg responded sympathetically.[54] The panic in Kenya intensified; British Asians in Nairobi tendered their resignation, gathered what few belongings they could, and left the country within twenty-four hours. By noon on the day following the announcement of the immigration bill, all direct flights from Nairobi to London were fully booked until early March, and connecting flights were filling quickly.[55] On 27 February, the Conservative Shadow Cabinet agreed to support the government's bill.[56] Macleod again made clear his intention to vote against any restrictive measure.[57] Edward Boyle had expressed unease about the discriminatory nature of the bill,[58] and he and Robert Carr made their support conditional on no Conservative vote against the government's promised Race Relations Bill, which strengthened a similar act adopted in 1965. The Conservatives supported the second reading of the bill, but no whip was used. Fifteen Conservatives, including Macleod, Nigel Fisher, Norman St John-Stevas, and Michael Heseltine, voted against it. The second reading of the Commonwealth Immigrants Bill was moved on 27 February, and it was passed by Parliament on 1 March 1968.[59]

The bill restricted the rights of Asians to enter the United Kingdom by adding an additional prerequisite for entry. In addition to holding a passport issued under the authority of London or by Dublin, those exempted from control must have had a 'qualifying connection' to the United Kingdom: only individuals, or their children or grandchildren, born, naturalized, or adopted in the United Kingdom could enter the country. As the vast majority of Kenyan Asians enjoyed no such connection, their right to enter the United Kingdom was effectively withdrawn. In addition to the quotas under the 1962 legislation, the 1968 Act allowed 1,500, a figure slightly higher than Callaghan's preferred 1,000, Kenyan Asian heads of households and

---

[53] *CPA, LCC 68/218,* 'Leader's Consultative Committee', 21 Feb. 1968. Macleod made it clear that he would vote against the bill.

[54] *Hansard (Commons)* (759), col. 661, 22 Feb. 1968.

[55] *The Times,* '4,000 Expected on Extra Flights', 24 Feb. 1968.

[56] M. Thatcher, *The Path to Power* (London: HarperCollins, 1995), 145; *CPA, LCC 68/219,* 'Leader's consultative committee', 27 Feb. 1968.

[57] Thatcher, *Path,* 145.

[58] *Edward Boyle papers,* the Brotherton Library, University of Leeds, *MS 660/28031,* Letter from Edward Boyle to A. J. Doherty, 27 Feb. 1968.

[59] *Hansard (Commons)* (759), cols. 1241–368, 27 Feb. 1968 and col. 1917, 1 Mar. 1968.

dependants (i.e. approximately 6,000 to 7,000 in total) to enter the UK each year.[60]

Like immigration restrictions in 1962 and 1965, the legislation was loathed by liberal opinion and loved by the public.[61] Students, migrants, civil libertarians, and immigrant organizations organized mass protests.[62] Anthony Lester successfully challenged the act before the European Commission on Human Rights. The National Committee on Commonwealth Immigrants (NCCI), which advised on Commonwealth immigration and made recommendations on local community development,[63] accused the government of irreparably damaging race relations and hinted at collective resignation.[64] Callaghan was undaunted. The public demanded action, he was under pressure from Labour MPs and others from the Midlands, and he claimed—though the argument was self-serving—that a failure to act could encourage racism in Britain.[65] The Home Secretary took the decision in favour of restrictions without consulting the NCCI, and when he met them on 27

[60]   Those Asians who left Kenya after 1 Mar. 1968 without an entry certificate were refused entry to the UK and had no right to return to Kenya. As a result, individuals were jetted back and forth between the two countries until the Home Office secured Kenyan agreement to accept the return of Asians without certificates. Interview with a Home Office official, Aug. 1995.

[61]   Gallup, which tracked public attitudes from 1958 to 1982 (*Coloured People in Britain* (London: Gallup, 1982), found consistent majority support for immigration restrictions. Support for the Commonwealth Immigrants Act, 1962 ranged from 62% to 76% (question 35); support for 'a strict limitation on the number of immigrants' from the Commonwealth was 87% in 1965 (question 50); support for the Commonwealth Immigrants Act, 1968 was 72% (question 56); and support for the Immigration Act, 1971 was 59%, with 25% not knowing (question 85). In 1968, *The Times* and the *Spectator* accused the government of shirking an obligation willingly accepted by the British government in 1962. See *The Times*, 'Hasty law makes bad cases', 23 Feb. 1968 and the *Spectator*, 'A shameful and unnecessary act', 1 Mar. 1968.

[62]   *The Times*, 'Demonstrator tears up her British passport', 26 Feb. 1968.

[63]   E. J. B Rose et al., *Colour and Citizenship* (London: Oxford University Press, 1969), 522. The Home Office, in an effort to ward off criticism from the Community Relations (liaison) Officers, sent a letter to each claiming that the only reason the bill had been enacted was to prevent a deterioration in race relations (*PRO, HO 376/118*, Letter from David Ennals, 13 Mar. 1968). The file contains many responses. One of those receiving letters, Ann Dummett, later became one of the sharpest critics of the government. She writes of her disappointment with the 1968 legislation in M. Dummett and A. Dummett, 'The Role of Government in Britain's Racial Crisis', in   C. Husband (ed.), *'Race' in Britain: Continuity and Change* (London: Hutchinson, 1982).

[64]   *The Times*, 'Race relations work put back 10 years!', 2 Mar. 1968; *PRO, HO 376/125*, 'Statement by the Archbishop of Canterbury, Chairman of the National Committee for Commonwealth Immigrants', 27 Feb. 1968. Only two resignations in fact occurred. Richard Titmuss claims to have played a role in this, cynically admitting to the government that he made a 'melodramatic' statement to the press in order to retain the confidence of black members of NCCI. *PRO, PREM 13/2157*, Letter from the Lord President of the Council to Harold Wilson, 8 Mar. 1968.

[65]   *PRO, CAB 129/135*, 'Memorandum by the secretary of state for the Home Department,' C(68) 34, 12 Feb. 1968. Callaghan, *Time*, 264–5.

February, he found it difficult to contain his impatience. The decision of the European Commission on Human Rights, whose negative decision had been anticipated by the government,[66] was simply ignored.[67]

THE ORIGINS OF THE KENYAN EXEMPTION

With this political history in the background, it is now time to return to the two questions raised at the outset of the chapter—the reasons for the Asians' ability to circumvent the 1962 immigration controls and the question of pledges made by Macmillan's last Conservative government. Behind the controversy surrounding the 1968 legislation lay disagreement and confusion about the source of the Asians' right to enter the United Kingdom. Public debate developed in a curious manner. The front bench of the Labour Party, despite its professed commitment to the Commonwealth, was publicly—and it seems privately—united in support of the legislation.[68] It was joined, in keeping with the bipartisan consensus that characterized the parties' approach to immigration in the late 1960s, by the leader of the Conservative Party and the majority of the front bench. As a result, the fundamental questions concerning the United Kingdom's obligation to the Commonwealth, the status of a pledge that might have been given by the Conservative government and the implications of international law principles on/against statelessness were addressed by two members of the Conservative Party: Iain Macleod, and Duncan Sandys.

Sandys, who had served as Commonwealth and Colonial Secretary in the Conservative government, argued that he and his government had 'certainly never intended to provide a privileged backdoor entry into the U.K.'.[69] A few

---

[66] The Attorney-General noted in a memorandum to the Cabinet that the European Commission on Human Rights (which first hears individual petitions) or the European Court of Human Rights might deem the legislation a violation of article 3 of the fourth protocol (right of a national to enter his/her territory) or article 8 (right to respect for family life). He noted, however, that the UK had not ratified the protocol, and that, though it would be a 'serious step', the government could simply refuse to obey the committee of ministers (which receives the Commission's report) or the Court. *PRO, CAB 129/135*, Attorney-General's memorandum on the immigration legislation, C(68) 36, 14 Feb. 1968.

[67] The case did not reach the European Court of Human Rights because the UK did not challenge the decision. In Feb. 1975, Roy Jenkins, again Home Secretary, raised the quota to approximately 5,000 individuals per year with the goal of speeding the Asians' entry to the UK. For the European Commission's decision, see *East African Asians* v. *United Kingdom* European Human Rights Reports 3 (1981), 76–103. I owe my thanks to Lord Lester of Herne Hill QC for clarifying this issue.   [68] Interview with Peter Shore, Sept. 1995.

[69] *Daily Telegraph*, 4 Feb. 1968.

days later, Enoch Powell, who would later deliver the 'rivers of blood' speech, publicly endorsed Sandys's position.[70]

Iain Macleod, previously a close friend of Powell, fellow founding member of the 1950s 'One Nation' Group, and Colonial Secretary in this decade, came as close as he politely could to calling Sandys a liar. He argued that the Conservatives had willingly accepted an obligation to all CUKCs in Kenya that they were now bound to fulfil. Under the pretext of responding to Duncan Sandys attempt to initiate a private member's bill, Macleod sent an open letter for publication in the *Spectator*.[71] He wrote to Sandys that

[t]he true question must be whether such a [restrictive] Bill as you propose would break an undertaking given freely by this country and her Conservative Government. More specifically did you give your word? Did I? . . . If I understand your position correctly it is . . . that 'it was certainly never intended to provide a privileged back-door entry to the UK.' Leaving aside the emotive words that is exactly what was proposed: special entry in certain circumstances which have now arisen. We did it. We meant to do it. And in any event we had no other choice. . . . We cannot ignore the past nor the pledges we gave. In what we did for the minorities communities we were supported by all political parties and by the press. . . . It is, of course, true that no one said in terms to the Asian community 'we are providing for you a privileged backdoor entry, etc.' But your Kenyan constitution is devastatingly clear. So is Hansard. So are all the statutes. And so is, therefore, my position. I gave my word. I meant to give it. I wish to keep it.[72]

Duncan Sandys denied the charge: 'I', he argued, 'can assure the House that no such pledge was given, either in public or in private';[73] James Callaghan argued that it was a 'loophole' in the 1963 Kenya Independence Act that gave all inhabitants of the territories the right to a British passport on request;[74] and Enoch Powell claimed until his death to be entirely mystified by Macleod's intervention.[75]

---

[70]   E. Powell, speech made at Walsall, 9 Feb. 1968. Reproduced in full in B. Smithies and P. Fiddick, *Enoch Powell on Immigration* (London: Sphere, 1969), 19–22.

[71]   Cleverly, Macleod sent the letter *before* the next Shadow Cabinet meeting (21 Feb. 1968), but—because of printing time—it did not appear until after the meeting (23 Feb. 1968). Macleod was able to criticize the Shadow Cabinet's call for 'phasing the entry of these immigrants' without being accused of either (*a*) attempting to influence the Shadow Cabinet decision by speaking in advance of it or (*b*) violating collective solidarity by breaking with the decision afterwards. R. Shepherd, *Iain Macleod* (London: Pimlico, 1995), 495.

[72]   *Spectator*, 23 Feb. 1968, 225–6.

[73]   *Parliamentary Debates (Commons)*, (759), col. 1274, 27 Feb. 1968.

[74]   Callaghan, *Time*, 264. The term 'loophole' was used frequently at the time. David Steel, who claimed that '[n]ever has such a mischievous and misguided piece of legislation been introduced into Parliament and then steamrollered through in record time as the Commonwealth Immigrants Act, 1968,' agrees with Callaghan's interpretation. See David Steel, *No Entry* (London: C. Hurst & Co., 1969), 63 (quotation from the preface).

[75]   Interview with Enoch Powell, Aug. 1995.

The debate over the 1968 Act has remained largely where Macleod and Sandys left it in 1968. Scholars have generally endorsed Macleod's position, but they have not furnished the evidence that would carry his argument against Sandys's.[76] It is still, as it were, Macleod's word against his. In the last section of the chapter I provide primary evidence that partially resolves the argument in favour of Macleod, although his 1968 argument would have to be modified. The exemption of Kenyan Asians from the 1962 Commonwealth immigration act resulted *unintentionally* from the mechanism on which the act based immigration control. As this outcome was an accident, Macleod's argument that the British government 'meant to do it' seems exaggerated. Nonetheless, primary evidence establishes that the British government—and Duncan Sandys himself—both recognized and agreed to respect the Asians' exemption from the 1962 controls. In denying this de-cision, Sandys appears to have, as Macleod all but claimed he had, lied, or at the very least very selectively remembered his party's very recent history.

Before turning to these documents, it is worth noting that the legal texts cited by Macleod himself in his letter to the *Spectator* do not, in fact, support his argument. The texts he cites—the Kenyan constitution, the statutes, and Hansard—are anything but 'devastatingly clear'. The Kenyan constitution gives no guarantees to citizens of the United Kingdom and colonies. It grants citizenship automatically to those born in Kenya of at least one parent born there,[77] makes the acquisition of Kenyan citizenship conditional on the renunciation of all other citizenships,[78] and provides CUKCs, Irish citizens, and residents the opportunity to apply for citizenship.[79] The constitution grants to all Kenyans the status of 'Commonwealth citizen', and it recognizes all British subjects as Commonwealth citizens,[80] but it provides no guarantees to anyone not acquiring Kenyan citizenship. It is of course silent on the rights of Commonwealth citizens in the United Kingdom, as authority over the matter rested in Westminster alone.

The British statutes also contain no promises. Macleod cites three: the British Nationality Acts, 1958 and 1964, and the Kenya Independence Act, 1963. The first allowed CUKCs in Ghana, which gained independence in

---

[76] See, for example, Spencer, *British Immigration Policy*, 142.

[77] Kenyan constitution, Section 1. This citizenship scheme was in fact more inclusive than what Kenya originally wanted. Kenya, like Uganda before it, first proposed a citizenship scheme granting citizenship only to Africans. The British government, notably the Commonwealth Relations and the Colonial Office, insisted on its modification. See *PRO, HO 344/177*, Letter from J. M. Ross to Governor's Office, Nairobi, 26 Aug. 1963.

[78] Kenyan Constitution, Section 12.   [79] Ibid., Section 2 (4).

[80] Ibid., Section 9 (1) and (2).

[81] Section 2 (1) of the Kenya Independence Act, 1963 added Kenya to the list of Section 1

1957, to retain this citizenship if their family had been in the country for less than three generations, and allowed individuals with an 'ethnic' connection to the UK to acquire CUKC. It was passed, however, in 1958, when all British subjects still enjoyed unrestricted entry to the United Kingdom. All CUKCs outside the United Kingdom came under control through the 1962 Commonwealth Immigrants act. As this latter act took precedence over previous legislation, the provisions of the 1958 Act grant no right of entry to the Kenyan Asians.

Section 3 of the Kenya Independence Act, 1963 ensured that anyone not acquiring Kenyan citizenship would retain CUKC.[81] This is the broad provision to which Callaghan refers.[82] The British Nationality Act of 1964 extends the right to reacquire CUKC to two categories: (i) those who could not have become or remained a citizen of an independent Commonwealth country without making such a renunciation and (ii) those individuals, and their spouses, whose father or grandfather was born in the United Kingdom and colonies or in a protectorate state, was registered or naturalized as a CUKC, or acquired British subjecthood through the annexation of a territory.[83] The latter legislation enabled (usually white) British settlers in any colony, protectorate, or protected state to reclaim British[84] citizenship. It also, through provisions for those who had no choice but to renounce CUKC in order to acquire local citizenship, allowed those few Kenyan Asians (under 20,000) who had successfully applied for Kenyan citizenship to renounce it and resume their British citizenship.

Despite their expansive approach to citizenship, the acts did not attribute the right of entry to Kenyan Asians. The acts granted to the Asians and others the right to acquire a British passport, but this passport did not, by itself, guarantee entry to the United Kingdom. As discussed, one of the peculiarities of British nationality law and immigration policy was that, between 1962 and 1983, colonial British subjects still retained British citizenship (CUKC), but did not have the right freely to enter the UK. Nothing in either the British Nationality acts or the Kenya Independence Act gave, as Macleod claimed, Kenyan Asians unrestricted access to the UK.

It is unclear why Macleod cites these acts, when they do not, from a legal point of view, support the argument he wished to make. Macleod's argument

<hr/>

(3) countries of the British Nationality Act, 1948 (for the independent Commonwealth countries). From 1963, Kenyans were considered as CICCs by BNA 1948. In addition, Kenya did not tolerate dual nationality, and it would have been impossible to be both a CUKC and a Kenyan citizen.   [82]   Callaghan, *Time*, 264.

[83]   British Nationality Act, 1964, Section 1 (1) *(a)* and *(b)*.

[84]   For papers concerning the settlers in Kenya, see *PRO, HO 213/1685*.

[85]   Given the strength of the 'settler lobby' within the Conservative Party in the 1960s, intu-

really rests not on the content of these documents, but on the question of intent. His central claim is that the Conservative government knew of the Asians' situation and accepted their right to come to the UK should the situation in Kenya sour: 'I gave my word. I meant to give it. I wish to keep it.' This is the flaw in his argument. None of Macleod's evidence demonstrates that the British government intended either to exempt Asians from immigration controls in 1962 (it did not) or to offer them free entry to the United Kingdom in the event of African hostility and discrimination.[85] It could be that constitutional conventions against revealing the substance of Cabinet discussions, which were stronger in years before Crossman's diaries, led him to provide this not entirely sound evidence. In any case, their availability now, in conjunction with other official documents, provides a degree of retrospective credence to Macleod.

BRITISH PASSPORTS, THE 1962 ACT, AND KENYAN INDEPENDENCE

To develop this point, it is necessary to return to the Commonwealth Immigrants Act, 1962, and to consider the question of why the Asians found themselves exempt from immigration control in the 1960s. The legislation was passed under an assumption that had guided British policy on imperial nationality since the War. The British Nationality Act, 1948 was based on the belief that all CUKCs outside the UK would move from the status of dependent colonial subjects to citizens of an independent Commonwealth country.[86] The eventual independence of the colonies was envisaged by British policy-makers (although they expected the process to take much longer than it did), and all persons within a given colony, including Kenyans of course, were to graduate from citizenship of the United Kingdom and colonies to citizenship of an independent Commonwealth country. As this process repeated itself throughout the Empire, United Kingdom citizenship—possessed exclusively by those born within the UK or direct descendants of those born

ition suggests that the eyes of the Conservative government in 1963 and 1964 were on the fate of Europeans, their 'kith and kin', within Kenya, and not on that of the Asians. During the second reading of the Kenya Independence Bill, very little was said about the Asians. See *Parliamentary Debates Commons* (684), cols. 1329–400, 22 Nov. 1963. Sandys discussed the opportunity (enshrined in the British Nationality Act of 1964) for Britons to reclaim CUKC status after its renunciation (cols. 1393–4); no mention was made of the Asians as such.

[86] Interview with Lord Merlyn Rees, Dec. 1995, *PRO, HO 213/1704*, 'Draft note as a basis for a submission to Ministers', 18 Aug. 1952, 'British Nationality Act, 1948', undated.

[87] Interview with Sir Geoffrey Otton (retired Home Office official), Aug. 1995.

therein—would emerge gradually, as the residual remaining after all colonies had become independent nations.

This assumption proved to be false for reasons that were central to the Kenyan Asians crisis. At independence, as seen, non-African CUKCs generally chose not to opt for Kenyan citizenship, retaining instead their CUKC status, and others who applied for Kenyan citizenship were denied it. The Home Office attempted to ensure inclusive citizenship laws after independence, but, keen to secure a rapid settlement, did not make agreement conditional upon them,[87] and the Africans themselves were adamantly opposed to inclusive citizenship. Ghana, Nigeria, Sierra Leone, Uganda, and Tanganyika also refused to grant automatic citizenship to Asians born in these countries.[88] When the Home Office addressed Kenyan nationality, it felt that Uganda and Tanganyika created a force of precedent it was unable to resist.[89] For its part, the Commonwealth Relations Office felt that the citizenship provisions in Kenya, which were at least not entirely based on race, were the best it could do.[90] Finally, the British government did not pressure non-African CUKCs to apply for local citizenship. The result across East Africa was large numbers of individuals who had only citizenship of the UK and colonies after independence.[91]

Such a situation would have had few consequences for immigration (from 1962, the possession of a British passport did not guarantee entry to the UK) were it not for the mechanism chosen to restrict immigration: British passports issued *under the authority* of the government of Britain were free from control, while British passports issued under a colony's authority were subject to control.

It was this decision that led, in conjunction with Kenyan independence, to the 'release' of Kenyan Asians from immigration control. When the Commonwealth Immigrants Act, 1962 was adopted, Asian CUKCs in Kenya, despite frequent claims to the contrary,[92] *were* subject to the 1962 immigration controls. According to the legislation, individuals were free to enter the UK if they were born in the country or if they held a passport 'issued in the

---

[88] *PRO, HO 213/2292*, 'Background note for the minister of state. Position under the Commonwealth Immigrants Act of citizens of the United Kingdom and colonies who do not acquire citizenship of Uganda on Independence Day', undated.

[89] *PRO, HO 344/177*, Letter from G. Otton to Sandars, 26 Feb. 1968.

[90] *PRO, HO 344/177*, Letter from W. F. G. Le Bailly to H. S. H. Stanley, 1 Nov. 1963.

[91] Although estimates were unreliable, it was thought that some 20,000 Asians in South Africa, 25,000 in Tanganyika (Tanzania after 1961), and 200,000 in Kenya were in this situation. *PRO, CO 1032/322*, Extract of a letter from Cleary to Ross, Home Office, 28 Nov. 1961.

[92] Dummett and Nicol, *Subjects*, 199; Holmes, *John Bull's Island*, 265–7, Mason, *Race and Ethnicity*, 28, Solomos, *Race and Rascism*, 54.

[93] In practice, this often related to location of issue—most passports issued under the

United Kingdom or the Republic of Ireland [Section 1(2)]'. 'Passport', however, was strictly defined by the legislation: 'In this section "passport" means a current passport; and "United Kingdom passport" means a passport issued to the holder by the Government of the United Kingdom, *not being a passport so issued on behalf of the Government of any part of the Commonwealth outside the United Kingdom*' (emphasis added).

These provisions restricted entry of CUKCs by distinguishing among their passports, but not their citizenship. If CUKCs' passports were issued under the authority of the colonial governments, they were subject to control; if CUKCs received them under London's authority (all CUKCs—British-born or not), then they were not. Because the government had not created a distinctive United Kingdom citizenship in 1962, the mechanism for distinguishing among the entry rights of CUKCs depended *on the authority under which the passports were issued.*[93] As Kenya was a colony in 1962, all British subjects in Kenya who were not issued a passport under London's authority had no right to enter the UK. Had the Kenyan Asians applied for a passport in 1962, the vast majority would have been issued one by the colonial government in Kenya, and they would, therefore, have been subject to immigration control.

Approximately one year later, the situation changed. When Kenya achieved independence in 1963, the colonial governor naturally gave up his post and became the High Commissioner, the UK's direct representative in independent Kenya. Had all Kenyan CUKCs received local citizenship, this process would have been of no consequence. As they had not, the implications were profound: passports previously issued under the authority of the colonial governor (and subject to control as such) were from 1963 issued directly by and *under the authority* of the British government. They were thus no longer subject to immigration controls. Immediately following Kenyan independence, all CUKCs in Kenya, including the Asians, were freed from the immigration controls set in place by the 1962 Act.

There were thus two causal steps leading to the Kenyan Asians crisis: first, the complications associated with replacing the 1948 citizenship scheme led policy-makers to opt for a bizarre control mechanism based on the issue of passports in 1962; and, second, in the absence of inclusive citizenship provisions (on the eventual existence of which BNA itself was premissed), this

---

authority of the United Kingdom would be issued in London, while most dependent subjects' passports would be issued in the colonies. There were exceptions, however, such as a London-born Briton renewing a passport in Hong Kong while travelling overseas, or a Hong Kong student renewing a passport in London while a student in the UK. In the latter case, the passport would be stamped to the effect of 'issued on behalf of the overseas territory of Hong Kong'. As such, it would be subject to immigration control.

[94] *PRO, CO 1032/322*, Extract of a letter from Cleary to Ross, Home Office, 28 Nov. 1961.

mechanism released CUKCs from immigration controls at independence. Since this outcome was a secondary consequence of the control mechanism, it is difficult to argue that the Conservatives intended to grant rights to Kenyan Asians in the robust sense suggested by Macleod. To this degree, Sandys's claim that Macleod misrepresented the Macmillan government's intentions in 1962, at least when judged against the available primary evidence, is sound.

What is not sound, however, is the claim that the Kenyan's exemption was unforeseen, and that the British government made no pledges to the Asian community. At least three archival documents demonstrate both that the Asians' position was recognized and accepted, before and after the passage of the 1962 Act, and that at least one promise was made to members of the Kenyan Asian community.

The possibility of a post-independence exemption for CUKCs was noted by the Home Office during the Commonwealth Immigrants Bill, 1962's passage through Parliament. As one Home Office official noted:

Another point that worries me is the fact that about 20,000 people of Indian origin in South Africa, about 25,000 in Tanganyika and an even greater number in Kenya, after that country becomes independent, will be eligible as things stand for United Kingdom passports. I believe that there is also a great number of British subjects without citizenship in Northern Rhodesia, who can also get United Kingdom passports. It seems to me to be undesirable that they should have freer access to this country than Canadians, Australians or New Zealanders, seeing that it is only in a technical sense that they can be said to belong to this country.[94]

The bill was not amended to prevent this development, and when passed, the mechanism through which Asians would enjoy entry rights after independence was entrenched in statute.

The position of Asians in Kenya was thus not a secret;[95] indeed, it was so well known in Whitehall that one Commonwealth Relations Office official discussed the Asians and the source of their right to enter the UK with the Indian Official at a dinner party.[96] What, though, of the pledges made? Shortly after the passage of the Commonwealth Immigrants Act, the Senior Civil Servants' Association of Kenya asked the Colonial Secretary about their access to the United Kingdom. In his response (transmitted through the colonial governor), the Colonial Secretary noted that the position (seven months

---

[95] The analogous situation of Asians in Uganda, Tanganyika, Nigeria, Sierra Leone, and Ghana was also recognized. *PRO, HO 213/2292*, 'Background note for the minister of state. Position under the Commonwealth Immigrants Act of citizens of the United Kingdom and colonies who do not acquire citizenship of Uganda on Independence Day', undated.

[96] *PRO, HO 344/177*, Letter from H. S. H. Stanley to H. K. Hickman, 8 Oct. 1968.

[97] *PRO, CO 1032/322*, Savingram from the Secretary of State for the Colonies to the offi-

after the passage of the Commonwealth Immigrants Act) then meant that all those in Kenya who did not 'belong' to the UK would have to apply for an entry certificate. Following independence, however, the matter changed. The Colonial Secretary's response is worth quoting:

So far as the position after independence is concerned, it is not of course possible at this stage to forecast what form the citizenship laws which will be enacted at independence will take, but in any event those who do not acquire citizenship of Kenya will retain their citizenship of the U.K. and Colonies; and *I can confirm that those who retain their citizenship of the U.K. and colonies will after independence become entitled to U.K. passports from the British High Commission, and that such passports will confer exemption from U.K. immigration control.*[97] (emphasis added)

The Colonial Secretary in 1962 was none other than Duncan Sandys. Since all those born in the United Kingdom (i.e. most of the European Kenyans) were exempted from the 1962 controls, Sandys most likely had the Asians in mind during the drafting of this passage. However, as the document is not clear on the matter, it is technically possible that Sandys was thinking only of white civil servants. This is highly unlikely for two reasons.[98] First, although the highest positions within the civil service were dominated by Britons, Asians made up the bulk of the middle and lower ranks;[99] these individuals would have been represented by the Association. Second, even if this was not the case, Sandys demonstrates in the passage an understanding of the mechanism leading to the Kenyan exemption. As it was widely known at independence that the Asians were unlikely to apply for local citizenship, the Kenyans' position was known to Sandys.[100] In 1968, while Sandys was speaking of loopholes, the Commonwealth Secretary reminded him of this fact in a private letter: 'The present situation [i.e. the Asians' free entry] has followed necessarily and directly from the Kenya independence settlement which was negotiated by you in the knowledge of the Commonwealth Immigrants Act passed in the previous year; and it is misleading to dismiss the rights to which a substantial number of U.K. citizens then became entitled as a "loophole in the law". . . . I venture to suggest

cer administering the Government of Kenya, 26 Nov. 1962. Sandys became Secretary of State for Commonwealth Relations and Secretary of State for the Colonies following the 'night of long knives', 12–13 July 1962, when Macmillan sacked seven full members of the Cabinet as well as four junior members.

[98] A conversation with Richard Coggins, Lecturer in Politics at Christ Church, Oxford, clarified this point.

[99] Himbara, *Kenyan Capitalists*, 116.

[100] See the note from the Kenyan High Commissioner to Sandys discussing it. *PRO, HO 344/177*, Telegram from Malcolm Macdonald to the Colonial Secretary, 26 Oct. 1963.

[101] *PRO, PREM 13/2157*, Letter from George Thomson to Duncan Sandys, 20 Feb. 1968.

that your share of responsibility for [the current problem] is greater than one would judge from your public utterances.'[101]

Should any doubt have remained about who enjoyed which rights, the issue was clarified a year later. The Home Secretary, Henry Brooke, raised the question of Asians in Kenya before the Commonwealth immigration committee during the passage of the Kenya Independence Bill. He noted that while East African Asians had no tradition of emigration to the United Kingdom, a number had begun to consider the possibility of doing so. The Home Secretary's judgement, in the full view of Duncan Sandys (Commonwealth and Colonial Secretary), Joseph Godber (Minister of Labour), Sir John Hobson, QC (Attorney-General), Maurice Macmillan (Economic Secretary, Treasury), and Margaret Thatcher (Joint Parliamentary Secretary, Ministry of Pensions and National Insurance), was unequivocal: 'It would be out of the question to withdraw their United Kingdom citizenship, so making them stateless; nor could the normal facilities for obtaining a passport be withheld from them as this would plainly be discrimination based on racial origin.'[102] The position taken by the Conservative Party, and above all by Sandys, in 1968 was a wilful denial of this commitment; it was a betrayal of a basic pledge.

The Labour Party, by contrast, was not involved in the independence negotiations; the government was uncertain about the content of promises made by the Conservatives;[103] and it could claim, however feebly, that no Parliament can bind its successor.[104] Callaghan defended the bill as necessary to avoid deterioration in race relations,[105] and he argues today that the decline in political controversy surrounding immigration after 1968 is a reflection of its

---

[102]   *PRO, CAB 134/1468*, Commonwealth immigration committee meeting, 7 Nov. 1963. Also see *PRO, CAB 134/1468*, Cabinet memorandum by the Home Secretary on the Asians' position, 30 Oct. 1963. Quoting the Home Secretary: 'It is . . . out of the question not to accord normal passport facilities to United Kingdom citizens of Asian origin in independent African States, with the object of rendering them subject to our immigration control. Such action would be, and would be seen to be, a discrimination based on racial origin, and would be tantamount to a denial to these persons of one of the basic rights of a citizen, namely to enter the country of which he is a citizen.' Also see *PRO, HO 344/177*, Letter to L. E. T. Storar, undated, and *PRO, HO 344/177*, Letter to the Secretary of State, undated. The latter outlines the Asians' position exactly as above, and notes that 'the United Kingdom has always acted on the principle in granting independence that we could not abandon such people and make them stateless by withdrawing their citizenship to the United Kingdom and Colonies'.

[103]   See *PRO, PREM 13/2157*, 'Asian immigration from Kenya', Letter from Burke Trend to Wilson, 21 Feb. 1968.

[104]   Callaghan defended the bill on these grounds. See the *Spectator*, 'A shameful and unnecessary act', 1 Mar. 1968.

[105]   *PRO, CAB 129/135*, 'Memorandum by the secretary of state for the Home Department', C(68) 34, 12 Feb. 1968.

[106]   Callaghan, *Time*, 267.   [107]   These are figures based on settlement.

success.[106] The implicit premiss is that the indigenous community will only accept strangers in its presence when it feels that it is no longer under the threat of continued mass immigration; good race relations, as countless policy documents state, require strict immigration. The argument, although difficult to verify or falsify, is not entirely implausible. New Commonwealth immigration was less of a political issue in the 1970s and 1980s, and the statutory framework constructed by the Labour and Conservative governments since the 1960s (the latter offering only restrictive legislation) may well have contributed to its decline. The stabilization in overall levels of immigration (alien and Commonwealth) at some 46,000 immigrants per year (through a combination of restrictive legislation and a finite source of dependants),[107] along with the provision of statutory mechanisms through which ethnic minorities can secure a degree of protection against racism, has probably contributed to the contemporary state of race relations.[108] Racially motivated attacks continue, but the anti-immigrant hysteria of the 1960s and 1970s has faded, and the extreme-right National Front[109] never recovered from its 1979 collapse in national support. The 1968 Commonwealth Immigrants Act reduced the number of East African Asians eligible to enter yearly to 6,000–7,000, and so contributed to this process.[110]

The argument, however, cannot end here. The Kenyan Asians were not immigrants like any other for the simple but crucial reason that they lacked any other citizenship.[111] The manner in which the Kenyans attained British

[108]   This is a controversial statement; the relationship between immigration control, on the one hand, and racism and race relations, on the other, has been a matter of debate for decades. For those taking the contrary position, see Rose et al., *Colour and Citizenship*, 228 and S. Saggar, *Race and Politics in Britain* (London: Harvester Wheatsheaf, 1992), 175. Also see R. Miles, *Racism and Migrant Labour* (London: Routledge & Kegan Paul, 1982); Solomos, *Race and Racism*; J. Solomos and L. Back, *Racism and Society* (Houndmills: Macmillan, 1996), ch. 1. See also S. Spencer, 'The Implications of Immigration Policy for Race Relations', in Spencer (ed.), *Strangers & Citizens: A Positive Approach to Migrants and Refugees* (London, 1994). The issue is not of central importance to this chapter, but it is worth noting that, for all the arguments about migration control's role in legitimating racism, attitudes to ethnic minorities in Britain have improved considerably since restrictions were first applied to Commonwealth immigration in the 1960s. See L. Brook and E. Cape, 'Libertarianism in Retreat?' in R. Jowell et al. (eds.), *British Social Attitudes: the 12th report* (Aldershot: Dartmouth Publishing Co., 1995), 201–4.

[109]   Now the British National Party.

[110]   It should be noted, however, that the nadir in race relations—following Powell's 1968 speech—came after the act, not before. In his memoirs, Callaghan fudges the chronology, and suggests that the government was responding to the extremism encouraged by Powell's intervention. Callaghan, *Time*, 267.

[111]   Callaghan conceded this point when he admitted later that if Kenyatta did not allow the Asians to physically remain in Kenya, Britain could not refuse them entry. Shepherd, *Iain Macleod*, 498. A further mark of the extent to which the language of citizenship was poorly implanted in British discourse is the fact that debate was more concerned with whether or not the legislation was 'racialist' than the fact that they were citizens (though the two issues were

citizenship involved a series of historical contingencies, and it was not foreseen by the drafters of the British Nationality Act of 1948, but it was none the
less known by 1963 (if not earlier) and accepted by the government of the
day. Had the government in 1963 told all non-European CUKCs in Kenya that
the British government would not honour their passports if they refused local
citizenship, the decision would have been harsh but justifiable. They did not;
instead, they relied on the naive hope that the Asians would not exercise their
right to enter Britain, a lesson they should have learned during the first large-
scale arrival of Commonwealth immigrants in the 1950s. To have pretended,
when these rights were exercised, that the Kenyan Asians were an unpre-
dictable side-effect of empire that no government could have reasonably been
expected to accept was hypocrisy.

CONCLUSION

In summary, the Asians' access to the UK resulted neither from a 'loophole'
in British legislation on independence or nationality, nor from an explicit
British decision to exempt Asians from immigration control. The Asians'
exemption resulted from the combined effect of, first, the 1962 decision to
base immigration control on a passport's issuing authority (rather than on the
possession of a passport as such), and, second, the granting of independence
to Kenya in the absence of inclusive local citizenship. This highly contingent
outcome cannot in any sense be said to be the result of a manifest aim on the
part of those negotiating Kenyan independence and defining the content of
British nationality law. Equally, though, archival evidence makes it clear that
the British Cabinet, and above all Duncan Sandys himself, understood the
rights that would be granted to Asians in post-independence Kenya and, on
several occasions, affirmed them. As seen, at least one pledge was made by
Sandys to members of the Kenyan Asian community. In denying these
commitments, he and those members of the Conservative Shadow Cabinet

---

obviously linked). I am doubtful that even the law's critics fully appreciated the absolute
centrality of the Asians' citizenship. In an Ealing-based campaign against the legislation, one
organization entitled a protest leaflet 'Justice for British Citizens?' but then went on to argue
within the government's own terms. The legislation was unjustified because of numbers: 'the
total number of Asians ever likely to come here from Kenya has been estimated as few as
40,000.' If the force of their citizenship were taken seriously, it would carry the argument irrespective of how many—20,000 or 200,000—came to the UK. *PRO, HO 376/118*, Letter from
Martyn Grubb, Ealing International Friendship Council, to David Ennals, 1 Apr. 1968. Also see
PRO, HO 376/118, Letter from David Ennals to Martyn Grubb, 2 Apr. 1968.

supporting him misrepresented their actions to the British public and abandoned the Kenyan Asians to political expediency. In condemning this policy, Iain Macleod stood by his and his government's promises in the face of public pressure and his own party's censure. For these actions, the historical record owes him credit.

The legislation was also a central instance of BNA 1948's powerful influence on subsequent policy and politics. Viewed in a broader historical context, the Kenyan Asians crisis was the consequence of decisions taken in 1962, which were in turn encouraged by the character of the citizenship arrangement created in 1948. The British Nationality Act was founded on the (very British) assumption that exclusion would occur gradually as the colonies progressed to independence and all persons therein graduated from CUKC status to citizenship of an independent Commonwealth Country (Kenyans, Nigerians, Indians, etc.). The possibility that there would be large pockets of non-citizens within the newly dependent nations, who would retain CUKC under BNA, was not considered.[112]

The existence of these groups of individuals without local citizenship would have been irrelevant for immigration except for the 1962 decision to base immigration control on the authority under which passports were issued. When, in conjunction with this mechanism, the independence process released CUKCs in Kenya from the 1962 restrictions, the Labour government could only limit the influx created by the Kenyan crisis through publicly devaluing the citizenship of CUKCs distinguishable by the colour of their skin. The institutional framework created by the British Nationality Act shaped policy decisions made in 1962, and these decisions structured the subsequent evolution of the immigration issue itself.

The dilemma was exacerbated by the government's approach to decolonization. In the early 1960s, the Colonial Office, in its eagerness to achieve an agreement, was willing to accept settlements which left a large residue of persons whose nationality status was uncertain and precarious; the Office never sought the guarantee of citizenship.[113] The question was viewed as peripheral to the central issue of peaceful independence. The UK might have seized the issue then—as it should have in 1962—and ensured that all persons who meaningfully belonged to one or another of the colonies (i.e. those such as Asians born in Uganda and Kenya) were granted citizenship of the independent nation. In those instances, (including Kenya) when the offer

---

[112] The precedent, to the extent that there was one, was Canada, Australia, and New Zealand, polities that respected the principle of *ius soli*, nationality through birth. As past patterns of migration were a poor precedent for future ones, the largely tolerant policy of these liberal democracies in respect of access to nationality was a wholly inadequate guide to their New Commonwealth successors.   [113] Interview with a Home Office official.

of citizenship was made, however resentfully, the UK should have made it clear that such persons could not claim UK citizenship. They might well have still been expelled in an ethnic cleansing of the Ugandan sort, and the UK would have found itself involved, but the country could then have accepted individuals as refugees rather than second-class citizens. It would have gained a reputation for tolerance and liberality rather than their opposites, and it would have been in a far better position to encourage other nations to do so. The responsibility would have rested where it belonged: on the illiberality and racism of Kenya.

By 1968, the consequences of the 1948 citizenship scheme were abundantly clear: over a million people outside the UK, without the right to enter the country, possessed no citizenship but CUKC.[114] It was equally clear that large numbers might attempt to come to the United Kingdom. Yet in those countries which were independent (most by 1968) it was too late to ensure that they took local citizenship. CUKC status could not be withdrawn, for these would leave them stateless. British governments found themselves in a situation in which immigration control could only be exercised by making distinctions among people who were in a legal sense full British citizens. The lessons of the Kenyan Asians crisis had been drawn, but they were drawn too late, and British policy-makers could do little but maintain the framework created by the 1968 Commonwealth Immigrants Act and hope that no further crises were on the horizon. They of course were, but the vicissitudes of electoral politics would pass them to the Conservatives.

[114] These were in Africa (approximately 200,000), the West Indies (approximately 40,000), and Malaysia (1,000,000). *Parliamentary Debates (Commons)*, (759), col. 1278, 27 Feb. 1968.

8

Heath, Powell, and Migration Policy, 1968–1974

To the displeasure of the British government, the Kenyan Asians' experience repeated itself four years after the passage of the Commonwealth Immigrants Act of 1968. In August 1972, Idi Amin announced the expulsion of all Asian CUKCs from Uganda. The legal position of the Ugandan Asians was identical to their Kenyan counterparts: they were originally controlled by the 1962 Commonwealth Act, were released from the restrictions through the independence process and were placed under a new set of controls through Callaghan's 1968 Act. Their social and political experience in Uganda was broadly similar: they were a largely skilled, professional class whose presence was resented by Africans and who found themselves facing a series of discriminatory measures culminating in an expulsion order.

The treatment they received at the hands of the British government was, however, markedly different: whereas Wilson's government recognized the Asians as citizens legally, yet differentiated between them and those with a close ethnic connection to the UK, Heath accepted the consequences of their citizenship—that they could not be denied entry to the UK—while making clear that the experience would not be repeated. It was a politically riskier move, and led to a temporary resurgence in support for the extreme right, but it spared Heath the shame visited upon Wilson. This decision, which was taken in the midst of Enoch Powell's meteoric rise to national prominence, is the subject of this chapter.

Heath's approach to Powell and the Ugandan Asians has implications for the traditional critique of British governments' policies towards Commonwealth immigrants. The 1970–4 period brings into sharp focus the relative liberality of British governments. Taken as a whole the stance of both parties was until the 1980s considerably less restrictionist than that demanded by the British public. The contrast was, however, most striking under Heath, during a period in which anti-immigration sentiment reached near-hysterical levels, and the government faced restrictionist pressure more intense than that faced by any British Prime Minister, before or since. Although, as we shall see, Heath surrendered something to the restrictionist case, his resolve and his claim to relative liberality are founded on two points: first, Powell's extremist demand for repatriation was, despite the man's public support, resisted; and, second, Heath granted, against the demands of the public and of Powell himself, immediate entry rights to all CUKCs expelled by Uganda's Idi Amin.

The Uganda Asians crisis occurred, somewhat ironically, two years after Heath's Conservative government adopted legislation designed to avoid a repetition of the Kenyan episode. The 1971 Immigration Act, which effectively equated for the purposes of immigration control Commonwealth citizens with aliens, was aimed at clarifying once and for all the legal position of CUKCs abroad. As in 1962, however, the tentacular effects of the 1948 citizenship scheme rendered this goal illusory. The daunting task of redefining the various citizenships created by the scheme, and Commonwealth hostility that would probably have been incurred, led the government to retain the British Nationality Act's underlying scheme. It instead distinguished between those admitted and those excluded through a novel and contentious legal concept: 'patriality'. In a second irony, patriality created more problems than it solved; driven to it by the complications linked with BNA, policymakers succeeded only in instituting one the most reviled concepts in British nationality law.

POWELL, HEATH, AND COMMONWEALTH IMMIGRATION

Ironically, behind the many differences between Powell and Heath lay a fundamental agreement. Both Powell and Heath believed, although the latter would not have expressed it in these terms, in the need to redefine nationality in a post-imperial age.[1] They shared a disillusionment with the Commonwealth; Heath saw it as an impediment to Britain's national interest in the Common Market,[2] and Powell viewed it as an absurd monstrosity, that 'great and glorious heir of Empire', which prevented the United Kingdom from articulating a sense of its own national identity free from the shackles of

---

[1] Interview with Enoch Powell, Aug. 1995. Powell also had a specific constitutional objection to the Commonwealth. Powell was alone in opposing the Royal Titles Bill of 1953, which granted the Queen the title 'Head of the Commonwealth' (and allowed India to remain in this organization as a republic), a position which he maintained until his death. The Queen can exercise no power as Head of the Commonwealth, he argues, because there are no ministers capable of responsibly advising her on the Commonwealth (because the Commmonwealth as such has no government and no ministers). The Commonwealth is therefore a constitutional fiction. See E. Powell, 'What Commonwealth?' and 'End this Fiction', *Reflections of a Statesman: The Writings and Speeches of Enoch Powell* (London: Bellew, 1991), 601–4.

[2] On this, see J. Campbell, *Edward Heath: A Biography* (London: Jonathan Cape, 1993), 336–41.

its former imperial commitments. 'Nations live by myths,' as Powell was fond of saying, and the Commonwealth was an errant myth and a dangerous myth.

Beyond this general agreement, there was little uniting the two, on immigration or anything else. For Heath, the privileges accorded Commonwealth immigrants were a historic relic which had lost their relevance, and he made it a priority for his government to equalize as much as it could the rights of aliens and Commonwealth immigrants. Beyond that, the numbers themselves were a technical question to be worked out efficiently, humanely, and dispassionately. For Powell, as he consistently argued, numbers were the essence of the question, and mass immigration was itself a threat to nationhood. It created an alien presence[3] in the national community.

But immigration meant more than such abstract stuff; it was a question of political power. Immigration was one of several points from which Powell launched an attack on Heath's leadership. This dualism in Powell's approach, this combination of idealism and instrumentalism, is something that scholars of Powell and 'Powellism' have difficulty grasping. Accounts of him range from reverential to the reductionist. For Patrick Cosgrave, Powell was a high Tory who selflessly placed his principles above party;[4] he ends his 1989 biography with the cloying injunction to '[l]ook upon him. Learn from him. You will not see his like again.'[5] For Paul Foot, he was an opportunist who belatedly seized on immigration as an unscrupulous means for political advancement.[6] Listing a series of contradictory claims over twenty years, he concludes that Powell demonstrated a 'degree of inconsistency, uncertainty and opportunism which would put most politicians on their guard'.[7] The truth of the matter lies somewhere in the middle: Powell was motivated by the pursuit of principle and the pursuit of power. He made quite clear his interest in the party leadership,[8] and yet took decisions—such as urging his supporters to vote Labour in 1974—that could only be justified on rational grounds with great difficulty. Rather like Roy Jenkins in the Labour Party, Powell was a skilful politician with a clear interest in advancing his position within the

---

[3] Powell has always claimed to be ignorant of the meaning of the term 'race'. The question, he argues, is one of numbers, and a cluster of thousands of Italians or Germans in British cities would constitute the same sort of alien presence. Interview with Enoch Powell, Aug. 1995; Powell interview with BBC, 9 Sept. 1969, *Reflections of a Statesman*, 367.

[4] P. Cosgrave, *The Lives of Enoch Powell* (London: The Bodley Head, 1989). For a similar view, see R. Lewis, *Enoch Powell: Principle in Politics* (London: Cassell, 1979).

[5] For a review of Cosgrave, see R. Jenkins, 'Enoch Powell', in Jenkins, *Portraits and Miniatures* (London: Macmillan, 1993).

[6] P. Foot, *The Rise of Enoch Powell: An Examination of Enoch Powell's Attitude to Immigration and Race* (Harmondsworth: Penguin, 1969).

[7] Ibid. 8.

[8] See his 3 Jan. 1969 interview with David Frost, reproduced in B. Smithies and P. Fiddick, *Enoch Powell on Immigration* (London: Sphere, 1969), ch. 5.

party hierarchy, but one who viewed certain fundamental issues—British membership of the EEC—as above political strategy and, indeed, above party.

POWELL AND THE BIRMINGHAM SPEECH

Powell's intervention in the immigration debate began actively in early 1968; it lasted until the end of the Conservative 1970–4 government, and succeeded in continually manœuvring Heath and the Conservative Party towards a more restrictionist position: by galvanizing public and party support for a restrictionist position, Powell forced the party's front bench reluctantly to adopt a firmer anti-immigration stance; in turn, Powell responded by declaring himself in favour of a still more restrictionist position; the Conservatives again followed, and so on. As Douglas Schoen has argued, through a series of strategic moves, Powell was able to tug Conservative Party policy along his restrictionist path.[9] The motivation of Heath and the front bench was not, as so many have also argued, mere cowardice; the Conservatives, as we shall see in the context of the Ugandan Asians crisis, displayed at times considerable courage. It was rather that Powell tapped into and channelled powerful and diffuse anti-immigrant support which had not previously been given expression in the mainstream political parties; his success made it imperative for Heath to follow, to a degree, Powell's lead.

On 10 April 1968, the Conservative Shadow Cabinet agreed to move a Reasoned Amendment when the government's Race Relations Bill was before Parliament, and that the Whip would be used. When the meeting ended, Hogg said to Powell on the way out, 'I hope I explained it fairly.' Powell, according to Hogg, replied, 'You could not have put it more fairly.'[10] The Shadow Cabinet was intensely concerned about their ability to maintain party unity on the vote, but no one, it seems, expected Powell to intervene at such a delicate moment. Ten days later, Powell did just that. On 21 April, Quintin Hogg was summoned to the television to hear an abridged version of Powell's speech on the BBC. Powell looked stern, but not emotional, and spoke slowly, apocalyptically:[11]

---

[9]   See D. E. Schoen, *Enoch Powell and the Powellites* (London: Macmillan, 1977).

[10]   Lord Hailsham of St Marylebone, *A Sparrow's Flight* (London: Collins, 1990), 369. Also see E. Heath, *The Course of My Life: My Autobiography* (London: Hodder & Stoughton, 1998), 292.

[11]   Powell's speech is generally quoted only in passing, with emphasis on the most controversial passages. I provide a fuller sample of the speech, one which includes Powell's efforts, subsequently the basis of the claim that he was poorly treated, to link his arguments with Conservative Party policy.

The supreme function of statesmanship is to provide against preventable evils. In seeking to do so, it encounters obstacles which are deeply rooted in human nature. One is that by the very order of things such evils are not demonstrable until they have occurred: at each stage in their onset there is room for doubt and for dispute whether they be real or imaginary. By the same token, they attract little attention in comparison with current troubles, which are both indisputable and pressing: whence the besetting temptation of all politics to concern itself with the immediate present at the expense of the future. Above all, people are disposed to mistake predicting troubles for causing troubles and even for desiring troubles: 'if only,' they love to think 'if only people wouldn't talk about it, it probably wouldn't happen.'...[T]he discussion of future grave but, with effort now, avoidable evils is the most unpopular and at the same time the most necessary occupation for the politician. Those who knowingly shirk it, deserve, and not infrequently receive, the curses of those who come after.

A week or two ago I fell into conversation with a constituent, a middle-aged, quite ordinary working man employed in one of our nationalised industries. After a sentence or two about the weather, he suddenly said: 'If I had the money to go, I wouldn't stay in this country.' I made some deprecatory reply, to the effect that even this government wouldn't last forever; but he took no notice; and continued: 'I have three children, all of them been through grammar school and two of them married now, with family. I shan't be satisfied till I have seen them all settled overseas. In this country in fifteen or twenty years time the black man will have the whip-hand over the white man.'

I can already hear the chorus of execration. How dare I say such a horrible thing? How dare I stir up trouble and inflame feelings by repeating such a conversation? The answer is that I do not have the right not to do so. Here is a decent, ordinary fellow-Englishman, who in broad daylight in my own town says to me, his Member of Parliament, that this country will not be worth living in for his children. I simply do not have the right to shrug my shoulders and think about something else. What he is saying, thousands and hundreds of thousands are saying and thinking—not throughout Great Britain, perhaps, but in the areas that are already undergoing the total transformation to which there is no parallel in a thousand years of English history. . . .

The natural and rational first question with a nation confronted by such a prospect is to ask: 'How can its dimensions be reduced?' Granted it be not wholly preventable, can it be limited, bearing in mind that numbers are of the essence: the significance and consequences of an alien element introduced into a country or population are profoundly different according to whether that element is 1 percent or 10 percent. The answers to the simple and rational question are equally simple and rational: by stopping, or virtually stopping, further inflow, and by promoting the maximum outflow. Both answers are part of the official policy of the Conservative Party.

It almost passes belief that at this moment twenty or thirty additional immigrant children are arriving from overseas in Wolverhampton alone every week—and that means fifteen or twenty additional families of a decade or two hence. Those whom the Gods wish to destroy, they first make mad. We must be mad, literally mad, as a nation to be permitting the annual inflow of some 50,000 dependants, who are for the most part the material of the future growth of the immigrant-descended population. It is like watching a nation busily engaged in heaping its own funeral pyre. . . .

I turn now to re-emigration. If all immigration ended tomorrow, the rate of growth of the immigrant and immigrant-descended population would be substantially reduced, but the prospective size of this element in the population would leave the character of the national danger unaffected. . . . Hence the urgency of implementing now the second element of the Conservative Party's policy: the encouragement of re-emigration. . . .

It can be no part of any policy that existing families should be kept divided; but there are two directions in which families can be reunited, and if our former and present immigration laws have brought about the division of families, albeit voluntarily or semi-voluntarily, we ought to be prepared to arrange for them to be reunited in their countries of origin. In short, suspension of immigration and encouragement of re-emigration hang together, logically and humanely, as two aspects of the same approach. . . .

The third element of the Conservative Party's policy is that all who are in this country as citizens should be equal before the law and that there shall be no discrimination or difference made between them by public authority. As Mr Heath put it, we will have no 'first-class citizens' and 'second-class citizens.' This does not mean that the immigrant and his descendants should be elevated into a privileged or special class, or that the citizen should be denied his right to discriminate in the management of his own affairs between one citizen and another. . . . [Those who support the Race Relations Bill] have got it exactly and diametrically wrong. The discrimination and deprivation, the sense of alarm and of resentment, lies not with the immigrant population but with those among whom they come and are still coming. This is why to enact legislation of the kind before Parliament at this moment is to risk throwing a match on to gunpowder. . . .

Powell then spoke of the many letters he received from frustrated constituents, and he read aloud 'just one':

Eight years ago in a respectable street in Wolverhampton a house was sold to a Negro. Now only one white (a women old-age pensioner) lives there. This is her story. She lost her husband and both her sons in the war. So she turned her seven-roomed house, her only asset, into a boarding-house. She worked hard and did well, paid off her mortgage and began to put something by for her old age. Then the immigrants moved in. With growing fear, she saw one house after another taken over. The quiet street became a place of noise and confusion. Regretfully, her white tenants moved out.

The day after the last one left, she was awakened at seven am by two Negroes who wanted to use her phone to contact their employer. When she refused, as she would refuse any stranger at such an hour, she was abused and feared she would have been attacked but for the chain on her door. . . .

The telephone is her lifeline. Her family pay the bill, and help her out as best they can. Immigrants have offered to buy her house—at a price which the prospective landlord would be able to recover from his tenants in weeks, or at most a few months. She is becoming afraid to go out. Windows are broken. She finds excreta pushed through her letter-box. When she goes out to the shops, she is followed by children, charming, wide-grinning piccaninnies. They cannot speak English, but one word they know. 'Racialist,' they chant. When the new Race Relations Bill is passed, this woman is convinced she will go to prison. And is she so wrong? I begin to wonder. . . .

After another spirited attack on the Race Relations Bill, Powell concluded his speech with his infamous words:

As I look ahead, I am filled with foreboding. Like the Roman, I seem to see 'the River Tiber foaming with much blood.' The tragic and intractable phenomenon which we watch with horror on the other side of the Atlantic but which is there interwoven with the history and existence of the States itself, is coming upon us here by our own volition and our own neglect.[12]

By structuring his speech around three Conservative policies on immigra-tion—strict immigration control, voluntary repatriation, and equal treat-ment—Powell could claim (and claimed until his death) that he was simply articulating and explaining official policy. Certain commentators have endorsed this position and suggested that Heath used the speech as a pretence for removing an intimidating rival.[13] Such a view ignores the extent to which Heath's anger was shared by others in the Shadow Cabinet. Hogg was enraged,[14] and Whitelaw felt that Powell had betrayed the party and could not be trusted.[15] Iain Macleod, an old friend of Powell's, broke definitively with him. Heath shared their anger, and resolved to remove Powell from the Shadow Cabinet. He telephoned the other members and found almost univer-sal backing; Boyle Hogg, Peter Carrington, and Macleod refused to remain in the Shadow Cabinet with Powell, the last three being especially adamant.[16] Powell would go, or they would. As Carr, generally a mild-mannered man, put it to Heath, 'we have only been putting up with this lonerism because it's Enoch, but this is going too far. You either get rid of him or you get rid of

---

[12] Speech to the Annual General Meeting of the West Midlands Area Conservative Political Centre, Birmingham, 20 Apr. 1968, in Powell, *Reflections of a Statesman*, 373–9.

[13] Lewis, *Enoch Powell*, 105–9. Edward Boyle, Lewis concludes, was allowed to remain in the Cabinet despite his abstention on the Second Reading of the Race Relations Bill because he did not threaten Heath. For press comment, see *The Times*, 'An Evil Speech', 22 Apr. 1968, *Guardian*, 'Mr Enoch Powell Dismissed', 22 Apr. 1968, and *Daily Telegraph*, 'The Powell Affair,' 22 Apr. 1968. The *Telegraph*, though not supportive, offered the most ambiguous reac-tion to the speech. It viewed the most 'sinister' aspect of the affair to be the calls, from Jeremy Thorpe among others, for prosecution of Powell under the Race Relations Act's provisions on racial incitement. Nothing, of course, came of this.

[14] Cosgrave, *Lives of Enoch Powell*, 251.

[15] W. Whitelaw, *The Whitelaw Memoirs* (London: Aurum, 1989), 64.

[16] See Campbell, *Edward Heath*, 243; Heath, *Course of My Life*, 293; and R. Shepherd, *Iain Macleod: A Biography* (London: Pimlico, 1995), 500.

me.'[17] Heath sent a message to Powell's Wolverhampton home (which was without a telephone) to ring him. When Powell rang, Heath told him that the speech was racist in tone, and that he was being sacked with the agreement of the Shadow Cabinet; Powell took the news without protest, and the two men never exchanged another word.[18] Heath issued a statement an hour later, at 10.00 p.m.:

I have tonight been in touch with Mr. Enoch Powell and told him of my decision, taken with the greatest regret, that he should no longer be invited to attend the Shadow Cabinet. I have told Mr. Powell that I consider the speech he made in Birmingham yesterday to have been racialist in tone and liable to exacerbate racial tensions. This is unacceptable from one of the leaders of the Conservative Party and incompatible with the responsibility of a member of the Shadow Cabinet.[19]

The speech and its reception were quite unlike anything seen in British post-war history, before or since.[20] The front bench was fully behind Heath's decision; the liberal wing—Macleod, Carr, Boyle—was infuriated by Powell's February intervention on Commonwealth migration and was more so over the Birmingham speech. All agreed that Powell's consistent flouting of collective responsibility (which Powell refused even to recognize), and his quixotic interventions on topics outside his jurisdiction—inflation, incomes policy, sterling, and immigration—rendered him unsuitable for the cooperative work of the Shadow (and the real) Cabinet.

Although Heath's action was viewed by the political world as brave and decisive,[21] in the public it met extensive and often bitter hostility. Citizens

[17]   Quoted in S. Heffer, *Like the Roman: The Life of Enoch Powell* (London: Weidenfeld & Nicolson, 1998), 455.   [18]   Heath, *Course of My Life*, 293.

[19]   Quoted in *The Times*, 'Dramatic Prelude to Clash on Bill', 22 Apr. 1968. Conservative Central Office drafted a similar letter for publication in the *Express*. CPA, CCO4 10/142, 'Mr. Heath Writes to the Express', 25 Apr. 1968.

[20]   The Labour Party kept deliberately quiet after the speech. In the immediate aftermath, Wilson instructed his Cabinet to make no speeches in the country about either the Race Relations Bill or the Opposition's difficulties with it. He later said that ministers were free to make comments, if they, first, emphasized the positive aspects of the RRB and, second, gave facts about immigration that dispelled prevailing ignorance. In all cases, they were to 'steer clear of personalities and of getting involved in party political approaches. The general line should be the need for bipartisanship on this grave national problem.' *PRO, PREM 13/2314*, Letter from Private Secretary to Michael Halls, 25 Apr. 1968.

[21]   Campbell, *Edward Heath*, 244. The one exception to this may have been Margaret Thatcher, who claims to have attempted to dissuade Heath (M. Thatcher, *The Path to Power* (London: HarperCollins, 1995), 146–7). 'I', she states, 'strongly sympathized with the gravamen of his argument about the scale of New Commonwealth immigration into Britain. I too thought this threatened not just public order but also the way of life of some communities, themselves already beginning to be demoralized by insensitive housing policies, Social Security dependence, and the onset of the "permissive society" ' (146). Her colleagues view this as entirely revisionist; she did not object to Heath's decision and never strayed from her education brief to voice an opinion in the Shadow Cabinet on immigration. Confidential interview.

spontaneously took to the street in Powell's support, including the Smithfield meat porters who marched to Parliament in Powell's defence, their placards proclaiming 'Keep Britain White' and 'Don't Knock Enoch!'[22] Powell's post-bag, his own delivered in front of the television cameras, contained thousands of letters, the vast majority of which were supportive. Conservative Central Office was flooded with letters in praise of Powell and in condemnation of Heath; many were obscene and some contained excrement. Gallup found that 69 per cent of respondents disapproved of Heath's action.[23] The British political establishment was shaken by the response, and there existed a genuine fear that politics would be dominated by an ugly populism of a sort unseen since Mosley. Calls were made for Powell's prosecution under the 'incitement to hatred' provisions of the Race Relations Act, 1965, but these were resisted by the Attorney-General, ostensibly on the grounds of insufficient evidence and improbability of conviction.[24]

Powell has since referred to his dismissal as the greatest boon granted him.[25] Above all, it gave him autonomy. Within the Shadow Cabinet, he was forced, as much as he resented it, to restrain his attacks on Heath. With these shackles removed, he employed his rhetorical skills to the fullest in a damning indictment of the British establishment's approach to immigration.

The public response to Powell's dismissal, the maverick politician's continuing popularity, and his campaign against immigration encouraged Heath, who, while moderate, felt no particular post-imperial obligation to Commonwealth citizens, to harden his position. John Campbell, Heath's biographer, put it thus:

[P]aradoxically, Heath needed Powell. Even though he was no longer a member of the Shadow Cabinet, Powell was now the best-known and most-admired figure in the Tory Party, with enormous appeal to precisely that section of the electorate—the patriotic working and lower-middle class—which the Tories needed if they were to win the election. Polls continued to show Powell's popularity running ahead of Heath's, while the Party's huge leads over Labour could be plausibly attributed at least in part to Powell's influence. Reluctantly, therefore, and without appearing to embrace his views, Heath was bound to trim his sails over the next two years to catch the Powellite wind.[26]

[22] *Guardian*, 'Mixed motives of "non-racialist" dock marchers', 24 Apr. 1968.
[23] *Attitudes towards Coloured People in Great Britain 1958–1982* (London: Gallup, 1968), Question 66.
[24] *PRO, PREM 13/2315*, Draft Press Statement for Law Officers Department, 24 Apr. 1968. For a marvellous example of bureaucratic feet-dragging in the face of demands for prosecution, see the correspondence in this file.
[25] Interview with Enoch Powell, Aug. 1995.
[26] Campbell, *Edward Heath*, 245.

He did so for the first time publicly at York, on 2 September 1968. There he outlined his proposals on migration: he promised to equate Commonwealth citizens with aliens and to restrict the right of dependants to join heads of families in the country; and he reiterated the pledge to offer a limited scheme of assisted—but strictly voluntary—repatriation.

Powell again spoke on immigration to a Rotary Club meeting at Eastbourne, on 16 November 1968. He defended his Birmingham speech and argued for a 'a programme of large-scale voluntary but organised, financed and subsidised repatriation and re-emigration'.[27] He rejected integration and predicted that, without mass repatriation, social violence would result:

Sometimes people point to the increasing proportion of immigrant offspring born in this country as if the fact contained within itself the ultimate solution. The truth is the opposite. The West Indian or Asian does not, by being born in England become an Englishman. In law he becomes a United Kingdom citizen by birth; in fact, he is a West Indian or an Asian still. Unless he be one of a small minority—for number, I repeat again and again, is of the essence—he will by the very nature of things lose one nationality without acquiring a new one. Time is running against us and them. With the lapse of a generation or so we shall have at last succeeded—to the benefit of nobody—in reproducing in 'England's green and pleasant land' the haunting tragedy of the United States.[28]

Like all of Powell's interventions, this speech contained a more extreme element than the previous one: the impossibility of assimilation. And like all of Powell's interventions, Heath soon followed with further restrictionist promises. Referring to a public fear that politicians were unable to control immigration, Heath promised in January 1969 four initiatives to curb immigration: (i) Commonwealth citizens once admitted would no longer have the right to permanent settlement, and they would only be admitted for specific jobs in specific locations, (ii) Commonwealth immigrants' work permits would have to be renewed every year, and, unlike labour vouchers, they would not carry the automatic right of settlement, (iii) those admitted would only be able to bring their dependants at the discretion of British authorities, and (iv) the decision on an immigrant's right to enter should be taken in the country from which he or she originates, rather than upon arrival in the United Kingdom.[29]

---

[27] Quoted in Smithies and Fiddick, *Enoch Powell on Immigration*, 76.

[28] Quoted ibid. 77.

[29] *CPA, CCO 505/4/63*, 'Conservative Policy on Immigration', 25 Jan. 1969. The speech was welcomed by Sandys, who competed with Powell for the restrictionist crown of the Conservative Party, and was viewed by immigrant and race relations organizations as an implicit embrace of Powell's position. *The Times*, 'Race workers see Heath speech as Powellism', 27 Jan. 1969.

The restrictionist drift in Conservative Party policy seemed to be confirmed by the departure of Edward Boyle, Shadow Education Secretary, from the Shadow Cabinet. Although Boyle's departure most likely reflected hostility within the party, particularly among the Tory shires, to his sympathy for Labour's comprehensivization programme,[30] Boyle had been a strong supporter of race relations legislation. Against considerable constituency pressure to vote against it,[31] Boyle abstained on the Second Reading of the Race Relations Bill,[32] and he consistently defended it against critics in his Midlands constituency and in the party.[33] His decision to leave politics, in which the hostility he experienced on immigration no doubt played a part, created an impression of a party lurching to the right, one which was not countered by Heath's decision to replace him with Margaret Thatcher.

Powell's attack continued until the election. In June, Powell accused Heath of 'sheer incomprehension of the very magnitude of the danger'.[34] In response to many challenges to state his position in Parliament, Powell told a packed House of Commons on 11 November 1969 of whole areas of British cities taken over by a foreign and alien population, a 'prospect [which] is fraught with the gravest danger of internecine violence', and he appealed for government-sponsored repatriation.[35] Two months later, he told the Young Conservative Conference at Scarborough that positive measures for immigrants should only be accepted as part of a 'voluntary and assisted' repatriation scheme; without such, 'they will encourage all concerned to deceive themselves for longer and longer as to the true magnitude and nature of the

---

[30] On this, see *The Times*, 29 Mar. 1990, and Lord Blake and C. S. Nicholls, *Dictionary of National Biography, 1981–85* (Oxford: Oxford University Press, 1990), 50.

[31] As early as 1964, the chairman of the Handsworth Conservative Party urged Norman Pannell, who had lost his seat in the 1964 election, to consider a move to Boyle's constituency. Referring to the latter as, with Patrick Gordon Walker, one of the two most unpopular Midland politicians, he promised to campaign against him. *The Private Papers of Edward Boyle, MS 660/24994/7*, Letter from John Sanders, Chairman, to Norman Pannell, 19 Oct. 1964.

[32] Boyle's private papers contain large files of extremely hostile letters. See *MS 660/27990–28050* on his liberalism and supposed lax attitude to control and *MS 660/28051–28101* on his support for the Race Relations Act of 1968.

[33] It is a mark of Powell's success in galvanizing anti-immigration support that even this humane, liberal patrician felt it necessary to concede something to the Powellite position. In a standard letter defending the Race Relations Act as necessary to ensure that all hard working persons have equal opportunities irrespective or race, he reiterated his support for strict immigration control: 'I *am* in favour of the strictest control of numbers coming in. There is no disagreement between Mr. Enoch Powell and myself on this point—though I personally regretted some of the language which he used.' *Private Papers of Edward Boyle, MS 660/19237*, 30 Apr. 1968.

[34] *The Times*, 'Powell's challenge to Heath on immigration', 10 June 1969. For *The Times*'s reaction, see 'Mr Powell's Policy', 10 June 1969.

[35] *Parliamentary Debates (Commons)* (791), col. 256, 11 Nov. 1969.

prospect, and to squander these few remaining precious years when it might still be possible to avert disaster.'[36]

Heath responded to this intervention with a force that had not character-ized his earlier approach to Powell, which had been to disassociate himself from Powell's language while identifying himself more closely with his basic position. Powell's Scarborough speech was, Heath told a London interviewer, 'an example of man's inhumanity to man which is absolutely intolerable in a Christian, civilised society'.[37] A few days later he took the step of stating that Powell could have no place in a future Conservative government.[38] This firm stance delighted Heath's supporters, and it was useful for a candidate who was too often viewed as bland and characterless. But the 'inhumanity' comment enraged Powell at the same time as his exclusion from any future government removed the last constraint on his behaviour. Powell became Heath's tireless enemy on a whole range of policies: the EEC, incomes policy, sterling, and defence.[39]

There is little doubt that Heath accepted that the public support enjoyed by Powell necessitated a greater restrictionism in Conservative policy.[40] Heath's September 1968 speech promising to equate the rights of Commonwealth citizens with those of aliens, his January 1969 speech outlining four curbs on immigration, and his frequent claim that he and Powell were separated by tactic and tone rather than underlying aim[41] all reflected Heath's effort to move Conservative policy towards the restrictionist position demanded by Powell and supported by the public. Powell skilfully exploited this potential by following each of Heath's speeches on immigration with a further (and more restrictionist) intervention chastising Heath for his ignorance of the problem's scope and outlining further specific measures. In doing so, Powell maximized the latent public support for his position and left Heath, a prag-matic politician, with little choice but to follow. Given the level of support enjoyed by Powell, if anything in Heath's behaviour is surprising, it is that he did not go further.[42]

---

[36] *The Times*, 'Powell wants Commons to debate immigration "without flinching".' 19 Jan. 1970.

[37] *The Times*, 'Powell view is inhuman, Heath says', 19 Jan. 1970.

[38] *The Times*, 'Heath sees no answer to rift with Powell', 24 Jan. 1970.

[39] For Powell's critique of British membership in the EEC, see Powell, *Reflections of a Statesman*, 465–85. For his views on the EEC and economic policy, see J. Enoch Powell, *Still to Decide* (London: B. T. Batsford, 1972), chs. 11 and 8; J. Enoch Powell, *A Nation or No Nation?: Six Years in British Politics* (London: B.T. Batsford, 1978), chs. 2, 1, and 8.

[40] Campbell, *Edward Heath*, 245; Schoen, *Enoch Powell and the Powellites*, 43.

[41] See, for example, Heath's comments in the *Daily Express*, 25 Apr. 1968.

[42] The available evidence suggests that Powell's position enjoyed considerable support in the lead-up to the 1970 election. In June 1969, Gallup undertook a study of public attitudes to Powellism and immigration. 54% agreed with Powell's call for grants to repatriate 'coloured

THE 1970 ELECTION

The 1970 election was the only one, before or since, in which immigration and race may have played a significant role. With the exception of Smethwick, immigration had no appreciable influence on the size of the swing to Labour in the majority of 1964 constituencies affected by it,[43] and it all but disappeared in the 1966 election.[44] A certain mythology has grown up around Powell's influence in the 1970 campaign. After much criticism of Heath and his policies, Powell offered an eleventh-hour endorsement. He chastised the Conservative leadership for its poor treatment of him, but urged his 19 June audience to vote Conservative:

On Thursday your vote is about a Britain that, with all its faults and failings, is still free, and great because it is free. On Thursday your vote decides whether that freedom shall survive or not. You dare not entrust it to any Government but a Conservative Government.[45]

Since Powell's intervention coincided with a last-minute shift in support from Labour to the Conservatives, which translated into a forty-three-seat majority, Powell's supporters and some commentators have concluded that he delivered the victory to Heath.[46] Others suggest that evidence for a 'Powell effect' is, in

immigrant families' (38% disagreed); 38% preferred to see money spent on repatriation than aid (vs. 24% who wished money to be spent on neither and 13% who did not know); and 42% felt that those who stayed in the country should not be given what they had—full citizenship rights (40% thought they should, 18% did not know). In early 1970, 33% felt themselves more favourable to Powell's views (vs. 22% who were less favourable and 33% felt the same), and 42% thought that restricting immigration would raise the Conservatives' chances of winning the election (second only to reducing direct taxation). See *Attitudes towards Coloured People in Britain*, questions 74–80.

[43] D. Butler and A. King, *The British General Election of 1964* (London: Macmillan, 1965), Appendix III. The effect of Smethwick, as I argued in Chapter 6, was symbolic.

[44] D. Butler and A. King, *The British General Election of 1966* (London: Macmillan, 1966), 117 and 249–54.

[45] Quoted in D. Butler and M. Pinto-Duschinsky, *The British General Election of 1970* (London: Macmillan, 1971), 162.

[46] For those that argue for a significant 'Powell effect', see R. Crossman, 'Understanding the Profusion of Shrinking Violets', *The Times*, 6 Sept. 1972; J. Wood (ed.), *Powell and the 1970 Election* (Kingswood, Surrey: Elliot Right Way, 1970); and D. Schoen and R. W. Johnson, 'The "Powell Effect"; or How One Man Can Win', *New Society*, 22 July 1976, 168–72. For a critical view of the thesis, see N. Deakin, 'Powell, the Minorities, and the 1970 Election', *Political Quarterly*, 41 (Oct.–Dec. 1970), 399–415; Butler and Pinto-Duschinksy, *British General Election of 1970*, 1970), 341, 405–7; and G. Hoinville and R. Jowell, 'What Happened in the Election', *New Society*, 2 July 1970, 14. The strongest case for the salience of immigration in the 1970 election is put by Studlar, who measures the perception of party difference on immigration. Although he detects no public perception of a difference between the parties on immigration in 1966 and 1970, there was a significant perception in 1970. After controlling for socio-economic attributes, economic contexts (region, percentage of New Commonwealth

fact, inconclusive.[47] At the very least, Powell's effect was likely to have firmed up the Conservative vote in constituencies which would have voted Tory in any event.[48]

THE IMMIGRATION ACT OF 1971

Shortly after the election, the government turned its attention to its promised reform of immigration law. The 1970 Conservative manifesto, *A Better Tomorrow*, stated that:

We will establish a new single system of control over all immigration from overseas. The Home Secretary of the day will have complete control, subject to the machinery for appeal, over the entry of individuals into Britain. We believe it right to allow an existing Commonwealth immigrant who is already here to bring his wife and young children to join him in this country. But for the future, work permits will not carry the right of permanent settlement for the holder or his dependants. Such permits as are issued will be limited to a specific job in a specific area for a fixed period, normally twelve months. We will give assistance to Commonwealth immigrants who wish to return to their countries of origin, but we will not tolerate any attempt to harass or compel them against their will.[49]

immigrants, cars per household, percentage of males engaged in agricultural occupations), and the appeal of the candidates, he argues that the Conservatives enjoyed an average 7.5% increase in voting among those who saw the party as more restrictive. He then concludes that 'the Conservatives gained a net of 6.7% of the vote on the basis of the immigration issue alone.' See D. T. Studlar, 'Policy Voting in Britain: The Coloured Immigration Issue in the 1964, 1966 and 1970 Elections', *American Political Science Review*, 72 (1978), 46–72; I. Mclean, *Changing Directions: Rhetoric and Manipulation in British Politics since 1846* (Oxford: Oxford University Press, forthcoming).

[47] Campbell, *Edward Heath*, 285. Campbell highlights the fact that, although the swing in Wolverhampton and a few neighbouring constituencies was somewhat larger than the average 4.8%, Heath's swing was consistent across the country, in constituencies where immigration was an issue and in those where it was not. There does seem to be some evidence to support this claim. Leeds (with a high concentration of immigrants) recorded a swing to the Conservatives of 3.3%, Edinburgh (with a low concentration) one of 2.8%. In Cardiff (high concentration) the figure was 4.1%, in East Anglia (low concentration) 5.5%. Leicester recorded the highest swing against the government: 6.8%, with East and West Midlands second and third at 5.9% and 5.8%. The differences between these figures are not large, and show no consistent correlation between high-immigrant constituencies and a high swing to the Conservatives. For the rest of the regional results, see Butler and Pinto-Duschinsky, *British General Election of 1970*, Appendix I, 356–7.

[48] Edward Heath maintains that Powell's goal was to place himself in a better position for a leadership challenge following the loss of the election, which he, Powell, fully expected. Heath, *Course of My Life*, 455–6.

[49] F. W. S. Craig (ed.), *British General Election Manifestos 1959–1987* (Aldershot: Dartmouth, 1990), 127; CPA, ACP 3/20, 'Manifesto. Spring 1970. Fourth Draft'. For a background paper laying out the Conservatives' approach to immigration and integration while in opposition, see CPA, CC04/10/257, 'Race Relations', undated.

In implementing this promise, the government had to choose the mechanism on which to base the new system of control. As in 1962, the institutional framework created in 1948 discouraged its own replacement, despite the legion arguments in favour of doing so. BNA's assumption that an exclusive UK citizenship would emerge as a post-independence residual proved spectacularly false, and, as the 1968 Commonwealth Immigrants Act made clear, the UK had no intention of fulfilling a legal obligation to admit the hundreds of thousands of CUKCs, the 'detritus of Empire', without a qualifying connection to the United Kingdom.[50] The withdrawal of all but a handful of privileges, such as the right to vote in the UK and to reside in the UK without registering with the police, from Citizens of the United Kingdom and Colonies meant that the normative principles underlying the 1948 Act—the attachment to the traditional rights of British subjects—would be entirely undermined.

Although the obsolescence of the 1948 scheme was recognized,[51] the government felt unable to replace it with an alternative control mechanism, such as a new definition of British citizenship. The legal complexities involved in a massive redefinition of the various citizenships created by the 1948 scheme would incur the hostility of Commonwealth governments.[52] Instead, a three-person group, including the former Home Secretary, Henry Brooke, was asked to consider the matter. It recommended the retention of BNA 1948 and the repeal of the Aliens Restrictions Act, 1914 and 1919 and the Commonwealth Immigrants Acts.[53] BNA would remain in statute, but it would be largely superseded by the new legislation.

Although the new legislation had the advantage of rationalizing a series of acts passed since the beginning of the century, it was a testament to the constraining influence of the 1948 citizenship scheme. As the introduction of a new citizenship scheme was excessively complicated and costly, the government opted instead to rely on the notion of 'patriality', or a certain familial connection to the United Kingdom. The result was a delay in the introduction of a distinctive United Kingdom citizenship, for which the case was abundantly clear, and the introduction of an apparently racist concept into British legislation. The latter served as a focus of attack in Parliament.

[50] *CPA, CRD 3/16/4*, Memorandum by Patrick Cosgrave for Edward Heath', 19 Mar. 1970.
[51] *CPA, CRD 3/16/4*, 'Integration of the Law Relating to Aliens and Commonwealth Immigrants', undated.
[52] *CPA, CRD, 3/16/4*, Memorandum by Patrick Cosgrave for Edward Heath, 19 Mar. 1970.
[53] *CPA, CRD 3/16/4*, 'Integration of the Law Relating to Aliens and Commonwealth Immigrants', undated.

THE IMMIGRATION ACT, 1970 IN PARLIAMENT

The broad provisions of the Immigration Bill, 1971 were announced in July 1970,[54] and the Home Secretary, Reginald Maudling, moved the second reading of the bill on 8 March 1971.[55] The act itself does not specify the mechanism through which immigration is regulated; it rather empowers the Home Secretary to lay such rules before Parliament.[56] It introduces the term patrial, and equates it with one having the 'right of abode'.[57] It defines those who have the right of abode—UK CUKCs and other CUKCs resident in the UK for more than five years and their wives.[58] It applies the same system of control to all those who lack it.[59] It allows the Home Secretary and the courts to make a deportation order against non-patrials.[60] Finally, the act includes a number of modest provisions for voluntary repatriation.[61]

---

[54]   In response to the announcement, India ended its policy of allowing British citizens to enter India without visas or entry certificates. *The Times*, 'Britons to need visas for India', 14 July 1970.

[55]   *Parliamentary Debates (Commons)* (813), col. 42, 8 Mar. 1971.

[56]   Section 3 (2). These rules were placed before Parliament in 1973, and the government was defeated on them. The defeat is discussed later in the chapter.

[57]   Section 2 (6).   [58]   Section 1 (2).   [59]   Section 3 (5).

[60]   Sections 2 (6).

[61]   Section 29 (1) authorizes the Secretary of State, with treasury approval, to make payments for the expenses of non-patrials leaving the United Kingdom for a country in which they intend to reside permanently. Section 29 (2) instructs the Secretary of State not to make these payments unless 'it is shown that it is in that person's interest to leave the United Kingdom and that he wishes to do so'. The section fulfilled the election pledge, but transformed a potentially sinister programme into a limited, almost benign, programme. It should be noted that a repatriation programme of sorts had already existed under Labour. In the 1960s, the National Assistance Board had the power to repatriate Commonwealth citizens who had not been able to settle 'successfully' in the country if doing so would lead to a saving in National Assistance and if they wished to go. The initiative was generally taken at the request of the immigrants themselves, though the National Assistance Board could suggest repatriation in exceptional circumstances. (It is unclear how often such suggestions were made.) Old Dominion governments paid for the repatriation of their citizens, and the British government paid for New Commonwealth citizens. In the mid-1960s, approximately 100 left under the scheme. The Ministry of Health could also repatriate Commonwealth citizens who wished to leave when it was shown to be medically desirable (see *PRO, HO 376/134*, 'Repatriation of Commonwealth and Colonial Immigrants by the National Assistance Board,' undated). The possibility of expanding this programme was considered at the time of the 1965 Osborne Bill, and Maurice Foley was interested in expanding the scheme (see *PRO, HO 376/134*, 'Repatriation of Commonwealth and Colonial Citizens', Mar. 1965 and 'Repatriation at Public Expense of Commonwealth citizens who fail to settle well in the UK', 24 June 1966, respectively). The proposal was opposed by the Colonial Relations Office (*PRO, HO 376/134*, Repatriation at Public Expense of Commonwealth citizens who have not settled down well in this country', 9 June 1966) and by some sections of the Home Office. The latter opposed the scheme because it would be open to abuse, it would probably make little difference in numbers of departures (since most Commonwealth citizens wished to remain), and it

The fact that patriality originally included, in the bill, grandparents caused great controversy. During the debate, it met considerable criticism for its alleged racialism and for its introduction of 'patriality' into British statute.[62] Powell likened the test to a Nazi law disqualifying Germans with a Jewish grandparent from certificates of German purity (*'Grossmutter nicht in Ordnung,'* 'Grandmother not in order').[63]

To some degree, the comparison is suspect. The difference between granting citizenship rights to first- and second-generation descendants born abroad is one of degree rather than kind. European and North American nationality law is generally based on a mix of *ius soli* (citizenship by territory) and *ius sanguinis* (citizenship by descent), and the right to pass one's citizenship to descendants born abroad is generally accepted. The terminus of this right is a matter of debate, but there is no obvious reason why granting citizenship to the first generation is acceptable but granting it to the second is objectionable. For its part, 'patriality' was only adopted as the legal basis of belonging because the British government could not, or at least felt that it could not, replace CUKC with an exclusive definition of British citizenship. The Home Office was in fact quite pleased with itself in having found a legal status that got around the problem of reforming 1948 and yet still succeeded in equating Commonwealth citizens with aliens for the purposes of immigration; it was wholly unprepared for the chorus of opprobrium directed at the concept.[64]

The bill none the less contained a racial element. The patriality provisions were clearly designed to secure access for Australians, Canadians, and New Zealanders while denying it to the rest of the Commonwealth.[65] They were also, however, a mechanism for distinguishing between Britons and those denied entry rights without recourse to a new definition of British citizenship. Enoch

would involve taking full responsibility for costs that the British government wished to see Commonwealth governments assume (*PRO, HO 376/133*, 'Measures to reduce coloured Commonwealth immigration', Document for the Secretary of State, 11 Sept. 1964).

[62] The patriality clause was criticized both for its racialism (by, for example, granting rights to grandchildren of persons who left the UK 150 years ago while denying them the East African CUKCs) and for its generosity, particularly the possibility that one million plus Anglo-Indians could enter the UK. See *Parliamentary Debates (Commons)* (813), cols. 112–13, 8 Mar. 1971 (David Steel). The bill itself was said to be a sop to racial prejudice because it would have little effect on the number of immigrants (cols. 120–4, John Fraser), while the registration proposals (subsequently dropped) would encourage police harassment of black immigrants (cols. 134–5, Renée Short). The bill was also criticized by *The Times* as unnecessary, given the government's limited ability to further restrict immigration while respecting the rights of dependants, and by the National Council for Civil Liberties, as a destruction of the remaining advantages of Commonwealth citizenship. *The Times*, 'Tighter control over immigrants', 9 Oct. 1970.

[63] *Parliamentary Debates (Commons)* (813), col. 80, 8 Mar. 1971.

[64] Interview with a Home Office official.

[65] I. Macdonald, *The New Immigration Law* (London: Butterworths, 1972), 4; R. Maudling, *Memoirs* (London: Sidgwick & Jackson, 1978), 158–9.

Powell and James Callaghan argued that precisely such a new definition was required.[66] The Commonwealth Immigrants Act, as Powell pointed out, legislated by exception ('all CUKCs may enter the country except . . .'). Having faced the opportunity to replace the 1948 scheme, which used the language of citizenship (CUKC) without defining its content (who belonged to the UK and who did not), policy-makers in 1962 balked. Almost a decade later, Powell charged, they committed the same error; they tinkered further with the categories of persons which could claim entry (Australians with British grandparents—yes, other Australians—no; dependants of current immigrants—yes, dependants of future immigrants—no), but they left untouched the fundamental redefinition of British citizenship. This failing led him to conclude that 'although I sympathise with [Maudling's] aspiration to finality . . . I am convinced that we shall soon again have to legislate, and have to legislate fundamentally.'[67] In whatever else Powell was wrong, he was in this claim, exactly right.

As governments often did on immigration bills, the Conservatives faced a difficult—but not debilitating—time in committee. Labour's overall opposition was tepid, limited to the argument that a full-scale review of citizenship was required.[68] The original bill contained the requirement that Commonwealth citizens, in addition to aliens, would have to register with the police. A number of backbenchers had expressed at a private meeting with the Home Secretary reservations about the effect of registration on community relations,[69] and Maudling expressed flexibility on this point during the bill's second reading.[70] The requirement was dropped in committee.[71] More seriously, the government received a defeat on the patrial clause.[72] The liberal wing on the party—represented by the Bow Group and Pressure for Economic and Social Toryism—had been unhappy with the bill from the beginning, particularly its failure to make better provisions for the Kenyan Asians,[73] and the patriality clause was opposed by a coalition of the left

[66]   As one would suspect, Powell supported certain provisions, such as repatriation, which Callaghan did not.

[67]   *Parliamentary Debates (Commons)* (813), col. 81, 8 Mar. 1971. For Callaghan's comments, see cols. 62–6.

[68]   S. Saggar, *Race and Politics in Britain* (London: Harvester Wheatsheaf, 1992), 116–17.

[69]   *The Times*, 'Tory fears on registration with the police', 2 Mar. 1971.

[70]   *Parliamentary Debates (Commons)* (813), cols. 50–1, 8 Mar. 1971.

[71]   This concession was probably eased by the fact that the police opposed registration because of its possible consequences for police-immigrant relations. *The Times*, 'Police do not want to have to register immigrants', 28 Apr. 1971. Freedom from the requirement to register is now, along with the right to vote, one of the few residual rights enjoyed by Commonwealth citizens resident in the United Kingdom.

[72]   For press comment, see *The Times*, 'A government defeat over the patrials', 7 April 1971.

[73]   *The Times*, 'Bow Group chief says bill ignores case of Asians', 26 Apr. 1971. Rather ironically, given his approach in the 1990s to Hong Kong, the chairman of the Bow Group was Michael Howard.

(which saw it as racist) and the right (which feared an open door for persons of 'mixed blood').[74] In response to these concerns, the right of abode was limited to persons with parents born in the UK (its application to those with grandparents was reinstated when the immigration rules of 1973 were published). The bill received the Royal Assent on 21 October 1971.

THE UGANDAN ASIANS CRISIS

As the act left CUKC status intact, it did not address the conundrum created by the Commonwealth Immigrants Act of 1962: British subjects in the UK, those in the few remaining colonies, and those without local citizenship all possessed the same legal status. The Commonwealth was effectively littered with second-class British citizens. The Conservative government discovered in this fact, as Labour had before it, the seeds of a political crisis.

In January 1971, Milton Obote of Uganda was deposed in a military coup executed by Idi Amin. Heath, who had disagreed with Obote (and much of the African Commonwealth) on defence sales to South Africa, was not sorry to see him go.[75] He soon would be; on 4 August 1972 Amin announced that there was 'no room in Uganda' for the Asians. He accused the Asians of economic sabotage, appealed to the army for help against them, and bluntly stated that they were now a British responsibility.

The situation in Uganda was a mirror image of Kenya a few years earlier. The Ugandan constitution granted citizenship to those born in Uganda to a father born there, and it offered wives of citizens the opportunity to register.[76] To apply for citizenship, one had to renounce any other nationality and apply within two years from 9 October 1962. Of the approximately 73,000 Asians in Uganda, one-half retained their CUKC status; the applications of 12,000 were not processed or not properly completed; a few thousand retained Indian or Pakistani nationality; and the rest became Ugandan citizens.[77] As in Kenya, non-citizens found themselves the target of Africanization. The 1969 Trade Licensing Act increased controls on trading licenses, limited non-citizens to

---

[74] In opposition to the patrial provisions, Powell found himself united, in Parliament, with a collection of generally liberal MPs—David Steel (Liberal), Sir George Sinclair (Conservative, Dorking), and Stanley Clinton Davis (Labour, Hackney Central)—and, outside it, the National Council for Civil Liberties. *The Times*, 'Liberty Powell', 8 Apr. 1971.

[75] Campbell, *Edward Heath*, 338.

[76] The Constitution of the Republic of Uganda, Section 4 (1) and (4).

[77] H. H. Patel, 'Indians in Uganda and Rhodesia—Some Comparative Perspectives on a Minority in African', *Studies in Race and Nations* (Center on International Race Relations, University of Denver), 5, No. 1 (1973–4), 26.

specific areas, and often restricted their work to particular occupations, and a 1970 Immigration Act required non-Ugandans to possess one of several types of entry permits if they were to remain in the country.[78] Obote, however, had been slow to implement these policies, responding to the carrot of British aid.[79] When Kenyan Asians found themselves squeezed out of the economy, their Ugandan counterparts were still relatively secure. This tranquillity ended with Amin, whose announcement of the expulsion was quick and brutal: all Asians from Britain, India, Pakistan, Bangladesh, Kenya, Tanzania, and Zambia were told they had three months to leave Uganda.[80]

The British government had feared a deterioration in the Ugandan Asians' situation,[81] but such a sudden and brutal action was entirely unpredicted.[82] The decision was followed by days of intense diplomatic negotiations, and the government threatened a cut-off of foreign aid, as well as other vague economic punishments, if the Asians were expelled.[83] The government originally stuck to its electoral pledge not to allow any further large-scale immigration, and repeatedly stated over the days immediately following Amin's announcement that the quota system established for Kenyan Asians could not be altered. India stated that it would accept no more than a limited number of Asians,[84] provided they remained Britain's responsibility,[85] and Kenya announced two days later that its border with Uganda would be sealed to prevent the crossing of any Asian refugees.[86] Still hoping to change Amin's mind, Geoffrey Rippon, Chancellor of the Duchy of Lancaster, flew to Uganda on 11 August for talks with the President.[87] The effort was futile; Amin was beyond reasonable persuasion,[88] and he brushed Rippon aside with the claim that he was too busy to see him.

Nine days after Amin's announcement, the British government stated that it would accept full responsibility for Asian CUKCs. The UK government

---

[78] K. Ingham, *Obote: A Political Biography* (London: Routledge, 1994), 122.

[79] *CPA, CRD 3/16/4*, Memorandum by Patrick Cosgrave for Edward Heath, 11 Mar. 1970.

[80] *Guardian*, 'Britain could face influx of 80,000 Asians', 5 Aug. 1972; *The Times*, 'Gen Amin confirms other Asians will be affected', 8 Aug. 1972.

[81] *CPA, CRD 3/16/14*, Memorandum by Patrick Cosgrave for Edward Heath, 11 Mar. 1970.

[82] Confidential interview.

[83] *The Times*, 'Asian policy may cost Gen Amin British aid', 8 Aug. 1972; *Guardian*, 'Amin says stopping aid would not save Asians', 8 Aug. 1972.

[84] These restrictions were lifted when the British government announced it would accept the Ugandan Asians.

[85] *The Times*, 'India bars 40,000 Ugandan Asians', 7 Aug. 1972.

[86] *The Times*, 'Kenya seals border with Uganda to keep out expelled Asians', 9 Aug. 1972.

[87] *The Times*, 'Mr. Rippon flies to Uganda in effort to stop expulsion of 50,000 British Asians', 12 Aug. 1972; *Guardian*, 'Rippon's visit risks a snub from Amin', 12 Aug. 1972.

[88] Amin had announced a few days earlier that the plan was given to him by God. See Ingham, *Obote*, 142; *The Times*, 'Kenya seals border with Uganda to keep out expelled Asians', 9 Aug. 1972.

abandoned any hope of influencing Amin, and turned its attention to encouraging other nations to accept them. Over fifty were approached; Canada ultimately agreed to accept 5,000 Asians,[89] and several other nations, including India,[90] the United States, West Germany, and Sweden accepted a smaller number. A Resettlement Board was created to ease the Asians' integration into the UK, and airlifts began at the end of August. By the 8 November deadline, all approximately 50,000 Asian CUKCs had been evacuated from Uganda, and—thanks in part to last-minute offers from Greece, Malta, Spain, and Morocco—only 800 stateless Asians, under UN protection, remained in Uganda.[91]

Although the term was not in common usage, Amin's treatment of the Ugandans was a clear instance of ethnic cleansing. Asians, many of whom were born to families that had lived in Uganda for generations,[92] were forced to leave their homes and businesses and were prevented from selling them to anyone but Africans, who had every incentive to wait until they were freely obtainable after the expulsion. They were prevented from taking their savings, and even the shillings in their pockets and jewellery on their bodies were wrested from them at the airport.[93] At least half of the 20,000 Asians with Ugandan citizenship found themselves stripped of it (Amin felt the figure to be too high[94]). Following the deadline, Amin first ordered all Asian citizens left (numbering approximately 500) to be transferred to rural areas to cultivate plots of land granted by the government,[95] but then later extended the

[89] *The Times*, 'Canadian Government agrees to take some Ugandan Asians', 25 Aug. 1972. Canadian immigration policy is based on a 'points system' which rewards linguistic skills, education, capacity for investment, and so forth. The Asians were an exceptionally skilled and well-educated group, and many would probably have gained entry without Canada's decision. On the Canadian system, see M. García y Griego, 'Canada: Flexibility and Control in Immigration and Refugee Policy', in W. A. Cornelius et al. (eds.), *Controlling Immigration: A Global Perspective* (Stanford, Calif.: Stanford University Press, 1994).

[90] Soon after the British government announced its decision, India reversed its limited and temporary access for Ugandan Asians. The Indian High Commission in Kampula was instructed to grant entry visas to all Asian CUKCs willing to renounce their passports and reside permanently in India. Few availed themselves of this new right. See A. Gupta, 'India and the Asians in East Africa', in M. Twaddle (ed.), *Expulsion of a Minority: Essays on Ugandan Asians* (London: Athlone, 1975).

[91] *The Times*, 'Only 800 stateless Asians left as Amin deadline expires', 9 Nov. 1972.

[92] For a discussion of the Ugandan Asian community's history in Uganda, as well as its character shortly before the expulsion, see H. S. Morris, *The Indians in Uganda* (London: Weidenfeld & Nicolson, 1968).

[93] *The Times*, ' "Not a single Ugandan shilling" to leave, airport notice says', and 'Asians tell of passports cut, broken-glass haircuts,' 1 Sept. 1972.

[94] *The Times*, 'Professional men and technicians preparing to leave Uganda with their expelled fellow-Asians', 11 Aug. 1972.

[95] *The Times*, 'Uganda's remaining Asians must work on the land', 13 Nov. 1972.

expulsion order to include 'any person of Indian, Pakistan or Bangladesh origin, extraction or descent'.[96]

While Heath's action was successful, it did not come without cost. The most immediate threat to the Conservative government was an attack from the Tory right on Heath's leadership. The Monday Club organized a 'Halt Immigration Now' campaign within the Conservative Party,[97] and Enoch Powell again attacked the government. Accusing it of lying to the British public over the country's obligations under international law and capitulating to Amin, Powell told a 13 September audience that '[i]f the overriding purpose had been to humiliate the people of this country and show complete indifference to their interests, feelings and wishes, the tactics could not have been better devised.'[98]

Powell carried his attack to the October Annual Conference. Against the wishes of the party leadership, he secured through a ballot of constituency delegates the inclusion on the conference agenda of a resolution on immigration. The resolution was deceptively uncontroversial: it declared '[t]hat this Conference is convinced that the Conservative Party's declared policy on immigration is the only solution likely to be successful and should be implemented by this Government at the earliest opportunity.'[99] The implication, which Powell made quite clear in his address, was that the government should fulfil its promise of 'no large-scale immigration' and refuse entry to the Ugandan Asians.

Facing the very real possibility that the motion might be carried, Heath challenged Powell on the eve of the conference. Although the government recognized public anxiety over immigration, it 'knew that we had no choice but to stand by Britain's obligation. . . . [The British people] have refused to be scared into supporting the attitude of meanness and bad faith towards the refugees. They have responded in accordance with our traditions of honouring our obligations and holding out a friendly hand to people in danger and distress.'[100]

Although the Conservative Party, unlike—at least theoretically—the Labour Party, is not bound by conference resolutions, support for the resolution would have been a serious symbolic blow to the government. In addition, the media had in the weeks preceding the conference built the matter up to be

[96]   *The Times*, 'General Amin issues decrees on Asians from hospital', 26 Nov. 1972.

[97]   Layton-Henry, 'Immigration and the Heath Government', 229.

[98]   *The Times*, 'Decision shows yawning gap between government and nation, Mr Powell says', 13 Sept. 1972. Powell's campaign had begun with a letter to *The Times* on 15 Aug. 1972, shortly after the decision to accept them was announced.

[99]   *Nineteenth Annual Conference of the National Union of Conservative and Unionist Associations*, 72.

[100]   *The Times*, 'Mr. Heath takes up Powell's challenge', 11 Oct. 1972.

a clash of immeasurable importance, one which would be crucial to both men's political futures.[101] The party leadership responded by encouraging David Hunt, the Chairman of the Young Conservatives, to move an amendment replacing all the words after 'successful' with 'and congratulates the Government on its swift action to accept responsibility for the Asian refugees from Uganda'. Hunt's speech, which denounced Powell in naked terms, was followed with a speech by Robert Carr, who succeeded Maudling as Home Secretary, affirming the Conservative Party's fundamental restrictionism.[102] The strategy worked; the Young Conservatives' amendment was carried by 1,721 to 985.[103]

Ultimately, approximately 28,000 Ugandan Asians settled permanently in the United Kingdom. They were a sophisticated and talented group of individuals who integrated without difficulty into British society.[104] As was the case with past migrations (Polish migration after the War standing out as an example), the success of their integration is proved by the fact that their arrival has largely been forgotten.

THE IMMIGRATION RULES

After routing Powell at the conference, the government promulgated its new immigration rules. Schoen suggests that this was a further concession to Powellism,[105] but they had in fact been promised by Maudling when he presented the 1971 Immigration Bill to Parliament, and they contained no further restrictions.

The rules, as promised, placed Commonwealth citizens on the same legal footing as aliens; non-patrial Commonwealth citizens were only allowed the enter the UK for six months and could only work with permission. Alone, these rules would probably have been approved by Parliament. The government, however, linked them with new rules for European nationals, which

---

[101] Schoen, *Enoch Powell and the Powellites*, 94.

[102] *Nineteenth Annual Conference of the National Union of Conservative and Unionist Associations*, 73 (Hunt) and 76–80 (Carr). This is not to suggest that the government failed to stick by his commitment. In December, Heath staunchly defended the decision to a London audience. If the UK had not accepted the Ugandans, '[t]hey would be rotting in concentration camps prepared by President Amin and they would be there simply because of the colour of their skin and the fact that they held British passports. That would have been the sight presented to us on our television screens night after night this Christmas.' *The Times*, 'Mr. Heath: Triumph will emerge after "setbacks, mistakes" ', 1 Dec. 1972.

[103] For his efforts, Hunt found himself deselected as a parliamentary candidate by Plymouth.

[104] Campbell, *Edward Heath*, 394.

[105] Schoen, *Enoch Powell and the Powellites*, 95.

gave effect to the Treaty of Rome's provisions on the free movement of European workers. This decision earned the government the hostility of parliamentarians opposed to any further retrenchment of Commonwealth citizens' rights (particular citizens from the Old Commonwealth), those who remained opposed to Britain's membership in the European Economic Community and a larger, more diffuse, group of individuals who could tolerate either action on its own, but could not bring themselves to strip Commonwealth citizens of rights at precisely the moment they granted them to Europeans. The government created the conditions for a cross-party coalition against it. In retrospect, it seems extraordinary that the front bench failed to foresee this possibility.

Against a three-line Whip, the assurances of Robert Carr, and the prestige and charisma of Sir Alec Douglas-Home, the government was defeated by thirty-five votes (240 for, 275 against). Forty Conservative MPs abstained, and seven—including Enoch Powell—voted against the government.[106] Against calls for his resignation, Heath calmly promised new rules, and left the chamber white with anger.

The vote was the first time, with one minor wartime exception, that a British government had been defeated on a matter of importance since 1895,[107] and it reflected broader backbench dissatisfaction with Heath's abrasive style and the inability of the government to overcome Britain's chronic economic difficulties.[108] In terms of migration, it was more of a final, angry, ineffectual protest. Parliament had acceded to the Treaty of Rome, and there was little scope, promised or delivered, for alterations in either these or the immigration rules. When the new rules were laid before Parliament on 25 January 1973, the changes were cosmetic: an extension, for example, of the length of time granted to Commonwealth citizens on the working-holiday scheme. Non-patrial Commonwealth citizens faced the same basic restrictions as aliens, and they were in a disadvantageous position vis-à-vis European nationals.

POWELL, HEATH, AND POST-WAR MIGRATION

This chapter has considered three aspects of the 1968–74 period: the passage of the Immigration Act of 1971, the role of Enoch Powell in shaping immigration

---

[106] For the debate on the rules, and the division, see *Parliamentary Debates (Commons)*, (846), col. 1343–59, 22 Nov. 1972.

[107] A. King, 'How to Strengthen Legislatures—Assuming that We Want to', in N. J. Ornstein (ed.), *The Role of the Legislature in Western Democracies* (Washington, DC: American Enterprise Institute for Public Policy Research, 1981), 87.

[108] On this, see P. Norton, 'Intra-Party Dissent in the House of Commons: A Case Study. The Immigration Rules 1972', *Parliamentary Affairs*, 29, No. 3 (1976), 404–20.

policy, and the implications of the Ugandan Asians crisis for the scholarly judgement of post-war governments' approach to Commonwealth immigration. The Immigration Act of 1971 constitutes a further instance in which the efforts of a British government to articulate immigration policies were constrained by previous policy decisions. The aim of the act was clear: to equate as much as possible the position of non-UK Commonwealth citizens with that of aliens. The instruments with which to achieve this aim were, however, constrained, and the government was unable to articulate an exclusive definition of British citizenship. It instead opted for a controversial legal concept which served to further its legislative difficulties, including a legislative defeat, while failing to obviate the future need for legislation. In consequence of the continuing effects of BNA, the government's aspiration to achieve finality was frustrated.

The effect of Powell in the 1970–4 period is a matter of some debate. When I put the question to him, he stated that causality in politics is most difficult to determine; when I suggested he try to determine it, he concluded that he had no effect at all. His view is shared by the Home Office, which saw the 1971 Act as the simple execution of a manifesto commitment. Powell's effect should not be exaggerated, but it is none the less important. The support he galvanized in the two years preceding the 1970 election worried Heath, and in a series of statements—in September 1968, January 1969—he explicitly moved party policy in a Powellite direction. Significantly, each intervention followed one by Powell and each was more restrictive than previous policy. In the first of these, moreover, Heath promised to equate the position of aliens with those of Commonwealth citizens; this equation was at the foundation of the Immigration Act of 1971. In setting the broad terms of debate, then, Powell's influence was felt.

Powell's project was supported and delimited by his institutional position. Powell's place within the party, as a member of the Shadow Cabinet, gave him a privileged position from which to exercise influence;[109] yet, his failure to bring the party with him ensured that this influence would ultimately be limited.[110] After the Birmingham speech, it would have been difficult to name more than a few MPs, such as John Biffen, who supported him in the parliamentary party. He enjoyed widespread support in the public, as demonstrated in marches and public opinion polls, and considerable support among

---

[109]   A. M. Messina. *Race and Party Competition in Britain* (Oxford: Clarendon, 1989), 189.

[110]   This conclusion should not be surprising. As Powell himself remarked, the basis of Westminster politics and British parliamentary government is party; it is from this institution that the executive is formed and within this institution that individuals exercise their influence. See E. Powell, Speech to South Kensington Young Conservatives, 30 Sept. 1976 and Speech to the Croydon South Conservatives Annual Conference, 10 Nov. 1973, *Reflections of a Statesman*, 255 and 471–3, respectively.

party activists, as reflected in the 1972 Annual Conference. But without supporters on the front bench, and without significant support on the back bench, he guaranteed that, despite the large and passionate support once enjoyed, his influence after the passage of the 1971 Act would be limited. On repatriation, and more importantly on the Ugandan Asians crisis, it was not Powell but Heath who left his signature on immigration policy in the early 1970s.

The Ugandan Asians crisis is in itself significant for the extent to which it highlights the 1970–4 Conservative government's liberality relative to that of Harold Wilson. It has been claimed that Heath did nothing more than fulfil the United Kingdom's duty under international law.[111] This claim is only partially true, and it trivializes the accomplishment of the Heath government. International law is a vague term referring to a series of international conventions, treaties, and norms[112] that become binding on particular states through accession by a state or through incorporation by a state into domestic law. Since enforcement mechanisms in the case of the former remain weak, incorporation is the surest means to ensure that international agreements are respected.

The UK was said to have an obligation under international law because no citizen is to be deprived of his citizenship. The Labour government, however, did precisely that, denying Asian CUKCs with no other citizenship the right to enter the United Kingdom. Their case was argued by Anthony Lester before the European Commission of Human Rights, and the British action

---

[111] Dummett and Nicol, *Subjects, Citizens, Aliens and Others*, 234. There is a general reluctance in the literature to concede the laudable and, given the hysterical anti-immigrant sentiment that reigned at the time, brave character of Heath's action, most likely because it complicates an otherwise simple history of racism, cowardice, and capitulation. A. Sivanandan, for instance, devotes pages to the Kenyan Asians, but mentions the Ugandan Asians in one line and does not note the government's decision to grant them entry. A. Sivanandan, 'From Resistance to Rebellion', in Sivanandan, *A Different Hunger: Writings on Black Resistance* (London: Pluto Press, 1982), 29.

[112] The core of these provisions is the United Nations Charter (which has brief references to human rights and questions of self-determination), the Universal Declaration of Human Rights (United Nations General Assembly Resolution 217A (111), 1948), the International Convenant on Civil and Political Rights and the International Covenant on Economic Social and Cultural Rights (both 1976). The last three form the International Bill of Rights. Added to these are the Hague Resolutions of 1907, the Geneva Convention of 1949 (both concerning conduct of war and treatment of war prisoners), and the European Convention on Human Rights. In the case of refugees, for whom there is the strongest international human rights regime, there is the 1951 Geneva Convention relating to the status of refugees and the 1967 Protocol relating to the status of refugees. See G. Goodwin-Gill, *The Refugee in International Law* (Oxford: Clarendon, 1996); M. Theodor, *Human Rights in Internal Strife: Their International Protection* (Cambridge: Grotius, 1987); H. J. Steiner and P. Alston, *International Human Rights in Context: Law, Politics, Morals* (Oxford: Clarendon, 1996); and P. Thornberry, *International Law and the Rights of Minorities* (Oxford: Clarendon, 1991).

was found to contravene the European Convention on Human Rights.[113] As the Ugandan situation was legally identical to the Kenyan, international law would presumably have applied in the same manner (although those who claim that the UK was bound by such law rarely specify which). The only differences between the two cases were that the number of Asians in Uganda was smaller, thus making the problem a more limited one, and Amin was more brutal than Kenyatta. These considerations made it at once more imperative and politically less risky to accept the Ugandans than the Kenyans, but it did not alter the legal question. Two points are relevant to this question. First, the Commission's decision was effectively ignored; Kenyan Asians were on queues well into the 1990s. Second, the Heath government did far more than refrain from impeding the Ugandan Asians entry. It organized a massive airlift to remove all Asian CUKCs from Uganda, and it worked with the United Nations to secure the safety of other Asians without Ugandan citizenship. In its response to the Ugandan Crisis, the Heath government acted— against hysterical anti-immigrant sentiment—with bravery and determination; it did not passively follow the dictates of external constraints.

It is salutary to end the dissertation's empirical investigations with a few reflections on the broad state of nationality law and immigration policy at the end of the Heath government. The Immigration Act, 1971 equated, with the exception of a few residual rights, Commonwealth citizens with aliens; it ended, with a few exceptions, the privileges enjoyed by British subjects outside the United Kingdom. Although the creation of British citizenship as a legal status would have to wait for Margaret Thatcher's first government, Heath facilitated the process politically (by ending the majority privileges enjoyed by British subjects abroad) and symbolically (by reducing the Commonwealth's importance and effect to symbol and sentiment). Although the language was not yet invoked, there existed for the first time a legally recognizable category of distinctively British citizens, persons with a qualifying connection to the UK. The confusing term 'patrials', a consequence of the constraining effect of the 1948 legislation, was the basis for an ultimate definition of British citizenship.[114]

At the same time, the importance of redefining citizenship gained broader recognition in Parliament. A Labour Study Group on Immigration, the membership of which included Anthony Lester, Eric Heffer, Tom Driberg,

---

[113] *East African Asians* v. *United Kingdom* European Human Rights Reports 3 (1981), 76–103. Britain ratified the Convention, but did not incorporate it into British law until 1999. See R. Brazier, *Constitutional Reform* (Oxford: Clarendon, 1991).

[114] Politically, the need for such a definition was recognized. The discussions leading up to the Immigration Act, 1971 emphasized the argument in its favour, and it was repeated by Callaghan and Powell (generally not allies) in Parliament.

and Ian Mikardo, recommended the creation of a separate United Kingdom citizenship;[115] the cross-party committee on United Kingdom citizenship had reached the same conclusion earlier;[116] and the 1972 Opposition Green Paper, 'Citizenship, Immigration and Integration', saw the merits, if not the necessity, of a distinctive conception and definition of UK citizenship. The lesson of the Kenyan and Ugandan Asians crises—that the possession of the same citizenship status with differential rights was legally untenable—had begun to be internalized by both parties.

At the end of the Heath government, the basic conditions for the institution of United Kingdom citizenship, and for an end to the legal and political crises associated again and again with immigration, were in place. Commonwealth citizens were equated in practice—though not in status as CUKC still existed—with aliens, and the final wave of mass migration, in the form of Ugandan Asians, had passed. It was left for the next Conservative government to replace the shell that remained on CUKC status for non-patrials with a legal status commensurate with their extremely attenuated rights.

---

[115] *LPA, Study Group on Immigration: Minutes and Papers 11 June 1969–29 April 1971*, 'Immigration to Britain: Report of the Study Group on Immigration', May 1971. The implications of distinctive citizenship were recognized by the Group: 'The effect of this proposal would be to recognize legally that the withdrawal of the right of colonial citizens to free entry to the UK is now inevitable. It would also follow that citizens of the United Kingdom and Colonies who are resident in the remaining UK colonies and dependencies, would have citizenship of the colony in which they are resident. Citizens of the United Kingdom and Colonies who are ordinarily resident in the independent countries of the Commonwealth, but who also have local citizenship, would become, solely, citizens of the country of residence.' Labour did not implement this proposal when it returned to power.

[116] Ibid., 'A Three Point Plan Proposed Concerning Citizenship & Migration within the Commonwealth', Jan. 1969.

9

Citizenship's Late Entrance: The British Nationality Act, 1981

TEN years after the passage of the Immigration Act, 1971, Margaret Thatcher's Conservative government finally overhauled British nationality law. The British Nationality Act, 1981 (BNA 1981) abolished the category of CUKC, all but abolished the status of British subject, and introduced a definition of citizenship exclusively for the United Kingdom. British citizenship was, for the first time, linked with membership in the political entity of the United Kingdom and, for the first time since 1962, linked with the full exercise of civic and political privileges enjoyed by members of the British political community.

The British Nationality Act marked a turning-point in another sense. The creation of a British citizenship not only ended the legal anomaly that had existed, with disastrous results, since 1962; it also decoupled nationality law and immigration. Immigration and citizenship are now governed by distinct legal regimes, and the UK finds itself broadly convergent with the rest of Europe in that it combines relatively easy access to nationality with strict migration control. The main remaining difference between the UK and the rest of Europe is in its liberal and restrictionist thrusts: nationality law is slightly more liberal in policy and practice than the rest of Europe, while migration policy is more restrictive. This chapter will consider the former; the next will turn to the latter, returning again to the issue of how a policy that was once so liberal became so restrictive.

Following a well-trodden path, scholars of migration have bitterly attacked BNA 1981. For John Solomos, the legislation, like the Immigration Act, 1971 before it, amounted to an 'attempt by the government to further circumvent the rights of those black Commonwealth citizens with a legal right to enter Britain and to construct the question of nationality along racial lines'.[1] The verdict is echoed by Ian Macdonald and Nicholas Blake, who argue that the legislation 'merely enshrines the existing racially discriminatory provisions of immigration law under the new clothing of British citizenship and the right

---

[1] J. Solomos, *Race and Racism in Britain* (Houndmills: Macmillan, 1993), 71.

of abode'.[2] Zig Layton-Henry, always more reserved in his judgements, favourably quotes Roy Hattersley's and David Steel's attacks on the legislation as a 'shabby' measure institutionalizing racism.[3] Most recently, Kathleen Paul concluded that 'despite its territorial appearance these [provisions of BNA 1981] in fact placed greater significance on parentage than on geography and so position the 1981 act within the larger postwar discourse of blood, family, and kith and kin'.[4] For its critics, the 1981 legislation was the culmination of decades of racism and state-sponsored 'racialization'.

This chapter examines the legislation in the context of this charge. It also considers nationality issues since 1981, particularly the citizenship status of Hong Kong 'Belongers'. It is designed as a descriptive exercise completing the examination of British nationality since 1948. It is meant to end the story of British nationality law, rather than to launch a new inquiry.

THE LABOUR PARTY AND NATIONALITY LAW

In 1977, the Labour government published a Green Paper entitled *British Nationality Law: Discussion of Possible Changes*.[5] The document proposed a substantial reform of British nationality law, including the introduction of 'British citizenship' (for those belonging to the United Kingdom) and 'British Overseas Citizenship' (for the remainder holding British nationality) as replacements for CUKC. Once in government, the Conservatives followed the basic structure of the Green Paper, and adopted a law that was more the product of William Whitelaw than Thatcher. Shortly after coming to power in 1979, the Conservatives published a White Paper containing similar proposals to Labour's; indeed, the paper itself emphasizes the common points between the two documents.[6] *British Nationality Law: Outline of Proposed Legislation* formed the basis of an act introduced a year later.

---

[2] I. Macdonald and N. Blake, *Immigration Law and Practice in the United Kingdom* (London: Butterworths, 1995), 144.

[3] Z. Layton-Henry, *The Politics of Race in Britain* (London: George Allen & Unwin, 1984), 159.

[4] K. Paul, *Whitewashing Britain: Race and Citizenship in the Postwar Era* (Ithaca, NY: Cornell University Press, 1997), 183.

[5] (London: HMSO, 1977), Cmnd. 6795.

[6] *British Nationality Law: Outline of Proposed Legislation* (London: HMSO, 1980), Cmnd. 7987, 1–2. The major differences between the documents were twofold: the Green Paper proposed granting citizenship to anyone born in the United Kingdom, while the White Paper rejected this proposal, and the White Paper proposed three categories of citizenship rather than two.

MARGARET THATCHER AND IMMIGRATION

Although the 1981 Act was not simply the product of Thatcher,[7] it is worth devoting a few words to her approach to immigration, as it was a policy area she claimed to take seriously, though she devoted little time to it in her long parliamentary career.

In her memoirs, she claims that on immigration—like so much else—she was dissatisfied with the patrician centrism of the Tory grandees, which expressed itself in 'civilized high-mindedness' and a desire to keep migration out of politics. Thatcher wished to carve out a policy more in line with popular demands:[8]

Nothing is more colour-blind than the capitalism in which I placed my faith for Britain's revival. It was part of my credo that individuals were worthy of respect *as individuals*, not as members of classes or races; the whole purpose of the political and economic system I favoured was to liberate the talents of those individuals for the benefits of society. I felt no sympathy for rabble rousers, like the National Front, who sought to exploit race. . . . At the same time, large-scale New Commonwealth immigration over the years had transformed large areas of Britain in a way which the indigenous population found hard to accept. It is one thing for a well-heeled politician to preach the merits of tolerance on a public platform before returning to a comfortable home in a tranquil road in one of the more respectable suburbs, where house prices ensure him the exclusiveness of apartheid without the stigma. It is quite another for poorer people, who cannot afford to move, to watch their neighbourhoods changing and the value of their house falling. Those in such a situation need to be reassured rather than patronised . . . The failure to articulate the sentiments of ordinary people . . . had left the way open to the extremists.[9]

Others, including senior Labour politicians, viewed her stand on immigration as a cynical effort to attract votes irrespective of the cost to relations between migrant and local communities. In truth, Thatcher's efforts reflected two factors, as Hugo Young noted in a masterful study of the Thatcher years. By disposition, Thatcher was, 'without effort or much apparent thought', as Young put it, strongly anti-immigration, on the Powellite right of the Conservative Party.[10] Her attitudes on immigration were similar to those she held on other social issues. She saw no contradiction between holding, steadfast and with little inclination towards tortured doubt about the complexity of most issues, to simplistic platitudes—'an end to immigration'—yet quietly

---

[7] Both parties and the Home Office agreed on the need to bring some rationality to immigration laws that had been piled onto the anachronistic British Nationality Act, 1948.

[8] M. Thatcher, *The Path to Power* (London: HarperCollins, 1995), 405–6.

[9] Ibid. 406.

[10] H. Young, *One of Us* (London: Pan Books, 1993), 233.

dispensing with them in instances that did square with her general principle. Thus, her firm anti-immigration stance was softened, while in Heath's Cabinet, to allow the entry of the Ugandan Asians, for whom she later claimed respect and even fondness.[11] By contrast, Enoch Powell, whose unyielding logic was usually his political downfall, led an almost viscous public campaign against the Asians. Likewise, Margaret Thatcher saw no contradiction between her moral opposition to homosexuality, pronounced several times during the 1980s, and her support for its decriminalization in 1967, following the experience of seeing a gay man humiliated for 'engaging in homosexual conduct', as only the British would call it.[12] Like many people, Margaret Thatcher had only good to say about actual immigrants, and nothing good to say about immigration.

Beyond armchair psychology, Thatcher's approach to immigration reflected the pursuit of an explicit political aim. Throughout her career as leader of the Opposition and Prime Minister, Thatcher was not, and could not be, as far to the ideological right as she claimed, and her strongest supporters expected her, to be. Her Cabinet colleagues and, on matters such as privatizing the NHS, the country would not have it. More or less ritual hard-line comments on the unions, social policy, and immigration allowed Margaret Thatcher to combine a recognition of the limits of the possible with a retention of her hard-core support of the party's far right. As Young argued,

> While the official position . . . was cautiously expressed and often more pleasing to the left than the right of the party, the right gained confidence from their belief, which was rarely contested, that in her heart the leader agreed with them. [Anti-immigration comments, quoted below] were not followed by a serious policy commitment to introduce a more repressive regime of immigration control. . . . But the text encouraged anyone who wanted to believe that Thatcher was a repressor of immigrants, just as numerous private conversations made it perfectly clear where she would honestly stand if she didn't have political reality to cope with on union privileges and welfare scroungers.[13]

On immigration, these efforts reached a peak in an infamous 1978 interview. On 30 January, during a period in which opinion polls were not in her favour, Thatcher told her *World in Action* interviewer that immigration was excessively high and that the British people were 'rather afraid that this country might be rather swamped by people with a different culture. . . . We do have to hold out the prospect of an end of immigration, except, of course, for compassionate cases.' Asked if she wished to bring National Front supporters back to the Tories, she replied, 'Oh, very much back, certainly, but I think that

---

[11]   Thatcher, *Path*, 212.   [12]   Ibid. 150–1.
[13]   Young, *One of Us*, 111.

the National Front has, in fact, attracted more people from Labour voters than from us. But never be afraid to tackle something which people are worried about. We are not in politics to ignore people's worries; we are in politics to deal with them.' The comment provoked an outcry, and some have suggested that Thatcher's decision to 'play the race card' succeeded in undermining National Front support and delivering the Conservatives a victory.[14]

It has also been interpreted as a 'repoliticization' of race and migration, the death knell of a decades-long effort to keep migration and race out of party competition.[15] Like similar claims about Enoch Powell,[16] the argument is exaggerated. Thatcher met a storm of criticism from within her party, and she did not return to the issue.[17] Whatever desire she might have had to chase a few votes or shore up her support among the Tory right wing by anti-immigrant rhetoric, William Whitelaw, Shadow Home Secretary and a powerful figure in the Conservative Party, refused to let her do it.[18] Migration had no effect in the 1979 election,[19] and William Whitelaw ensured that it was kept entirely out of the 1983 campaign.[20] At no point since the 1970s has Commonwealth immigration been more than a fleeting issue.[21] As Ivor Crewe noted at the time, the 1983 general election demonstrated that immigration had

[14] Layton-Henry, *Politics of Immigration*, 184–7.

[15] A. Messina, *Race and Party Competition in Britain* (London: Clarendon Press, 1989), 128.

[16] See Layton-Henry's argument that Powell's 'river of blood' speech 'saw [Labour's] carefully constructed bipartisan policy smashed to smithereens.' Layton-Henry, *Politics of Immigration*, 81. In fact, the consensus survived Powell's attack.

[17] D. Kavanagh, 'Enoch Powell: Vision and Waste', in *Politics and Personalities* (Houndmills: Macmillan, 1990), 173. Even Enoch Powell was dismissive: Thatcher 'could not see a live wire until she has hit it. Only touch electric fuses when you understand them.' Quoted ibid. [18] H. Young, *One of Us*, 111.

[19] See B. Särlvik and I. Crewe, *The Decade of Dealignment: The Conservative Victory of 1979 and Electoral Trends in the 1970s* (Cambridge: Cambridge University Press, 1983), 242–6. The public perceived the Conservatives to be more restrictionist than Labour, and this might have influenced the small minority (14%) who felt the issue to be important. This effect, the authors conclude, is likely to have been cancelled by the opposite minority—those immigrants and liberals who were repelled by the Conservatives' stricter stance.

[20] Confidential interviews.

[21] It is possible that Hong Kong, should China treat the former colony illiberally, might become such an issue. As it stands, the British Nationality (Hong Kong) Act of 1990 grants full British citizenship to 50,000 individuals and their families (to a total of 225,000). These quotas have been filled, but the interest in migration to the UK has been less than expected, and there has been little pressure on the UK to relax them. I discuss the Hong Kong situation in R. Hansen, 'The United Kingdom and Nationality Law in China's Hong Kong', *Oxford International Review*, 7, No. 3 (1996), 38–43. For the 1983, 1987, and 1992 elections, see D. Butler and D. Kavanagh, *The British General Election of 1983* (London: Macmillan, 1983), *The British General Election of 1987* (London: Macmillan, 1987), and *The British General Election of 1992* (London: Macmillan, 1992). Only in the 1992 election, when Kenneth Baker (Home Secretary) earned a front-page *Express* headline ('Baker's migrant flood warning', 7 Apr. 1992) by accusing Labour of laxity on asylum controls, is immigration mentioned.

'dropped off the political agenda'.[22] Since then, issues that would have been defined in terms of immigration in the 1960s—the 1981 Brixton riots, the 1985 Toxteth riots, the 1989 Rushdie affair—have been understood as issues of 'race relations', referring both to attitudes towards ethnic minorities and to their economic and social integration into British society.[23] Repatriation, once half-seriously discussed, has dropped off the political agenda, raised only, and oddly, by black MPs and activists. In the 1997 general election, neither immig-ration nor asylum were issues in the campaign, and the British National Party's performance, despite a strategy or concentrating efforts on poor communities with large migrant concentrations, was so derisory as to not even merit a mention in David Butler's and Dennis Kavanagh's analysis of the results.[24]

THE BRITISH NATIONALITY ACT, 1981

By far the most significant development in the last two decades, in national-ity or migration policy, was the enactment of the British Nationality Act, 1981. A number of concerns motivated the legislation. Above all, politicians in both parties believed that the contradictions surrounding nationality law had become intolerable. The Labour and Conservative Parties and the Home Office agreed that the nationality status of CUKCs without the right of abode had to be clarified, and that nationality legislation had to be brought into line with immigration rules and legislation.[25] Most importantly, this meant repeal-ing the British Nationality Act, 1948. The Ugandan Asians' crisis served as further proof—were any needed—of the need to place nationality law on a clearer foundation. In addition, gender played a minor role; before 1983, only British men could pass their citizenship to children born abroad. The Cabinet agreed that it was time to end the tradition of paternal descent, and to extend the right to transfer British citizenship to women. Although this reform has been seldom emphasized, it is one of the most important liberalizing initi-atives in nationality law in the post-war period. Finally, of course, the govern-ment wished to respond to public concerns over immigration by appearing to

---

[22]   I. Crewe, 'How Labour was trounced all around', *Guardian*, 14 June 1983.
[23]   On this see, S. Saggar, *Race and Politics in Britain* (London: Harvester Wheatsheaf, 1992), 126–9, D. Studlar, ' "Waiting for the catastrophe": Race and the Political Agenda in Britain', *Patterns of Prejudice*, 19, No. 1 (1985), 3–15. Also see B. D. Jacobs, *Black Politics and Urban Crisis in Britain* (Cambridge: Cambridge University Press, 1986).
[24]   D. Butler and D. Kavanagh, *The British General Election of 1997* (Houndmills: Macmillan, 1997).   [25]   Interviews with Home Office officials, May 1998.

take decisive action on the issue; the Prime Minister continued to feel particularly strongly about migration and nationality.[26]

The British Nationality Act of 1981 repealed the British Nationality Act, 1948 and created a new citizenship scheme based on three main categories. The most fundamental of these was British citizenship, which was defined to the exclusion of the colonies for the first time. All persons who had the right of abode were granted British citizenship, and 'patriality' was replaced as a legal concept by citizenship.[27] The concept thus no longer exists, though many people still cite it as evidence of the ethnic character of British migration law. In addition to the legal definition of British citizenship, BNA 1981 defined two additional categories: British Dependent Territories Citizenship (BDTC) and British Overseas Citizenship (BOCs). British Dependent Territories Citizenship was granted to persons in the remaining territories.[28] The majority of these individuals were residents of Hong Kong,[29] the largest remaining colony, but the territories also included Bermuda, the British Virgin Islands, and Gibraltar.[30] British Overseas Citizenship was granted as a residual category to all CUKCs who received neither of the other two citizenships. They were in practice stateless persons within independent members of the Commonwealth, mainly East African Asians still waiting to enter the United Kingdom, as well as a considerable number of individuals in Malaysia.[31]

[26] Confidential interview.

[27] More specifically, 'patriality' was subsumed under the category of 'right of abode', as all those who were the former retained the latter.

[28] In essence, those colonies that had not achieved independence.

[29] For discussion of the Hong Kong provisions, W. S. Clarke, 'Hong Kong Immigration Control: The Law and the Bureaucratic Maze', *Hong Kong Law Journal*, 16, No. 3 (Sept. 1986), 341–8; R. A. Hansen, 'The United Kingdom and Nationality Law in China's Hong Kong'; and R. M. White, 'Hong Kong Nationality, Immigration and the Agreement with China', *International and Comparative Law Quarterly*, 36, No. 3 (July 1987), 482–503.

[30] At BNA 1981's passage, members of the Falkland Islands were BDTCs. Following the Falkland's War, British citizenship was granted to all Falklanders through the British Nationality (Falklands Islands) Act, 1983. Citizens of Gibraltar remain BDTCs, but they are able to claim British citizenship at any time. Section 5 states that 'A British Dependent Territories citizen who fails to be treated as a national of the United Kingdom for the purposes of the Community Treaties shall be entitled to be registered as a British citizen if an application is made for his registration as such a citizen.'

[31] R. M. White and F. J. Hampson, ' "What is My Nation? Who Talks of My Nation?" British Nationality Act 1981', *International and Comparative Law Quarterly*, 31 (Oct. 1982), 849–55. The government retained the 'special quota' scheme established by the Commonwealth Immigrants Act, 1968 for BOCs who received that status in a former East African territory. To apply, an applicant must (1) be a 'head of a household'—a man or a woman, if the latter is single, widowed, divorced, or married to a mentally or physically incapable man, (2) be under pressure to leave, and (3) have neither citizenship nor the right to reside in any other country. The quota, which is established annually, is approximately 5,000, which includes the wife and dependent children under 25 of the head of household. At the Green Paper's publication, there were an estimated 190,000 individuals who would become British Overseas Citizens.

British Dependent Territories and British Overseas Citizenship were the hollow shells of Citizenship of the United Kingdom and Colonies; such citizens did not possess the right to enter the United Kingdom and, in the case of British Overseas Citizenship, were effectively stateless if they did not possess local citizenship.[32] The two categories essentially granted one of two impoverished legal identities to any former CUKC without local citizenship.

The act all but abolished the status of British subject, which had been used synonymously with 'Commonwealth citizen' until this point. After the passage of BNA 1981, the term was reserved for British subjects without citizenship (that is, stateless individuals within the Commonwealth), Irish citizens born before 1 January 1949 who express, or have expressed, the desire to remain British subjects[33] and women who were British subjects by virtue of the British Nationality Act of 1965.[34]

Acquiring British Citizenship

The act parted somewhat from the tradition of *ius soli*, which had underpinned previous nationality law.[35] Whereas birth in the United Kingdom or any dependent territory had traditionally meant, before 1 January 1949, the acquisition of British subject status and, after then, the acquisition of CUKC, British cit-izenship is now attained through a combination of birth and descent. A child born in the United Kingdom is granted British citizenship if either its mother or father is a British citizen or settled in the United Kingdom.[36] All others born in the United Kingdom, unless abandoned,[37] do not acquire British citizenship automatically. They may, however, be able to register as British citizens while still minors if one of two conditions obtain: first, their mother or father becomes a British citizen or settles in the United Kingdom; or, second, they are resident in the United Kingdom for ten years without being absent from the country for more than ninety days in any of the years.[38]

---

[32] BDTC, however, naturally carries the right to enter the dependent territory in question and acts as a sort of proxy citizenship for it.

[33] This amounted to respecting formally a commitment made under BNA 1948 (Section 2).

[34] The British Nationality Act, 1965 provided for the acquisition of British subject status by alien women who married British subjects without citizenship.

[35] Under the 'natural-born' subject provisions of the 1914 Act, children of both British subjects and aliens became British subjects if born within the United Kingdom or the Empire's jurisdiction.   [36] Section 1 (1).

[37] Section 1 (2) stated that abandoned children found in the UK shall be assumed to have been born in the UK to either a British citizen or a settled resident. They are, in other words, granted automatic citizenship.

[38] Section 3 (*a*) and (*b*) and Section 4, respectively. The act also limited citizenship by descent to the second generation. Children of male and (for the first time) female citizens born abroad acquired citizenship by descent. This provision, however, does not apply to children born

A tremendous scholarly outcry followed the 1981 legislation's abandonment of pure *ius soli*. For Dummett and Nicol, incongruously adopting quasi-Powellite discourse with which they seem less than entirely comfortable, this provision 'marked the formal abandonment of a tradition encompassing English and British history and identity, the tradition of the land'.[39] In fact, the measure changed very little.[40] All individuals born in the UK to someone legally resident in the country are British at birth. In Europe, only Ireland, reflecting in part that country's historical fears of depopulation, operates a more liberal policy, granting citizenship automatically to anyone born in the country.[41] Few political theorists defend the claim that illegal migrants, students, or tourists should be able to claim citizenship for their children born in the country.[42] In the rest of Europe, birth in the country to a permanent resident gives no immediate claim on citizenship.[43] The policy is even more liberal than that of France, cited by historians as the example *par excellence* of an expansive, inclusionary nationality.[44] Outside Europe, only the USA, Canada, and Australia, traditional countries of migration, have more expansive policies.

The provisions granting citizenship by birth to children of legal residents ensure that all migrants resident in the country for more than four years, if they apply for permanent residency, will secure for their children British citizenship. Those who are not residents but later naturalize have an entitlement

of female British citizens before 1981; instead, they would have to apply for discretionary registration during their minority. If, however, the parent(s) of a child born of the third generation abroad returns to and resides in the UK, the child benefits from reduced residence requirements: three years, without being absent for more than 270 days overall. Both parents must consent to the registration. See N. Blake, 'British Nationality Law', in B. Nascimbene (ed.), *Nationality Laws in the European Union* (London: Butterworths, 1996), 690.

[39] Dummett and Nicol, *Subjects, Citizens, Aliens and Others*, 244.

[40] As, oddly, Dummett and Nicol admit when they note that the measure would probably effect only a few thousand each year. Ibid. 246.

[41] In 1999, Germany adopted a new nationality law that is in some ways similar to the British. Once defined purely on the basis of lineage, German citizenship is granted to anyone born in Germany of an individual who has been resident for eight years and held an unlimited legal residence permit for three years. The citizenship is, however, conditional in that, to retain it, dual nationals must give up any other citizenship(s) at the age of 23. See S. Green, 'Citizenship Policy in Germany: The Case of Ethnicity over Residence?', in R. Hansen and P. Weil (eds.), *Towards a European Nationality: Citizenship, Immigration and Nationality Law in the EU* (Houndmills: Macmillan, forthcoming).

[42] See J. Carens, 'Citizenship and Civil Society: What Rights for Residents?', in R. Hansen and P. Weil, *Dual Citizenship, Social Rights and Federal Citizenship in the US and Europe* (Oxford: Berghahn, forthcoming).

[43] Though, across most of Europe, birth in the country leads to a right to citizenship at the age of majority. R. Hansen, 'A European Citizenship or a Europe of Citizens?'

[44] R. Brubaker, *Citizenship and Nationhood in France and Germany* (Cambridge, Mass.: Harvard University Press, 1992). I owe this point to a conversation with Patrick Weil.

to claim citizenship for their children under 18.[45] For those that become residents but not citizens after their children are born, British citizenship will automatically be conferred on them at 10 years of age. In short, the only individuals denied British citizenship—illegal migrants, temporary workers, tourists, and students (many of whom are of course white)—are those with the weakest claim to it.

Naturalization

The requirements for naturalization were broadly similar to those specified by the Immigration Act, 1971. In addition to the requirement of 'good character' and a sufficient knowledge of the English, Welsh, or Scottish Gaelic languages,[46] BNA 1981 requires that either (i) the applicant's principal home be the United Kingdom or (ii) the applicant intend to enter or continue in employment in the United Kingdom, in Crown service, or in an international organization of which the United Kingdom is a member.[47] After four years' residence, applicants can apply for settled (permanent residence) status, and they may apply for citizenship after five.[48] These requirements are squarely within the European norm. The requirement is the same in Belgium, France, the Netherlands, Finland, Sweden, but it is higher in Austria (ten years), Denmark (seven years), Germany (eight),[49] Italy (ten years), Luxembourg (ten years), Portugal (seven years).[50] The UK policy is close to that of Canada and the USA. Elsewhere, Australia has less stringent residency requirements.

Residual citizenships

The rules for acquiring the BDTC and BOC are almost identical to those for British citizenship,[51] and both BNOs and BDTCs were treated basically as

---

[45] L. Fransman, *Fransman's British Nationality Law* (2nd edn.) (London: Butterworths, 1998), 296.

[46] In practice, this means a functional grasp of the spoken language, and exceptions are made for the ill and aged. On this requirement, and the vague 'good character requirement', see the minister's comments in *Official Reports*, cc 691–9, 19 Mar. 1981.

[47] Section 1(*d*).

[48] Satisfaction of the residence requirement depends on the following: applicants must have lived in the United Kingdom for five years, generally in full-time employment; they may not be absent from the United Kingdom for more than 450 days in total, and no more than ninety days in the year preceding application (Schedule 2 (*a*)(*b*)); and they pay a fee for naturalization upon application. Before 1981, the fee was paid upon approval.

[49] Eight years if current SPD/Green proposals are adopted.

[50] See the chapters in Hansen and Weil, *Towards a European Nationality*.

[51] Thus, for example, a child born abroad to BDTCs *by descent* could register as a BDTC after the age of 10 years, if he or she was not absent more than 90 days in any one of these years. Section 15 (1).

aliens for the purposes of immigration control and naturalization. The sole difference between the two is that individuals in these groups have the right to register as British citizens after five years' residence in the United Kingdom, whereas other Commonwealth citizens and aliens may apply and are granted it on a discretionary basis.

NATURALIZATION IN PRACTICE

It is worth devoting a few words to the acquisition of British citizenship in practice, as the implementation of policy is constitutive of its content.[52] The practical operation of naturalization policy is inclusionary and expansive. The language requirement is interpreted liberally; individuals must only have a grasp of rudimentary English necessary to function in daily life.[53] The requirement of 'good' behaviour is interpreted essentially as obeying the law, and it exists everywhere in Europe and in the USA. Unlike in the majority of European states, individuals are not obligated to provide any further evidence of their integration. In some respects, British nationality law's implementation is more liberal than the US: whereas lengthy interviews are necessary to acquire US citizenship, the Home Office approves citizenship applications without even meeting the applicants unless there is any reason to suspect irregularities. Critics of British nationality law have provided no evidence establishing that non-white migrants have more difficulty naturalizing than white migrants. Compare current British policy on naturalization with Germany's pre-1993 policy, in which 'foreigners' who were born in Germany, and whose parents, grandparents, and so on were also born in the country, had absolutely no legal claim to citizenship.[54] Relative to what was in fact a genuine ethno-cultural model of nationality, British citizenship is an instance *par excellence* of territorial citizenship.

NATIONALITY LAW SINCE 1981

The major nationality issue has involved the remnants of empire, especially in Hong Kong. The national status of the colony was originally settled

[52] I discuss British naturalization practice in greater detail in R. Hansen, 'From Subjects to Citizens: Immigration and Nationality Law in the United Kingdom', in Hansen and Weil, *Towards a European Nationality*.

[53] In both France and Germany, the language requirement varies according to one's social position (more so for a teacher, less so for a manual worker).

[54] On German nationality law before liberalizing 1993 and 1999 reforms, see R. Brubaker, *Citizenship and Nationhood in France and Germany*, ch. 8.

through bilateral negotiations between China and Britain. The product of these negotiations, the Hong Kong (British Nationality) Order, 1986 granted the status of British National (Overseas) to Hong Kong BDTCs who registered before 1 July 1997 (the date on which sovereignty reverts to China). Those who obtain the status have no rights in the United Kingdom, but they may travel on a UK-endorsed passport and claim consular protection abroad.[55]

Despite pressure from the Hong Kong lobby, Hong Kong BDTCs were to have no privileged access to UK citizenship. Following the Tiananmen massacre, however, public and elite fear for economic and political instability in the colony, and perhaps for human rights in China's Hong Kong, led the British government to grant, through the British Nationality (Hong Kong) Act, 1990, full British citizenship to 50,000 Belongers and their dependants. There was Cabinet discussion about increasing this figure, and some members argued for the benefits of Hong Kong entrepreneurs for the British economy,[56] but fears of a public reaction against another large wave of migration prevented endorsement of the higher figure. Applicants were judged according to a Canadian-style 'points-system' (rewarding skill and entrepreneurial talent). As it happened, politicians and bureaucrats overestimated the UK's appeal; applications were far fewer than expected, and the quota was only just filled. Hong Kong BDTCs preferred the more prosperous shores of Australia, Canada, and the USA.

In addition to the BDTCs, who made up the clear majority of Hong Kong Belongers, there were also BOCs, mostly of Indian of Pakistani descent, in the colony. No one knows the exact figure, but it is estimated at between 5,000 and 15,000. Originally, no provision was made for these individuals, and they were to be effectively stateless following the transfer of sovereignty to Hong Kong. In early 1997, however, the British government announced that it would offer them citizenship on a case-by-case basis. A team of Home Office officials took applications in Hong Kong. To qualify, applicants had to have had no other citizenship and to have been regularly resident in Hong Kong. The last provision was added to prevent BOCs and BDTCs elsewhere (Asians on the queue in Kenya, BDTCs who left Hong Kong and had children in Nepal) from taking advantage of the provisions. In the end, 5,500 applied, and approximately half of these did not fit the criteria.[57] Given the general fear among British elites of

---

[55] For a critical discussion of the provisions for Hong Kong, see Sir William Goodhart et al., *Countdown to 1997: Report of a Mission to Hong Kong by an International Committee of Jurists* (Cambridge: E & E Plumridge, 1992).

[56] Confidential interview.

[57] Interview with an Immigration & Nationality Department official, Home Office, Jan. 1999.

an explosion of anti-immigrant sentiment of the sort seen in the 1960s and 1970s, this and the 1990 decision granting 50,000 Belongers citizenship were liberal measures offering some degree of protection against the possibility of post-independence discrimination. They belie the frequent claim that British nationality law is the story of one restriction after another.

These two exceptions aside, the residual citizenships of BDTC, BOC, and BNO are legal identities for those who fell through the cracks of decolonization. Policy-makers defined these categories so that they would be temporary, or at least as limited as possible. As British Overseas Citizenship can, at the most, be passed on to one more generation, it will disappear. BDTC mostly disappeared in July 1997, though there are of course other colonies whose citizens will keep it and pass it on, and British subject status will do the same.

An announcement in late 1998 confirmed this trend. Breaking with previous policy, the government announced that the dependent territories will be renamed overseas territories, and that all members of them will receive British citizenship. The details are yet to be worked out—whether they will postal vote in UK elections, whether the territories will be considered parts of the UK and thus the EU, and so forth—but BDTCs within them will become British citizens. In the light of the history outlined above, the decision's implications are double-sided. On the one hand, it furthers the shift towards British citizenship as the basic foundation of British 'belonging'. The match between nationality and citizenship is not quite perfect—BOCs and BDTCs will continue to exist—but it is closer than ever before. Most likely sometime early in the next century, British citizenship will be, if not the sole, then incontestably the main basis of British belonging. On the other hand, the provision contains a nod towards British citizenship's cosmopolitan origins. Some forty-eight years after the UK withdrew the right of 'colonial' subjects to enter the UK, the British government restored it: although the overseas territories are of course a fraction of the former empire, those who remain will soon enjoy rights not held since the 1950s. As CUKCs in the colonies enjoyed full rights in this country, so will British citizens in the territories.

CONCLUSION: BRITISH CITIZENSHIP

Given the tortured history of British nationality law, and the constraints created by the 1948 British Nationality Act, BNA 1981 was a noteworthy accomplishment. The legislation was above all a massive effort at rationalization and clarification, and this aim was largely realized. For the first time in British history, policy-makers defined British citizenship exclusively for the 'imagined community' of England, Scotland, Wales, and Northern

Ireland. There is no sense in which this community, as entrenched in naturalization policy, is an ethnically exclusivist one. All migrants from the colonies arrived with full citizenship rights; all migrants from independent Commonwealth countries who arrived before 1962 acquired citizenship automatically after one year; all migrants since 1971 have been able to acquire it after five years. When one compares these requirements with the fifteen years necessary in Austria or the ten years required in Italy, and with pre-1993 German law providing no right of naturalization to anyone who was not of German descent, the claim that legislation is nested in a discourse of blood, family, and kith and kin is absurd.

This rationalizing logic extended as well to the residual citizenships created by the legislation—BDTC and BOC. These residual citizenships are legal identities for those who fell through the cracks of decolonization. The drafters of the British Nationality Act, 1948 assumed that all British subjects would eventually become citizens of independent Commonwealth countries, and that a distinctive United Kingdom citizenship would emerge as the consequence of this process. This assumption proved false, and these individuals were left with a legal status with little practical significance in relation to UK nationality. The 1981 legislation defined the categories so that they would be temporary. As British Overseas Citizenship can, at the most, be passed on to one more generation, it will disappear. BDTC mostly disappeared in 1997, and British subject status will disappear. Some time in the next century, all that will remain of the various legal categories created by the British Nationality Act, 1948 will be a small and indeterminate number of BDTCs.[58] The rest will be, as they are and likely have long thought themselves to be, British citizens.

These categories were criticized for their emptiness, and empty they are. In this respect, however, BNA 1981 changed nothing. Such individuals have had no right to enter the UK since 1962 and, in the case of Kenyan Asians, since 1968. It is true that the legislation continued a bipartisan policy of quietly ignoring 1963 pledges made by the Conservative government to the Asians. In this limited sense, the legislation did entrench a racially discriminatory policy. There is, however, no evidence to support John Solomos's claim that the legislation 'further circumvent[ed] the rights of those black Commonwealth citizens with a legal right to enter Britain.'[59] No one, black or white, with a legal right to enter the UK lost that right because of BNA

---

[58] Fransman, *British Nationality Law*, 207. As Fransman suggests, the dependent territories may become independent, may be incorporated into the adjacent territories, or may remain indefinitely as dependent territories populated by BDTCs.

[59] Solomos, *Race and Racism*, 71.

1981, and those mild restrictions imposed by legislation—ending the automatic acquisition of citizenship after five years' residence and a pure *ius soli* policy—applied to all residents. The claims of Paul, Solomos, and Carter about 1981 are, as they are for claims about the 1950s and 1960s, as unsubstantiated as they are colourful.

10

Migration Policy in the 1970s and 1980s: The Institutional Origins of British Restrictionism

As seen in previous chapters, British governments ended a centuries' old tradition rapidly and completely. Open borders to the Commonwealth came to an end in 1962; quotas for work permits were halved in 1962 and primary migration was definitively halted in 1971. The following two decades contained further restrictions, formal and in implementation, that made British migration policy about as restrictive as it can possibly be. The aim, if not zero immigration (an illusory goal), has been the strict control on numbers. 'Firm but fair' migration polices have been the goals of both parties in government. Labour, following a century-old tradition, has criticized restrictive migration policies in opposition and extended them in office. The only individuals who can migrate, legally and permanently, to the UK are family members, asylum seekers, and those few who obtain a work permit and permanent leave to remain after four years.[1] Most recently, asylum seekers have experienced the efficiency of Britain's restrictionist migration policy: a (pan-European) rise in numbers was met with a series of restrictive acts that made the UK's refugee policy barely consistent with its obligations under the 1951 Geneva Convention. The United Kingdom's policies are more European than their critics recognize—there has been a European convergence in migration, asylum laws since the 1970s[2]—and there have been liberalizing measures (predictably ignored), but the country still remains a model of restrictiveness. This penultimate chapter briefly outlines these developments leading to this outcome and offers an explanation of them.

MIGRATION IN THE 1970S

After the Ugandan Asians crisis, the major migration-related issue was the extreme right's rise in support. The National Front participated in a series of

---

[1] I am excluding temporary workers (such as those on the holiday working scheme for the Commonwealth), illegal migrants, and overstayers.

[2] J. F. Hollifield, *Immigrants, Markets, and States: The Political Economy of Postwar Europe* (Cambridge: Harvard University Press, 1992).

demonstrations against the Ugandan Asians; among the most memorable of these was the Smithfield porters, who marched on the Home Office chanting 'Enoch is Right', 'Stop Immigration', and booing passing African and Asian pedestrians.[3] The National Front accused the government of betrayal, and presented itself to the electorate as the only party with a credible restrictionist stance.[4] Membership of the movement grew to an alleged peak of 14,000 in 1973,[5] reached an electoral high of 16 per cent in a West Bromwich by-election, and reached 15 per cent in several May 1976 municipal elections.[6] In 1976, the National Front secured a number of seats in local elections, and their success led to the formation of the Anti-Nazi League.[7] Cobbled together from various Marxist groups within and outside the Labour Party, civil libertarians, and campaigners for unilateral nuclear disarmament, the Anti-Nazi League met National Front demonstrations with counter-demonstrations, the result often being violence. The movement peaked in the late 1970s, and fell to internal factionalism (though Anti-Nazi League demonstrations continued into the 1990s). In 1977, the National Front reached its peak in support, garnering 19.2 per cent of the vote in the Bethnal Green and Bow County constituency in Greater London's Country Council elections.[8] Although apocalyptic predictions of a surge in National Front support proved greatly exaggerated,[9] it remained a source of concern to both parties until its decisive failure in the 1979 general election.[10]

[3] *The Times*, 'Immigration march brush with police', 25 Aug. 1972 and 'Smithfield men in new protest', 8 Sept. 1972.

[4] Z. Layton-Henry, 'Immigration and the Heath Government', in S. Ball and A. Seldon (eds.), *The Heath Government 1970–74: A Reappraisal* (London: Longman, 1996), 229. This article was first presented as a paper at St Antony's College, Oxford, 25 Apr. 1996. I am grateful to Professor Layton-Henry for sending me a copy in advance of publication.

[5] The figure is cited in N. Nugent and R. King, *The British Right: Conservative and Right-Wing Politics in Britain* (London: Saxon House, 1977), 175. Layton-Henry suggests that this figure, given the number of National Front branches at the time, is exaggerated. *The Politics of Race in Britain*, 94–5.

[6] See H. Kitschelt, *The Radical Right in Western Europe: A Comparative Analysis* (Ann Arbor: University of Michigan Press, 1995), 251. See 250–6 for a discussion of the National Front's decline. Also see S. Taylor, *The National Front in English Politics* (London: Macmillan, 1982).

[7] A. Dummett and A. Nicol, *Subjects, Citizens, Aliens and Others: Nationality and Immigration Law* (London: Weidenfeld & Nicolson, 1990), 237.

[8] D. Matas, 'The Extreme Right in the United Kingdom and France', in A. Braun and S. Scheinberg (eds.). *The Extreme Right: Freedom and Security at Risk* (Boulder, Colo.: Westview Press, 1997), 86. In addition, a year earlier, in May 1976, two extreme-right candidates were elected as councillors in Blackburn.

[9] See M. Walker, *The National Front* (London: Macmillan, 1977).

[10] For a discussion of the British National Party's fortunes since 1979, see R. Eatwell, 'Britain: The BNP and the Problem of Legitimacy', in H.-G. Betz and S. Immerfall, *The New Politics of the Right: Neo-Populist Parties and Movements in Established Democracies* (London: Macmillan, 1998).

Today, the relative weakness of Britain's extreme right stands in contrast with the rest of Europe.[11] The membership of the various extreme-right organizations in the UK amounts to around 5,000 individuals: the British National Party (BNP) (2,500 members), the Ku Klux Klan (an American offshoot, 400 members), Blood and Honour (a Nazi skinhead organization, 2,000 members), and Combat 18 (the most violent organization, eighty members).[12] The National Front collapsed in the 1979 general election, earning less than 2 per cent of the vote; since then, the BNP's support in any electoral contest has almost always been below 5 per cent of the vote, usually hovering in the 1–2 per cent range. The one exception was 1992, when Derek Beackton won a subcouncil seat in the Millwall ward, the Isle of Dogs, Tower Hamlets with 34 per cent support (among 480 individuals voting) on a protest vote over housing.[13] In contemporary Britain, the far right is close to politically irrelevant. This does not make the situation of black Britons subjected to racist chants at football matches, or black players who see bananas thrown from the stands, any less intolerable. But it does make the BNP, and the far right more generally, of limited political significance.

By contrast, the 1980s have witnessed a renaissance in far-right support in the rest of Europe.[14] In France, Jean Marie le Pen's Front national earned a derisory 0.3 per cent of the vote in 1980; four years later, it won 11 per cent of the vote at the European elections (leading to ten seats), 8.8 per cent in the March 1985 departmental elections, and 9.7 per cent in the 1986 legislative elections.[15] Its support in the last two presidential elections has hovered around 15 per cent; its fourth mayoral candidate succeeded in 1997,[16] and 1998 was a banner year for the Front. In March, five UDF (Union pour la Démocratie Française) candidates were elected to the presidency of regional councils, on the second ballot, with votes of Front national candidates.[17] In Austria, Jörg Haider's Freiheitliche Partei Österreichs (FPÖ) has exploited

[11]   With some exceptions, notably the Netherlands, in which the extreme right is also weak and fragmented. See G. Voerman and P. Lucardie, 'The Extreme Right in the Netherlands', *European Journal of Political Research*, 22 (1992), 35–54.

[12]   D. Matas, 'The Extreme Right in the United Kingdom and France', 87–8. The figures are from 1997.   [13]   Ibid. 90.

[14]   H. G. Betz, *Radical Right-Wing Populism in Western Europe* (Houndmills: Macmillan, 1994).

[15]   On the Front National, see G. Durand, *Enquête au cœur du Front National* (Paris: Jacques Grancher, 1996); N. Mayer *Le Front National à découvert* (Paris: Presse de la Fondation National des Sciences Politiques, 1996); and M. A. Schain, 'Immigration and Politics', in P. A. Hall, J. Hayward, and H. Machin (eds.), *Developments in French Politics* (Houndmills: Macmillan, 1994).

[16]   Toulon, Orange, Marignane, and Vitrolles are now run by the *Front National*.

[17]   R. Hansen, 'The Evolution of Nationality Law in France and Germany', in C. Joppke and E. Morawska (eds.), *Integrating Immigrants in Liberal States: From Postnational to National* (work under review, 1999).

antipathy towards immigrants, multiculturalism, and European integration to become the EU's most electorally successful extreme-right party (scoring 22.5 per cent and 21.89 per cent, respectively, in the 1994 and 1995 federal elections).[18] Even Germany, where the far right has been moribund for most of the post-war period, has witnessed a post-unification rise in far-right support. In April 1992, the Republikaner received 10.9 per cent of the popular vote in the Baden-Württemberg *Land* election.[19] The Republikaner's star has been fading since then, but the far-right Deutsche Volksunion achieved an unprecedented 13 per cent of the vote in the local *Sachsen-Anhalt* elections in May 1998. This relative success has led the centre right, and above all the Bavarian CSU (Christliche Soziale Union), to call for a range of repressive security measures against foreigners.

MIGRATION AND RACE RELATIONS POLICY UNDER LABOUR

Roy Jenkins's return to the Home Office heralded a restrained liberalism. To the fury of Enoch Powell and the National Front, he announced an amnesty for illegal Commonwealth/Pakistani migrants since 1971 (February 1974), and he raised the quota for CUKCs (mostly Kenyan Asians) from 3,600 to 5,000 (February 1975).[20]

The Race Relations Acts

These measures were matched by a third Race Relations Act 1976, again the product of Jenkins. The 1968 Race Relations Act had extended the 1965 legislation (limited to 'places of public resort'—public houses, restaurants, theatres, dance halls, etc.) to include employment, housing, credit and insurance facilities, education, all places of public resort, and the Crown; discrimination in all these areas, on the grounds of colour, race, ethnic or national origin, was made illegal.[21] Although the 1965 Act's use of conciliation rather

[18] M. Riedlsperger, 'The Freedom Party of Austria: From Protest to Radical Right Populism', in Betz and Immerfall, *The New Politics of the Right*.

[19] V. Hans-Joachim et al., *The Republikaner Party in Germany: Right-Wing Menace or Protest Catchall?* (Westport, Conn.: Praeger, 1993), 9. Also see B. Westle and O. Niedermayer, 'Contemporary Right-Wing Extremism in West Germany', *European Journal of Political Research*, 22 (1992), 83–100.

[20] Layton-Henry, *The Politics of Race in Britain*, 152–3.

[21] A number of exemptions were written into the legislation. Discrimination was tolerated when it: was done in good faith to retain a reasonable racial balance; involved employment in

than criminal law was supported by lobbyists in favour of the legislation—the Society of Labour Lawyers and CARD—the entire bill was widely felt to be far too limited in scope. They redoubled their efforts after the 1965 legislation's adoption, and were aided by the young Roy Jenkins's appointment as Home Secretary in 1966. Jenkins was, in his words, 'resolved to strike a more upbeat note on race relations than had hitherto been forthcoming from the Home Office'.[22] He began by appointing Mark Bonham Carter as Chair of the Race Relations Board. Bonham Carter made his acceptance of the position conditional upon his ability to press for further legislation within a year.[23] Jenkins made a series of public speeches committing himself and the Cabinet to further legislation, and he was aided by continuing efforts on the part of the Society for Labour Lawyers and the NCCI.[24] The case in favour was all but sealed by the publishing of the Political and Economic Planning (PEP) survey on racial discrimination, which reported extensive discrimination in employment and housing, the Race Relations Board's first annual report, and the Labour working party on race relations; all were in favour of further legislation.[25] When the legislation was passed, by James Callaghan following his post-devaluation swap with Jenkins, it expanded the Race Relations Board to twelve members and gave it the duty to secure compliance with the act through a graduated process of investigation, conciliation, and, failing all else, legal proceedings.[26]

Although a significant improvement on 1965 legislation, the 1968 Act was felt to have serious flaws: discrimination was difficult to prove; the complaints-based approach relied on ethnic minorities (or others) coming forward, which they were often reluctant to do; the two-tier structure in which the Race Relations Board reviewed the decisions of conciliation committees was time-consuming; and the courts were conservative in their judgments.[27]

---

private households and on merchant ships in which sleeping and eating facilities are shared; concerned employers of twenty-five or fewer employees in the first two years following the act, employers of ten or fewer employees in the following two years; concerned the private sale of property by the owner-occupier without using an estate agent or shared accommodation involving six or fewer people. L. Kushnick, 'British Anti-discrimination Legislation', in Kushnick, *Race, Class & Struggle: Essays on Racism and Inequality in Britain, the US and Western Europe* (London: Rivers Oram Press, 1998), 109–10.

[22]   R. Jenkins, *A Life at the Centre* (London: Macmillan, 1991).

[23]   E. J. B Rose, et al., *Colour and Citizenship: A Report on British Race Relations* (London: Oxford University Press, 1969), 520.

[24]   See A. Lester and G. Bindman, *Race and Law* (London: Longman, 1972), 122–30.

[25]   The working party proposed dividing enforcement between the Race Relations Board, which would be responsible for conciliation, and in the event that it failed, an independent Race Relations Tribunal. For the archives of the Labour Party study group on immigration, see *LPA, Study Group on Immigration. Minutes and Papers*, 6 June 1968–14 May 1969.

[26]   Lester and Bindman, *Race and Law*, 134.

At the same time, the Home Secretary and his legal advisers, notably Anthony Lester, shifted their concern from direct discrimination to indirect discrimination[28] and the possibility of addressing it through positive action. As Erik Bleich has argued, British thinking in 1976, as in 1965 and 1968, was heavily conditioned by American experience.[29] The legislation extended the definition of 'discrimination' to include indirect discrimination; allowed individuals to take complaints to the county courts (except in the case of employment, where they go to tribunals); and abolished the Race Relations Board and Community Relations Commission, replacing them with the Commission for Racial Equality.[30] In a smart strategic move, Jenkins linked, for presentational purposes, the racial discrimination legislation with similar measures against sex discrimination.[31] The Conservatives had backed the sex discrimination measures and thus found it difficult to oppose analogous measures for ethnic minorities.[32] Importantly, the legislation, like the Sex Discrimination Act, 1975,[33] empowered the Commission for Racial Equality to identify discriminatory practices and to issue legally binding non-discrimination notices.[34]

As Christian Joppke has pointed out, the 1976 legislation did not embrace affirmative action;[35] it provides in Sections 37 and 38 the opportunity for employers to place special job advertisements in the minority press, but it

---

[27] C. McCrudden, 'Racial Discrimination', in G. McCrudden and G. Chambers (eds.), *Individual Rights and the Law in Britain* (Oxford: Clarendon Press, 1994), 415–17. In Feb. 1973, for instance, the House of Lords ruled that a club operating a genuine selection procedure was, for purposes of admission to membership, outside the scope of the Act. In Oct. 1974, it decided that guests and associates of clubs were not covered by the Act; in doing so, it reversed an Oct. 1973 Court of Appeal decision that the Preston Dockers' Labour Club's refusal to admit the complainant, as associate member and guest, was unlawful. See *Race Relations and Immigration: Report of the Race Relations Board for 1974* (London: Sessional Papers, 1974–5 [XXXIII]), 3–4. Also see *Racial Discrimination* (Cmnd. 6234).

[28] That is, situations where racial discrimination is not necessarily intentional but practices and procedures applying to everyone put a particular racial group at a disadvantage. I. Macdonald, *Race Relations—The New Law* (London: Butterworths, 1977).

[29] E. Bleich, 'Problem-Solving Politics, Ideas and Race Policies in Britain and France' (Ph.D. dissertation, Harvard University, Apr. 1999). Also see, though the point is less developed, J. Gregory, *Sex, Race and the Law: Legislating for Equality* (London: SAGE, 1987).

[30] Layton-Henry, *Politics of Race*, 59.

[31] Adopted through the 1975 Sex Discrimination Act. See *Sex Discrimination: A Guide to the Sex Discrimination Act 1975* (London: Home Office, 1975).

[32] Interview with a Home Office official, Aug. 1995.

[33] Through the Equal Opportunities Commission.

[34] A. Lester, 'Discrimination: What Can Lawyers Learn from History', *Public Law* (Summer 1994), 224–37, 226. For the Select Committee, see *Select Committee on Race Relations and Immigration: Organisation of the Race Relations Administration, i: Report* (London: HMSO, 1974–5).

[35] C. Joppke, *Immigration and the Nation-State: The United States, Germany, and Great Britain* (Oxford: Oxford University Press, 1998), 230.

does not require them to guarantee ethnic minority representation. It has none the less transformed, in large measure informally, the way in which issues of ethnic minority representation are addressed. In a manner that was inconceivable twenty years ago, and is non-existent in France today, government departments, government-sponsored committees, and even some private enterprises consider the importance of securing female and (perhaps to a lesser degree) ethnic minority participation.[36] Most broadly, the 1976 Act has become the second pillar of Britain's 'fair but firm' immigration regime. In the same way that strict immigration control has been the goal of every government, no government has considered the possibility of repealing or modifying the Race Relations Act or questioning the goal of anti-discrimination. As Adrian Favell notes, it was one of the few bipartisan policies to survive Margaret Thatcher's war on all things consensual.[37] If there is a home for elite progressivism in 1990s British migration and integration policy, it is the Race Relations Act.

FAMILY REUNIFICATION

The 1970s were the years in which the second-generation migrants bore the brunt of Britain's tight control policy. Primary immigration had all but ended with the 1971 Act, and government policy sought to limit the number of dependants as much as possible. In line with a cross-party belief that families could not permanently be kept apart, no government seriously considered attempting to prohibit family reunification.[38] All governments, however, kept

---

[36]   Interview with a Home Office official.

[37]   A. Favell, 'Multicultural Race Relations in Britain: Problems of Interpretation and Explanation', in C. Joppke (ed.), *Challenge to the Nation-State: Immigration in Western Europe and the United States* (Oxford: Oxford University Press, 1998); Favell, *Philosophies of Integration: Immigration and the Idea of Citizenship in France and Britain* (Houndmills: Macmillan, 1998), ch. 4.

[38]   There was a general recognition that a core of family unification was inevitable, and that such limitations as could be applied could not be racially discriminatory. A 1975 working paper from the Conservative Research Department, which provided the raw material for Tory party policy before Thatcher's first government, made this point: 'Most acceptable options for restricting immigration would tend to affect as many whites as non-whites. Any restriction which aimed directly at reducing non-white rather than total immigration would be discriminatory and would undoubtedly antagonise non-white communities, thereby undermining rather than improving race relations. Restrictions on immigration, therefore, are not likely to reduce substantially the rate of growth of the non-white population or to improve race relations. . . . Immigration restrictions are a very poor policy tool for dealing with these problems and any attempt to use immigration as a high-profile, partisan political issue is likely to be counter-productive in this respect. . . . While immigration under the present Labour government has

the definition of the family strict and operated immigration rules on dependants with an eye to keeping numbers to a minimum.[39] Before the 1970s, legislation and administrative practice treated dependants liberally. Between 1962 and 1965, wives and children under 16 of a Commonwealth citizen ordinarily resident in the United Kingdom could freely enter the country.[40] Children between 16 and 18 were, in practice, admitted on a discretionary basis. A 1965 White Paper restricted this practice to instances of hardship.[41] The 1971 Immigration Act entrenched the right of migrants who arrived in the UK before 1 January 1973 (when the act took effect). From then, however, the logic of tight immigration control began to squeeze dependants.[42]

risen substantially, it cannot be expected in light of past Conservative obligations that a Conservative Government would be able to alter the picture substantially. Two immigration categories alone, those admitted for settlement by reason of their marital status and UKPH [United Kingdom Passport Holders], account for nearly 85 per cent of the total increase in immigration between 1973 and 1975, and including dependants would account for a still higher proportion. . . . [F]urther restriction of these categories would be difficult.' CPA, CRD 3/16/3, 'Immigration into Britain: Some Options for Restriction', 16 Dec. 1975.

[39] There is some indication that politicians during the 1970s were again learning, as they did in the 1960s, that migration patterns at time t produce further migration at time $t+1$, following chain migration of the sort familiar to demographers. The 1970s' assumption among some politicians and policy-makers that family/dependant migration would soon end was false. Quoting a report from an Assistant Under-Secretary of State, 'The present position is unsatisfactory because current procedures and instructions are based on a Home Office assumption that the immigration problem in the sub-continent is finite and that we are in the last stages of clearing up a backlog of "entitled" dependants. All the Heads of Mission and Post are convinced that this assumption is wrong and I share their view.' CPA, CRD 3/16/3, 'Report of a Visit to Posts in the Sub-Continent Made by Mr D F Hawley, CMG, MBE, Assistant Under-Secretary of State—November/December 1975', 4.

[40] Commonwealth Immigrants Act, 1962, Section 2. The term 'ordinarily resident' could not be specified and was entirely up to Home Office discretion. People could be absent from the United Kingdom for considerable periods and still be ordinarily resident. Before the clause was replaced in 1981, it was common for applicants to ask how long they could be absent from the United Kingdom before violating the provision; they were told that no reply could be given. 'Children' included stepchildren, adopted children, and, in the case of the mother, illegitimate children.

[41] Immigration from the Commonwealth (London: HMSO, 1965). Until 1968, children of either parent could enter the United Kingdom (Commonwealth Immigrants Act, 1962: Instructions to Immigration Officers (London: HMSO, 1962), paragraph 26). After 1968, both parents had to be resident in the United Kingdom, both accompanying the children to the United Kingdom, or one resident and one accompanying. Commonwealth Immigrants Acts, 1962 and 1968: Instructions to Immigration Officers (London: HMSO, 1968), paragraph 1. Under 1994 immigration rules, unmarried, dependent children under the age of 18 may accompany or join their parents when both are settled in the UK, or in the process of being settled. When only one is settled, 'compelling' reasons must be provided. See Rule 297 of the 1994 Immigration Rules in M. Phelan, Immigration Law Handbook (London: Blackstone, 1997), 211–12.

[42] Technically, the first restriction on family unification was introduced with the 1969 Immigration Appeals Act. It provided a right of appeal to an independent tribunal, but required spouses and children under 16, who retained their legal right to enter the UK, to obtain an entry certification in advance of travelling to Britain. Although the Labour government argued that the

The restrictionist cycle began with Roy Jenkins's announcement of immigration rules designed to crack down on male migrants entering or remaining in the UK through marriages of convenience.[43] At the same time, the application of the rules focused squarely on reducing numbers: discrepancies between the husband's and wife's claims were seized upon; little allowance was given for linguistic difficulties, and claims of marriage were viewed with suspicion. These efforts reached their grotesque extreme in the infamous 'virginity tests' of the late 1970s: women arriving from India claiming to marry were forced to undergo a vaginal examination to determine whether they were virgins;[44] if these unreliable tests determined that they were not, they were denied entry on the grounds that the marriage was disingenuous. Several dozen of these tests were carried out before being abandoned in the face of public and media outcry.[45]

In the 1980s, the entitlement of permanent residents and citizens to family unification ended altogether. Part of the legislation's general principles, Section 1 (5) of the Immigration Act, 1971 had given male spouses who had entered before 1973 the right to bring their spouses to the UK without hassle. It reflected the belief in both parties that denying family entry to those who arrived in the 1960s and 1970s would be, as Frank Soskice put it, a 'breach of faith'.[46] The provision, and related immigration rules, were challenged by settled women who wished to bring their husbands to the UK without going through complicated application and interview procedures. In two separate suits, three women argued that the rules amounted to discrimination by birth, race, and sex and that they constituted degrading treatment (Article 3). The European Court of Human Rights declared the rule, in *Abdulaziz, Cabales and Balkandali* v. *UK* (1985),[47] sexually discriminatory.[48] The government

requirement was not designed to impede entry, it did exactly that. Queues soon developed, and the average waiting time for the first overseas interview in the main settlement queue reached, between 1974 and 1980, an average of 38 months in Bangladesh (1974), 23.75 months in Pakistan (1980), and 16 months in India (1975–6). The queues fell by 1981 (to 22, 20.25, and 10–12 months, respectively), but remain high into the 1990s. See S. Juss, *Discretion and Deviation in the Administration of Immigration Control* (London: Sweet & Maxwell, 1997), 41–7. For a report of the Cabinet discussions leading to the original decision, see R. Crossman, *The Diaries of a Cabinet Minister, iii: Secretary of State for Social Services 1968–1970* (London: Hamish Hamilton and Jonathan Cape, 1977), 214–15.

[43] At the same time, however, he lifted 1969 restrictions on the admissions of husbands and fiancés of women resident in the UK (June 1974). Layton-Henry, *Politics of Race*, 154

[44] Dummett and Nicol, *Subjects, Citizens, Aliens and Others*, 252.

[45] Ibid. 252.

[46] *PRO, CAB 129/21*, 'Cabinet. Commonwealth Immigration: Memorandum by the Secretary of State for the Home Department', 7 July 1965.

[47] *East African Asians* v. *United Kingdom* European Human Rights Reports 3 (1981), 76–103.

[48] Under article 14 (on enjoying rights and freedoms without discrimination on grounds of sex, among other things), taken together with article 8 (right to respect for private and family life). Article 8 alone was deemed insufficient.

responded—respecting the law but certainly not the spirit of it—with a 1985 rule change and 1988 legislation that removed the privileges enjoyed by pre-1973 male New Commonwealth migrants. Under immigration rules last changed in 1994, all applicants must satisfy the following requirements:

- the applicant is married to a person present and settled in the United Kingdom or who is on the same occasion being admitted for settlement;
- the parties to the marriage have met;[49]
- each of the parties intends to live permanently with the other as his or her spouse and the marriage is subsisting;
- there will be adequate accommodation, which the parties own and occupy exclusively, for them and any dependants;[50]
- the parties will be able to maintain themselves and any dependants adequately without recourse to public funds; and
- the applicant holds a valid United Kingdom entry clearance (obtained in the country of origin) for entry in this capacity.[51]

After meeting these requirements, individuals may join their spouses in the UK. They are generally granted 'leave to remain' for twelve months; after this period, they must go through the process again, applying for 'indefinite leave to remain'. The Home Secretary, who has full discretion in accepting or refusing, may grant indefinite leave if he is satisfied that the marriages continue and the couples live together.[52]

THE PRIMARY PURPOSE RULE

Until recently, one of the most controversial aspects of family reunification policy was the now-infamous 'primary purpose' rule. The rule originated in the 1970s, following Labour's decision in 1974 to allow either the husband or wife to seek clearance for permanent residence for spouses abroad. The rules only spoke of 'husbands' and 'wives', however, and this opened the possibility for marriages of convenience. The government promulgated new rules in 1977, which allowed the Home Office to refuse an application if the applicant(s) married to obtain settlement and without the intention of living

---

[49] This rule does not preclude arranged marriages as such, as the meeting does not have to be in the context of marriage; casual meetings suffice.

[50] According to the immigration rules, the sponsor may be required to given an undertaking in writing that the person's maintenance and accommodation will be secured. *Statement of Changes in Immigration Rules* (London: HMSO, 1994), paragraph 320 (14).

[51] Ibid., paragraph 284. The paragraph also contains the primary purpose rule, abolished in 1997.   [52] Ibid., paragraphs 285 and 287.

together. The burden of proof, however, was on the Home Office. Another rule was added giving men (to whom the rules applied alone) leave to enter only for twelve months; indefinite leave was only to be given at the end of the one-year period if the couple was still living together.

The Home Office argued that the rules were too weak, allowing for several avenues for abuse: first, the burden of proof made it too difficult to prove marriages of convenience;[53] second, even if this could be established, applicants could get around it by living together; and, third, the refusal of settlement if the marriage broke down within one year was only discretionary—the husband had the right to argue that discretion should be exercised in his favour because of hardship he would suffer on return to his country of origin.[54] In 1980, the Conservative government responded with rules that tightened family reunification overall, and introduced the primary purpose rule:[55]

1. An applicant had to fulfil all requirements in order to obtain entry clearance; failure on any one meant mandatory refusal. Discretion could not be exercised in an applicant's favour either at the time of decision or on appeal.
2. The applicant was obligated to satisfy the entry clearance officer both that the parties intended to live together as man and wife and that the primary purpose of the marriage was not to obtain admission to the United Kingdom; there were thus two distinct tests against marriages of convenience.
3. A husband could be admitted only if the female sponsor was a British citizen, who either had been born in the United Kingdom or had a parent who was born there.[56]

In 1982, the government faced a European Court of Human Rights challenge, and it attempted to remove the last requirement.[57] The proposal was defeated in January 1983; the government responded by reintroducing its proposal with a new condition attached to the primary purpose rule: the burden of proof was on the applicant, who had to satisfy the entry clearance officer that the primary purpose of his marriage to a British citizen was not to obtain admission to the UK.[58] In another example of post-1970s restrictiveness vis-à-vis the rest of

---

[53] CPA, CRD 3/16/3, 'Report of a Visit to Posts in the Sub-Continent Made by Mr D. F. Hawley, CMG, MBE, Assistant Under-Secretary of State—November/December 1975', 9.

[54] D. Pannick et al., The Primary Purpose Rule: A Rule with no Purpose (London: Justice, 1993), 5.

[55] Statement of Changes in Immigration Rules (London: HMSO, 1980), 20 Feb. 1980.

[56] Pannick et al., The Primary Purpose Rule, 6.

[57] Macdonald and Blake, Immigration Law and Practice, 336.

[58] Statement of Changes in Immigration Rules (London: HC Paper 169, 1983), rule 54.

Europe, whereas the spouse of an EU national can refuse to answer prying questions into his or her personal life, both parties could suffer intrusive questions on how and why they met and suffer rejections on those grounds.[59] Following the ECHR decision, the rule applied to both men and women.

The rule was widely viewed as arbitrary and unjust, and there is little doubt that genuine spouses were denied entry clearance as a result. The chief avenue for abuse stemmed from the fact that the two conditions were separate: applicants had to establish that they would live together and that their primary purpose was not to gain entry to the UK.[60] If living together did not make a marriage genuine, it was not clear what did; the result was intrusive and insinuating questions, subjective judgements by entry clearance offers, and a bias in favour of rejection. A typical question asked by entry clearance officers illustrates the point. Concerning whether the marriage would survive if entry was refused, applicants were asked 'what will you do if the appeal does not succeed?' Those who said they would *not* leave jobs, homes, and contacts in the UK to live in India and Pakistan were faulted for insufficient devotion to marriage; applicants who said they *would* return to the subcontinent, were either disbelieved or, where the woman was the sponsor, it was suspected that the husband abroad was dictating the UK as the primary matrimonial home for marriage purposes.[61] Applicants could be forgiven if they thought they were trapped in a Kafkaesque nightmare.

One of the (1997–present) Labour government's first initiatives was to abandon the primary purpose role. The measure constitutes a significant liberalization, and again proves that policy evolution is rarely unidirectional. None the less, the UK remains in a highly anomalous position as the only European country not to recognize a right of a citizen to have his or her spouse join him or her in the country of his or her citizenship. Moreover, the remaining requirements mean, in conjunction with the considerable discretion granted to the Home Secretary, that there are multiple rejection points.

Refugees and asylum seekers

Another area of exceptional restrictiveness in the UK is asylum policy.[62] The country admits many fewer refugees than France and, in particular, Germany;

---

[59] Implied by Imm AR 50, *R* v. *IAT, ex p Bhata* [1985], 52. Also see M. Chatwin, *Immigration, Nationality & Refugee Law Handbook* (London: JCWI, 1999), ch. 2.

[60] Affirmed, for instance, in Imm AR 39, *R* v. *IAT, ex p Vinod Bhatia* [1985], 42–3.1

[61] I take these examples from Macdonald and Blake, 340–1. For the cases, see, respectively, *Rajput* v.*IAT* [1989] Imm AR 350, CA at 365 and *R* v. *IAT, ex p Aurangzeb Khan* [1989] 524 at 528.

[62] Asylum is generally outside the scope of this inquiry, but I cite it here as an example of the UK's restrictive policy.

it uses detention camps and expulsions are frequent and uncompromising. From 1980 until 1988, Britain received a minuscule number of annual applications, around 5,000 per year. From 1988, applications began to rise, increasing sharply, following a pan-European trend, in 1991. Between 1988 and 1991, applications jumped from 3,998 to 44,840, falling somewhat in the next two years before reaching an almost identical figure in 1995.[63] Figures for 1996 and 1997 were 27,930 and 32,500, respectively.[64] Despite this, acceptance rates remain very low. Those accepted as refugees increased marginally from 1,059 in 1988 to 1,115 in 1996, with a somewhat larger increase in those not recognized as refugees but given 'exceptional leave to remain': from 483 (1988) to 3,080 (1996).[65]

Appeals rights have been restricted in the 1990s. Until 1993, asylum seekers had rights to appeal under the immigration appeal system, set up in the 1969 Immigration Appeals Act. As such, they were subject to broader critiques of the appeal system, particularly that the success rate was low and there were no appellant appeals from abroad.[66] In 1993, anticipating a European Court of Human Rights challenge,[67] the 1993 Asylum and Immigration Appeals Act introduced a separate right of appeal for asylum seekers, providing for special adjudicators who hear cases.[68] It also, however, introduced a category of 'claims without foundation',[69] for which the time frame for appeal is sharply reduced, and removed rights of appeal for visitors, students coming for courses lasting six months or less and prospective students. The result of the asylum appeals has been unremarkable: successful appeals totalled 240 in 1995, and 570 in 1996.[70] The

---

[63]   *Asylum Statistics. United Kingdom 1996* (London: Home Office Press, 1997), table 1.1.

[64]   Ibid.; *Financial Times*, 'Britain: New rules urged for detention centres'.

[65]   *Asylum Statistics*, table 1.1.

[66]   C. Blake. 'Immigration Appeals—The Need for Reform', in A. Dummett (ed.), *Towards a Just Immigration Policy* (London: Cobden Trust, 1986).

[67]   Ironically, the ECHR, in *Vilvarajah*, declared that the UK had satisfied its obligations under the Convention. The *Yearbook of the European Convention on Human Rights*, *Vilvarajah and Others* v. *UK*, Series A, Vol. 215, paras. 125–7. C. Randall, 'An Asylum Policy for the UK', in S. Spencer (ed.), *Strangers and Citizens: A Positive Approach to Migrants and Refugees* (Concord, Mass.: Institute for Public Policy Research/Rivers Oram Press, 1994), 220–2.

[68]   Joppke, *Immigration and the Nation-State*, 133. Unsuccessful appellants can have a further appeal to the second-tier Immigration Appeal Tribunal and the Court of Appeal; these are rarely successful.

[69]   Those arriving from countries where there is no general fear of persecution; people arriving without passports; those whose fear of persecution is not one of the five listed in the UN Convention on Refugees (race, religion, nationality, membership of a particular social group or political opinion); people whose fear of persecution is 'manifestly unfounded'; people applying for asylum after being refused leave to enter; people whose cases are 'manifestly fraudulent' or for which the evidence adduced is 'manifestly false' and cases that are 'frivolous or vexatious'. Chatwin, *Immigration, Nationality and Refugee Law Handbook*, 352.

[70]   *Asylum Statistics. United Kingdom 1996*, table 8.1.

Asylum and Immigration Act, 1996 removed appeal rights for those deemed to have come through a safe-third country, and it expanded the number of cases that could be dealt with through 'fast-track procedures'; in such cases, applicants have *one* opportunity to appeal to an adjudicator within ten days of the appeal's filing.[71] Finally, the 1999 Immigration and Asylum Bill promises to replace the entire appeal process with a 'one-stop' comprehensive appeal for those in the country lawfully; clandestine migrants will have no right of appeal and will be subject to detention and deportation.[72]

Laid against these restrictions were measures designed to make life as a refugee in the UK less attractive. Were the possibility of facing Campfield's grim barbed wire not enough, asylum seekers were from 5 February 1996 denied income supplement and housing benefits. The measure was attacked by the Joint Council for the Welfare of Immigrants as 'petty and vindictive', and attempt to '[starve] people out of the country'.[73] A 1999 Immigration and Asylum Bill removed all benefits, with the exception of small amounts of pocket money, from asylum seekers, giving them vouchers instead. The bill also provides for the forced housing of asylum seekers in different parts of the country; they have no say in the matter.[74] In a touch of irony, Tony Blair listened with earnestness and sympathy to the stories of Kosovar refugees as the bill passed through Parliament. Although the UK is again not entirely out of line with the rest of Europe—many of the 1996 measures are part of a broader harmonization on European policy[75]—asylum policy appears to be in a cycle of unending restrictionism.

---

[71] *Providing Protection: Towards Fair and Effective Asylum Procedures* (London: Justice, ILPA, ARC asylum research project, 1997), 16. On the 1996 Act, see R. Cholewinski, 'Enforced Destitution of Asylum Seekers in the United Kingdom: The Denial of Fundamental Human Rights', *International Journal of Refugee Law*, 10 (1998), 462–98.

[72] The bill also extends the Home Office's power to require airline carriers to provide information about passengers, particularly those who are not nationals of the European Economic Area, and to impose civil penalties (above existing airline fines) on any carrier of clandestine migrants. Immigration and Asylum Bill, introduced in the House of Commons on 9 Feb. 1999. Website: http://www.parliament.the-stationary-office.co.uk.

[73] *Financial Times*, 'Asylum benefit "will starve people out of Britain" ', 19 Dec. 1995.

[74] Website: http://www.parliament.the-stationary-office.co.uk.

[75] Notably, the refusal to entertain asylum applications from a country deemed 'safe', and from applicants who have passed through another EU country. On this, see P. De Bruycker, 'D'un système européen d'asile vers un droit européen des réfugiés', in *Europe and Refugees: A Challenge? / L'Europe et les réfugiés: un defi?* (The Hague: Kluwer Law International, 1997); L. Leigh and C. Beyani, *Blackstone's Guide to the Asylum and Immigration Act 1996* (London: Blackstone Press, 1996), J. van Selm-Thorburn, *Refugee Protection in Europe* (The Hague: Martinus Nijhoff Publishers, 1998), ch. 3.

The turn to restrictionism

Post-1960s restrictionism has been detailed and condemned endlessly,[76] and there is little to be added to the chorus of execration. What remains lacking, however, is an adequate account of why policy-makers succeeded in slamming the door so firmly. The arguments that lie at the root of scholarly condemnation can be summarily dismissed. Current restrictiveness cannot be a simple function of anti-immigrant sentiment, racism, and politicians' responsiveness to both because all three exist across Europe. All publics have wanted an end to immigration since Europe's dazzling economic growth halved in the early 1970s, and all governments have sought to restrict migration as much as possible. Indeed, in attempting to suspend family reunification and to organize forced repatriation, some countries—notably France and Germany—attempted to go further than the UK ever did.[77] This result is unremarkable. European publics oppose immigration, this opposition intensifies in conditions of economic downturn; under conditions of electoral and even political saliency, democratic governments have a strong rational interest in responding.

If political intent cannot account for British exceptionalism, neither can public attitudes. The man on the Clapham omnibus (who might well work in the City today) is, to be sure, restrictionist.[78] But so is the woman on the métro or Strassenbahn. The most recent Eurobarometer statistical survey of attitudes on race and immigration across the European Union found the UK squarely in the middle, with a small overall range.[79] The study has been

---

[76] A citation list would be too long. See anything published by the Institute of Race Relations, and scholarly work by Ann Dummett, Kathleen Paul, and John Solomos.

[77] Hollifield, Immigrants, Markets and States; P. Weil, La France et ses étrangers: l'aventure d'une politique de l'immigration de 1938 à nos jours (Paris: Gallimard, 1991).

[78] Current policy—indeed even stricter control—has the strong support of public opinion, and has for decades. (L. Brook and E. Cape, 'Libertarianism in retreat?' in R. Jowell et al. (eds.), British Social Attitudes: The 12th Report (Aldershot: Dartmouth Publishing Co., 1995), 202). Liberal academics have trouble reconciling themselves to this fact, as they have trouble reconciling themselves to many things that they do not wish to be true, but a fact it remains.

[79] To the question 'Generally speaking, how do you feel about foreigners living in (OUR COUNTRY): are there too many, a lot but not too many, or not many?', 42% of Britons thought there were too many, 40% a lot but not too many, and 12% not many. These attitudes placed the country eighth in Europe on a tolerance ranking, and above France, Germany, and Italy. In Germany, 52% thought there were too many, 39% a lot but not too many and only 1% not too many. The figures for France are 46% (too many), 40% (a lot but not too many), and 4% (not many). To the statement, 'Some people are disturbed by the opinions, customs and way of life of people different from themselves. Do you personally find the presence of people of another race disturbing in your daily life?', 86% of Britons said that such a presence was not disturbing, 12% that it was. In the rest of Europe, the median was 81% (not disturbing) and 15% (disturbing); Portugal was ranked highest, with 94% answering 'not disturbing' and 5% 'disturbing'. France, Germany, and Italy were somewhat below the UK, though the difference

confirmed by scholarly research. A recent comparative study of Australia, Canada, Germany, Japan, and the UK concluded that

the one major and consistent theme that is sharply and clearly defined in each country's responses to national public opinion polls is that in no country—those with long histories of admitting immigrants, those with more restrictionist policies, and those who have consistently kept a lock on their doors—does a majority of citizens have positive feelings about their current cohort of immigrants.[80]

Throughout the post-war period, large pluralities have supported decreasing the number of immigrants being admitted.[81] If the British are racist or restrictionist, so are all Europeans.

The institutional origin of British restrictiveness

The source of restrictiveness of migration policy is found not in public attitudes or government intention but rather in British institutions. Four factors, well known to political scientists,[82] distinguish the Westminster model from continental Europe: a powerful executive, a weak legislature, a timid judiciary, and an absence of a bill of rights. Of these, the last two are the most important.

Under conditions of majority government, the British executive is unconstrained by Parliament. Its Cabinet is bound by collective responsibility; its

was only statistically significant in the French case: 15% of German respondents found such a presence disturbing, while 16% of Italian and 19% of French respondents felt the same. Respondents in Greece, Belgium, and Denmark were the least tolerant, markedly less so than Britons: 29%, 30%, and 31%, respectively, found the presence of people of another race disturbing *Eurobarometer: Public Opinion in the European Union* (Brussels: European Commission, DG X), vol. 48: Autumn 1997), released Mar. 1998, Section 6.2, 71–2.

[80] J. Simon and L. Lynch, 'A Comparative Assessment of Public Opinion toward Immigration and Immigration Policies', *International Migration Review*, 30, No. 2 (1999), 455–67, 458.

[81] G. P. Freeman, 'Democratic Politics and Multi-lateral Immigration Policy', in L. F. Tomasi (ed.), *In Defence of the Alien*, vol. 21 of the Proceedings of the Annual Legal Conference on Immigration and Refugee Policy (in press). Also see K. Betts, 'Immigration and Public Opinion in Australia', *People and Place*, 4, No. 3 (1996), 9–20 and *The Great Divide: Immigration Politics in Australia* (Sydney: Duffy & Snellgrove, 1999). The country that stands out as more positively disposed towards, though not massively enthusiastic about, immigration is Canada (R. Holton and M. Lanphier, 'Public Opinion, Immigration and Refugees', in H. Adelman et al. (eds.), *Immigration and Refugee Policy: Australia and Canada Compared* (Toronto: University of Toronto Press, 1994)). The reasons for greater Canadian tolerance are not clear, but the presence of Quebec and state support, since the 1970s, for official bilingualism and multiculturalism may have accustomed the population to diversity and promoted the perception that immigration is good for the country.

[82] The fact that this has gone largely noticed is probably a reflection of the limited interest political scientists have shown in Commonwealth migration, the analysis of which has been dominated by sociologists, lawyers, and activists.

backbenchers are bound by the Whip and the desire for future promotion; and the Opposition can do little but voice an ineffectual, if loud, protest, generally designed to gain political advantage rather than to change policy radically. Amendments can be pressed in committee, but these are generally technical and do little to alter the basic policy aims, instruments, or outcomes.

Whatever exceptions there are to this simple model of executive dominance, it is borne out in migration policy. The number of changes that the legislature secured on British migration legislation was minuscule. In 1962, the government agreed, in response to backbench pressure, to publish a survey of Irish immigration to the UK and to emphasize that the Irish would be subject to a symbolic control when arriving from somewhere other than Ireland. In 1968, the Commonwealth Immigrants Act was passed within a week and without amendment, and the fifteen Conservatives who voted against it were easily ignored. In 1971, the requirement of police registration was dropped for Commonwealth citizens. Following the easy passage of the Immigrant Act, 1971,[83] Heath's Conservative government actually did face a significant defeat on immigration rules, though only because it linked them with the ever-emotive issue of Europe. On the one hand, the defeat was one of the most significant (of the few) defeats this century; on the other, it was further proof of the legislature's weakness: the rules were adopted by Parliament a few months later, without meaningful change and without any difficulty. These minor exceptions aside, British governments got what they wanted: free entry ended in 1962, Asians with British passports were excluded in 1968, Commonwealth citizens lost their privileged place in migration law in 1971 and Britons and settled persons lost the right to bring family members to the UK in 1988. The executive's power is further augmented by the fact that some of the most important instruments have been immigration rules. These are not debated in Parliament as bills are; they are laid before Parliament and take force immediately unless MPs object. If they do, the rules are then debated in committee, where the option is acceptance or rejection, but not amendment.

In contrast, the US Congress's efforts to crack down on illegal immigration in the 1980s led to an *expansion* of overall migration. A 1986 bill that began as a control measure, combining stiff employer sanctions with a limited compensating amnesty for illegal migrants, ended up—following the usual lobbies, trade-offs, and deal-making that are essential to American policy— sharply expansionist. The sanction was limited to those 'knowingly' hiring illegal immigrants (i.e. no pressure to check for forged documents) and subject to strict anti-discrimination limits; millions of illegal migrants were granted

---

[83]   On this, see Edward Heath, *The Course of My Life: My Autobiography* (London: Hodder & Stoughton, 1998).

amnesty and access to citizenship; agricultural workers in a seven-year temporary workers' programme were also given access to citizenship; and one billion dollars was granted to state governments to cover public assistance, health, and education services, a form of federal support for migrant advocacy networks in densely populated areas.[84] As a control measure, the law was an absolute failure. All the while, the American public remained concerned about losing control of US borders and opposed to further immigration.[85]

The British executive's strength would not translate directly into successful policy restrictionism if UK policy provided for other institutional or procedural checks. Canada, for instance, combines an equally strong executive with an assertive judiciary that has used the 1982 Charter of Rights and Freedoms to articulate a broad range of rights for migrants and, especially, asylum seekers.[86] In Britain, there is no bill of rights and the judiciary has weak powers and exercises them with restraint. The British Court of Appeal and the House of Lords may rule against legislation on the basis of common law—i.e. because legislation is consistent with other statues—but they may not strike down legislation with reference to overarching legal principles (*Grundnormen*) or a bill of rights, whether statutory or constitutional. The result is that such jurisprudence as there has been is limited. An illustrative example occurred in the judicial reaction to the primary purpose rule.[87] Parallel to the ECHR challenges were a series of domestic cases, turning on the two separate requirements: (*a*) that the man and wife be living together and (*b*) that the primary purpose not be entry to the UK. In *Ravinder Singh* and *Lambikhar Singh*, the Immigration Appeal Tribunal[88] extended an earlier decision (*Naresh Kumar*) and held that if (*a*) were satisfied, this would

---

[84] Joppke, *Immigration and the Nation-State*, 29–38.

[85] On this, see T. J. Espenshade and K. Hempstead, 'Contemporary American Attitudes toward U.S. Immigration', *International Migration Review*, 30, No. 2 (1996), 535–57, who find 64.5% of respondents wanting the level of immigration to the USA decreased (546). Also see G. P. Freeman, 'Immigration as a Source of Political Discontent and Frustration in Western Democracies', *Studies in Comparative International Development*, 32, No. 3 (1997), 42–64.

[86] N. Kelley and M. J. Trebilcock, *The Making of the Mosaic: A History of Canadian Immigration Policy* (Toronto: University of Toronto Press, 1998), G. Stobo, 'The Canadian Refugee Determination System', *Texas International Law Journal*, 29, No. 3 (1994).

[87] This section is meant to be illustrative and is not a comprehensive review of jurisprudence on migration or family reunification.

[88] The Immigration Appeal Tribunal was set up in 1969. Although 1999 legislation may alter the situation, appeals first went to adjudicators, who only had the power to decide if the decision made by the Home Office, an entry clearance officer, or an immigration officer was in accordance with the law and immigration rules. A refusal could then be appealed to the Tribunal, within fourteen days of the adjudicator's decision if the applicant is in the UK, within forty-two if he/she is abroad. A rejection may then go to the Court of Appeal, but, since the 1993 Asylum and Immigration Appeals Act, only on legal grounds. See Chatwin, *Immigration, Nationality & Refugee Law Handbook*, ch. 16.

amount to satisfaction of (*b*).[89] In *Vinod Bhatia*, however, the Tribunal retreated, and held by a majority that it, and two other liberalizing decisions, were wrong.[90] As the government intended, the Tribunal maintained that the burden of proof was on the applicants to satisfy both conditions; the satisfaction of one did not imply satisfaction of the other.[91] Finally, the High Court and the Court of Appeal upheld the burden of proof .[92] In the High Court decision, a further restrictive twist was added: it was suggested that entry clearance officers should approach their task of assessing the primary purpose of a marriage against the background of their knowledge of Hindu customs and should take into account the fact that many marriages in the subcontinent had admission to the UK as their primary purpose; the proper approach should thus be one of 'cautious pessimism'. Although the Court of Appeal suggested that this had pejorative overtones and should be disregarded, it in turn referred to a 'presumption' to be derived from the Rules that the primary purpose of the intended marriage was always to obtain admission to the UK unless the applicant proved the contrary.[93] The Court retreated somewhat in *ex p Arun Kumar*,[94] in which it was stated that all it actually does is to place the applicant under the burden of satisfying the entry clearance officer that, on the balance of probability, the primary purpose and other requirements of the marriage rule are duly satisfied. The goal, said the Master of the Rolls, should be for the 'entry clearance officer to consider the question as would a jury, that is to say by impression based on the evidence as a whole, rather than on legalistic analysis'.[95] Following Home Office appeal, the decision was reaffirmed, but the Court of Appeal added a series of guidelines that reaffirmed

---

[89]   Quoted in Macdonald and Blake, 337.

[90]   Imm AR 39, *R* v. *IAT, ex p Vinod Bhatia* [1985].

[91]   They proposed instead a scale. At one extreme, there were cases in which the applicant has previously made repeated unsuccessful attempts to enter the UK; in such instances, the onus on the applicant should be formidable. At the other, there were cases in which the families of the proposed bride and groom had known one another for a long time and there was a history of intermarriage between them. In such cases, the burden of proof could be easily satisfied. See Macdonald and Blake, *Immigration Law and Practice*, 338.

[92]   Imm AR 50, *R* v. *IAT, ex p Bhata* [1985], 52, affirming decision reported at [1985] Imm AR 39.

[93]   O'Conner LJ: 'In my judgement the wording of the rule is straightforward and clear. The rule presumes that it is the primary purpose of the intended marriage to obtain admission of the applicant to the United Kingdom.' Imm AR 50, *R* v. *IAT, ex p Bhata* [1985], 52–3.

[94]   Imm AR 446, *R* v. *IAT ex p Arun Kumar* [1986].

[95]   Ibid. 455. That is, officers should avoid taking conclusions to their logical extreme, since a British woman who wishes to remain in the UK *and* marry a man without right of abode by definition has to marry someone who wishes to obtain admission to the UK; as the rules are distinct, this could be (and probably has been) in itself taken as violation of the primary purpose rule.

the essence of primary purpose: the burden of proof lay on the applicant; the entry clearance officer was not limited in his inquiries to answers given by the parties; and satisfaction of intent to cohabit is insufficient, as is proof of cohabitation.[96] At the beginning of the 1990s, following significant legal action, primary purpose looked broadly as it did at the beginning of the 1980s. One of the few substantial changes to it was announced by the government itself. In response to judicial rulings, the Home Office announced in 1992 that 'genuine' marriages having lasted five years or having produced one or more children with the right of abode would be treated as, in principle,[97] having satisfied the primary purpose rule.[98]

In all this detail lies the fact that British jurisprudence affected the rule only on the margins, being bound, as courts are in the UK, by the original wording of the legislation. The decisions had consequences, and perhaps slightly liberalizing consequences, but the debate was constructed within the government's terms. The French and German courts, by contrast, delivered a number of judgements that blocked efforts at preventing family unification and facilitating compulsory return.[99] Only another government, with a large majority and thus an unassailable executive, would overturn a migration policy considered to be one of the gravest violation of individual rights in British legislation. This is of course not to say that British judges as such are unsympathetic individuals, or that British legal advocates lack commitment to their cause; on the contrary. Yet, the latter are sharply limited by their inability to appeal to a right to privacy (violated by intrusive questioning), to equality (discrepancies between British who have worked abroad and those who have not), to mobility (limited by divided families), to respect for private and family life (available in European conventions[100]), or to any other clause found in other domestic constitutions.

Other decisions stand out as evidence of impotence of British courts. The 1968 Commonwealth Immigrants Act effectively stripped Britons of one of the most basic rights of citizenship; UK courts did not mutter a word. It is inconceivable that such a decision in the USA,[101] Canada, or Germany would

---

[96] *R* v. *IAT, ex p Hoque and Sing* [1988] Imm AR 216, CA

[97] That is, entry clearance could still be refused along other grounds, such as criminal record, accommodation, or maintenance.

[98] D. Jackson, *Immigration Law and Practice* (London: Sweet & Maxwell, 1996), 399.

[99] For details, see Hollifield, *Immigrants, Markets and States*; C. Joppke, 'Why Liberal States Accept Unwanted Immigration', *World Politics*, 50 (Jan. 1998), 266–93, 269; D. Lochak, 'Les Politiques de l'immigration au prisme de la législation sur les étrangers', in D. Fassin et al., *Les Lois de l'inhospitalité: les politiques de l'immigration à l'épreuve des sans-papiers* (Paris: La Découverte, 1997); Weil, *La France et ses étrangers*.

[100] Article 8, European Convention on Human Rights.

survive judicial scrutiny, to say nothing of public outcry. The 1988 Immigration Act removed, with no judicial protest, the right of Britons to bring spouses to the country of their citizenship, a right that all EU citizens enjoy.

CONCLUSION: BRITISH RESTRICTIONISM

In the 1960s, it was customary to lavish praise on the British for their love of liberty and their success in protecting it. Commenting on an unwritten constitution, Sartori argued that '[T]he drawbacks and dangers of this solution are so serious, that only the British can afford the luxury of not formalizing the constitution.'[102] Memories of the Second World War and European fascism still in mind, Britain was the land of Churchillian avowals to never surrender, of quiet streets, quaint bowler caps, and polite, gun-less British bobbies. Thirty years later, following Enoch Powell, hysterical opposition to Commonwealth migrants and its legislative results have, above all among migration scholars, created another image: one of vindictive pettiness, a ceaseless pursuit of restrictionism, and, of course, near-rampant racism. The former myth was probably never true, as the latter is not today. Although accepting the inevitability of Commonwealth immigration, and, among the young at least, even recognizing and enjoying the benefits of a multicultural society, the British public overall remains adamantly opposed to further immigration. British governments, like all European governments, have an interest in limiting immigration as much as possible. The only difference is that while German, French, and—across the Atlantic—American governments find their efforts frustrated by legislative and judicial checks, the UK enjoys a largely free hand. Although a number of American and European scholars[103] have recognized this point, not a single British scholar of migration has linked British restrictionism with the UK's legislature, executive, and

---

[101]   Article 6 of the German basic law and article 10 of the Dutch constitution protect private life; in 1978, the Conseil d'État ruled that the suspension of family reunification violated the *principe général du droit* (general legal principle) protecting an individual's right to a normal family life. V. Guiraudon, 'Third country nationals and European law: obstacles to rights' expansion', *Journal of Ethnic and Migration Studies*, 24, No. 4 (1998), 657–74, 665.

[102]   G. Sartori, 'Constitutionalism: A Preliminary Discussion', *American Political Science Review*, 56 (1962), 853–64, 862.

[103]   The point is made particularly forcefully by Joppke, 'Why Liberal States Accept Unwanted Immigration', 287–91. Also see Gary P. Freeman, 'Britain, the Deviant Case', in W. A. Cornelius, P. L. Martin, and J. F. Hollifield (eds.), *Controlling Immigration: A Global Perspective* (Stanford, Calif.: Stanford University Press, 1994).

courts. There is in this fact a noteworthy irony: those who are most willing to condemn Britain in the most uncompromising terms betray their essential Britishness: they recognize the faults of individuals, but are blind to those of their institutions.

11

Conclusion

COMMONWEALTH migration has transformed the demographic make-up of the UK and irreversibly altered its politics. In offering an account of this unprecedented migration, the study has sought to explain three features of it: the late adoption of migration controls in 1962, the rapid and complete adoption of restrictions after 1962, and the legal peculiarities linked with the experience of Commonwealth immigration. The account can be briefly summarized:

- The deferral of migration restrictions until 1962, which ensured (via family reunification) the development of multicultural Britain, resulted from the intersection of ideology and partisan power. Both parties, but especially the Conservatives, were profoundly attached to the Old Commonwealth and its citizens' right to enter Britain; no politician wished to see this movement blocked. At the same time, a few politicians, and above all the Colonial Secretary, refused to countenance racist immigration restrictions. The resulting veto, carried in 1955, guaranteed further non-white migration and the emergence of British multiculturalism.

- Once the first restrictions had been adopted (following the weakening of the Colonial Office and the attenuation of policy-makers' attachment to the Commonwealth), the door to the Commonwealth closed so quickly because policy-makers faced few constraints on pursuing the tight migration policy demanded by the public. A strong executive, weak legislature, and tightly constrained judiciary allowed governments to respond to public demands with a single-minded success unknown in the rest of Europe or North America.

- The peculiar features of British migration policy and politics—the decoupling of citizenship and the right to enter from 1962 to 1981, the Kenyan Asians crisis of 1968, the derided concept of patriality—were determined, wholly or in part, by the path-dependent feedback effects of the British Nationality Act, 1948.

Following the structure outlined at the outset, this conclusion returns to and expands upon the three issues—immigration policy between 1948 and 1962, policy after 1962, and the legal peculiarities of Commonwealth migration—and it considers broader questions relevant to the study of Commonwealth immigration.

POLICY BEFORE 1962

The 1950s were the defining years in the development of multicultural Britain; they have accordingly received a great deal of attention in scholarly work over the last decade. They were once viewed, no doubt naively, as years in which Conservative politicians, imbued with a profound sense of imperial obligation and *noblesse oblige*, supported open borders in the name of empire and against the wishes of the British public. Today, a group of revisionists—self-described 'challengers' of this myth—have recast our picture of this decade in favour of a far more sinister one in which these politicians were the generators of British racism. Taking 1954 as the turning-point, Kathleen Paul provides an 'alternative reading' of these years:

[D]uring this year ... some Conservative ministers, along with some officials, became convinced that the solution to their problem lay in publicizing the dangers of uncontrolled 'coloured immigration' to a general public perceived to be as yet too liberal to initiate change on their own behalf. The language and content of various committees, reports, parliamentary speeches, and Cabinet debates suggest that ministers and officials envisioned an educational campaign designed to produce a majority public opinion opposed to continuing colonial migration, and in favour of controlling legislation. Fostering a climate of public hostility in this way enabled ministers to escape responsibility for legislation curtailing colonial immigration and to attach the blame instead to an apparently illiberal public clamouring for control. It is my contention that this campaign is the key to understanding the shift from private to public sphere and from open to closed borders. Thus, according to this interpretation, the infamous 'race riots' resulted not from a desperate *popular* hostility toward people of colour but from the policy-making *elite's* racialized understanding of the world's population and their propogation of this belief to the rest of society.[1]

Thus, the 1950s, when 'no coloureds' signs hung in London hotels, black Britons could only find accommodation with slumlords, and white thugs beat West Indians with bottles and bats, were years when a liberal, xenophile public was talked into racism by elite duplicity. During 1958 riots, the worst racially motivated violence in the UK since the war, one saw 'in the whites' reported chants that the blacks should "go home" the success of policy makers' reconstruction of subjects into aliens and proof that the language of the Cabinet room and parliamentary chamber had finally moved to the public highway'.[2]

Along with other work in the same vein,[3] the thesis is a rejection of a position that enjoyed support in the 1960s, which Paul refers to as the 'Whitehall version of events': 'namely, that a liberal UK government was forced by a frightened and hostile public to impose immigration controls on subjects and citizens of colour'.[4]

Paul's thesis is not merely intuitively implausible; it is, as the archives on which she bases her hypothesis make clear, wholly untenable. The 'language and content' of committees, reports, parliamentary speeches, and Cabinet debates demonstrate a constellation of preferences that one would expect on any difficult issue: a few had strong preferences one way or another, and most were uncertain of how to act and/or viewed the immigration issue through the lens of other considerations: its consequences for decolonization, the Old Commonwealth, Britain's reputation abroad, and so on. The empirically defensible element of the argument, its premiss, is that British politicians were not keen on the emergence of multiculturalism in Britain. This is true; even Alan Lennox-Boyd was suspicious of indefinite open borders. Cabinet opinion overall was tinged by a modest anti-restrictionist tendency, but this is a far cry from a duplicitous campaign in racism's favour. From the ivory tower, Paul, Carter, Solomos, and others have recreated a world that we never had, in which politicians, aiming at apartheid by the back door, slyly indoctrinated a liberal public into xenophobia and racism. It makes a tantalizing story, but it simply did not happen.[5] British policy-makers did not expect New

---

[2] Paul, *Whitewashing Britain: Race and Citizenship in the Postwar Er*, 155–6.

[3] B. Carter, C. Harris, and S. Joshi, 'The 1951–1955 Conservative Government and the Racialization of Black Immigration', *Immigrants and Minorities*, 6, No. 3 (1987), 335–47; B. Carter et. al., 'The 1951–55 Conservative Government and the Racialization of Black Immigration', in W. James and C. Harris, *Inside Babylon: The Carribean Diaspora in Britain* (London: Verso, 1993); B. Carter et al., 'Immigration Policy and the Racialization of Migrant Labour: The Construction of National Identities in the USA and Britain', *Ethnic and Racial Studies*, 19, No. 1 (1996), 135–57; L. Kushnick, 'The Political Economy of White Racism in Britain', in Kushnick, *Race, Class & Struggle: Essays on Racism and Inequality in Britain, the US and Western Europe* (London: Rivers Oram Press, 1998); A. Sivanandan, *A Different Hunger: Writings on Black Resistance* (London: Pluto Press, 1982); J. Solomos, *Race and Racism in Britain* (Houndmills: Macmillan, 1993), 56–61.

[4] Paul, *Whitewashing*, 133. She suggests that this thesis has gained such unearned currency because scholars did not have access to official documents, which only became open from mid-1980s.

[5] Among the many factors that render the thesis untenable is the fact that such a campaign would require an immense amount of effort. Even if politicians had wanted to racialize immigration, they simply would not have had the time. All scholars suffer from professional myopia; they exaggerate the importance, to other scholars, politicians, and the public, of their special-

Commonwealth migration and they, in the main, did not want it. The 'Whitehall version', which was in fact the product of meticulous historians and other academics with an intimate hands-on knowledge of Commonwealth immigration,[6] got it wrong insofar as it attributed, in the absence of official records, too much indifference to policy-makers. When migration began, however, the convergence of universal support for *Old* Commonwealth migration and selective anti-racism resulted in its resigned acceptance. The fundamental piece of evidence that Paul and others cite in favour of their conspiracy theory—informal discouragement of non-white migration—renders it in fact less plausible. The measures adopted were limited; they did not repudiate British subjects' fundamental right to enter the UK; and some of those implementing them, particularly the Colonial Office, hoped that they would deflect anti-restrictionism within the Cabinet enough to keep the door formally open. Anything more ambitious and pernicious than this—public speeches against the 'evils' of immigration, open support within the Cabinet for racist restrictions—was, in the decade before Powell, restricted to a few politically impotent extremists.

The laissez-faire years, and they were largely laissez-faire, ended with the Commonwealth Immigrants Act, 1962. A number of political historians have suggested that the decision should have been taken sooner,[7] but the majority of commentary has been scathing. One scholar, closely connected with the Institute of Race Relations, argued that '[t]his racial scapegoating [of immigrants, for housing, education and heath problems] legitimised, and was legitimised by, a series of racist immigration laws that emerged in the 1960s and 1970s. One such law was the 1962 Conservative Government's Commonwealth Immigration Act [*sic*] which marked the institutionalisation of racism.'[8] Others concur, holding that the legislation 'was the first of a series of acts of appeasement of the racialists, and, of course, could not serve

---

ized subject. What strikes anyone who has conducted elite interviews is how low immigration was, with the exception of the late 1960s, on the list of government priorities. This was especially the case in the 1950s, but even in the early 1970s the Conservatives were more preoccupied with inflation, a collapsing pound, entry to Europe, and the Cold War. A glance through any of the major Cabinet diaries of the period—of Tony Benn, Barbara Castle, Denis Healey, Edward Heath, Quintin Hogg, Roy Jenkins, Margaret Thatcher—invariably produces only a few pages on immigration.

[6] N. Deakin, *Colour, Citizenship and British Society* (London: Panther, 1970); K. Morgan, *The People's Peace* (Oxford: Oxford University Press, 1990), 202–4; P. B. Rich, *Race and Empire in British Politics* (Cambridge: Cambridge University Press, 1990), 189–90.

[7] R. Lamb, *The Macmillan Years, 1957–1963: The Emerging Truth* (London: John Murray, 1995), 416–17; A. Roberts, *Eminent Churchillians* (London: Weidenfeld & Nicolson, 1994), ch. 4.

[8] L. Kushnick, *Race, Class & Struggle: Essays on Racism and Inequality in Britain, the US and Western Europe* (London: Rivers Oram Press, 1994), 175.

this purpose unless its intention and effect, of restricting "coloured" immigration, was plainly recognizable . . . [E]ach restrictive measure had upon the crypto-racialists a far graver effect than that of allowing them to continue to disguise the real situation [in which those who support immigration control are racists] from themselves: it acted as the most powerful possible *education* in racialism.'[9]

RACISM AND IMMIGRATION POLICY

The claim that immigration laws are racist is often bandied about, and it needs to be unpacked. There are at least four possible claims underpinning it: first, that any restriction on immigration disproportionately affecting non-whites is racist; second, that Britain's immigration laws are formally racist; third, that, while formally not racist, the operation of them has been racist; and, fourth, that the way in which Britain's immigration laws were implemented (in response to public anti-immigrant sentiment) legitimized racism. The first claim is not tenable, as it collapses the distinction between racist—an assumption of ethnic or racial inferiority—and 'racialist'— disproportionately affecting non-whites. British immigration law and policy have certainly been 'racialist', but so have French, German, Danish, Canadian, American, and all other liberal democratic policies. As emigration pressure stems today from countries that are in the main non-white, the position either reduces to a naive appeal for open borders or to the claim that all liberal democratic immigration policies are racist. The latter, radical-structuralist critique is fine so far as it goes, but it provides no standard for distinguishing (relatively) liberal policies (Canada, Australia) from relatively restrictive ones (the UK), and no standard for policy improvement. Jeannette Money draws our attention to the fact that when large-scale immigration was predominantly white—German and Irish in nineteenth-century America, Jewish in early twentieth-century Britain, Italian in Switzerland after the Second World War—it met with intense anti-immigration pressure and was similarly demonized.[10] The second argument is simply false; all immigration laws and rules have applied to both the Old and the New

[9]   M. Dummett and A. Dummett, 'The Role of Government in Britain's Racial Crisis', in C. Husband (ed.), *'Race' in Britain: Continuity and Change* (London: Hutchinson, 1982), 103, 109–10.

[10]   J. Money, *Fences and Neighbours: The Political Geography of Immigration Control* (Ithaca, NY: Cornell University Press, 1999), 213–15.

Commonwealth.[11] From 1971, they have been largely equivalent to policies applying to all aliens, whatever their origin.

The third and fourth arguments are more complicated and are impossible to resolve definitively. There is little doubt that certain immigration rules are more rigorously enforced when the applicant is from a traditional source country, such as India or Pakistan.[12] At the same time, these countries are the largest sources of legal and illegal migrants, and all countries use policy instruments, such as mandatory visas, to discourage their entry. In the UK's case, white migrants have also experienced the rigour of UK asylum laws: gypsies attempting to enter the country to claim asylum in early 1998 were summarily returned, and asylum seekers—whatever their origin—are given an unwelcome reception. If such accusations are to be carried, moreover, the level of analysis must be shifted from a condemnation of the immigration system as a whole, or even a given parliamentary act, to focus on which rule or rules are objectionable. In many cases—the primary purpose rule standing out—it would be more productive to reject them as violations of principles of equality, privacy, or fairness than as instances of racism.

The broader issue of the relationship between immigration control, on the one hand, and racism and race relations, on the other, has been a matter of debate for decades. It is not possible in the last few pages to establish whether immigration restrictions have legitimized racism[13] or, as the government claims, improved 'race relations'. The issue is likely to be essentially contestable. It is worth noting, however, that, for all the arguments about migration controls' role in legitimating racism, attitudes to ethnic minorities in Britain have improved considerably (however far they still have to go) since restrictions were first applied to Commonwealth immigration in the 1960s.[14]

---

[11]   Although the opposite is often claimed: 'current [1984] immigration policy and practice keep West Indians and Asians out of Britain and yet allow large numbers of Canadians and Australians freedom of entry (R. Miles and A. Phizacklea, *White Man's Country: Racism in British Politics* (London: Pluto Press, 1984), 6). In fact, a cursory glance at migration patterns since the 1970s (see the appendices) demonstrates that New Commonwealth migration has consistently dominated Old.

[12]   M. Chatwin (ed.), *Immigration, Nationality & Refugee Law Handbook* (London: JCWI, 1999), chs. 2–4.

[13]   As is argued by Dummett and Dummett, 'The Role of Government in Britain's Racial Crisis'; E. J. B Rose et al., *Colour and Citizenship: A Report on British Race Relations* (London: Oxford University Press, 1969), 228; and S. Saggar, *Race and Politics in Britain* (London: Harvester Wheatsheaf, 1992), 175. Also see R. Miles, *Racism and Migrant Labour* (London: Routledge & Kegan Paul, 1982); Solomos, *Race and Racism*; John Solomos and Les Back, *Racism and Society* (Houndmills: Macmillan, 1996), ch. 1. See also S. Spencer, 'The Implications of Immigration Policy for Race Relations', in Spencer (ed.), *Strangers & Citizens: A Positive Approach to Migrants and Refugees* (London: Institute for Public Policy Research, 1994).

[14]   See L. Brook and E. Cape, 'Libertarianism in Retreat?' in Roger Jowell et al. (eds.), *British Social Attitudes: The 12th Report* (Aldershot: Dartmouth Publishing Co., 1995), 201–4.

The turn to control

Returning to the first instance of immigration control, the legion attacks on the Commonwealth Immigrants Act are puzzling. The legislation applied to both the New and Old Commonwealth, and created a skill-based quota system that now appears positively generous. By 1962, public opposition to migration was clear, and the economic gains of further migration, during a period in which labour shortages were sectoral and limited to skilled professions, were dubious. Commonwealth migrants, though naturally and understandably interested in migration to the UK, could claim no right to it. International law confers on individuals the right to leave the country of their nationality, but it grounds no corresponding duty on any other state to admit them.[15] Leaving aside a purely normative defence of open borders, the only justification for unfettered immigration was imperial.

THE IMPERIALIST FOUNDATIONS OF EXPANSIVE POLICY

The last point needs to be textured. As argued in Chapter 2, the right of British subjects to enter the UK stemmed from a pre-democratic theory of allegiance to the monarch. To the extent that there was a clear idea behind *Civis Britannicus sum*, it was simple:[16] all British subjects, because they

---

[15] Or, as Jeannette Money put it, control of exit is governed by rules of human rights, while control of entry is governed by rules of national sovereignty. Money, *Fences and Neighbours*, 217.

[16] The phrase was first invoked, to my knowledge, in the 'Pacifico Affair'. Pacifico was Spanish and normally resident in Portugal. He, through his birth in Gibraltar, enjoyed British subject status. In 1847, his house in Greece was pillaged by a Greek mob, including well-connected youths. Pacifico appealed to the British government for aid in securing recompense. The Greek action was followed by a period of difficulty for the British Prime Minister, Palmerston, who was under attack from Peelites, protectionists, and the Manchester liberals. Three years after the incident, Palmerston used Pacifico's dubious claims against the Greek government as the pretence for establishing a naval blockade and seizing Greek ships in compensation. The action enraged the great powers (France withdrew its ambassador in protest) and led to an attack in Parliament. Lord Stanley, hoping to unseat Palmerston, succeeded in moving a vote of censure against him in the Upper House, and a counter-resolution was moved in the Commons by Roebuck. Palmerston's position was weak. While there was some constitutional question about how British subjects resident in foreign countries were to be treated under British law, it was generally accepted that, if the law of the country in question applied, then first resort should have been to domestic tribunals; as the Greek courts had not been resorted to by Pacifico, no diplomatic action was justified. Gladstone made this point in an attack on Palmerston's speech, whose action he declared a violation of international law, an interference in the domestic affairs of a sovereign state. Were it not for the invocation of the Roman Empire's ghost, Palmerston would probably have been defeated. In the Commons debate on the blockade,

enjoy an identical relationship with the sovereign, could claim full privileges in and the full protection of the United Kingdom. The year 1948 was the high-point of this ideal: there was no question of ending the formal right of all British subjects to enter the UK; in 1954, Henry Hopkins, the Colonial Secretary, told the House of Commons that '[i]n a world in which restrictions on personal movement and immigration have increased we can still take pride in the fact that a man can say *Civis Britannicus sum* whatever his colour may be, and we take pride in the fact that he wants and can come to the mother country;'[17] by 1962, the tradition was abandoned with agonizing regret; by 1971, no one was prepared to defend such a position publicly; and by 1991, it is doubtful that few people could even conceive of such an argument ever being made.

In light of the rapidity with which restrictions were enacted, it may be tempting to conclude that *Civis Britannicus sum* was empty. Such a conclusion is hasty for two reasons. First, as argued throughout this book, the primary commitment of policy-makers was to a pattern of migration dominated by movement between the Old Commonwealth and the United Kingdom. The documents repeatedly attest to British politicians' support for this movement as an expression of the linguistic, historical, and institutional ties between these countries and Britain.[18] Non-white British subjects were, in

---

Palmerston uttered the famous words: 'I therefore fearlessly challenge the verdict which this House, as representing a personal, a commercial, a constitutional country, is to give on the question now brought before it; whether the principles on which the foreign policy of Her Majesty's Government has been conducted, and the sense of duty which has led us to think ourselves bound to afford protection to our fellow subjects abroad, are proper and fitting guides for those who are charged with the government of England; and whether, as the Roman, in the days of old, held himself free from indignity, when he could say *Civis Romanus sum*; so also a British subject, in whatever land he may be, shall feel confident that the watchful eye and the strong arm of England will protect him against injustice and wrong.' On the affair, see J. Brooke and M. Sorensen (eds.), *The Prime Minister's Papers: W. E. Gladstone*, i: *Autobiographica* (London: HMSO, 1971), 67; E. Eyck, *Gladstone* (London: George Allen & Unwin, 1938); R. Shannon, *Gladstone*, vol. i (London: Hamish Hamilton, 1982), 222–3; R. Jenkins, *Gladstone* (London: Macmillan, 1995), 117; H. W. Paul, *The Life of William Ewart Gladstone* (London: Thomas Nelson & Sons, 1901); G. B. Smith, *The Life of the Right Honourable William Ewart Gladstone* (London: Cassell, Petter, Galpin & Company, 1880), 114, 55. The speech carried the argument.

[17] *Parliamentary Debate (Commons)* (532), col. 827, 5 Nov. 1954.

[18] It is tempting to think of this commitment, for which there is abundant evidence, as an example of ideas influencing politics. See, for example, P. A. Hall, 'Policy Paradigms, Social Learning and the State: The Case of Economic Policymaking in Britain', *Comparative Politics*, 25, No. 3 (1993), 275–96, P. A. Hall, *The Political Power of Economic Ideas* (Princeton: Princeton University Press, 1989); and J. Goldstein and R. O. Keohane, *Ideas and Foreign Policy: Beliefs, Institutions, and Political Change* (Ithaca, NY: Cornell University Press, 1993). This conclusion should, however be reached hesitantly, for, as is often the case, ideas—an attachment to the traditional right of British subjects—traded upon interests—the close strategic and economic ties between Britain and the Commonwealth, particularly the Old.

small numbers, welcomed in the UK as an expression of the indivisibility of British subjecthood, and there was arguably even a residual sentimental attachment to a small colonial presence in the United Kingdom.[19] Policy-makers' primary commitment was, none the less, unquestionably to the Old Commonwealth and its citizens' right of entry. As patterns of migration changed, and the Old Dominions sought to pursue their interests within a regional framework rather than within the Commonwealth, it is unsurprising that support for *Civis Britannicus sum* withered.

The point, however, runs deeper than this. Immigration controls were not a betrayal of *Civis Britannicus sum*; on the contrary, they were justifiable with reference to its terms. The historic and theoretical justification for the right of all British subjects to enter the United Kingdom stemmed from the *allegiance* of each individual to the sovereign. Although colonial subjects were deemed citizens after 1948, citizenship was instrumental to subjecthood, the mechanism through which it and its privileges were sustained. Yet, after the British Nationality Act was passed, nation after nation repudiated allegiance and remained in the Commonwealth as Republics.[20] This 'pragmatic nonsense', originally designed for India in 1950, was made possible by the Royal Titles Act of 1953, which stripped the Queen of all power and prerogative over the Commonwealth;[21] she was from that point its symbolic head. Given the traditional justification of laissez-faire, immigration controls could be defended *according to the logic and principles of* 'Civis Britannicus sum'. If individual nations proclaimed no allegiance to the British Crown, if they did not embrace the principles that underlined the 1948 scheme, then they could not claim a historic right which they engendered. It would have naturally been possible to refound the principles on which an open immigration policy for the Commonwealth rested; but, as no such process was undertaken, it is impossible to claim that the decision to end the historic right was anything

---

[19] An internal Commonwealth Relations Office document speaks favourably about ambitious Indians' and Pakistanis' desire to send their sons to the United Kingdom for an education. The document, equally revealingly, makes no mention of the existence or possibility of permanent Asian immigration. *Private Papers of Patrick Gordon Walker*, GNWR 1/7, 'Some Considerations on the Question of India's and Pakistan's Association with the British Commonwealth of Nations', Information Department, CRO, 28 May 1948. Reginald Maudling makes a similar point. See R. Maudling, *Memoirs* (London: Sidgwick & Jackson, 1978), 157–8.

[20] In 1962, for example, India, Pakistan, South Yemen, and Somalia were Republics. Today, sixteen independent Commonwealth nations, in addition to the United Kingdom, recognize the Queen as Head of State, including Canada, Australia, New Zealand, Jamaica, Barbados, Papua, and New Guinea. See J. Darwin, *Britain and Decolonisation: The Retreat from Empire in the Post-War World* (London: Macmillan, 1988), 326–7.

[21] G. Marshall, *Constitutional Conventions: The Rules and Forms of Political Accountability* (Oxford: Clarendon Press, 1984), 170–1. The phrase in quotes is Marshall's.

but the United Kingdom's full prerogative.[22] It is a historical irony that the bitterest critics of empire were the strongest defenders of an open migration policy that derived its only justification from imperialism.[23]

POLICY AFTER 1962

The (admittedly limited) historiography on immigration policy in the 1960s has thus constructed a moral condemnation of British governments that is undeserved. It is based on empirical research that is, at best, selective and, at worse, simply false. The 1960s and subsequent decades, however, are another matter, and it is essential to distinguish between the two. There are two points worth developing in the post-1962 period.

The first concerns the Commonwealth Immigrants Act, 1968. The act has been treated in all descriptive accounts of immigration policy as a piece of post-1960s restrictionism, a trend encouraged by appellative similarities with the 1962 Act. The implication of this study is that it should be viewed as an aberration; the Commonwealth Immigrants, Act 1968 is the sole immigration law (as distinct from rule) since 1945 that stands out as truly indefensible. The legislation was not, however, indefensible either because it was an immigration restriction (nothing exceptional in that) or because the Kenyan Asians had been exempted from 1962 controls (they had not). As argued in Chapter 7, the Asians' exemption from the 1962 controls resulted from a series of feedback effects; in the absence of any one, there would have been no exemption. Had the 1962 Act created a distinctive British citizenship, the Asians would have possessed another legal status that would have remained unchanged at independence. Had the 1962 Act been based on some other

[22]   There is the argument, made more in the popular press than scholarly work, that the UK's exploitation of the Empire placed it under a special obligation to aid nations from which it benefited. The argument, which has a certain appeal, has never to my knowledge advanced beyond the emotive level; no one has articulated the theory of historical culpability which it presupposes, and no one has convincingly demonstrated why, if such an obligation exists, the UK is bound to maintain an open-door policy rather than, for example, supporting economic development in the former colonies themselves.

[23]   Those who are in favour of open borders will find this claim unsatisfactory. See, for instance, J. H. Carens, 'Aliens and Citizens: The Case for Open Borders', *Review of Politics*, 49 (1987), 251–73. It is tenable to argue that the 1962 and subsequent restrictions were unacceptable because any restriction on migration is unacceptable. I do not consider the position convincing, but cannot develop the point here. The point I wish to make is that if immigration restrictions are accepted in principle, the objection against the 1962 Act (but *not* the 1968 Act) collapses. In this context, it is worth nothing that most students of Commonwealth immigration find restrictions on the Commonwealth more objectionable than those on aliens.

control mechanism than the issue of passports, the transformation of the Kenyan Governor into a High Commissioner would have conferred no right of entry. Had inclusive local citizenship been introduced, either because Kenya pursued different policies or because the UK insisted on such provisions as a condition of independence, any attack on the Asian community would have been an attack on individuals with no legal, as distinct from moral, claim on the United Kingdom. Kenya, rather than Britain, would have been the target of shame, and the British government could have accepted a limited number of persecuted Asians as refugees. As in 1972, the UK would have gained a reputation for liberality rather than its opposite, and the criticism would have fallen where it belonged: on the illiberality of Kenyatta.

As none of these obviating steps were taken, responsibility rested firmly with the UK. The Asians' exemption was known to civil servants and Cabinet members in the early 1960s, and it was accepted by them. When the Asians were driven out after 1965, with a brutality that critics of the British government have ignored,[24] they possessed no citizenship but British. The British government denied them entry to this country, ignored the promises a previous government had given, and left them languishing in East Africa, unwelcome and with few rights.

Although the 1968 legislation was qualitatively different from other post-war legal and policy measures, it shared ease of legislative passage. On one level, it is extraordinary that such a draconian law was subject to so little legal resistance. For ammunition, its critics possessed only the legally correct, but politically ineffectual, claim that it violated international law. There was no domestic remedy because, as argued in Chapter 10, the courts could only measure the legislation's consistency with the common law and the Home Secretary's administrative competence; it violated neither and faced no judi-

---

[24]   At the time and now, the vehement attacks on Wilson, Callaghan, and the Labour government are not matched by similar attacks on Kenya, which of course orchestrated the ethnic cleansing. There is even in certain writings the implication that they had it coming. Paul Foot, in a polemic against Enoch Powell, writes that an escape clause 'designed solely for Kenya whites . . . was complicated by the position of Asians in Kenya, most of whom were merchants [read: capitalists, author's note] and who, as a community, had played an ambiguous role in the Kenyan Africans' long struggle for independence' (P. Foot, *The Rise of Enoch Powell* (Harmondsworth: Penguin Books, 1969), 105). As pointed out in Chapter 7, this is false; a significant part of the Asian community was sympathetic to independence, and others were neutral. Foot goes on to provide an apologist's defence of the Kenyan government, claiming it 'denied no one who was living in Kenya at the time of independence citizenship' (ignoring bureaucratic delays and rejected applications) and that it 'had merely made it clear that they would not tolerate dual citizenship' (106–7). It would be illuminating to witness Foot's reaction if the British government enacted a policy revoking the right of non-white permanent residents who had not taken British citizenship, but who had an entitlement to it, to work in this country. One is left with the impression that racism perpetrated by Africans is more acceptable, or at least more difficult to condemn, than racism perpetrated by Europeans.

cial censure until challenged at the European Commission of Human Rights. The ease with which the 1968 legislation was passed, and the overall restrictiveness of UK immigration policies reflected the strength of the British executive and, above all, the absence of a strong judiciary and a bill of rights.

THE EUROPEANIZATION OF BRITISH MIGRATION POLICY

As stated in the introduction, there is little likelihood that Britain's tight migration control policies will change in the absence of an entrenched bill of rights. In the late 1980s, there was a strong movement, led by 'Charter 88', in favour of such a bill, but the issue is no longer high on the political agenda. The one possibility for the development of significant institutional constraints on the executive centres around developments at the European level. The 'Europeanization' of migration policy, to use a fashionable term, has three components: the abolition of borders within the EU; the harmonization of asylum policy across it; and the articulation of minimum asylum and immigration standards by the European Court of Justice and the European Court of Human Rights. The last of these is most significant.

To summarize their content briefly, migration and asylum policy in the EU have been organized around harmonization through the 1985 Schengen Agreement (and its 1990 Implementing Convention) and the 1990 Dublin Convention. Schengen was designed to reinforce European border control through extending the borders of Europe to its outer periphery.[25] For participating members, border checks were abolished in the EU and a common visa, valid for three months, was established for an (almost wholly) harmonized list of countries requiring visas. The Dublin Convention was designed to reduce asylum applications, which sky-rocketed from the end of the 1980s and, particularly, to crack down on 'asylum shopping': applying for asylum at multiple points across the EU in the hope of gaining access somewhere.[26] The core of Dublin is a mechanism allowing EU member states to transfer asylum

[25] On the Schengen agreement, see G. Brochmann, *European Integration and Immigration from Third Countries* (Oslo: Scandinavian University Press, 1996), ch. 4.

[26] In asylum, there has also been considerable interest, following the break-up of Yugoslavia, in offering asylum seekers temporary protection on the condition that they return home when conditions improve. See K. Kerber, 'Temporary Protection: An Assessment of the Harmonisation Policies of the European Union Member States', *International Journal of Refugee Law*, 9 (1997), 453–69. On asylum, also see K. Koser, 'Out of the Frying Pan and into the Fire: A Case Study of Illegality amongst Asylum Seekers', in K. Koser and H. Lutz, *The New Migration in Europe: Social Constructions and Social Realities* (London: Macmillan, 1997).

seekers to another member state for processing. The main criterion is first country of passage (i.e. an asylum seeker travelling through Belgium to Germany is returned to Belgium for processing), but there are others—past residence, past receipt of a visa, and the existence of family members. In the 1992 Maastricht Treaty, all these measures were intergovernmental. The 1998 Maastricht Treaty partially 'communitarizes' Schengen, providing for eventual Commission proposals and European Court of Justice jurisprudence,[27] both of which tend to be more sympathetic than nation-states to migrants and third country nationals.

The United Kingdom's approach to European migration policy has been characteristic of its broader approach to the EU—it remains in principle suspicious of transfers of power, entirely mystified by appeals to harmonization's role in constructing Europe and willing to participate wholeheartedly when it is clear that British interests will be served.[28] Accordingly, the UK has resolutely refused to participate in border abolition but has been an enthusiastic participant in the harmonization of asylum policy. The United Kingdom signed and incorporated the Dublin Convention, and some of the post-1990s asylum legislation, particularly provisions on safe third countries, has been necessary to its implementation. It has also participated in the spate of intergovernmental measures adopted in the 1990s on the basis of the Maastricht Treaty's Third Pillar.[29]

---

[27] K. Hailbronner, 'The New Title on Free Movement of Persons, Asylum and Immigration in the TEC', in M. Boer (ed.), *Schengen, Judicial Cooperation and Policy Coordination* (Maastricht: European Institute of Public Administration, 1997).

[28] One striking (and faintly amusing) feature of the European dimension to migration policy is the extent to which migrant lobbies reproduce the infamous British suspicion of continental Europe. Justifying the Conservatives' 1995 rejection of harmonized anti-racist, anti-discrimination laws across Europe, the Eurosceptic Home Secretary, Michael Howard, said that 'The UK already has effective legislation. It would mean changing our laws in a very significant way for reasons that do not have much to do with the circumstances we encounter in Britain. We have a longer history of laws affecting race relations than almost any other country in the EU and better race relations than almost any other country.' A few years earlier, the Commission for Racial Equality, which shares little politically with the former Home Secretary, shares his views on the merits of splendid isolation: 'When you travel in Europe you are not protected by the Race Relations Act. Travel in Europe can often be a traumatic experience for Britain's ethnic minorities—even when they have British passports. You could be hassled by an immigration officer, the police or racists in the country you are visiting. Unfortunately, there's not a lot that can be done to help you from here . . .' Both quoted in A. Favell, 'Multicultural Race Relations in Britain: Problems of Interpretation and Explanation', in C. Joppke (ed.), *Challenge to the Nation-State: Immigration in Western Europe and the United States* (Oxford: Oxford University Press, 1998).

[29] Among them, the 1992 Council resolution on manifestly unfounded applications for asylum (London, 30 Nov.–1 Dec.); the 1995 Justice and Home Affairs Council Resolution on minimum guarantees for asylum seekers (*OJ C 274/25, 19 9 1996*); the 1996 Joint Position concerning harmonized application of the term 'refugee' in Article 1 of the 1951 Geneva Convention (*OJ L 63, 13 03 1996*); the 1998 Joint Action introducing a programme of training,

Although there are important exceptions, the broad thrust of these measures has been restrictionist.[30]

From the migrants' point of view, the most promising aspect of Europeanization concerns the European Court of Human Rights (ECHR). Although questions of migrants' rights have accounted for only 2.5 per cent of the Court's jurisprudence, a handful of important decisions has been decided in favour of third country nationals. Efforts by France and Belgium to expel foreigners raised in these countries were rejected on the basis of article 8 (right to lead a normal family life), and article 3 (protection against inhuman treatment) was successfully invoked in an asylum case, leading the Court to rule that protection of asylum-seekers cannot be ruled out by questions of public security alone.[31]

In the UK, the record of the appeals to ECHR has been mixed at best. The most infamous ECHR challenge to British migration law occurred in 1985. Under the 1980 non-statutory immigration rules, a foreign husband wishing to join his wife settled in the UK could not do so unless she was a British citizen born in the UK.[32] By contrast, Section 1 (5) of the Immigration Act, 1971 gave male spouses who had entered before 1973 the right to bring their wives to the UK. In two separate suits, three women argued that the rules amounted to discrimination by birth, race, and sex and that they constituted degrading treatment (Article 3). The European Court of Human Rights ruled, in *Abdulaziz, Cabales and Balkandali* v. *UK* (1985), that the rules did not discriminate on the basis of birth or race, or did so with legitimate aims, and that they did not constitute degrading treatment, but that they were sexually discriminatory.[33] The government, relieved that the legislation had not been deemed racially discriminatory, responded by making the entry rules as difficult for women as they are for men. All spouses must now apply for prior

exchange, and cooperation in the field of Justice and Home Affairs for the period from 1 Jan. 1998 to the day of entry into force of the Treaty of Amsterdam (*JO L 99/2, 31 3 1998)*; and the 1998 Joint Action concerning the financing of specific projects in favour of asylum seekers and refugees (*OJ L 138/8*, 9 5 1998).

[30] I discuss them in detail in R. Hansen, 'Dublin and Schengen: The Emergence of an EU Migration Policy?' Paper presented at the European Community Studies' Associations conference, Pittsburgh, 2–5 June 1999.

[31] V. Guiraudon, 'Third Country Nationals and European Law: Obstacles to Rights' Expansion', *Journal of Ethnic and Migration Studies*, 24, No. 4 (1998), 657–74, 664. As Guiraudon points out (p. 665), the most successful ECHR jurisprudence has concerned article 8, which mirrors similar constitutional protections and domestic judicial decisions in France, Germany, and the Netherlands.

[32] V. Berger, *Case Law of the European Court of Human Rights*, i: *1960–1987* (Dublin: The Round Hall Press, 1989), 293.

[33] Under article 14 (on enjoying rights and freedoms without discrimination on grounds of sex, among other things), taken together with article 8 (right to respect to private and family life). Article 8 alone was deemed insufficient.

entry clearance before leaving for the United Kingdom, and no spouse can claim an automatic right to join his or her partner in the United Kingdom. Christian Joppke commented that, vindictive though the decision perhaps was, 'one must admire the cleverness of turning a European court indictment into a means of even firmer immigration control.'[34] At the very least, it was further evidence, if more were needed, of the ability of a state lacking sufficient domestic constraints to assert its interests in the face of weak international norms and actors.[35]

It is possible that the approach may in the future soften. One of the first promises of the 1997–present Labour government was the incorporation of the European Convention on Human Rights, to which Britain is a signatory, into domestic legislation. The measure was viewed with suspicion by Jack Straw, the Home Secretary, but he was talked into by activists and sympathetic members of the Cabinet. From a rational point of view, incorporation allows the government to throw something to the left of the party, which doubts that there is much more than the name connecting the Labour Party to its social democratic past.[36] It also, the government hopes, will depoliticize convention-based decisions, providing them with legitimacy when delivered by domestic judges. As it stands, any ECHR ruling against the British government, and there have been many, has been followed by a tedious and predictable tabloid rant against unelected and (worse still) foreign judges. From a rights point of view, incorporation will provide the UK with a regional bill of rights, and the result may be greater judicial activism on the part of British courts. The government, not unaware of the Convention's implications for migration, did not incorporate several of its provisions.[37] Noteworthy among these are protocol 4, including article 3 (right not to be deprived of the right to enter the country of which one is a national) and article 5 (equality of the spouses in marriage).

Scholars, advocates, and migrants themselves will probably have to wait for the next government to know if incorporation proves the foundation for a robust pro-migrant jurisprudence. For the moment, appeals to Europe, whether to the European Court of Human Rights or the European Court of Justice, have led either to a reduction in citizens' rights (*Abdulaziz, Cabales and Balkandali* v. *UK*, 1985) or to bizarre anomalies. In 1992, the European Court of Justice ruled that British citizens who had travelled and worked

---

[34] C. Joppke, 'Why States Accept Unwanted Immigration', *World Politics*, 50 (Jan. 1998), 266–93, 291.

[35] R. Hansen, 'Migration, Citizenship and Race in Europe: Between Incorporation and Exclusion', *European Journal of Political Research*, 35 (1999), 415–444.

[36] And to, in the form of Roy Jenkins, its classical liberal past.

[37] Articles 13–18, protocol 1, articles 4–6, protocols 2–5, protocol 6, articles 3–5, protocols 7–11. See website: http://www.hmso.gov.uk/acts/acts1998/80042—a.htm.

elsewhere in the EU are governed by Community law (*R* v. *IAT and Surinder Singh, ex p Secretary of State for the Home Department,* 1992). The result is that British citizens who have so travelled and worked have a right to bring their spouses to the UK (as well as to elsewhere in the EU if they are employed), whereas British citizens who have not lack, under British law, such a right.[38] This decision came on top of another perverse outcome: under EU law concerning intra-Union mobility, member state nationals working in Britain have the right to bring their spouses to the UK, whereas Britons (who have not worked elsewhere in the EU) are denied this right. Such an outcome should raise a few eyebrows among even those with a highly developed English scepticism of Cartesian logic.

THE POVERTY OF GLOBALIZATION AND POST-NATIONALISM

The British case serves as a particularly powerful test case of claims that globalization and the internationalization of human rights discourse have undermined the power of the nation-state over immigration and third country nationals, or set it irrevocably on a path towards decline. Such arguments, particularly under the guise of post-nationalism, hold that the limits faced by the state in the treatment of migrants and resident third country nationals derive in large, if not complete, measure from international norms ('universal personhood') and institutions (human rights conventions and courts). As Yasemin Soysal argued, post-national citizenship 'reflects a different logic and praxis: what were previously defined as national rights become entitlements legitimized on the basis of personhood. The normative framework for, and legitimacy of, this model derive from transnational discourse and structures celebrating human rights as a world-level organising principle.'[39] David Jacobson, in a work published two years later, makes a similar point: '[t]ransnational migration is steadily eroding the traditional basis of nation-state membership, namely citizenship. As rights have come to be predicated on residency, not citizen status, the distinction between "citizen" and "alien" has eroded. The devaluation of citizenship has contributed to the increasing importance of international human rights codes, with its premise of "universal personhood." '[40] Such theses are part of a broader 1990s intellectual

---

[38] Macdonald and Blake, *Immigration Law and Practice in the United Kingdom,* 316.

[39] Y. Soysal, *The Limits of Citizenship: Migrants and Postnational Membership in Europe* (Chicago: University of Chicago Press, 1994), 3.

[40] D. Jacobson, *Rights across Borders: Immigration and the Decline of Citizenship* (Baltimore: Johns Hopkins University Press, 1997), 9 (2nd edn.).

movement, which sees in globalization the beginning of the end of nation-states as the dominant actors in society and the economy.

As noted in the introduction, the globalization and post-nationalist theses have generated, respectively, two related claims: globalization has robbed the state of sovereignty over immigration and (permanently resident) third country nationals (and even illegal immigrants) enjoy extensive socio-economic rights against the state because they are legitimized at the international level. Both theses, coming out of the international relations and sociology literature, have been challenged by North American and European comparativists who have marshalled detailed evidence in favour of two opposing claims. First, the nation-state retains considerable control over entry to its borders and its welfare state; and second, such limitations as there are have been self-imposed by domestic institutions and/or the domestic political process.[41]

The British case is a confirmation of these counter-arguments. For the globalization/post-nationalist claims about 'lost control' and the constraining effects of universal personhood to stand, they must apply, at the very least, across Europe and North America. The UK, of course, is subject to all the 'globalizing' pressures associated with the European Union, GATT-led tariff reduction, increasing international capital movements (much of which flows through London) and so on, and it takes pride in one of the oldest traditions of individual liberty in the world. None of this stood in the way of firm immigration control. When it belatedly asserted control of its borders, it did with success and with little successful opposition from international norms or institutions. The UK has either pursued restrictive policies consistent with the latter (thus suggesting that they are at best a weak control on domestic immigration policy) or brushed these aside when they conflicted with domestic objectives. The government's reaction to both the 1985 *Abdulaziz* ruling (harmonization downwards) and the 1972 *East African Asians* v. *United Kingdom* decision (effectively ignored) are evidence of that. As a reflection of the propensity to imprecision and error inherent in levels of analysis that ignore domestic politics, Jacobson and Soysal incorrectly cite both as

---

[41] G. P. Freeman, 'Modes of Immigration Politics in Liberal Democratic States', *International Migration Review*, 29, No. 4 (1995), 881–902; G. P. Freeman, 'The Decline of Sovereignty? Politics and Immigration Restriction in Liberal States', in C. Joppke (ed.) *Challenge to the Nation-State: Immigration in Western Europe and the United States* (Oxford: Oxford University Press, 1998); C. Joppke, *Immigration and the Nation-State: The United States, Germany and Great Britain* (Oxford: Oxford University Press, 1999), C. Joppke, 'Immigration Challenges the Nation-State', in Joppke (ed.), *Challenge to the Nation-State: Immigration in Western Europe and the United States* (Oxford: Oxford University Press, 1998); Joppke, 'Why Liberal States Accept Unwanted Immigration', 266–93.

evidence of their post-nationalist theses.[42] That nation-states should be the source of expansive or restrictive migration policies is unremarkable. International institutions and human rights norms are laudable and expressive of normative intent, but they are ultimately froth on the ocean of nations. Even the strongest international regime governing migration—the refugee system—was created and persists in order to protect the state system, not to challenge or undermine it.[43] International norms institutions are in the end only efforts, and not always successful ones, to institutionalize at the international level values best protected in liberal constitutions and national democratic politics.[44] They are expressive, not determinative, of (national) liberal democratic values. Migrants facing nation-states that wish to adopt, as the UK has done, a less than generous reading of them will find little support at the international level.

THE LEGAL PECULIARITES OF COMMONWEALTH MIGRATION

Drawing inspiration from path-dependence theory, the study offered an account of three legal oddities of the Commonwealth experience—reflected in the Commonwealth Immigrants Act 1962, 1968 legislation of the same name, and the Immigration Act, 1971—with reference to the tentacular effects of the British Nationality Act, 1948. A related feature, silent and unnoticed but no less powerful for it, was contingency. Proponents of 'garbage can models' of public policy have emphasized how policy problems, information, solutions, and so forth do not follow in the predictable sequence suggested by models of policy cycles, but rather arrive chaotically and independently of

---

[42] Jacobson, claiming that nation-states are 'accountable to international rules and institutions for the treatment of people in its jurisdiction', notes that the UK government 'subsequently amended the immigration law to take account of this ruling', but does not mention how (Jacobson, *Rights across Borders*, 89–90); Soysal cites 'some East African Asians, [who,] by appealing to the European Convention of Human Rights, were able to contest their exclusion from the United Kingdom under the 1968 Commonwealth Immigrants Act, which subjected populations from the New Commonwealth to immigration controls (Soysal, *Limits of Citizenship*, 150); they were not, or at least not much with success.

[43] C. Keely, 'How Nation-states Create and Respond to Refugee Flows', *International Migration Review*, 30, No. 4 (1996), 1046–66, 1057. Also see G. P. Freeman, 'Democratic Politics and Multi-lateral Immigration Policy', in L. F. Tomasi (ed.), *In Defence of the Alien*, Vol. 21 of the Proceedings of the Annual Legal Conference on Immigration and Refugee Policy (in press) and D. Papademetriou and K. Hamilton, *Managing Uncertainty: Regulating Immigration Flows in Advanced Industrial Countries* (Washington, DC: Carnegie Endowment for International Peace, 1995), 24.

[44] R. Hansen, 'Migration, Citizenship and Race in Europe'.

each other.[45] There is an important truth in this metaphor. The British Nationality Act, 1948, which institutionalized a free entry policy for 600,000,000 individuals across the globe, was enacted before—just, but before none the less—large-scale, non-white migration was (for reasons of economics and infrastructure) a possibility. The timing of the 1948 legislation was in turn determined by Canada's impatience for a new citizenship. Had the Canadian Citizenship Act, 1946 been adopted as little as five, and certainly ten, years later, it is nearly inconceivable that a resulting British Nationality Act would have left British subjects' right of entry unrestricted. In the absence of BNA 1948, there would have been no need for a migration control mechanism based on passports in 1962; no automatic entry for East African Asians in 1963; and no need for patriality in 1971. The entire history of Commonwealth immigration would have been radically different.

So perhaps would our perception of the relationship between citizenship, race, and racism. The UK's approach to migration policy in the 1960s appears, in large measure, so unproblematicly racist because it applied entry restrictions to its own citizens. What is often overlooked is that it did so because the country lacked what every other liberal democracy possessed: a definition of citizenship that distinguished those who belonged from those who did not. In the absence of what Rogers Brubaker has called citizenship as 'social closure', an 'internally inclusive, externally exclusive'[46] mechanism for assigning members of the national community the rights and duties associated with it, British governments had no choice but to adopt a policy that was not racist in design but was racist in effect. In restricting the entry of third world migrants, the UK did in 1962 what every other European nation did approximately a decade later. Gary Freeman has written that, in ending labour and colonial migration in the early 1970s, governments 'have done little more than end a set of policies that were of recent vintage, were uncharacteristic and devoid of public support, produced undesired outcomes, and by most indicators were no longer economically wise'.[47] The UK's policy towards the Commonwealth, unlike guestworker policies, was ancient, but the points about public support and undesired (though not undesirable) outcomes could not be truer.

[45] J. G. March and J. P. Olson, 'The New Institutionalism: Organisational Factors in Political Life', *American Political Science Review*, 78 (1989), 734–749; J. G. March and J. P. Olson, *Rediscovering Institutions* (New York: Free Press, 1993).

[46] R. Brubaker, *Citizenship and Nationhood in France and Germany* (Cambridge, Mass.: Harvard University Press, 1992), especially ch. 1.

[47] Freeman, 'The Decline of Sovereignty', 100.

THE IMPLICATIONS OF THE UK EXPERIENCE: BRITISH DEVIANCY REVISITED

In ending this study, it is worth considering the political and scholarly implications of Britain's post-war experience of migration. If the exceptional
degree of restrictiveness achieved by British governments from the 1960s to
the 1980s—reaching its culmination, perhaps, in the primary purpose rule—
had an institutional source, then British 'deviancy' loses its puzzling character. British policy was restrictive because elite preferences are channelled into
policy outcomes more directly in Britain than in any other liberal democracy.
Once the constraining influence of the Old Commonwealth and the Colonial
Office withered, governments were able to deliver the public what it wanted.
Perhaps paradoxically, this history provides solace for both immigration
alarmists and enthusiasts. For those who feel that global migration movements threaten economies and social solidarity in liberal democracies,[48] the
British case shows that a polity which gets its institutions right—namely, does
not place too many checks in front of the executive—can gain control of its
borders.[49] For those who feel that impediments on immigration control
violate our basic liberal democratic commitments, then the path to challen-
ging this lies in strengthening precisely these checks.

What is almost entirely unhelpful—for purposes both of explanation and
political change—is throwing accusations of racism at the government.[50] The
British government did what any rational government would have done—
attempted to be responsive to the demands of its electorate.[51] There were of
course individual politicians, even within the mainstream, who pushed policy
further than other politicians would have dared: Margaret Thatcher, whose

---

[48] P. Brimelow, *Alien Nation: Common Sense about America's Immigration Disaster* (New
York: Random House, 1995). The starkest version was presented in a 1973 novel, Jean Raspail,
Camp des saints; translated into English (*The Camp of Saints* (New York: Scribner, 1975)).
Cited in G. P. Freeman, 'The Politics of Race and Immigration in Britain (Faculty Seminar in
British Studies, University of Texas, Austin, 1994). Also see M. Wiener, *The Global Migration
Crisis: Challenge to States and to Human Rights* (New York: HarperCollins, 1995) and (though
it concerns multiculturalism and identity politics) A. M. Schlesinger Jr, *The Disuniting of
America* (New York: W. Norton & Company, 1992).

[49] I am referring here to legal immigration. There is no question that the UK's position as
an island makes the prevention of clandestine immigration easier.

[50] For the most egregious example of this, see Dummett and Dummett, 'The Role of
Government in Britain's Racial Crisis'.

[51] There were of course extra-institutional limits on this: coerced repatriation enjoyed
majority support [*Attitudes towards Coloured People in Britain* (London: Gallup, 1982), questions 74–6], but the government viewed it as unthinkable; the public wished to prevent family
reunification, but there was a Cabinet consensus against it; the Ugandan Asians were met with
intense public opposition, but their entry was guaranteed.

antipathy towards immigrants was well known, is an instance of this. Their presence, however, says nothing about the character of elite attitudes more broadly. All political systems will throw up restrictionist politicians like Thatcher, and provide opportunities for extremists such as Powell to carry thinly veiled racist campaigns against immigration. Only in some polities—those in which the executive is divided from the legislature, or in which there are other veto points, or in which there are entrenched constitutional limits on political action, or in which there is an activist bill of rights—will there be a guarantee that these individuals' plans will burn themselves out before being realized.

As in the case of the discussion of the UK's institutions, this is nothing new to modern political science. As long ago as the federalist papers, students of politics have argued that without institutions that divide power and lengthen the political process, popular passions will lead to illiberal/draconian political outcomes. In 1787, James Madison wrote that '[a]mong the numerous advantages promised by a well-constructed Union, none deserves to be more accurately developed than its tendency to break and control the violence of faction . . . [In the absence of a separation of official functions,] a common passion or interest will, in almost every case, be felt by a majority of the whole; a communication and concert results from the form of government itself; and there is nothing to check the inducements to sacrifice the weaker party or an obnoxious individual. Hence it is that such democracies have been spectacles of turbulence and contention; have ever been found incompatible with personal security or the rights of property; and have in general been as short in their lives as they have been violent in their deaths.'[52] In the light of the anti-immigrant hysteria that reigned in the 1960s, and the consistent opposition towards immigration that has prevailed throughout the post-war period, the only remarkable element of Britain's current migration policies is that they are not more restrictive.

---

[52] A. Hamilton, J. Madison, and J. Jay, *The Federalist Papers* (New York: Mentor Books, 1961), 77 and 81.

Appendix A

APPENDIX 1: Net Immigration from the New Commonwealth, 1953-1961[1]

	West Indies	India	Pakistan	Others	Total
1953	2,000	2,000			
1954	11,000	11,000			
1955	27,500	5,800	1,850	7,500	42,650
1956	29,800	5,600	2,050	9,350	46,800
1957	23,000	6,600	5,200	7,600	42,400
1958	15,000	6,200	4,700	3,950	29,850
1959	16,400	2,950	850	1,400	21,600
1960	49,650	5,900	2,500	−350	57,700
1961	66,300	23,750	25,100	21,250	136,400

APPENDIX 1a: Labour Vouchers Issued, 1962–1965[2]

	Category A		Category B		Category C[3]		Depend-ants[4]
	Canada Australia New Zealand	New Common-wealth	Canada Australia New Zealand	New Common-wealth	Canada Australia New Zealand	New Common-wealth	
1962[5]	307	3,063	1,163	3,363	667	16,827	8,832
1963	460	7,002	1,369	9,618	470	22,182	26,234
1964	383	10,219	814	7,187	72	2,149	37,460
1965	283	8,361	842	6,560	6,427[6]	41,214	

[1] Source: Z. Layton-Henry, *The Politics of Immigration: Immigration, 'Race' and 'Race' Relations in Post-war Britain* (Oxford: Blackwell, 1992), 13.

[2] Sources for Appendices 5b and 5c: *Commonwealth Immigrants Act 1962: Statistics* (London: HMSO, 1962–7) and *Commonwealth Immigrants Acts 1962 and 1968: Statistics* (London: HMSO, 1968–71).

[3] Category C vouchers were discontinued 2 Aug. 1965.

[4] Recorded as dependants entering the UK for settlement.

[5] From 1 July until 28 Dec. 1963, during the first six months of control.

[6] 1965 statistics provide only total applications received and total numbers refused for Category C. No precise national breakdown is possible.

APPENDIX 1*b*: Labour Vouchers Issued, 1966–1971

	Category A		Category B		Dependants
1966	23	2,852	461	4,694	42,026
1967	26	3013	384	4,986	52,813
1968	24	2,865	429	4,802	48,650
1969	89	2,731	905	3,044	33,820
1970	130	2,736	1,295	2,654	27,407
1971	169	1,788	728	1,077	28,014

Appendix B

APPENDIX 2: Settlement by Origin,[1] Commonwealth Citizens & Foreign Nationals, 1972–1994[2]

	New Commonwealth[3]	Old Commonwealth	Foreign Nationals	Total
1972	68,500	4,100	19,700	92,300
1973	32,200	3,100	19,900	55,200
1974	42,500	3,900	22,500	68,900
1975	53,300	5,400	23,700	82,400
1976	55,000	6,000	19,700	80,700
1977	44,200	6,600	18,500	69,300
1978	42,900	7,400	22,000	72,300
1979	37,000	6,900	25,800	69,700
1980	33,620	6,880	29,250	69,750
1981	31,370	5,380	22,310	59,060
1982	30,390	5,160	18,330	53,880
1983	27,550	5,800	20,120	53,470
1984	24,800	7,440	18,720	50,960
1985	27,050	8,160	10,120	45,330
1986	22,670	6,600	18,520	47,790
1987	20,850	6,900	18,220	45,970
1988	22,800	7,380	19,100	49,280
1989	23,170	7,890	18,600	49,660
1990	25,670	6,030	20,700	52,400
1991	27,930	3,120	22,850	53,900
1992	27,710	3,120	21,760	52,590

[1] Settlement statistics are a poor indicator of population movement, as they include individuals who have been in the UK for several years in some other capacity, and do not include asylum seekers, temporary workers, students, working holiday-makers, and so forth. They are, however, a reasonably good indicator of permanent immigration as they measure, over several years, the number of people staying permanently.

[2] Sources: *Commonwealth Immigrants Act 1962: Statistics* (London: HMSO, 1962–7), *Commonwealth Immigrants Acts 1962 and 1968: Statistics* (London: HMSO, 1968–72), *Control of Immigration: Statistics* (London: HMSO, 1973–97). These figures include those accepted on arrival, and those whose time limits were removed. All figures are rounded to the nearest '100'.

[3] Including Pakistan, which left the Commonwealth on 31 Aug. 1973 and rejoined it on 1 Oct. 1989.

Appendix 2 (*Continued*):

	Europe	Americas	Africa	Asia	Oceania	Other	Total
	Acceptances for Settlement by Nationality and Region, 1993–1997						
1993	5,010	7,660	10,790	25,360	2,650	4,170	55,640
1994	4,650	7,890	11,920	25,900	2,850	1,890	55,010
1995	4,250	8,810	12,000	26,120	3,450	1,470	55,480
1996	7,500	8,470	12,790	27,880	3,520	1,400	61,730
1997	7,740	7,790	13,200	25,610	3,100	1,280	58,720

Select Bibliography

A. Manuscript Collection

1. Public Records

Cabinet: *CAB* 128–34.
Colonial Office: *CO* 1028–32.
Dominion Office: *DO* 35.
General: *GEN* 325.
Home Office: *HO* 213, 344, 276.
Ministry of Labour: *LAB* 8.
Prime Minster's Office: *PREM* 8, 11, 13.

2. Private Papers

Lord Attlee, Bodleian Library, Oxford.
Ernest Bevin, Churchill College, Cambridge.
Lord George-Brown, Bodleian Library, Oxford.
Lord R. A. Butler, Trinity College, Cambridge.
Lord Edward Boyle, Brotherton Library, University of Leeds.
James Chuter Ede, Surrey Record Office.
Arthur Creech Jones, Rhodes House Library, Oxford.
Sir Dingle Foot, Churchill College, Cambridge.
Lord George Brown, Bodleian Library, Oxford.
Patrick Gordon Walker, Churchill College, Cambridge.
Lord Noel-Baker, Churchill College, Cambridge.
Viscount Simon, Bodleian Library, Oxford.

3. Autobiography, Biography, Diaries, Memoirs

ADDISON, P., *Churchill on the Home Front, 1900–1955* (London: Jonathan Cape, 1992).
BENN, T., *Out of the Wilderness: Diaries 1963–1967* (London, Hutchinson, 1987).
BROOKE, J, and SORENSEN, M. (eds.), *The Prime Minister's Papers: W. E. Gladstone*, i: *Autobiographica* (London: HMSO, 1971).
BUTLER, R. A., *The Art of the Possible: The Memoirs of Lord Butler* (London: Hamish Hamilton, 1971).
CALLAGHAN, J., *Time and Chance* (London: Collins, 1987).
CAMPBELL, J., *Roy Jenkins: A Biography* (London: Weidenfeld & Nicolson, 1983).
—— *Edward Heath: A Biography* (London: Jonathan Cape, 1993).
CASTLE, B., *The Castle Diaries, 1964–1970* (London: Weidenfeld & Nicolson, 1984).
COSGRAVE, P., *The Lives of Enoch Powell* (London: The Bodley Head, 1989).

CROSSMAN, P., *The Diaries of a Cabinet Minister,* (London: Hamish Hamilton and Jonathan Cape, 1976).

EYCK, E., *Gladstone,* (London: George Allen & Unwin, 1938).

FISHER, N., *Harold Macmillan* (London: Weidenfeld & Nicolson, 1982).

HAILSHAM of St Marylebone, Lord (Quintin Hogg), *A Sparrow's Flight* (London: Collins, 1990), 369.

HEALEY, D., *The Time of My Life* (London: Penguin Books, 1989).

HEATH, E., *The Course of My Life: My Autobiography* (London: Hodder & Stoughton, 1998).

HEFFER, S., *Like the Roman: The Life of Enoch Powell* (London: Weidenfeld & Nicolson, 1998).

HOME, Lord, *The Way the Wind Blows* (London: Collins, 1976).

HORNE, A., *Macmillan* (London: Macmillan, 1989).

INGHAM, K., *Obote: A Political Biography* (London: Routledge, 1994).

JENKINS, R., *Nine Men of Power* (London: Hamish Hamilton, 1974).

—— *A Life at the Centre* (London: Macmillan, 1991).

—— *Portraits and Miniatures* (London: Macmillan, 1993).

—— *Gladstone* (London: Macmillan, 1995).

LEWIS, R., *Enoch Powell: Principle in Politics* (London: Cassell, 1979).

MACMILLAN, H., *At the End of the Day, 1961–1963* (London: Macmillan, 1973).

MAUDLING, R., *Memoirs* (London: Sidgwick & Jackson, 1978).

MURRAY-BROWN, J., *Kenyatta* (London: George Allen & Unwin, 1972).

PAUL, H. W., *The Life of William Ewart Gladstone* (London: Thomas Nelson & Sons, 1901),

PEARCE, R. (ed.), *Patrick Gordon Walker: Political Diaries, 1932–1971* (London: The Historians' Press, 1991).

PEARSON, L. B., *Memoirs, 1948–1957: The International Years* (London: Victor Gollancz, 1974).

PIMLOTT, B., *Harold Wilson* (London: HarperCollins, 1993).

POWELL, J. ENOCH, *Still to Decide* (London: B. T. Batsford, 1972).

—— *A Nation or No Nation? Six Years in British Politics* (London: B. T. Batsford, 1978).

—— *Reflections of a Statesman: The Writings and Speeches of Enoch Powell* (London: Bellew, 1991).

ROBERTS, A., *Eminent Churchillians* (London: Weidenfeld & Nicolson, 1994).

ROTHWELL, V., *Anthony Eden: A Political Biography, 1931–57* (Manchester: Manchester University Press, 1992).

SHANNON, R., *Gladstone,* vol. i (London: Hamish Hamilton, 1982),

SHEPHERD, R., *Iain Macleod: A Biography* (London: Pimlico, 1995).

SMITH, G. B., *The Life of the Right Honourable William Ewart Gladstone* (London: Cassell, Petter, Galpin & Company, 1880).

THATCHEr, M., *The Path to Power* (London: HarperCollins, 1995).

WHITELAW, W., *The Whitelaw Memoirs* (London: Aurum, 1989).

WILLIAMS, P. M., *Hugh Gaitskell: A Political Biography* (London: Jonathan Cape, 1979).

4. Government Publications, White Papers, Legislation

Aliens and British Protected Persons (Naturalization) (London: HMSO, 1952–1961).
British Nationality Act, 1948.
British Nationality Act, 1958.
British Nationality Act, 1964.
British Nationality Act, 1965.
British Nationality Act, 1981.
British Nationality Law: Discussion of Possible Changes (London: HMSO, 1977), Cmnd. 6795 (Green Paper).
British Nationality Law: Outline of Proposed Legislation (London: HMSO, 1980), Cmnd. 7987 (White Paper).
Citizenship Statistics: United Kingdom (London: Government Statistical Service, 1990).
Commonwealth Immigrants Act, 1962.
Commonwealth Immigrants Act, 1968.
Constitution of Kenya.
Constitution of the Republic of Uganda.
Commonwealth Immigrants Act 1962: Statistics (London: HMSO, 1962–7).
Commonwealth Immigrants Acts 1962 and 1968: Statistics (London: HMSO, 1968–71).
Control of Immigration Statistics (London: HMSO, 1973–1982).
Home Office Statistical Bulletin: Citizenship Statistics (London: Government Statistical Service, 1984–94).
Immigration Act, 1971.
Immigration from the Commonwealth, 1965 (White Paper, Cmnd. 2739).
Kenyan Independence Act, 1963.
Persons Acquiring British Citizenship: United Kingdom (London: Government Statistical Service, 1992, 1994).
Race Relations Act, 1965.
Race Relations Act, 1968.
Race Relations Act, 1976.
Racial Discrimination (Cmnd. 6234).
Report of the Race Relations Board for 1974 (London: Sessional Papers, 1974–75 [XXXIII]).
Select Committee on Race Relations and Immigration: Organisation of the Race Relations Administration, vol. i: *Report* (London: HMSO, 1974–5).
Statement of Changes in Immigration Rules (London: HMSO, 1994).
Statistics of Persons Acquiring Citizenship of the United Kingdom and Colonies (London: HMSO, 1962–81).
Tables of Persons Acquiring Citizenship of the United Kingdom and Colonies (London: HMSO, 1978–83).

5. Parliamentary Debates

House of Commons

Volume 214, June 1850
Volume 451, June 1948

Volume 453, July 1948
Volume 525, Mar. 1954
Volume 532, Nov. 1954
Volume 563, Jan. 1957
Volume 606, June 1959
Volume 634, Feb. 1961
Volume 649, Nov. 1961
Volume 654, Feb. 1962
Volume 684, Nov. 1963
Volume 701, Nov. 1964
Volume 702, Nov. 1964
Volume 705, 4 Feb. 1965
Volume 708, Mar. 1965
Volume 709, Mar. 1965
Volume 711, May 1965
Volume 717, Aug. 1965
Volume 759, Feb. 1968
Volume 791, Nov. 1969
Volume 813, Mar. 1971
Volume 846, Nov. 1972

House of Lords

Volume 155, May 1948
Volume 156, June 1948

6. Papers of Other Organizations

Conservative Party Archives, Bodleian Library, Oxford.
Home Office Library, Queen Anne's Gate, London, Commonwealth Immigrants Act—NCCI Statements.
Labour Party Archives, National Museum of Labour History, Manchester.
Trades Union Congress Papers, Modern Records Centre, University of Warwick.

8. Other Primary Sources

Eurobarometer: Public Opinion in the European Union (Brussels: European Commission, DG X), vol. 48: Autumn 1997), released Mar. 1998.
Coloured People in Britain (London: Gallup, 1982).
NOP (quoted in *LPA, Study Group on Immigration,* 'Public opinion and immigration, by Dr. Mark Adams', Jan. 1969).
Immigration and Race Relations (London: NOP, 1968).

B. Interviews

William Joseph Bohan (Home Office)
Anthony Butler (Home Office)

Sir Brian Cubbon (Home Office, by correspondence)
Richard Fries (Home Office)
M. E. Head (Home Office)
Sir Edward Heath
Wilfred Hyde (Home Office)
Lord Jenkins of Hillhead
Chris Kelly (Home Office)
Lord Lester of Herne Hill, QC (by correspondence)
Sir Geoffrey Otton (Home Office)
Anthony Pilgrim (Home Office)
J. Enoch Powell
Timothy Raison (Home Office)
Lord Merlyn Rees of Morley and South Leeds
Anthony Rawsthorne (Home Office)
The Right Honourable Peter Shore
Ralph Shuffrey (Home Office)
A. Sivanandan (Director, Institute of Race Relations)
Viscount Whitelaw of Penrith

C. Secondary Sources

ABRAHAM, H. J., *The Judicial Process* (New York: Oxford University Press, 1993).

ADELMAN, H. et al. (eds.), *Immigration and Refugee Policy: Australia and Canada Compared* (Toronto: University of Toronto Press, 1994).

ALIBHAI-BROWN, Y., *True Colours: Attitudes to Multiculturalism and the Role of the Government* (London: Institute for Public Policy Research, 1999).

ARTHUR, B., 'Competing Technologies, Increasing Returns, and Lock-in by Historical Events', *Economic Journal*, 99 (Mar. 1989), 116–31.

ARTHUr, W. B., 'Self-Reinforcing Mechanisms in Economics', P. W. Anderson et al., (eds.), *The Economy as an Evolving Complex System* (Reading, Mass.: Addison-Wesley, 1988).

BANNOCK, G. et al., *Dictionary of Economics* (London: Penguin, 1992).

BARNES, J., 'From Eden to Macmillan, 1955–1959', in P. Hennessy and A. Seldon (eds.), *Ruling Performance: British Governments from Attlee to Thatcher* (Oxford: Basil Blackwell, 1987).

BAUBÖCK, R. and ÇINAR, D., 'Nationality Law and Naturalisation in Austria', in R. Hansen and P Weil (eds.), *Towards a European Nationality: Citizenship, Immigration and Nationality Law in the EU* (Houndmills: Macmillan, 2000).

BERGER, S., (ed.), *Organizing Interests in Western Europe* (Cambridge: Cambridge University Press, 1981).

BERGER, V., *Case Law of the European Court of Human Rights*, i: *1960–1987* (Dublin: The Round Hall Press, 1989).

BETTS, K., 'Immigration and Public Opinion in Australia', *People and Place*, 4, No. 3 (1996), 9–20.

BETTS, K., *The Great Divide: Immigration Politics in Australia* (Sydney: Duffy & Snellgrove, 1999).

BETZ, H. G., *Radical Right-Wing Populism in Western Europe* (Houndmills: Macmillan, 1994).

BEVAN, V., *The Development of British Nationality Law* (London: Croom Helm, 1986).

BLAKE, Lord, and NICHOLLS, C. S., *Dictionary of National Biography, 1981–85* (Oxford: Oxford University Press, 1990).

BLEICH, E., 'Races or Racists: Ideas and Race Policies in Britain and France', Paper presented to the twenty-second meeting of the Social Science History Association (18 Oct. 1997).

—— Problem-Solving Politics: Ideas and Race Policies in Britain and France, 1945–1988', Paper delivered at the 1998 Annual Meeting of the American Political Science Association, 3–6 Sept. 1998.

—— 'Problem Solving Politics, Ideas and Race Policies in Britain and France' (Ph.D. dissertation, Harvard University, Apr. 1999).

BOGDANOR, V., and BUTLER, D., *Democracy and Elections: Electoral Systems and their Political Consequences* (Cambridge: Cambridge University Press, 1983).

—— and SKIDELSKY, R. (eds.), *The Age of Affluence: 1951–1964* (London: Macmillan, 1970).

BOOTH, H., 'Immigration in Perspective: Population Development in the United Kingdom', in A. Dummett (ed.), *Towards a Just Immigration Policy* (London: Cobden Trust, 1986).

BOSANQUET, N., and DOERINGER, P. B., 'Is There a Dual Labour Market in Great Britain?' *Economic Journal*, 330 (1973), 421–35.

BRAZIER, R., *Constitutional Reform* (London: Clarendon, 1991).

BRIMELOW, P. *Alien Nation: Common Sense about America's Immigration Disaster* (New York: Random House, 1995).

BROCHMANN, G., *European Integration and Immigration from Third Countries* (Oslo: Scandinavian University Press, 1996).

BROOK, L., and CAPE, E., 'Libertarianism in retreat?', in R. Jowell et al. (eds.), *British Social Attitudes: the 12 report* (Aldershot: Dartmouth Publishing Co., 1995).

BROOKE, S., 'The Conservative Party, Immigration, and National Identity, 1948–1968', in M. Francis and I. Zweiniger-Bargielowska (eds.), *The Conservatives and British Society, 1880–1900* (Cardiff: University of Wales Press, 1996).

BRUBAKER, R., *Citizenship and Nationhood in France and Germany* (Cambridge, Mass.: Harvard University Press, 1992).

BRUYCKER, P. De 'D'un système européen d'asile vers un droit européen des réfugiés', in *Europe and Refugees: A Challenge? / L'Europe et les réfugiés: un defi?* (The Hague: Kluwer Law International, 1997).

BUTLER, D., and KAVANAGH, D., *The British General Election of 1983* (London: Macmillan, 1983).

—— —— *The British General Election of 1964* (London: Macmillan, 1965).

—— —— *The British General Election of 1966* (London: Macmillan, 1966).

—— —— *The British General Election of 1987* (London: Macmillan, 1987)

―― ―― *The British General Election of 1992* (London: Macmillan, 1992).

―― ―― The British General Election of 1997 (Houndmills: Macmillan, 1997).

―― and PINTO-DUSCHINSKY, M., *The British General Election of 1970* (London: Macmillan, 1971).

―― and ROSE, R., *The British General Election of 1959* (London: Cass, 1960).

―― and STOKES, D., *Political Change in Britain: Forces Shaping Electoral Choice* (London: Macmillan,1969).

CARENS, J., 'Alternative Bases for Citizenship', Paper presented at the German Marshall Fund conference on Nationality Law, Immigration and Integration in Europe and the US, Paris, 25–7 June 1998.

―― Citizenship and Civil Society: What Rights for Residents?', in R. Hansen and P. Weil (eds.), *Dual Citizenship, Social Rights and Federal Citizenship in the US and Europe* (Oxford: Berghahn, forthcoming).

CARTER, B., HARRIS, C., and JOSHI, S.,' The1951–1955 Conservative Government and the Racialization of Black Immigration', *Immigrants and Minorities*, 6, No. 3 (1987), 335–47.

―― et al.,"The 1951–55 Conservative Government and the Racialization of Black Immigration', in W. James and C. Harris (eds.), *Inside Babylon: The Carribean Diaspora in Britain* (London: Verso, 1993).

―― et al., 'Immigration Policy and the Racialization of Migrant Labour: The Construction of National Identities in the USA and Britain', *Ethnic and Racial Studies*, 19, No. 1 (1996), 135–57.

CASTLES, S., and KOSACK, G., *Immigrant Workers and Class Structure in Western Europe* (London: Oxford University Press, 1973).

CHATWIN, M., *Immigration, Nationality & Refugee Law Handbook* (London: JCWI, 1999).

CHOLEWINSKI, R., 'Enforced Destitution of Asylum Seekers in the United Kingdom: The Denial of Fundamental Human Rights', *International Journal of Refugee Law*, 10 (1998), 462–98.

CLARKE, W. S., 'Hong Kong Immigration Control: The Law and the Bureaucratic Maze', *Hong Kong Law Journal*, 16, No. 3 (Sept. 1986), 341–68.

COLLIER, D., and COLLIER, R., *Shaping the Political Arena* (Princeton: Princeton University Press, 1991).

CRAIG, F. W. S. (ed.), *British General Election Manifestos 1959–1987* (Aldershot: Dartmouth, 1990).

CREWE, I., 'How Labour was trounced all around', *Guardian*, 14 June 1983.

DARWIN, J., *Britain and Decolonisation: The Retreat from Empire in the Post-War World* (London: Macmillan, 1988).

―― *End of the British Empire: The Historical Debate* (Oxford: Blackwell, 1991).

DAVID, P., 'Clio and the Economics of QWERTY', *American Economic Review*, 75, No. 2 (May 1985), 332–7.

de SMITH, S. A., STREET, H., and BRAZIER, R. (eds.), *Constitutional and Administrative Law* (London: Penguin Books, 1985).

DEAKIN, N., 'The Politics of the Commonwealth Immigrants Bill', *Political Quarterly*, 39 (1968), 25–45.

DEAKIN, N., The British Nationality Act of 1948: A Brief Study in the Political Mythology of Race Relations', *Race*, 11, No. 1 (1969), 77–83.

—— 'The Immigration Issue in British Politics' (unpublished D.Phil. dissertation, University of Sussex, 1972).

—— 'The Conservative Government and the 1961 Commonwealth Immigration Act: The Inside Story', *Race and Class*, 35, No. 2 (1993), 57–74.

DEAN, D. W., 'Conservative Governments and the Restriction of Commonwealth Immigration in the 1950s: The Problems of Constraint,' *Historical Journal*, 35, No. 1 (1993), 171–94.

DEEG. R., 'Institutional Transfer, Social Learning and Economic Policy in Eastern Europe', *Western European Politics*, 18, No. 4 (Oct. 1995), 38–63.

DILKE, C. W., *Greater Britain* (London: Macmillan, 1869).

DINES, M., 'British Asylum Law: Restricting Refugees', *Oxford International Review*, 7, No. 3 (1996).

DOWDING, K. and KING, D., 'Introduction', *Preferences, Institutions & Rational Choice* (Oxford: Clarendon Press, 1995).

DOWNING, B., *The Military Revolution and Political Change: Origins of Democracy and Autrocacy in Early Modern Europe* (Princeton: Princeton University Press, 1992).

DUMMETT, A., 'Immigration and Nationality', in C. McCrudden and G. Chambers (eds.), *Individual Rights and the Law in Britain* (Oxford: Clarendon, 1994).

—— and NICOL, A., *Subjects, Citizens, Aliens and Others: Nationality and Immigration Law* (London: Weidenfeld and Nicolson, 1990).

DUMMETT, M. and DUMMETT, A., 'The Role of Government in Britain's Racial Crisis', in C. Husband (ed.), *'Race' in Britain: Continuity and Change* (London: Hutchinson, 1982).

DURAND, G., *Enquête au cœur du Front National* (Paris: Jacques Grancher, 1996).

EATWELL, R., 'Britain: The BNP and the Problem of Legitimacy', H.-G. Betz and S. Immerfall, *The New Politics of the Right: Neo-Populist Parties and Movements in Established Democracies* (London: Macmillan, 1998).

ECKSTEIN, H. and APTER, D., *Comparative Politics* (New York: The Free Press, 1963).

ESPENSHADE, T., and HEMPSTEAD, K., 'Contemporary American Attitudes toward U.S. immigration', *International Migration Review*, 30, No. 2 (1996), 535–57.

FARRAN, S., *The UK before the European Court of Human Rights: Case Law and Commentary* (London: Blackstone Press, 1996).

FAVELL, A., *Philosophies of Integration: Immigration and the Idea of Citizenship in France and Britain*, (Houndmills: Macmillan, 1998).

—— Multicultural Race Relations in Britain: Problems of Interpretation and Explanation', in C. Joppke (ed.), *Challenge to the Nation-State: Immigration in Western Europe and the United States* (Oxford: Oxford University Press, 1998).

FEKETE, L., 'The Surrogate University', in C. Prescod and H. Waters (eds.), *A World to Win: Essays in Honour of A. Sivanandan*, special issue of *Race and Class*, 41, Nos. 1–2 (1999), 123–30.

FELDBLUM, M., 'Reconfiguring Citizenship in Western Europe', C. Joppke (ed.), *Challenge to the Nation-State: Immigration in Western Europe and the United States* (Oxford: Oxford University Press, 1998).

FOOT, P., *Immigration and Race in British Politics* (Harmondsworth: Penguin, 1965).

—— *The Rise of Enoch Powell: An Examination of Enoch Powell's Attitude to Immigration and Race* (Harmondsworth: Penguin, 1969).

FRANSMAN, L., *Fransman's British Nationality Law* (London: Fourmat, 1989).

—— *Fransman's British Nationality Law* (2 edn.) (London: Butterworths, 1998)

FREEMAN, G. P., *Immigrant Labor and Racial Conflict in Industrial Societies: The French and British Experience 1945–1975* (Princeton: Princeton University Press, 1979).

—— 'Britain, the Deviant Case', in W. A. Cornelius, P. L. Martin and J. F. Hollifield, (eds.), *Controlling Immigration: A Global Perspective* (Stanford, Calif.: Stanford University Press, 1994).

—— 'The Politics of Race and Immigration in Britain', Paper given to Faculty Seminar in British Studies, University of Texas, Austin, 1994.

—— 'Modes of Immigration Politics in Liberal Democracies', *International Migration Review*, 29 (1995), 881–902, 881–2.

—— 'Immigration as a Source of Political Discontent and Frustration in Western Democracies', *Studies in Comparative International Development*, 32, No. 3 (1997), 42–64.

—— 'Democratic Politics and Multi-lateral Immigration Policy', in L. F. Tomasi (ed.), *In Defence of the Alien*, vol. 21 of the Proceedings of the Annual Legal Conference on Immigration and Refugee Policy (in press).

FREEMAN, M. and SPENCER, S., 'Immigration Control, Black Workers and the Economy', *British Journal of Law and Society*, 6, No. 1 (1979), 53–81.

GARCÍA Y GRIEGO, M., 'Canada: Flexibility and Control in Immigration and Refugee Policy', in W. A. Cornelius *et. al.* (eds.), *Controlling Immigration: A Global Perspective* (Stanford, Calif.: Stanford University Press, 1994).

GEDDES, A., *The Politics of Immmigration and Race* (London: Baseline Books, 1996),

GERTH, H. H. and WRIGHT MILLS, C., *From Max Weber: Essays in Sociology* (New York: Oxford University Press, 1958).

GOLDBERG, E., 'Thinking about how Democracy Works', *Politics and Society*, 24, No. 1 (Mar. 1996), 7–18.

GOLDSTEIN, J., 'Ideas, Institutions, and American Trade Policy', *International Organization*, 42, No. 1 (1988).

—— and KEOHANE, R., *Ideas and Foreign Policy: Beliefs, Institutions and Political Change* (Ithaca, NY: Cornell University Press, 1993).

GOLDSWORTHY, D., *Colonial Issues in British Politics* (Oxford: Clarendon, 1971). Sir William Goodhart et al., *Countdown to 1997: Report of a Mission to Hong Kong by an International Committee of Jurists* (Cambridge: E & E Plumridge, 1992).

GOODHART, Sir William et al., *Countdown to 1997: Report of a Mission to Hong Kong by an International Committee of Jurists* (Cambridge: E & E Plumridge, 1992).

GOODWIN-GILL, G., *International Law and the Movement of Persons between States* (Oxford: Clarendon Press, 1978).

—— *The Refugee in International Law* (Oxford: Clarendon, 1996).

GRANTHAM, G., 'Path-Dependency and Historical Explanation: The Case of the Sickle and the Scythe', Paper presented to the twenty-second meeting of the Social Science History Association (17 Oct. 1997).

Green, S., 'Citizenship Policy in Germany: The Case of Ethnicity over Residence?', in R. Hansen and P. Weil (eds.), *Towards a European Nationality: Citizenship, Immigration and Nationality Law in the EU* (London: Macmillan, forthcoming).

GREGORY, J., *Sex, Race and the Law: Legislating for Equality* (London: SAGE, 1987).

GREGORY, R. G., *Quest for Equality: Asian Politics in East Africa, 1900–1967* (Hyderabad: Orient Longman, 1993).

GUPTA, A., 'India and the Asians in East Africa', in M. Twaddle (ed.), *Expulsion of a Minority: Essays on Ugandan Asians* (London: Athlone, 1975).

HALL, P. A., *Governing the Economy: The Politics of State Intervention in Britain and France* (New York: Oxford University Press, 1986).

—— *The Political Power of Economic Ideas* (Princeton: Princeton University Press, 1989).

—— 'The Movement from Keynesianism to Monetarism: Institutional Analysis and British Economic Policy in the 1970s', in S. Steinmo et al. (eds.), *Structuring Politics: Historical Institutionalism in Comparative Analysis* (New York: Cambridge University Press, 1992).

—— 'Policy Paradigms, Social Learning and the State: The Case of Economic Policymaking in Britain', *Comparative Politics*, 25, No. 3 (1993), 275–96.

—— and Taylor, R. C. R., 'Political Science and the Three New Institutionalisms', *Political Studies*, 44 (1996), 936–57.

HANSEN, R., 'The United Kingdom and Nationality Law in China's Hong Kong', *Oxford International Review*, 7, No. 3 (1996), 38–43.

——'The Politics of Citizenship in 1940s Britain: The British Nationality Act', *Twentieth Century British History*, 10, No. 1 (1999), 67–95.

—— The Kenyan Asians, British Politics, and the Commonwealth Immigrants Act, 1968', *Historical Journal*, 42, No. 3 (1999), 809–34.

—— Migration, Citizenship and Race in Europe: Between Incorporation and exclusion', *European Journal of Political Research* 35, No. 4 (1999), 415–44.

—— 'Dublin and Schengen: The Emergence of an EU Migration Policy?' Paper presented at the European Community Studies' Associations conference, Pittsburgh, 2–5 June 1999.

—— 'British Citizenship after Empire: A Defence', *Political Quarterly* (forthcoming).

—— and WEIL, P., *Towards a European Nationality: Citizenship, Immigration and Nationality Law in the EU* (Houndmills: Macmillan, 2000).

HANS-JOACHIM, V., et al., *The Republikaner Party in Germany: Right-Wing Menace or Protest Catchall?* (Westport, Conn.: Praeger, 1993).

HECLO, H., *Modern Social Politics in Britain and Sweden: From Relief to Income Maintenance* (New Haven: Yale University Press, 1974).

HENNESSY, P., *Never Again, Britain 1945–1951* (London: Vintage, 1992).

HIMBARA, D., *Kenyan Capitalists, the State, and Development* (Boulder, Colo.: Lynne Rienner, 1994).

HOBERG, G., 'Putting Ideas in Their Place: A Response to "'Learning and Change in the British Columbia Forestry Policy Sector" '. *Canadian Journal of Political Science*, 29, No. 1 (Mar. 1996), 135–44.

HOLLIFIELD, J. F., 'Immigration Policy in France and Germany: Outputs vs. Outcomes', *Annals*, 485 (May 1986), 113–28.

—— *Immigrants, Markets, and States: The Political Economy of Postwar Europe* (Cambridge, Mass.: Harvard University Press, 1992).

—— 'Migration, Trade, and the Nation-State: The Myth of Globalization', *UCLA Journal of International Law and Foreign Affairs*, 3, No. 2 (Fall/Winter 1998–9), 595–636.

—— 'Ideas, Institutions, and Civil Society. On the Limits of Immigration Control in Liberal Democracies', *IMIS-Beitraege*, 10 (1999), 57–90.

—— 'The Politics of International Migration: How Can We '"Bring the State back in"?', "Caroline Brettell and James F. Hollifield (eds.), *Talking across Disciplines: Migration Theory in Social Science and Law* (London: Routledge, forthcoming).

—— and ZUK, G., 'Immigrants, Markets, and Rights', in H. Kurthen et al., *Immigration, Citizenship, and the Welfare State in Germany and the United States: Welfare Polices and Immigrants' Citizenship* (London: JAI Press, 1998).

HOLMES, C., *John Bull's Island: Immigration and British Society 1871–1971* (Houndmills: Macmillan, 1988).

Human Rights Watch World Report 1998, 'Human Rights Developments: United Kingdom', website: *http://www.hrw.org/hrw/worldreport/Helsinki-26.htm#P1211_296656.*

IRELAND, P., *The Policy Challenge of Ethnic Diversity* (Cambridge, Mass.: Harvard University Press, 1994).

JACKSON, D., *Immigration Law and Practice* (London: Sweet & Maxwell, 1996).

JACOBS, D., *Black Politics and Urban Crisis in Britain* (Cambridge: Cambridge University Press, 1986).

JACOBSON, D., *Rights across Borders: Immigration and the Decline of Citizenship* (Baltimore: Johns Hopkins University Press, 1997).

JACOBSON, J. K., 'Much Ado about Ideas: The Cognitive Factor in Economic Policy', *World Politics*, 47 (Jan. 1995), 283–310.

JENSON, J., 'Paradigms and Political Discourse: Protective Legislation in France and the United States before 1914', *Canadian Journal of Political Science*, 22, No. 2 (1989).

JOHNSON, C., 'The Common Market: Way in for Britain?' *Crossbow*, 4, No. 1 (1961), 29–32.

JONES, T., *Britain's Ethnic Minorities: An Analysis of the Labour Force Survey* (London: Policy Studies Institute, 1993).

JOPPKE, C., (ed.), *Challenge to the Nation-State: Immigration in Western Europe and the United States* (Oxford: Oxford University Press, 1998).

—— 'Why Liberal States Accept Unwanted Immigration', *World Politics*, 50 (Jan. 1998), 266–93.

—— *Immigration and the Nation-State: The United States, Germany and Great Britain* (Oxford: Oxford University Press, 1999).

JUSS, S. *Discretion and Deviation in the Administration of Immigration Control* (London: Sweet & Maxwell, 1997),

KAHLER, M., *Decolonization in Britain and France: The Domestic Consequences of International Relations* (Princeton: Princeton University Press, 1984).

KATZENSTEIN, P. J., *Small States in World Markets: Industrial Policy in Europe* (Ithaca, NY: Cornell University Press, 1985).

KATZNELSON, I., *Black Men, White Cities: Race, Politics, and Migration in the United States, 1900–30 and Britain, 1948–68* (London: Oxford University Press, 1973).

—— *City Trenches: Urban Politics and Patterning of Class in the United States* (New York: Pantheon, 1981)

KAVANAGH, D., 'The Deferential English: A Comparative Critique', *Politics and Personalities* (Houndmills: Macmillan, 1990).

—— Enoch Powell: Vision and Waste', *Politics and Personalities* (Houndmills: Macmillan, 1990).

—— *British Politics: Continuities and Change* (Oxford: Oxford University Press, 1990).

KELLEY, N. and TREBILCOCK, M. J., *The Making of the Mosaic: A History of Canadian immigration policy* (Toronto: University of Toronto Press, 1998).

KESSLER, A. E., 'Immigration, Internationalization and Domestic Response: Toward an Explanation for the Rise of Restriction in the '"New World" ', Paper presented at the Center for the Study of Immigration, Integration and Citizenship (CEPIC)'s conference, sponsored by the German Marshall Fund, on Migration Controls in 19th Century Europe and America, La Sorbonne, Paris, 25–6 June 1999.

KING, A., 'How to Strengthen Legislatures—Assuming that We Want to', in N. J. Ornstein (ed.), *The Role of the Legislature in Western Democracies* (Washington, DC: American Enterprise Institute for Public Policy Research', 1981).

KING, D., *Actively Seeking Work? The Politics of Unemployment and Welfare Policy in the United States and Great Britain* (Chicago: Chicago University Press, 1995).

—— *In the Name of Liberalism* (Oxford: Oxford University Press, 1999).

KITSCHELT , H., *The Radical Right in Western Europe: A Comparative Analysis* (Ann Arbor: University of Michigan Press, 1995).

KOHLI, A., EVANS, P., KATZENSTEIN, P. J., PRZEWORSKI, A., HOEBER RUDOLPH, S., SCOTT, J. C., and SKOCPOL, T., 'The Role of Theory in Comparative Politics: A Symposium', *World Politics*, 48 (Oct. 1995), 1–49.

KOSER, K., 'Out of the Frying Pan and into the Fire: A Case Study of Illegality amongst Asylum Seekers,' in K. Koser and H. Lutz, *The New Migration in Europe: Social Constructions and Social Realities* (London: Macmillan, 1997).

—— and SALT, J., 'The Geography of Highly Skilled International Migration', *International Journal of Population Geography*, (1997), 285–303.

KRASNER, S. D., 'Sovereignty: An Institutional Perspective', *Comparative Political Studies*, 21, No. 1 (1988), 66–94.

KURTHEN H. et al., *Immigration, Citizenship, and the Welfare State in Germany and the United States: Welfare Polices and Immigrants' Citizenship* (London: JAI Press, 1998).

KUSHNICK, L., 'Race, Class & Struggle: Essays on Racism and Inequality in Britain, the US and Western Europe* (London: Rivers Oram Press, 1998).

LAMB, R., *The Macmillan Years, 1957–1963: The Emerging Truth* (London: John Murray, 1995).

LAYTON-HENRY, Z., 'Immigration', Layton-Henry (ed.), *Conservative Party Politics* (London: Macmillan, 1980).

—— *The Politics of Race in Britain* (London: Allen & Unwin, 1984).

—— 'Race and the Thatcher Government', in Z. Layton-Henry and P. Rich (eds.), *Race, Government and Politics in Britain* (Houndmills: Macmillan, 1986).

—— *The Politics of Immigration: Immigration, 'Race' and 'Race' Relations in Post-war Britain* (Oxford: Blackwell, 1992).

——'Immigration and the Heath Government', in S. Ball and A. Seldon (eds.), *The Heath Government 1970–74: A Reappraisal* (London: Longman, 1996).

—— and WILPERT, C., *Discrimination, Racism, and Citizenship: Inclusion and Exclusion in Britain and Germany* (London: Anglo-German Foundation for the Study of Industrial Society, 1994).

LEIGH, L., and BEYANI, C., *Blackstone's Guide to the Asylum and Immigration Act 1996* (London: Blackstone Press, 1996).

LESTER, A., 'Discrimination: What Can Lawyers Learn from History', *Public Law* (Summer 1994), 224–37.

—— and BINDMAN, G., *Race and Law* (London: Longman, 1972).

LEVI, M., *Of Rule and Revenue* (Berkeley and Los Angeles: University of California Press, 1988).

—— Social and Unsocial Capital: A Review Essay of Robert Putnam's *Making Democracy Work', Politics and Society*, 24, No. 1 (Mar. 1996), 45–55.

—— A Model, A Method, and a Map: Rational Choice in Comparative and Historical Analysis', in M. I. Lichbach and A. S. Zuckerman (eds.), *Comparative Politics: Rationality, Culture, and Structure* (Cambridge: Cambridge University Press, 1997).

LIEBOWITZ, S. J. and MARGOLIS, S. E., 'The Fable of the Keys', *Journal of Law & Economics*, 33 (Apr. 1990), 1–25.

—— —— 'Path-Dependence, Lock-in, and History', *Journal of Law, Economics, and Organization*, 11, No. 1 (1995).

—— —— 'Should Technology Choice be a Concern of Antitrust Policy?', *Harvard Journal of Law & Technology*, 9, No. 2 (1996), 283–318, 289.

LOCHAK, D., 'Les Politiques de l'immigration au prisme de la législation sur les étrangers', in D. Fassin, et al., *Les Lois de l'inhospitalité: les politiques de l'immigration à l'épreuve des sans-papiers* (Paris: La Découverte, 1997).

LUNN, K., 'The British State and Immigration, 1945–1951: New Light on the Empire Windrush', in T. Kushner and K. Lunn (eds.), *The Politics of Marginality: Race, the Radical Right and Minorities in Twentieth Century Britain* (London: Frank Cass, 1990).

MCCORD, N., *British History, 1815–1906* (Oxford: Oxford University Press, 1993).

MACDONALD, I., *The New Immigration Law* (London: Butterworths, 1972).

—— *Race Relations—The New Law* (London: Butterworths, 1977).

—— and BLAKE, N., *Immigration Law and Practice in the United Kingdom* (London: Butterworths, 1995).

MANGAT, J. S., *A History of the Asians in East Africa* (Oxford: Clarendon Press, 1969).

MARCH, J. G. and OLSON, J. P., 'The New Institutionalism: Organisational Factors in Political Life', *American Political Science Review*, 78 (1989), 734–49.

—— *Rediscovering Institutions* (New York: Free Press, 1993).

MARSHALL, G., *Constitutional Conventions: The Rules and Forms of Political Accountability* (Oxford: Clarendon Press, 1984).

MASON, D., *Race & Ethnicity in Modern Britain* (Oxford: Oxford University Press, 1995).

MATAS, D., 'The Extreme Right in the United Kingdom and France',in A. Braun and S. Scheinberg (eds.), *The Extreme Right: Freedom and Security at Risk* (Boulder Colo.: Westview Press, 1997).

MAYER, N., *Le Front National à découvert* (Paris: Presse de la Dondation National ds Sciences Politiques, 1996).

MERVYN JONES, J., *British Nationality Law and Practice* (Oxford: Clarendon Press, 1947).

MESSINA, A., *Race and Party Competition in Britain* (Oxford: Clarendon Press, 1989).

—— 'Ethnic Minorities and the British Party System in the 1990s', in S. Saggar (ed.), *Race and British Electoral Politics* (London: UCL Press, 1998).

MILES, R., *Racism and Migrant Labour* (London: Routledge & Kegan Paul, 1982).

—— 'Labour Migration, Racism and Capital Accumulation in Western Europe since 1945: An Overview', *Capital and Class*, 28 (1986), 49–86.

—— and KAY, D., *Refugees or Migrant Workers? European Volunteer Workers in Britain 1946–1951* (London: Routledge, 1992).

—— PHIZACKLEA, A., *White Man's Country: Racism in British Politics* (London: Pluto Press, 1984), 6.

MONEY, J., *Fences and Neighbours: The Political Geography of Immigration Control* (Ithaca, NY: Cornell University Press, 1999), 213–15.

MORDECAI, J., *The West Indies: The Federal Negotiations* (London: George Allen & Unwin, 1968).

MORGAN, K. O., *Labour in Power, 1945–1951* (Oxford: Clarendon Press, 1984).

—— *Callaghan* (Oxford: Oxford University Press, 1997).

MORRIS, H. S., *The Indians in Uganda* (London: Weidenfeld & Nicolson, 1968).

MORRISON, H., *Government and Parliament: A Survey from the Inside* (London: Oxford University Press, 1959).

MURRAY-BROWN, J., *Kenyatta* (London: George Allen & Unwin, 1979).

NNOLI, O., *Ethnic Politics in Nigeria* (Enugu, Nigeria: Fourth Dimension, 1978).

NORTH, D. C., *Institutions, Institutional Change, and Economic Performance* (Cambridge: Cambridge University Press, 1990).

NORTON, P., 'Intra-Party Descent in the House of Commons: A Case Study. The Immigration Rules 1972', *Parliamentary Affairs*, 29, No. 3 (1976), 404–20.

NUGENT, N., and KING, R., *The British Right: Conservative and Right-Wing Politics in Britain* (London: Saxon House, 1977).

OLSON, M., *The Logic of Collective Action* (Cambridge, Mass.: Harvard University Press, 1971).

PANNELL, N,. and BROCKWAY, F., *Immigration: What is the Answer?* (London: Routledge & Kegan Paul, 1965).

PARRY, C., *Nationality and Citizenship Laws of the Commonwealth and of the Republic of Ireland*, 2 vols. (London: Stevens, 1957).

PATEL, H. H., 'Indians in Uganda and Rhodesia—Some Comparative Perspectives on a Minority in African', *Studies in Race and Nations* (Center on International Race Relations, University of Denver), 5, No. 1 (1973–4).

PATTERSON, S., *Immigration and Race Relations in Britain, 1960–1967* (London: Oxford University Press, 1969).

PAUL, P., *Whitewashing Britain: Race and Citizenship in the Postwar Era* (Ithaca, NY: Cornell University Press, 1997).

PHELAN, M., *Immigration Law Handbook* (London: Blackstone, 1997).

PHILLIPS, J., *The Great Alliance: Economic Recovery and the Problems of Power 1945–1951* (London: Pluto, 1996).

PIERSON, P., 'The Path to European Integration: A Historical Institutionalist Account', *Comparative Political Studies*, 29, No. 2 (Apr. 1996), 123–63.

—— 'When Effect Becomes Cause: Policy Feedback and Political Change', *World Politics*, 45, No. 4 (1993), 595–628.

—— *Path Dependence, Increasing Returns, and the Study of Politics* (revised version of paper presented at European University Institute, Apr. 1997, 3 Oct. 1997).

PILKINGTON, E., *Beyond the Mother Country: West Indians and the Notting Hill White Riots* (London: I. B. Tauris, 1988).

PIORE, M., *Birds of Passage: Migrant Labor in Industrial Societies* (Cambridge: Cambridge University Press, 1979).

PORTES, A., 'Immigration Theory for a New Century: Some Problems and Opportunities', *International Migration Review*, 31, No. 4 (1997), 799–825.

POWELL, ENOCH, J., *A Nation or No Nation?: Six Years in British Politics* (London: B. T. Batsford, 1978).

—— *Reflections of a Statesman: The Writings and Speeches of Enoch Powell* (London: Bellew, 1991).

PUTNAM, R. D., *Making Democracy Work: Civic Traditions in Modern Italy* (Princeton: Princeton University Press, 1993).

RAMDIN, R., *The Making of the Black Working Class in Britain* (London: Gower, 1987)

RAMSDEN, J., *The Age of Churchill and Eden, 1940–1957* (London: Longman, 1995).

RANDALL, C., 'An Asylum Policy for the UK', in S. Spencer (ed.), *Strangers and Citizens: A Positive Approach to Migrants and Refugees* (Concord, Mass: Institute for Public Policy Research/Rivers Oram Press, 1994).

RASPAIL, Jean, *The Camp of Saints* (New York: Scribner, 1975).

RATH, J., 'Political Action of Immigrants in the Netherlands: Class or Ethnicity', *European Journal of Political Research*, 16 (1988), 623–44.

REX, J., *The Concept of a Multi-Cultural Society* (University of Warwick: Centre for Research in Ethnic Relations, Occasional Papers in Ethnic Relations No. 3, 1985).

RIEDLSPERGER, M., 'The Freedom Party of Austria: From Protest to Radical Right Populism', in H.-G. Betz, and S. Immerfall, (eds.), *The New Politics of the Right: Neo-Populist Parties and Movements in Established Democracies* (London: Macmillan, 1998).

ROBERTS, A., *Eminent Churchillians* (London: Weidenfeld & Nicolson, 1994).

ROSE, E. J. B. et al., *Colour and Citizenship: A Report on British Race Relations* (London: Oxford University Press, 1969).

ROTHCHILD, D., 'Citizenship and National Integration: The Non-African Crisis in Kenya,' *Studies in Race and Nations* (Center on International Race Relations, University of Denver, Working Papers), Vol. 1, No. 3, (1969–70).

—— *Racial Bargaining in Independent Kenya: A Study of Minorities and Decolonization* (London: Oxford University Press, 1973).

SABETTI, F., 'Path Dependency and Civil Culture: Some Lessons from Italy about Interpreting Social Experiments', *Politics and Society*, 24, No. 1 (Mar. 1996), 19–44.

SAGGAR, S. (ed.), *Race and British Electoral Politics* (London: UCL Press, 1998).

—— *Race and Politics in Britain* (London: Harvester Wheatsheaf, 1992).

SÄRLVIK, B., and CREWE, I., *The Decade of Dealignment: The Conservative Victory of 1979 and Electoral Trends in the 1970s* (Cambridge: Cambridge University Press, 1983).

SARTORI, G., 'Constitutionalism: A Preliminary Discussion', *American Political Science Review*, 56 (1962), 853–64, 862.

SASSEN, S., *Losing Control* (New York: Columbia University Press, 1996).

—— The *de facto* Transnationalizing of Immigration Policy', in C. Joppke, *Challenge to the Nation-State: Immigration in Western Europe and the United States* (Oxford: Oxford University Press, 1998).

SCHAIN, M. A., 'Immigration and Politic', in P. A. Hall, J. Hayward, and H. Machin, *Developments in French Politics* (Houndmills: Macmillan, 1994).

SCHLESINGER, A. M., Jr, *The Disuniting of America* (New York: W. Norton & Co., 1992).

SCHOEN, D. E., *Enoch Powell and the Powellites* (London: Macmillan, 1977).

SCHÖN, D. A., 'Generative Metaphor: A Perspective on Problem-Setting in Social Policy', A. Ortony (ed.), *Metaphor and Thought* (Cambridge: Cambridge University Press, 1993).

SEIDENBERG, D. A., *Uhuru and the Kenya Indians* (New Delhi: Vikas Publishing House, 1983).

SELDON, A., *Churchill's Indian Summer* (London: Hodder & Stoughton, 1981).

—— 'The Churchill Administration, 1951–1955', in P. Hennessy and A. Seldon (eds.), *Ruling Performance: British Governments from Attlee to Thatcher* (Oxford: Basil Blackwell, 1987).

SELM-THORBURN, J. van, *Refugee Protection in Europe* (The Hague: Martinus Nijhoff Publishers, 1998).

SHEPSLE, K. A., 'Studying Institutions: Some Lessons from the Rational Choice Approach', *Journal of Theoretical Politics* 1, No. 2 (1989), 131–47.

SHUTTER S., *Immigration, Nationality and Refugee Law Handbook: A User's Guide* (London: Joint Council for the Welfare of Immigrants, 1997).

SIMON, H., *Models of Man: Social and Rational* (New York: Garland, 1987).

—— Human Nature and Politics: The Dialogue of Psychology with Political Science', *American Political Science Review*, 79 (1985), 293–304.

SIMON, J., *The Economic Consequences of Immigration* (Oxford: Blackwell, 1989).

—— and LYNCH, L., 'A Comparative Assessment of Public Opinion toward Immigration and Immigration Policies', *International Migration Review*, 30, No. 2 (1999), 455–67.

SIVANANDAN, A., 'Race, Class and the State: The Black Experience in Britain', *Race and Class*, 17 (1976), 347–68.

—— *A Different Hunger: Writings on Black Resistance* (London: Pluto, 1982).

SKED, A., and COOK, C., *Post-War Britain: A Political History* (London: Penguin, 1993).

SKIDELSKY, R., 'The Choice for Europe', *Interests and Obsessions: Selected Essays* (London: Macmillan, 1993).

SKOCPOL, T., 'Bringing the State back in: Strategies of Analysis in Current Research', in P. Evans et al., *Bringing the State back in* (Cambridge: Cambridge University Press, 1985).

—— *Protecting Soldiers and Mothers: The Political Origins of Social Policy in the United States* (Cambridge, Mass.: Harvard University Press, 1992).

SMITH, R., *Civic Ideals: Conflicting Visions of Citizenship in U. S. History* (New Haven: Yale University Press, 1997).

SMITHIES, B., and FIDDICK, P., *Enoch Powell on Immigration* (London: Sphere Books, 1969).

SOLOMOS J., *Race and Racism in Contemporary Britain* (London: Macmillan, 1989).

—— *Race and Racism in Britain* (Houndmills: Macmillan, 1993).

—— and BACK, L., *Racism and Society* (Houndmills: Macmillan, 1996),

SOYSAL, Y. N., *Limits of Citizenship: Migrants and Postnational Membership in Europe* (Chicago: University of Chicago Press, 1994).

SPENCER, I. R. G., *British Immigration Policy since 1939: The Making of Multi-racial Britain* (London: Routledge, 1997).

STEINER, H. J., and ALSTON, P., *International Human Rights in Context: Law, Politics, Morals* (Oxford: Clarendon, 1996).

STEINMO, S., THELEN, K., and LONGSTRETH, F. (eds.), *Structuring Politics: Historical Institutionalism in Comparative Analysis* (New York: Cambridge University Press, 1992).

STOBO, G., 'The Canadian Refugee Determination System', *Texas International Law Journal*, 29, No. 3 (1994).

STOREY, H., 'International Law and Human Rights Obligations', in S. Spencer (ed.), *Strangers and Citizens: A Positive Approach to Migrants and Refugees* (Concord, Mass.: Institute for Public Policy Research/Rivers Oram Press, 1994).

STOUT, H. M., *British Government* (New York: Oxford University Press, 1953).

STRANGE, S., *Sterling and British Policy* (London: Oxford University Press, 1971).

STUDLAR, D. T., 'Policy Voting in Britain: The Coloured Immigration Issue in the 1964, 1966 and 1970 Elections', *American Political Science Review*, 72 (1978), 46–72.

—— 'British Public Opinion, Colour Issues, and Enoch Powell: A Longitudinal Analysis', *British Journal of Political Science*, 4, No. 3 (1978), 371–81.:

—— " 'Waiting for the catastrophe" Race and the Political Agenda in Britain', *Patterns of Prejudice*, 19, No. 1 (1985), 3–15.

TAYLOR, S., *The National Front in English Politics* (London: Macmillan, 1982).

THELEN, K., 'Historical Institutionalism in Comparative Politics', *Annual Review of Political Science*, 2 (1999).

—— and STEINMO, S., 'Historical Institutionalism in Comparative Politics', in S. Steinmo et al. (eds.) *Structuring Politics: Historical Institutionalism in Comparative Analysis* (New York: Cambridge University Press, 1992).

THEODOR, M., *Human Rights in Internal Strife: Their International Protection* (Cambridge: Grotius, 1987).

THORNBERRY, P., *International Law and the Rights of Minorities* (Oxford: Clarendon, 1991).

TIGNOR, R. L., *Capitalism and Nationalism at the End of Empire* (Princeton; Princeton University Press, 1998).

TSEBELIS, G., *Nested Games: Rational Choice in Comparative Politics* (Berkeley and Los Angeles: University of California Press, 1990).

TWADDLE, M., 'Was the Expulsion Inevitable?', in M. Twaddle (ed.), *Expulsion of a Minority: Essays on Ugandan Asians* (London: Athlone, 1975).

UNDERHILL, F. H., *The British Commonwealth: An Experiment in Co-operation* (Durham, NC: Duke University Press, 1956).

VEBLEN, T., *The Place of Science in Modern Civilisation and Other Essays* (New York: Russell & Russell, 1961).

VOERMAN, G., and LUCARDIE, P., 'The Extreme Right in the Netherlands', *European Journal of Political Research*, 22 (1992), 35–54.

WALKER, M., *The National Front* (London: Macmillan, 1977).

WALKER, P. G., *The Commonwealth* (London: Secker & Warburg, 1962).

WEIR, M., 'Ideas and the Politics of Bounded Innovation', in S. Steinmo et al., *Structuring Politics: Historical Institutionalism in Comparative Analysis* (New York: Cambridge University Press, 1992).

—— and SKOCPOL, T., 'State Structures and the Possibilities for "'Keynesian" Responses to the Great Depression in Sweden, Britain and the United States', in P. Evans et al., *Bringing the State back in* (Cambridge: Cambridge University Press, 1985).

WEIL, P., *La France et ses étrangers: l'aventure d'une politique de l'immigration de 1938 à nos jours* (Paris: Gallimard, 1991).

WESTLE, B., and NIEDERMAYER, O., 'Contemporary Right-Wing Extremism in West Germany', *European Journal of Political Research*, 22 (1992), 83–100.

WHITE, R. M., 'Hong Kong Nationality, Immigration and the Agreement with China', *International and Comparative Law Quarterly*, 36, No. 3 (July 1987), 482–503.

WISEMAN, H. V., *Britain and the Commonwealth* (London: Allen & Unwin, 1965).

YOUNG, H., *One of Us* (London: Pan Books, 1993).

YOUNG, O. 'International Regimes: Toward a New Theory of Institutions', *World Politics*, 39 (1986), 104–22.

Index